Best
Newspaper
Writing

Best Newspaper Writing
2006–2007 Edition

American Society of Newspaper Editors
Award Winners and Finalists

Edited by Aly Colón

The Poynter Institute for Media Studies
and

CQ PRESS

A Division of Congressional Quarterly Inc.
Washington, D.C.

The Poynter Institute for Media Studies
801 Third Street South
St. Petersburg, FL 33701
Phone: 727-821-9494; toll-free, 888-POYNTER (888-769-6837)
Web: www.poynter.org

CQ Press
1255 22nd Street, NW, Suite 400
Washington, DC 20037
Phone: 202-729-1900; toll-free, 866-4CQ-PRESS (866-427-7737)
Web: www.cqpress.com

Cover design, interior design and typesetting by Auburn Associates Inc.,
Baltimore

Cover photos, clockwise from top left: Todd Heisler/*Rocky Mountain News*;
Sora DeVore/*The Washington Post Magazine*; Vincent Laforet/*The New York Times*

Photos in the Community Service Photojournalism section were provided by the photographers. Photos of winners, finalists and contributors were provided by their news organizations.

Newspaper articles and photos are the exclusive property of the authors and their newspapers and are reprinted with permission.

⊗ The paper used in this publication exceeds the requirements of the American National Standard for Information Sciences—Permanence of Paper for Printed Library Materials, ANSI Z39.48-1992.

Printed and bound in the United States of America

10 09 08 07 06   1 2 3 4 5

ISBN-10: 0-87289-296-4
ISBN-13: 978-0-87289-296-5
ISSN 0195-895X

To Julie Moos,
whose work on the "Best Newspaper Writing" series
during the past two years has expanded its
range and helped it reach new readers.
As Poynter's publications manager,
Julie sets the standard for the enthusiasm, the
dedication to detail and the creative excellence it
takes to produce a book like this.

Contents

PART 1   Writing on Deadline   1

PART 4   Commentary/Column Writing   231

PART 5   Editorial Writing   269

Foreword: The Good, the Sad and the Enduring

BY KAREN BROWN DUNLAP

When I was an undergraduate at Michigan State University years and years ago, I spent cold afternoons and evenings listening to a Roberta Flack song.*

The third and fourth lines stay with me:

All the news is bad again
Kiss your dreams goodbye.

Life was good, but the melancholy beauty of that song lingered. The problem with listening to sad songs is that you can mistake the lyrics for your reality.

That is what's happening to journalists today. We're hearing too many sad songs.

You know the story: audience migration to new information sources, job layoffs and buyouts, ramped-up investor influence, news holes reduced, more infotainment than news and venerable news organizations bought and sold.

It's enough to give you the blues if you care about news in a democracy, but there's more to the story. James W. Carey was good at telling the rest of the story.

Jim Carey was known for teaching at the Columbia University Graduate School of Journalism and for years of leadership at the University of Illinois. He was a deep thinker who could weave humor and a distinctive laugh into his comments. When Carey died in 2006, Poynter's vice president, Roy Peter Clark, wrote a tribute. It included this Carey quote:

> Listen: You don't feel well, so you go to see the psychiatrist. And the doctor listens to your story. And, if he's a good doctor, he's listening for the parts of the story that are making you feel sick. His job is then to help you tell a new story about yourself, especially one that will make you well. Newspapers are the same way. Journalists are telling each other stories about themselves that are making them sick. So the remedy is to tell a new story about journalism that will help make journalism healthy again.

---

* "The Ballad of the Sad Young Men"

It's time for journalists and media leaders to tell a new story, one that stops expecting a future of declines, but instead focuses on opportunities. Audiences could use better online presentations, more thoughtful content and more creativity in how news is packaged and delivered. This is a time for energetic responses, innovation and growth.

Most of us could use a better understanding of electronic tools. Computer companies turn out devices that are constantly more powerful, smaller and less expensive. I could name a few new products, but even newer tools will replace them by the time you read this. Software developers and other entrepreneurs create new financial models as they reach audiences. News businesses need that kind of agility in reporting the news.

I saw a teenager standing on a street corner in Fort Lauderdale holding up a sign with the name of a fast-food place. Apparently he was being paid to advertise, so he held the sign with one hand while playing a video game with the other. Technology is a natural part of his world. What will he seek when he turns to the news? I'm convinced he *will* turn to the news. Will we be ready to engage him with useful formats and quality reports?

The burden of engaging him isn't limited to the technology. Nothing substitutes for excellence in the craft of reporting, writing, editing and producing the news. In the pages that follow you'll see outstanding journalism, representative of the great work that citizens see every day. Each day brings compelling stories, outstanding photojournalism, inspired design and producing by talented, committed and courageous journalists.

Let's be real, though: Much of the daily news report offers boring stories, confusing coverage and petty topics. We can do better. Nothing substitutes for excellence in craft skills.

Finally, to tell a new story we have to remember the mission of journalism. In a year of news media setbacks, the movie "Good Night, and Good Luck" captured an Academy Award nomination for best picture. The movie evoked the steel commitment of television newsman Edward R. Murrow.

Journalists warm to the story of news media taking on the powerful, standing for right and telling gripping stories that move the public. That mission didn't end in the 1950s; it is still important today.

The sense of mission brings joy and fulfillment to journalists even in uncertain times. Consider the career of Allan Johnson of the *Chicago Tribune,* whose story is told by colleague Rick Kogan and can be read at www.poynter.org/allanjohnson.

Johnson started as a copy clerk at the newspaper in 1979, served in several sections, even created a comic-club column. Johnson loved his job as reporter and critic at the *Tribune.* When he died suddenly this year,

Tribune editor Ann Marie Lipinski reflected on his strong presence in the newsroom and his good cheer. He enjoyed his life and his career as a journalist. At his funeral, attendees sang the song "Smile," she said.

This is no time for a sad song about the news business. The future of news rests in innovation, in finding new financial models and addressing audience migration. But the future also is determined by the attitudes of journalists and news media leaders, the quality of their work and their commitment to make a difference by serving their mission.

A quote often attributed to journalist-philosopher Walter Lippmann says the role of the press is to keep a community in conversation with itself. Jim Carey spoke of life as a conversation that never ends. In the interest of society we must think of news as a community's conversation that never ends. It is a conversation that's vital to democracy.

Let's re-engage the conversation and tell the good news of journalism.

Karen Brown Dunlap is president and managing director of The Poynter Institute as well as a Poynter trustee and a member of the board of directors of the Times Publishing Company. She is co-author of "The Effective Editor" with Foster Davis and co-author of "The Editorial Eye" with Jane Harrigan.

Preface

This annual celebration of the best American newspaper writing began as an idea nearly 31 years ago. At the time, Eugene Patterson was president of the American Society of Newspaper Editors (ASNE) and wanted to single out distinguished writing.

Patterson sought to highlight the "lilt and the loveliness" of the language, he told Keith Woods for an essay in "Best Newspaper Writing 2003." Such writing, he said, contained "clarity, grace, brevity. But clarity above all."

To honor exemplary work, ASNE created and still sponsors an annual contest that recognizes and rewards the finest writing in daily newspapers and wire services and the most outstanding community service photojournalism.

To produce "Best Newspaper Writing," ASNE partners with The Poynter Institute, a school for journalists in St. Petersburg, Fla. The book explores the work of winners and finalists in the annual competition.

This 2006–2007 edition of "Best Newspaper Writing" features the work of winners and finalists in the following categories: the Jesse Laventhol Prizes for deadline news reporting by a team and by an individual; the Freedom Forum/ASNE Award for Distinguished Writing on Diversity; Distinguished Writing Awards for non-deadline writing, commentary and column writing, editorial writing and watchdog reporting; and the Community Service Photojournalism Award.

In this edition, we have created a special section on Hurricane Katrina coverage. It features interviews with editors, teams and individuals who were finalists for an ASNE award. They offer insights into the organization it takes to cover a disaster of massive proportions. And it shows the journalistic dedication and courage involved when a hurricane threatened not only the lives and livelihood of their communities, but of the journalists and newspapers as well.

The evolving efforts on the part of newspapers to work on multiple news platforms encouraged us to provide a new feature: "Conversations about Convergence." These conversations ask some of our winners about what steps they took to translate their work to the online medium.

How to Use This Book

"Best Newspaper Writing 2006–2007" offers examples of excellent writing and photojournalism. In addition to the exemplary newspaper work produced by the winners and finalists, readers can turn to:

- **Interviews:** conversations with the winning writers and photojournalists about their craft, focusing on news judgment, reporting strategies, developing sources, collaboration, working with editors, writing with context, making photos and more
- **Lessons Learned:** essays by the finalists about the trials and techniques of producing their honored work
- **Writers' Workshop:** discussion questions and assignments that provide an opportunity to analyze and emulate winning work
- **X-Ray Readings:** Roy Peter Clark deconstructs the writer's language and rhetoric in five stories and offers a toolbox of techniques for reporting and writing.
- **Conversations about Convergence:** interviews with ASNE winners about how they dealt with, or sought out, online presentations for their work
- **Narrative Strategies:** Pulitzer Prize–winning journalist Thomas French examines the narrative techniques used by three reporters featured in "Best Newspaper Writing." He explains how the narrative style captures color and action and advances each story, and he highlights portions of the writing that show examples of narrative techniques at work.
- **Hurricane Katrina Coverage:** a special section that focuses on the work involved in covering Hurricane Katrina and its aftermath

Professors and professionals will see that "Best Newspaper Writing" has been broken into eight parts that represent different types of newspaper writing and photojournalism. The book was organized this way to better follow the structure of classroom teaching and the professional writer's desire to focus on the topics of greatest interest. The eight parts are: Writing on Deadline, Narrative Writing, Diversity Writing, Commentary/Column Writing, Editorial Writing, Watchdog Reporting, Hurricane Katrina Coverage and Community Service Photojournalism. The structure makes it easier to learn more about a particular form and to compare different forms of journalism.

The foreword, written by Karen Brown Dunlap, president of The Poynter Institute, and the introduction, written by Aly Colón, editor of "Best Newspaper Writing 2006–2007," set the stage for understanding how these winners and finalists fit into the journalism we practice.

About the Interviews and Other Material

Poynter faculty and fellows interviewed ASNE winners by e-mail, and, in some cases by phone. The interviews have been edited for clarity, flow and brevity. Faculty and fellows also wrote biographies of winners from information provided by the journalists and their news organizations.

ASNE provided Poynter with electronic versions of the winners' and finalists' stories for publication in this book. They may differ slightly from the stories that originally appeared in print. "Best Newspaper Writing" editors made minor changes for spelling and grammar. However, the newspapers' original styles remain. Stories were not edited to conform to AP style or Poynter style, even though other parts of this volume were.

Photos have been reprinted as they originally appeared, with captions edited for length, spelling and grammar.

The goal of this book is to help students of the craft become better journalists. Unfortunately, we could not publish all of the work that was honored by ASNE.

Community Service Photojournalism

News University (www.newsu.org), a project of The Poynter Institute and the John S. and James L. Knight Foundation, offers an interactive, in-depth look at the work honored in the Community Service Photojournalism category. The NewsU course, "Community Service Photojournalism: Lessons from a Contest (2006)," analyzes the three models of excellence featured in "Best Newspaper Writing." You will see and hear from the photojournalists and the judges as they discuss the work, and you will explore ways to strengthen your picture editing and critical thinking—improving your own photojournalism. The course is available online at News University at www.newsu.org/asne2006.

The Judging

The winners and finalists featured in this book were selected by the American Society of Newspaper Editors. We want to thank those members who served as judges. Here are their names and affiliations at the time the judging took place:

Amanda Bennett, *The Philadelphia Inquirer*
Francisco Bernasconi, Getty Images
Peter K. Bhatia, *The Oregonian*
Susan Bischoff, *Houston Chronicle*
Neil Brown, *St. Petersburg* (Fla.) *Times*
Jeffrey C. Bruce, *Dayton* (Ohio) *Daily News*
James N. Crutchfield, *Akron* (Ohio) *Beacon Journal*
Gregory Favre, The Poynter Institute
Charlotte H. Hall, *Orlando* (Fla.) *Sentinel*

Edward W. Jones, *The Free Lance-Star* (Fredericksburg, Va.)
W. Martin Kaiser, *Milwaukee Journal Sentinel*
Bill Keller, *The New York Times*
David A. Laventhol, retired, ASNE
Carolyn Lee, retired, *The New York Times*
Diane H. McFarlin, *Sarasota* (Fla.) *Herald-Tribune*
Christopher Peck, *The Commercial Appeal* (Memphis, Tenn.)
Tim Rasmussen, *South Florida Sun-Sentinel*
Rick Rodriguez, *The Sacramento* (Calif.) *Bee*
Sharon Rosenhause, *South Florida Sun-Sentinel*
Mark Silverman, Gannett News Service
Charlie Waters, *The Fresno* (Calif.) *Bee*
Janet Weaver, *The Tampa* (Fla.) *Tribune*
James P. Willse, *The Star-Ledger* (Newark, N.J.)
Patrick Λ. Yack, *The Florida Times-Union*

Acknowledgments

We want to thank the many people who helped make this book possible, beginning with the journalists whose work is featured in these pages. Without them, we would know less about reporting and writing.

Many others also helped.

We want to thank ASNE, its executive director, Scott Bosley, and his associates Suzanne Martin and Diana Mitsu Klos for their work on the contest.

This book benefited from the exceptional organizational skills and creative ideas of Poynter Online managing editor and publications manager Julie Moos. Candace Clarke, administrative assistant in Poynter's publications and online department, provided invaluable coordination, editing and coding efforts. She played a key role in keeping the book's production on track and on schedule with CQ Press, our publisher.

We are grateful to the Poynter faculty and fellows who contributed to this volume. I want to single out Poynter colleagues Bill Mitchell, Meg Martin, Vicki Hyatt and David Shedden for contributing their time and expertise. Their work made this book better. We offer a special thanks to Joe Grimm, *Detroit Free Press* recruiting and development editor, for editing help.

The people who work on News University (www.newsu.org), a project of The Poynter Institute, created an online course featuring the ASNE community service photojournalism winners. For that we thank Howard Finberg, Vicki Krueger, Ben Russell and Jen Wallace.

The following people at CQ Press made this a better book with their creativity, attention to detail and enthusiastic support: Brenda Carter, Charisse Kiino, Gwenda Larsen, Steve Pazdan, Paul Pressau, Dwain Smith, Erin Snow, Anna Socrates and Margot Ziperman.

—Aly Colón

About The Poynter Institute for Media Studies

The Poynter Institute is a school dedicated to teaching and inspiring journalists and media leaders. Through its seminars, publications and Web site (www.poynter.org), the Institute promotes excellence and integrity in the craft of journalism and in the practical leadership of successful news businesses. Poynter stands for a journalism that informs citizens, enlightens public discourse and strengthens ties between journalism and democracy.

Each year at its campus in St. Petersburg, Fla., the school offers approximately 50 seminars for professionals, educators and students including programs for high school students and recent college graduates. Poynter also teaches via the online training portal, News University (www.newsu.org). NewsU, as it is also called, offers interactive e-learning, as well as self-directed and faculty-led online seminars. Poynter faculty and staff also work with journalists at various locations around the nation and the world.

The Poynter Institute was founded in 1975 by Nelson Poynter, chairman of the *St. Petersburg Times* and its Washington affiliate, Congressional Quarterly. Poynter, who died in 1978, willed the controlling stock in his companies to the school. As a financially independent, nonprofit organization, The Poynter Institute is beholden to no interest except its own mission: to help journalists seek and achieve excellence.

About the Editor and Contributors

About the Editor

ALY COLÓN is The Poynter Institute's reporting, writing and editing group leader. He presents regularly at the Poynter-sponsored National Writers Workshops and consults with news organizations on diversity, ethics, writing and leadership.

Prior to joining Poynter, Colón worked at *The Seattle Times* as diversity reporter and coach. As a reporter, he focused on the intersections where people of different races, cultures, genders and abilities meet. As a coach, he helped reporters and editors address diversity issues. He also was a *Seattle Times* assistant metro editor for urban affairs, health care, ethics and values, religion and social issues. He worked at *The Herald* in Everett, Wash., as an executive editor responsible for business and features, and at *The Oakland Press* in Pontiac, Mich.

Colón is the recipient of a Knight-Bagehot fellowship in business from Columbia University, a National Endowment for the Humanities fellowship in ethics, Knight Center for Specialized Journalism fellowships in health care and race and a Robert Bosch study fellowship on European unity and German reunification.

Colón received his bachelor's degree in journalism from Loyola University in New Orleans and his master's degree in journalism from Stanford University.

About the Contributors

ROY PETER CLARK is vice president and senior scholar at The Poynter Institute, where he has taught writing since 1979. He founded the Writing Center at Poynter, lending support to the writing coach movement. He is the author of "Writing Tools: 50 Essential Strategies for Every Writer."

RICK EDMONDS is a researcher and writer at The Poynter Institute. His work centers on the future of the newspaper business and measurement of newsroom capacity. Earlier in his career, he was editor and publisher of several magazines for the *St. Petersburg Times* organization and managing editor of the paper's Tampa edition. Before that he worked as a reporter and editor at *The Philadelphia Inquirer* and was a finalist for the Pulitzer Prize for national reporting in 1982.

THOMAS FRENCH, The Poynter Institute's first writing fellow, began work as a *St. Petersburg Times* reporter soon after his graduation from

Indiana University. His first newspaper series, "A Cry in the Night," is an account of a murder investigation and trial that French turned into the book, "Unanswered Cries." A year spent reporting in a public high school produced the series and book "South of Heaven." His series "Angels & Demons," about the murder of three women visiting Florida, earned him a Pulitzer Prize for feature writing.

JILL GEISLER heads the leadership and management group at The Poynter Institute. Her lifelong love of writing has taken her from editor of her high school paper to broadcast news reporting to newsroom management. She was the country's first female news director of a major market affiliate, WITI-TV in Milwaukee, where she spent 25 years coaching a team of award-winning, enterprising journalists. She is the editor of Poynter Online's "Leading Lines" column and the author of many articles on journalism and leadership, as well as the book "News Leadership: At the Head of the Class." She holds a bachelor's degree in journalism from the University of Wisconsin and a master's degree in leadership and liberal studies from Duquesne University.

THOMAS HUANG, an ethics fellow at The Poynter Institute, is features editor of *The Dallas Morning News,* where he has worked since 1993. As a writer, Huang was a two-time finalist for the Livingston Award for Young Journalists and a two-time finalist for the Missouri Lifestyle Journalism Award for feature writing. Before moving to Dallas, Huang worked for five years as a metropolitan reporter for *The Virginian-Pilot* in Norfolk, Va. He contributes monthly to a column on diversity issues for Poynter Online (www.poynter.org/difference).

KENNY IRBY, visual journalism group leader and diversity director at The Poynter Institute, is the founder of Poynter's photojournalism program. Before joining Poynter, Irby worked as a photographer and deputy director of photography at *Newsday* and contributed as a photo editor to three Pulitzer Prize–winning projects there. Irby is the recipient of numerous awards from the National Press Photographers Association, including the 1999 Joseph Costa Award for outstanding initiative, leadership and service in photojournalism and the 2002 President's Award.

SCOTT LIBIN is a faculty member at The Poynter Institute. He specializes in leadership and ethical decision-making. He conducts training at news organizations and journalism conferences internationally in newsgathering, writing, producing and management. He has been a news director of KSTP-TV, the ABC affiliate in Minneapolis–St. Paul. He was vice president of news for WGHP-TV, serving Greensboro/High Point/Winston-Salem, N.C., where he also worked as a reporter, weekend anchor, managing editor and news director. Libin also has worked in Washington, D.C., as a congressional press secretary and as a national correspondent for an independent television news bureau serving stations around the country. He holds a master's degree in journalism and public affairs from American University and a bachelor's degree in English and journalism from the University of Richmond.

BILL MITCHELL is director of publishing at The Poynter Institute and editor of Poynter Online (www.poynter.org). Before joining Poynter in 1999, he was editor of Universal New Media (1995–1999) and director of electronic publishing at the *San Jose* (Calif.) *Mercury News* (1992–1995). Mitchell also has worked as a reporter, editor, Washington correspondent and European correspondent for the *Detroit Free Press,* and as Detroit bureau chief for *Time* magazine. He served as a juror for the Pulitzer Prizes in 2002 and 2003.

CHRISTOPHER SCANLAN is senior faculty in the reporting, writing and editing group at The Poynter Institute and director of the Poynter-sponsored National Writers Workshops. Scanlan joined the Poynter faculty in 1994 from the Knight Ridder Newspapers' Washington bureau, where he was a national correspondent. From 1994 to 2000, he edited the "Best Newspaper Writing" series. In two decades of reporting, he earned 16 awards, including a Robert F. Kennedy Award for international journalism. Scanlan is the author of "Reporting and Writing: Basics for the 21st Century" and co-editor of "America's Best Newspaper Writing: A Collection of ASNE Prizewinners."

BUTCH WARD is distinguished fellow at The Poynter Institute. He joined the staff of *The Philadelphia Inquirer* after working at *The News American* in Baltimore. At the *Inquirer,* he was New Jersey editor, assistant managing editor for the Sunday paper, assistant managing editor in features, metropolitan editor and managing editor. He left the *Inquirer* in 2001 and spent three years as vice president for corporate and public affairs at Independence Blue Cross.

KEITH WOODS is dean of the faculty at The Poynter Institute. In 16 years at *The Times-Picayune* in New Orleans, he worked as a sportswriter, news reporter, city editor, editorial writer and columnist. His professional writing won statewide and national awards, including the 1994 National Headliner Award, which he shared with colleagues for the 1993 series

"Together Apart/The Myth of Race." He joined Poynter in 1995 and led the Institute's teaching on diversity and coverage of race relations as part of the ethics faculty; he then served as reporting, writing and editing group leader. From 2001–2004, Woods edited the "Best Newspaper Writing" series.

Introduction:
The Value of Being There

BY ALY COLÓN

I rifled through the scraps of paper piled up on my newsroom desk. They bore names, phone numbers and hastily scribbled story ideas. As I tried to decide whom to call for a story, the phone rang.

The caller told me about a Korean-American businessman who planned to host a neighborhood block party to ease the tension that existed between Blacks and Korean-Americans. The strain stemmed from prickly interactions between Korean-American merchants and Black consumers at a small shopping center the businessman had just bought. The caller thought the businessman's outreach might make a good community interest story.

After I hung up, I thought about doing the story by phone. Call the businessman. Get some background on him and the party. Snag some good quotes. Contact a few other people for perspective. It would be what reporters call a "phoner." Quick. Tight. Ready for tomorrow's paper.

But as I spoke to the businessman on the phone, I changed my mind. I decided to get out of the office instead. I spent the afternoon with the businessman. We walked through his shopping center. I interviewed Korean-American merchants. I also came across a new tenant, a Black consumer with retailing ambitions who had just moved into the center. The shopping center's new owner had offered him retail space. I noticed some other retailers and went over to speak with them about relations between the two groups in the neighborhood.

I gathered good material. But when I got back to the newsroom and reviewed my notes, I felt something was missing. The businessman had been much more responsive and accessible to me because of my visit. But the look on his face, and the tone of his voice, made me feel there was something more.

I went back. I spent another afternoon with him. I pressed him for more information. He told me again that he wanted to bring the groups together. It was the neighborly thing to do. And, he acknowledged, he knew it could change his shopping center's image in the community. But when I prodded and probed some more, it finally came out. He revealed a deeper, more painful, more profound reason behind his mission.

After experiencing a devastating business failure some years earlier, he had found solace and support in his church. His faith renewed him. As a result, he committed himself to living out his faith in both his personal and professional life.

Then he read St. Paul's letter to the Galatians in which Paul wrote: "There is neither Jew nor Greek, slave nor free, male nor female, for you are all one in Christ Jesus." (Galatians 3:28)

"I suddenly realized that I was prejudiced. That I had bias against Blacks," the businessman said. "The only way to keep my promise to live out my faith was to battle these demons of prejudice." He viewed the purchase of the shopping center, with its Black customers and neighbors, as his opportunity to do that.

My prodding and probing helped him open up. This was not the kind of information I could have gotten from a phone, or e-mail, interview. The time I spent with him ultimately enabled me to see there was more to the story and made him comfortable enough to reveal to me what it was. It made the story more real, more human and more compelling. And that happened because I got out of the office.

Getting out of the office was one of the major themes that emerged as I edited "Best Newspaper Writing 2006–2007." Meeting people face to face, walking the streets and relating to the humanity in the stories being covered becomes evident in the conversations with the American Society of Newspaper Editors (ASNE) winners, and in the essays written by the finalists.

Here are the lessons these journalists share in this book:

Listen. Ask questions. Listen some more. Listen for what's being said. Listen for what's not being said. Observe. Be flexible. Be human. Immerse yourself in the environment you cover. Read. Write stories about people. Make pictures that capture their humanity.

These pieces of advice may seem obvious. But even the obvious bears repeating. Samuel Johnson, the English philosopher, wrote: "Always remind people of the obvious; it's the first thing they forget."

We have forgotten—in this age of technological tools, techniques and timing—what life looks like when we physically walk and talk our stories. I know the pressure the 24/7 news cycle presents. I appreciate the increasing demands for more production in newsrooms that are understaffed and facing even deeper cuts. I understand the benefit of using phones, the Internet and e-mail to get our reporting and writing done more quickly.

And yet, I want to remember why I got into journalism in the first place. I wanted to learn. And I wanted to share what I learned with others. I wanted to see people and places with my own eyes. I wanted to hear what was going on. I wanted to chronicle the journey of the people around me. And to do that, I needed to be among those making the journey.

Read the stories in this book. Read the "Lessons Learned" essays. They make it clear how valuable it is to *be* there. By witnessing what's taking place firsthand, journalists can find the words and images that make their stories credible and authentic. Their reporting lives and breathes.

You can see this in the stories by Jim Sheeler, the *Rocky Mountain News* reporter who won the ASNE non-deadline writing award and the Pulitzer Prize. He admits a failing that helped prepare him for making the "Final Salute" series so riveting:

"I'm a terrible telephone interviewer, which ended up working to my advantage: for the most part, I do almost everything in person," Sheeler tells "Best Newspaper Writing" interviewer Christopher Scanlan. Sheeler explains that when he started writing obituaries, he interviewed family members in person. It made him, and them, more comfortable. And it opened up the opportunity to know the story of a person's life.

In "Final Salute," he captures how Marines bring one of their own home for the last time. He shows how families receive their loved ones who have returned in coffins. The scenes he paints create a portrait of reality that makes your eyes water with pain—and with pride.

Read the conversations with the *Los Angeles Times* reporters who went to the scene of a devastating train derailment. Their presence yielded gripping interviews and descriptions. Erika Hayasaki tells "Best Newspaper Writing" interviewer Rick Edmonds how she "noticed a disoriented man, pulling a small suitcase on wheels." When she stopped him, she found out he had just escaped the train wreck.

The compelling, tight narrative written by John Simerman, of the *Contra Costa Times,* shows how striking the smallest of details can appear following an event as momentous as an execution. Simerman became the eyes and ears of the reader in "Watching Williams Die." In describing Stanley "Tookie" Williams' last moments, Simerman writes:

> As the drugs began coursing through his veins, Williams lifted his head. He held it there, tilted slightly left. It fell back and he raised it again, refusing to [lie] still. His breathing hitched. His stomach convulsed, lurching upward. Light shone across his damp temples.

Phuong Ly, the *Washington Post* reporter who won the Freedom Forum/ ASNE award for outstanding writing on diversity, offers a variety of fresh, original stories about people with different backgrounds and perspectives.

One way she finds such stories is by "always having lunch or coffee with someone, or asking people to take me through their neighborhoods," she tells "Best Newspaper Writing" interviewer Thomas Huang.

In the section on Hurricane Katrina coverage, reporters and photo-journalists tramped about on foot through flooded streets, rode bicycles and used boats and every other means possible to see what had happened and find the people struggling to survive the storm. Read the conversations that "Best Newspaper Writing" interviewer Butch Ward conducted with (New Orleans) *Times-Picayune* editor Jim Amoss and (Biloxi, Miss.) *Sun Herald* editor Stan Tiner. Then read about the personal dimensions of such coverage in the "Lessons Learned" essays written by Terri Troncale, Chris Rose, Margaret Baker, Don Hammack, Mike Keller, Anita Lee and Joshua Norman.

For Todd Heisler, the *Rocky Mountain News* photojournalist who won the ASNE community service photojournalism award and the Pulitzer Prize, recognizing the humanity of his subjects became an important lesson. He tells "Best Newspaper Writing" interviewer Kenny Irby: "It's important to truly care about your subjects and take time to put the camera down and listen. The photos you do not make can be as important as the ones you do make."

Get out of the office. Listen. Observe. Be human.

Lessons worth heeding—on any story.

Best
Newspaper
Writing

Writing on Deadline

Megan Garvey, Erika Hayasaki, Mitchell Landsberg, Jill Leovy, David Pierson and Richard Winton; and editor Shelby Grad

Team Deadline Writing

"Train wreck" has become a slightly overworked political and business metaphor for a particularly chaotic and shattering debacle.

On the morning of January 26, 2005, the staff of the *Los Angeles Times* was confronted with the real thing. One commuter train derailed, hitting a freight train on a siding, then jackknifed into the path of another commuter train headed in the opposite direction. The result was at least 11 deaths and about 180 injuries.

As the story unfolded, there was a bizarre twist. The accident had been caused by a despondent man who had parked his SUV on the tracks. He apparently intended to commit suicide. But he jumped out just before the first of the trains hit his vehicle.

That was a lot to sort out—even with a full working day to do so. But the *Times* has a well-established system for attacking this kind of challenge, known in-house as a "swarm" story.

Reporters and photographers rush to the scene. David Pierson was among the first from any news organization there, roughly half an hour after the 6 a.m. wreck. He quickly set to interviewing passengers sitting on benches and at picnic tables in an adjacent Costco parking lot, as well as official and volunteer rescuers.

Los Angeles Times

Erika Hayasaki headed to one of the hospitals receiving the injured. There she gathered, among other things, two finely detailed narrative accounts of individual victims and their families. Those two feeds would provide the conclusions for both the main bar and a scene-setting second story.

Back in the city room, a team of "catchers" had assembled to take feeds. These "catchers" are experienced feature writers, who transcribed and also interviewed reporters for specifics of detail and color. These feeds, fairly finished modules for the stories to be written later, go into a common basket and they are accessible for online updates through the day. The structure also avoids the breaking story trap of trying to do all the writing late in the day after the reporting has been completed.

Finally, rewrite specialists—Mitchell Landsberg, Megan Garvey and Jill Leovy—wrote the stories, each with an individual editor. Those three, and law enforcement writer Richard Winton, who did much of the reporting on a separate story about the suspect, have all been members of Pulitzer-winning breaking news teams at the *Times*.

Their collective effort—and those of dozens more—produced stories notable in a number of respects. The main bar brought clarity to basic facts that could have been confusing. The three stories provided a natural organizing principle for dividing material. The writing is crisp, free of clunky transitions or gushing and emotional adjectives. The tone is factual, but appropriately somber. The human dimensions of experiencing—or narrowly avoiding—disaster are at the forefront.

As Landsberg comments, if the segments of the story flow logically, it is all right to "pivot" now and then. The descriptive details speak for themselves—"the action is so powerful that you don't need to embellish it." Other elements—safety issues and details on the crime of intentionally derailing a train—were woven in without breaking the flow.

The stories were comprehensive without being indigestibly long. For those readers who wanted more, there was more. Readers could find additional inside stories (not included in the entry) about the experience of rescuers, or details on safety issues.

Finally, the stories reserved some rewards for readers who made it to the end—the two mini-narratives Hayasaki contributed as kickers, and the detail that the suspect's vehicle had skid marks, suggesting he may have tried to back it off the tracks but could not.

Members of the team lavish praise on the *Times* system in the e-mail interviews that follow the three stories. There is also ample evidence here of high-level execution, from energetic legwork in the early phases to a sure hand assembling the pieces at the end.

About the *Los Angeles Times* Team

Megan Garvey joined the *Times* in 1998. After several years in regional bureaus, she became a metro reporter in 2002. Earlier in her career, she worked at *The News & Observer* in Raleigh, N.C., and for *The Washington Post*. Like Landsberg, she was part of the team that won the 2004 Pulitzer Prize for breaking news covering the wildfires. She is a 1992 graduate of the University of Chicago.

Shelby Grad, who directed the train wreck coverage, became city editor of the *Times* in 2004, after a decade in other reporting and editing positions at the paper.

Erika Hayasaki has been a metro reporter at the *Times,* specializing in education and youth issues since 2001. She worked earlier for the *Tampa Tribune, Seattle Post-Intelligencer* and *News Gazette* of Champaign, Ill. She is a graduate of the University of Illinois in Champaign. She was a 2004 finalist in the Livingston Awards for Young Journalists.

Mitchell Landsberg is a reporter in the metro section and a rewrite specialist. He spent 19 years with the Associated Press as a reporter, writer and foreign correspondent before joining the *Times* in 1999. He was a member of Pulitzer Prize–winning teams at the *Times* in both 2004 and 2005, first for coverage of wildfires, then as part of the group winning the public service award for coverage of problems at King/Drew Medical Center. Landsberg is a 1976 graduate of the University of California at Los Angeles.

Jill Leovy joined the *Times* in 1993 and has been a crime and police reporter since 2001. Earlier in her career she worked for the *Seattle Times* and the *Morning News Tribune* of Tacoma. She was a member of the team that won the 1998 breaking news Pulitzer for coverage of a bank robbery and shootout.

David Pierson is a metro reporter. After two years at *Newsday,* he joined the *Times* as part of their Minority Editorial Training Program. He was first to the scene of the wreck and filed throughout the day.

Richard Winton covers law enforcement for the *Times.* He was part of the 2004 Pulitzer team covering wildfires and also part of a team that won a breaking news Pulitzer in 1998 for coverage of a bank robbery and shootout. He is a graduate of the University of Kent at Canterbury in the United Kingdom and the University of Wisconsin in Madison.

—Rick Edmonds

The Jesse Laventhol Prize for Deadline News Reporting by a team is funded by a gift from David Laventhol, a former Times Mirror *executive, in honor of his father.*

1. Chain-Reaction Crash Kills 11

JAN. 27, 2005

By David Pierson and Mitchell Landsberg

A man apparently intending to commit suicide parked his SUV in the path of a Metrolink commuter train Wednesday morning, then jumped out of the way in time to watch a chain-reaction wreck that killed at least 11 people and injured about 180.

The crash, which involved three trains, was the deadliest on a railroad in the United States since 1999. It shattered the predawn stillness near Griffith Park with what witnesses described as the sound of scraping gravel followed by a sustained boom that shook the ground.

"Before I knew it, there was a big, big bang. I looked out the window and saw fire," said Teresa Alderete, 50, of Reseda, a commuter whose train car was transformed in an instant from a rolling island of morning serenity into a nightmare of flying bodies, torn metal and shattered glass.

"I was one of the fortunate ones to walk out."

Officials said the carnage was caused by a despondent man from Compton, Juan Manuel Alvarez, 25, who parked his green Jeep Grand Cherokee on the tracks that run along the border of Glendale and the Los Angeles neighborhood of Atwater Village. As Metrolink's regular commuter train No. 100 from Moorpark to Union Station bore down on him just after 6 a.m., Alvarez leaped from the vehicle, Glendale Police Chief Randy Adams said. He was arrested at the scene and, after being taken to County-USC Medical Center, was booked on suspicion of murder. Prosecutors are weighing formal charges.

The lead passenger car of a three-car southbound train, which was being pushed from the rear by its locomotive, hit the truck, dragged it down the tracks, then derailed.

As the Metrolink train veered off the tracks, it crashed into an idle Union Pacific freight train that was on an adjacent siding. The impact caused the passenger train to jackknife. Its protruding end smashed into a three-car northbound Metrolink train as it passed on its way from Union Station to Burbank.

The rear two cars of the northbound No. 901 train—which was being pulled by its locomotive—also derailed.

"It was almost like a perfect storm of an accident," said Mary Travis, who oversees rail programs, including Metrolink, for the Ventura County Transportation Commission. "The timing of those three trains being at the same spot at the same time is just too horrible."

The crash renewed long-standing questions about rail safety in Southern California, where commuter lines share tracks with busy freight systems and intersect frequently with parts of the nation's most extensive urban road network.

Passengers aboard the Metrolink trains described how the roar of the crash gave way to isolated moans; the chaos of flying bodies and briefcases was followed by a stunned determination to survive. There was little panic, and those who were able helped those who were not.

"Most of the people in my car were fairly calm," said David McAfee, 50, an architect who works in downtown Los Angeles. "We gathered our thoughts and someone shouted to get us off the train."

At a makeshift triage center established in an adjacent Costco parking lot and, later, at a community room at the Glendale Police Department, anxious relatives waited for news of the missing.

Throughout the day, the families huddled around tables, speaking quietly with counselors and watching endless reports of the crash on a big-screen television. Periodically, police would enter to deliver the news that another body had been found.

There was no precise count by Wednesday night of the number of passengers aboard the two passenger trains, but Metrolink spokesman Francisco Oaxaca said the southbound train from Moorpark typically carried 200 to 250 people, and the northbound train carried about 30 to 50.

More than 120 people were taken to 14 hospitals, officials said. An undetermined number of others were treated at the scene or sought medical help on their own. As of Wednesday night, at least four people remained missing as rescue crews continued to search the wreckage, some of which burned after the crash.

Trains can attain up to 79 mph in the stretch where the wreck occurred. Officials said, however, they were probably traveling more slowly because the northbound train had just left the Glendale station and the other was approaching it.

Torn and twisted wreckage, yards from the Costco store on Los Feliz Boulevard, showed the force of the collision. The southbound Metrolink train had split into a mangled V, its passenger compartments ripped open in a tangle of roughly sheared metal.

Emergency crews examine the twisted metal and shattered remains of the Metrolink and Union Pacific trains in Glendale, Calif. (Photograph courtesy of Brian Vander Brug/*Los Angeles Times*)

The yellow Union Pacific freight train was knocked on its side, a toppled switching tower dangling above it.

About 20 yards from the train cars lay a wheel and axle, believed to be from the sport utility vehicle that caused the wreck.

Emergency exit panels, seat covers and bloody paper towels were strewn next to the rail cars, as were a jacket and backpack left behind by fleeing passengers.

Within minutes, rescuers—initially, Costco workers, then firefighters and police from Glendale, Los Angeles and elsewhere—were helping pull the dazed, the injured and the dead from the wreckage.

In one car, firefighters said, they found an injured man who had written a message in blood on a piece of metal under his seat. It read: "I (heart) my kids. (heart) Leslie."

The man, whom officials did not identify, was rescued and taken to a hospital.

Officials identified several of the dead: Scott McKeown, 42, who was in charge of the city of Pasadena's phone, radio and sound systems; Julia Bennett, a 44-year-old senior clerk-typist with the Los Angeles Fire Department; Manuel D. Alcala, 51, of West Hills, a senior general maintenance worker at the County Jail; and Elizabeth Hill, 65, who worked in the city of Glendale financial office.

Also among the dead was Los Angeles County Sheriff's Deputy James Tutino, a 47-year-old father of four who was on his way to work downtown at the Men's Central Jail.

"My empathy is with everyone on that train," Sheriff Lee Baca said. "When you lift up the body of a colleague who seconds earlier had been safe and secure on that train, and place it on a stretcher, and drape an American flag over him, and look down and you find blood on his hands, the blood that sustained his life only hours earlier, and then after that, you find out that some individual who was not happy with his life caused all this death and destruction... This is a thing to be extremely angry about."

Alvarez stabbed himself in the chest with a knife and tried to slit his wrists, police officials said, although it was not clear if that was before or after he parked on the tracks.

He apparently turned onto the tracks just south of a crossing at Chevy Chase Drive. Police said there were indications that he tried to back out but got stuck before abandoning the vehicle.

Adams, the Glendale chief, said Alvarez "will be charged with as many lives as were lost in this tragedy." He described Alvarez as "distraught and remorseful, but cooperative," and said he admitted leaving the vehicle on the tracks.

Adams added that Alvarez would be kept under close supervision in jail.

Los Angeles County Dist. Atty. Steve Cooley said that it was too early to discuss what charges may be brought against Alvarez, but that he could face multiple counts of murder. Under state law, intentional train wrecking could be the basis for a murder charge that would carry a potential death penalty, Loyola University law professor Laurie Levenson said.

Alvarez also could face separate charges under a law that makes derailing a train a federal crime. If the derailment results in fatal injuries, that law also provides for execution or life in prison without parole.

Wednesday's crash was the third fatal Metrolink crash in less than three years, and it brought fresh urgency to calls for costly projects that would put rails below or above roadways.

It also raised questions about Metrolink's practice—a common one among commuter railroads—of using a "push-pull" system in which locomotives are in the front of the train in one direction and in the rear the other.

In this crash, that meant a passenger car bore the brunt of the initial impact, but Metrolink spokeswoman Denise Tyrrell said the configuration is not inherently unsafe.

The southbound train that was the first to derail was operating on a route and at a time that were the first in the Metrolink system when it was established in 1992, according to Travis, the Ventura County official. Many of those on the train had been regular commuters for a decade or more, and had developed daily routines and friendships.

Russ Francis, 48, of Simi Valley, who has been taking the train several times a month, said he follows a personal safety plan he devised for train travel.

"I always sit in the second-to-the-last car from the back," he said. "I figured that you don't want to be in the front car if you get in a wreck, and you don't want to be in the very last car because of the whip."

Suddenly, the train jumped. "It was scary. I thought we either hit a car or ran over something really big on the tracks," he said.

For about 10 seconds, the scraping, screeching sound intensified. "It got faster and faster, louder and louder." Then the lights went out and there was more screeching.

Fearing an impact, Francis grabbed a nearby pole and braced a foot against the side of the car.

"Then we started hearing heavy metal," he said. "The metal sounded like it was being ripped around."

"I realized we were done, we were crashing."

The impact was strong and quick. And immediately following, silence. Francis looked around and saw passengers lying on the floor, eyeglasses strewn about. In the darkness he could make out a bloody forehead and a bloody neck.

The next-to-last car did not overturn.

Francis grabbed his rolling suitcase and started to make his way toward the door, watching a woman trying to help a man off the train.

"We've got to get out of this train right now," he remembered telling the couple. He estimated that it took him 10 seconds to get out of the car.

Outside, he trekked up to the first car and found a man in a uniform shirt lying on the ground. He reached out and grabbed his hand to help him, but the injured man fell back, unable to move.

Nearby, Francis saw another severely injured man lying on the ground, wearing what appeared to be a uniform jacket. His face was like "a hood of blood. It looked like a shell where his head should have been. He had no face."

2. A Troubled Past, a Startling Action

JAN. 27, 2005

By Richard Winton and Jill Leovy

Juan Manuel Alvarez's troubles had been building long before he drove his Jeep Cherokee onto the train tracks in an aborted suicide attempt that derailed two commuter trains and killed 11 people, according to family members, acquaintances and court records.

Alvarez, a pony-tailed sometime construction worker, had been separated from his wife for several months amid allegations that he had threatened her and her family.

Carmelita Alvarez alleged that drug use had addled his mind, according to court papers she filed in support of a restraining order. She described him as a jealous man possessed by paranoid fantasies that she was cheating.

Family members and acquaintances said he used drugs heavily.

Alvarez, 25, described as a devotee of ancient Mexican rituals, was in custody late Wednesday, booked on suspicion of murder.

Authorities disclosed little about his background, and even some of those close to Alvarez said they were mystified about what led him to a railroad crossing near Glendale early Wednesday.

Alvarez had never been convicted of a serious crime, but was arrested several times on suspicion of burglary and drug possession beginning in 1994, authorities said. A cocaine possession charge against him, dating from a 1999 arrest in Carson, was later dismissed, court documents show.

And while he had threatened his wife, he had never assaulted her nor their children, according to a questionnaire Carmelita Alvarez filled out last fall to get the restraining order.

"He threatened to take our kid away and to hurt my family members," she wrote. "He is planning on selling his vehicle to buy a gun and threatened to use it. He has caused damage to family property. ... He has primarily threatened my brother, saying that he would shoot and stab him."

The order was granted Dec. 14, court papers indicated. Its terms included a suspension of Alvarez's right to visit his two children: a stepdaughter, 6, and a 3-year-old son.

He and Carmelita met in Los Angeles about six years ago, said Carmelita's brother Ruben Ochoa, 26.

At that time, Alvarez was not working much, said Sergio Lopez, who manages an apartment complex in Bell where the couple had lived for several months.

But he played traditional drums used in ancient Mexican Indian ceremonies.

Lopez said Alvarez was in a group that performed such ceremonies in Aztec costume—headdresses, loincloths and sandals with bells.

When Alvarez's son was born, the couple gave him the middle name Nezahualcoyotl. The name is taken from a pre-Columbian warrior-poet and a Mexican city.

Relatives said the couple married about two years ago and moved into a converted garage behind the tidy, tan stucco home of his in-laws on a quiet, well-kept street in Compton.

Accounts of more recent events varied:

Alejandro Amaya, 50, who is married to Carmelita's sister and also lived in the Compton house, said Alvarez was "like a brother." Amaya said he sometimes drank beer with Alvarez but was not aware of any drug addictions. "He was never a problem," Amaya said.

But neighbors and Ochoa, Carmelita's brother, tell a different story. Ochoa said Alvarez was an alcoholic and used many drugs. In court papers, Carmelita alleged that Alvarez had been using drugs "a very long time," despite twice completing rehabilitation programs.

The couple split up several months ago, relatives said. On Nov. 24, Carmelita applied for the restraining order, alleging that Alvarez had begun hallucinating, convinced she was having affairs and making pornographic movies.

Alvarez accused her, she wrote, of setting up hidden cameras in the couple's bedroom. She said he told her he would buy a gun and take revenge on her, her family members and an imaginary lover.

Carmelita also described three incidents from Nov. 12 to Nov. 21 in which Alvarez made threats, including two menacing phone calls. He was especially hostile toward her brother, she said, who Alvarez believed introduced her to other men.

About 6 a.m. Wednesday, police said, Alvarez drove his Jeep Cherokee onto the tracks at the border of Los Angeles and Glendale east of the Golden State Freeway and north of Los Feliz Boulevard.

Authorities offered fragmentary accounts of what happened next:

According to some reports, Alvarez turned onto the tracks south of Chevy Chase Drive, hooking his front two wheels over the rails.

Later, police would find marks on the tires suggesting the Jeep had moved back and forth before the train hit. They concluded that Alvarez tried to drive forward over the tracks, but the car wouldn't move. So he tried to back up and failed. He was stuck.

As the train bore down on him, police said, he got out of the car.

He then stood by watching as the oncoming train flattened the car under its wheels. At first the car shattered easily—but then the train hit the Jeep's unyielding engine block.

That's when the train wheels lifted and it skipped the tracks, unleashing the collisions that followed.

Alvarez was arrested by police a few blocks away as he was being treated by paramedics, said Glendale Police Chief Randy Adams.

He was injured, not from the train crash but from self-inflicted wounds, police said.

He had tried to slit his wrists and had stabbed himself, police said. There were conflicting reports of when these injuries occurred—whether before the accident, or as police said some witnesses reported, afterward, while watching the disaster unfold.

Police described Alvarez as cooperative, suicidal and remorseful.

He was treated for his wounds and is being held at an undisclosed facility.

A man who described himself as one of Alvarez's relatives declined to answer questions about him, saying the family is trying to get a lawyer.

"We don't know what to do," said the man, speaking from a small home in Monterey Park. "We regret everything that happened."

3. Survival a Matter of Chance

JAN. 27, 2005

By Erika Hayasaki and Megan Garvey

They rode the southbound train in the predawn darkness, some napping, some reading, some chatting with the friends they had made over the years.

Los Angeles County Sheriff's Deputy James Tutino, 47, boarded at the first stop, Simi Valley, before 5:20 a.m. He needed to make it to downtown Los Angeles for an early meeting.

Tutino rode only a few times a month. He sat in the first car, with a group of fellow deputies. He told them his knee was bothering him and he didn't want to work the clutch of his Mustang in rain-soaked traffic.

About half an hour later, Steve Toby, 51, boarded the second car at the downtown Burbank station. A stranger was sitting in his regular seat. He chose another several rows back.

Theresa Gillen, 37, boarded at the same station, en route to her job at a Los Angeles day-care center. Her mother, Eleanor, had dropped her off, as she did each day. She got on the first car of Metrolink Train No. 100.

Minutes later, there was a loud noise, and then the sound of rocks striking the undercarriage.

Some screamed. Then, as the train careened off the track and the lights went out, the passengers fell silent. The only sound was the shriek of metal against gravel.

Derailed by an empty SUV left by a despondent man, Train No. 100 was hurtling toward a sidelined freight locomotive.

For the passengers on board, survival was a matter of chance.

The impact against the Union Pacific locomotive spun the lead car sideways, and popped Scott Cox's second-floor seat from its bolts.

Cox, 29, looked out a hole that had been ripped into the car to see the overturned yellow locomotive beside the train. Below, he saw fire. A woman's legs dangled out of the train. Cox pulled her in, to safety.

In the darkness of the wreckage, injured passengers cried for help—a scream that someone was pinned inside, a woman moaning that she could not move.

Cox walked with other passengers toward the back stairs.

He stepped over another woman sprawled on the floor. Then he compared his injuries to hers, and went back. Cox stayed with her until help arrived.

Still inside the train, Steve Toby had been thrown across the car.

Toby, who runs the audio for Los Angeles City Council meetings, landed on top of a woman who works for the Department of Water and Power, someone he saw regularly but had never met.

Ceiling tiles fell on them. Metal trapped his leg. They were close to where the train had jackknifed and collided with a northbound commuter train.

Toby broke free and hobbled to an exit. His usual seat was crushed and shredded. He wondered what had happened to the man who had been sitting there.

Outside, on the ground, he saw the body of a dead sheriff's deputy.

Tutino had been killed. The veteran deputy, an avid sports fan and part-time football coach, was carried away later, draped in an American flag. He left behind a wife and four children.

"Fate, it was just fate," said Sheriff's Sgt. Mark McCorkle, a longtime friend.

Others narrowly escaped.

Nearly every morning, Kenny Yi, 45, drove from Simi Valley to the Northridge Metrolink station, unloaded his bicycle and got on the first car. This time, the bike rack for the lead car was full. He got on the second car.

Usually, he got off at Burbank and bicycled the rest of the way to the Caltrans office downtown. But the rain persuaded him to stay aboard to Union Station.

He was napping on the second level when the sound of grinding rock woke him.

He was thrown into the aisle. When he saw the crumpled first car, he thought the overcrowded rack might have saved his life.

"Thank God. I guess someone was looking out for me," said the Simi Valley resident. "I was thinking about all the things I could have left, like my family."

Upstairs in the first car, Goddard Paialii, 53, of Woodland Hills had braced himself at the first loud noise. He thought that the train must be dragging whatever it had hit.

Around him, passengers were being tossed about.

One woman facing him ended up three seats away. A man seated across the aisle from him flew over and landed in a seat on the aisle.

The man, Paialii said, was unconscious. His eyes were open, but he didn't move.

Smoke filled the car. Someone yelled fire. But people weren't panicking.

"Everybody was trying to help everybody get out," Paialii said. The once-orderly passenger compartment seemed "ripped out"—laptops, seat cushions, briefcases, eyeglasses were scattered everywhere.

"We went out through the gaping hole," he said. The damage was so severe, he couldn't tell which side of the train was ripped open.

Someone made a step out of a piece of the broken train, to help passengers get out.

At Eleanor Gillen's Burbank home, the phone woke her about 7:30 a.m. It was her oldest daughter, Sarah Gillen.

"Mom," she said, "was Theresa on the train?"

"Yes," Eleanor told her.

"Mom," Sarah said, "the train wrecked."

Eleanor Gillen turned on the television, saw the jackknifed train cars, the injured people. She watched as rescue workers carried victims away on stretchers.

She dialed her daughter's cell phone. No answer. She tried again and again.

The home phone rang again, but it was a friend from Houston who had seen the news. Did she know anyone on board?

"I said, 'My daughter was there,' " Gillen said. "They said, 'We'll pray for her.' "

By 10 a.m., family members had fanned out to search.

A brother-in-law went to Glendale Memorial Hospital, where a dozen of about 180 injured were treated. There was no one there with her name, officials told him.

Unable to wait any longer, Gillen found her way to a makeshift information center near the crash site by 10:30 a.m. She brought a picture of her daughter.

Glendale police officers called hospitals and described Theresa Gillen: about 5 feet 5, long black hair, brown eyes. Wearing a black fleece jacket.

Glendale Memorial officials had a Jane Doe who matched.

Police drove Eleanor Gillen to the hospital.

Her daughter had undergone emergency brain surgery for a blood clot. Her head was shaved. Her arms were bruised. Three metal plates had been placed in her skull. She was heavily sedated. But by the afternoon, her family visited her in a recovery room.

"I have a myriad of emotions going from anger to sadness, to just relief that she's OK, to worry: What's she going to be like when she recovers?" said her younger sister, Leah Gillen, 35. "I'm angry that someone would be so selfish and would destroy the lives of so many people. These people were just going to work."

Conversations with

Megan Garvey, Erika Hayasaki, Jill Leovy and David Pierson; and editor Shelby Grad

An edited e-mail interview conducted by The Poynter Institute's faculty member Rick Edmonds with reporters Megan Garvey, Erika Hayasaki, Jill Leovy, David Pierson and editor Shelby Grad, members of the Los Angeles Times *team that won the ASNE team deadline news reporting award.*

The Reporting and Writing

RICK EDMONDS: When and how did you get to the story?

DAVID PIERSON: I was asleep when I got a call from an editor at around 6:15 a.m. to run out to the location where he had heard of a massive train derailment. How he first learned of the accident, I don't know. I didn't think much of it at first because I've been awakened for a variety of stories, including one about a tree-sitter being pushed out of his perch by developers in the middle of the night. My apartment at the time was only 10 minutes away from the crash site, so I got there around 6:30 a.m.

MEGAN GARVEY (left): I got a call at home in the morning from Shelby Grad—our city editor—asking me to start taking feeds from David Pierson, the first reporter on the scene, and talking to him about the sorts of detail we wanted and where we needed additional reporters to be sent. I think that was about 8 a.m.

JILL LEOVY: I got a call in the early morning from Shelby Grad, who mistakenly thought I lived nearby. In fact, I didn't. But I was already working. I was in the habit of starting work around 5:30 a.m. during that time because I was closely covering cops. And I was relatively nearby in a police station at the time Shelby called, I believe. I'm a big believer in starting early, even though that's not the usual thing for reporters.

ERIKA HAYASAKI: The morning assignment editor called me just after 6 a.m. and told me to head to the crash site immediately. On my way there, I received a second call from him telling me to go to the hospital instead. When I arrived, I didn't see other reporters. The injured were on their way.

I noticed a disoriented man, pulling a small suitcase on wheels. I stopped him, and he told me that he had just escaped the wreck. He wasn't injured, but he figured he would go to the hospital anyway. I followed him inside, and bought him a cup of coffee. As he waited for a doctor, he told me his story.

About 30 minutes later, a hospital security guard suspiciously eyed my notebook. He asked who I was. Then, he kicked me out of the hospital. But I already had enough material to compile a short narrative vignette. I jotted it down in loose story form quickly, and called the feed into a newsroom catcher.

One of the writers, Mitchell Landsberg, ended up using it as the kicker for the main story.

That anecdote is the following:

Russ Francis, 48, of Simi Valley, who has been taking the train several times a month, said he follows a personal safety plan he devised for train travel.

"I always sit in the second-to-the-last car from the back," he said. "I figured that you don't want to be in the front car if you get in a wreck, and you don't want to be in the very last car because of the whip."

Suddenly, the train jumped. "It was scary. I thought we either hit a car or ran over something really big on the tracks," he said.

For about 10 seconds, the scraping, screeching sound intensified. "It got faster and faster, louder and louder." Then the lights went out and there was more screeching.

Fearing an impact, Francis grabbed a nearby pole and braced a foot against the side of the car.

"Then we started hearing heavy metal," he said. "The metal sounded like it was being ripped around."

"I realized we were done, we were crashing."

The impact was strong and quick. And immediately following, silence. Francis looked around and saw passengers lying on the floor, eyeglasses strewn about. In the darkness he could make out a bloody forehead and a bloody neck.

The next-to-last car did not overturn.

Francis grabbed his rolling suitcase and started to make his way toward the door, watching a woman trying to help a man off the train.

"We've got to get out of this train right now," he remembered telling the couple. He estimated that it took him 10 seconds to get out of the car.

Outside, he trekked up to the first car and found a man in a uniform shirt lying on the ground. He reached out and grabbed his hand to help him, but the injured man fell back, unable to move.

Nearby, Francis saw another severely injured man lying on the ground, wearing what appeared to be a uniform jacket. His face was like "a hood of blood. It looked like a shell where his head should have been. He had no face."

How did you determine the focus of your part of the story?

DAVID PIERSON: When I arrived at the site—a massive parking lot for several retail stores like Best Buy and Costco—my first instinct was to head for the injured. There were dozens of them sitting on Costco picnic benches. The most severely wounded were being taken away to hospitals. I interviewed as many people on the benches as possible. Most were still shocked. They described the jolt of the crash and the panic that ensued.

I then fanned out looking for other witnesses. Some of the best were the early morning Costco employees who joined the rescue. They gave very detailed descriptions of what they saw and did. Next was finding the police and fire officials. These sources were invaluable throughout the day, dispersing updates for me, until I called it a night at around 11 p.m.

It wasn't much more complicated than that for me. I was lucky enough to get there early before most of the passengers were ushered away. Like most of the swarm stories we've done, there was always good communication with the desk. I gave them the meat and potatoes, as well as enough detail to construct the narrative. Being at the scene the entire time, all editors had to do was call if they needed clarification from an official or witness.

MEGAN GARVEY: In recent years, we've worked out a fairly consistent system of dividing up rewrite duties on big breaking news stories, usually breaking down—as this did—to Mitchell Landsberg handling rewrite on the mainbar, and me working on the main scene story. In this case, the drama of a mundane morning commute suddenly disrupted by a willful act—the car parked on the train tracks—seemed a clear place to focus a story that gave readers a sense of what had happened that day.

JILL LEOVY: I don't remember much thought going into this. It was a seat-of-the-pants, deadline situation, and we all just did what came our way. In the morning, I was sent to the scene. And it was lucky, because the accident happened just a few blocks from where I used to live. So I knew the area very well. And I knew a back way to get into the railroad tracks from an empty lot behind Costco. I never would have known this had I not lived in the area, so it helped. Later, I reported from the office, and  collated material called in from reporters in various places, and rewrote these into the story. I like doing rewrite, so I often volunteer for this.

Where and how did you collect information?

MEGAN GARVEY: We collected information from reporters at the scene, sources in various law enforcement communities, government studies of train accidents involving commuter trains being pushed by engines rather than pulled—as this one was—and transit officials.

JILL LEOVY: Through the usual means. I spent some time at the command post next to the tracks where many police sources who I cover all the time were gathered. They knew me, so it was an easy situation to get information in.

ERIKA HAYASKI: After getting kicked out of the hospital, I had to stand outside like the rest of the reporters, who had begun to arrive. We waited for periodic press conferences. We asked every person entering the hospital if they were family members of the injured.

    With every subject, I tried to get details to build short narratives. In getting feeds, I always walk the person I am interviewing through the beginning, middle and end of an event, because it is easier for the writer to build a strong anecdote for the story.

But it was hard. Reporters swarmed every family. They were surrounded by microphones, cameras and a dozen reporters scribbling in notebooks. Time was limited. It was hard to get personal.

I remember running into Eleanor Gillen. She arrived at the hospital looking for her daughter, Theresa Gillen, who had been badly injured in the wreck. Standing on the sidewalk in front of the hospital, Eleanor and her other daughter quickly recounted their morning phone conversation, when they discovered that Theresa had been a passenger on the smoldering train they were watching on television. They talked about the search to find Theresa, who had been listed as a Jane Doe.

I grabbed quotes and details. But the family, of course, was in a rush to see Theresa, who was in a recovery room after undergoing emergency surgery. The last thing they wanted to do was talk to a reporter. Before they entered the hospital, I got their cell phone numbers, in hopes that they would be willing to talk more, after things calmed.

I called them several hours later, and Megan Garvey, who was putting together the story, called them, too. The phone numbers helped us later get pertinent details about the Gillen family's experience, which turned into a powerful anecdote, with a beginning, middle and end.

The portion that ended up in the story is as follows:

At Eleanor Gillen's Burbank home, the phone woke her about 7:30 a.m. It was her oldest daughter, Sarah Gillen.

"Mom," she said, "was Theresa on the train?"

"Yes," Eleanor told her.

"Mom," Sarah said, "the train wrecked."

Eleanor Gillen turned on the television, saw the jackknifed train cars, the injured people. She watched as rescue workers carried victims away on stretchers.

She dialed her daughter's cell phone. No answer. She tried again and again.

The home phone rang again, but it was a friend from Houston who had seen the news. Did she know anyone on board?

"I said, 'My daughter was there,'" Gillen said. "They said, 'We'll pray for her.'"

By 10 a.m., family members had fanned out to search.

A brother-in-law went to Glendale Memorial Hospital, where a dozen of about 180 injured were treated. There was no one there with her name, officials told him.

Unable to wait any longer, Gillen found her way to a makeshift information center near the crash site by 10:30 a.m. She brought a picture of her daughter.

Glendale police officers called hospitals and described Theresa Gillen: about 5 feet 5, long black hair, brown eyes. Wearing a black fleece jacket.

Glendale Memorial officials had a Jane Doe who matched.

Police drove Eleanor Gillen to the hospital.

Her daughter had undergone emergency brain surgery for a blood clot. Her head was shaved. Her arms were bruised. Three metal plates had been placed in her skull. She was heavily sedated. But by the afternoon, her family visited her in a recovery room.

"I have a myriad of emotions going from anger to sadness, to just relief that she's OK, to worry: What's she going to be like when she recovers?" said her younger sister, Leah Gillen, 35. "I'm angry that someone would be so selfish and would destroy the lives of so many people. These people were just going to work."

How did you organize your story? Who wrote it?

JILL LEOVY: I wrote "A Troubled Past, a Startling Action"—organizing it completely on the fly. Just instinct.

MEGAN GARVEY: On breaking news stories when I know I'm doing rewrite I ask all reporters feeding from the field—and anyone taking feeds—to get specific details and times, asking for recollections about how things looked, smelled, sounded. In this case, I also asked everyone to also ask about normal routines—where did the passengers usually sit or disembark? Was the day routine, or was something different?

When you attach times to events you can put together a chronology of the day, even working under tight deadlines. A lot of the times when I work on these kinds of stories I find it helpful to print out all the feeds and order them by time. Although all stories don't end up working best by following a straight chronological order, doing so allows me to see what memories repeat among different witnesses, which quotes about the same moments are the strongest. It is also a way to fold in actions away from the scene—in this case allowing a smooth transition to the mother getting the phone call and turning on the television.

Did you do more than one draft?

MEGAN GARVEY: There was originally a much longer version of the story that wove together both the victims and the rescuers. Late in the day the top editor asked that we take out all of that material and create a separate story. That story ran much as it had been written in a separate 25-inch piece on rescuers that ran on an inside page.

I actually disagreed with that call, but was persuaded to let it go by my editor on the story, Geoff Mohan. I can remember being pretty unhappy about it since I felt like we had managed to put together a really comprehensive piece on deadline. Reading back on the stories now I still think it would have been great to have one story that really gave the overall feel of the entire scene, but understand concerns about length and readers' attention spans.

JILL LEOVY: No, there wasn't enough time. We did weave in new material through the day as it came in.

How were revisions made?

MEGAN GARVEY: Mostly I worked with Geoff to make sure we had used the strongest material and then, as I had the story in the shape I wanted it, I read back on the other pieces to make sure they were complementary and not repetitive.

All three stories seem to contain a mix of sympathy and outrage toward the perpetrator. How did you strike that balance in your profile of Juan Manuel Alvarez?

JILL LEOVY: For me, the detail about the skid marks indicating he may have had second thoughts, and tried unsuccessfully to get the vehicle off the tracks, was very significant. When Richard Winton told me that, I think I was cautious about what I wrote.

We really didn't know much about what happened, so it's always good to leave room for angles that haven't surfaced yet. Also, the perpetrator was clearly suicidal.

Did your portrait of Alvarez change as the day went on and more information became available?

JILL LEOVY: As I said, the skid mark detail was important. The paranoia was significant also—really gave a sense both of the depth of his psychological problems, and how much suffering he must have visited upon the woman who was the target of his delusions.

Did you have some piquant detail that didn't make it into the piece because it was not adequately verifiable?

JILL LEOVY: Many, I think. You just let 'em go until you have more. Period.

Both of these stories end with a fairly lengthy—10 grafs or so—narrative. Is that happenstance, or a shared writing strategy?

MEGAN GARVEY: It wasn't strategy. And I don't remember talking to Mitchell about it. But I do think having worked together as a team on these sorts of stories for a while, we use complementary approaches to breaking news stories. I do remember talking to him about who he wanted to use in the mainbar. The man who makes up the bottom portion of that story—Russ Francis—seemed like a great fit for the mainbar because he hit on many of the themes the story dealt with, including the element of chance in who lived and the question of safety.

How did you report where the victims were killed or injured? Or was that not known by the end of the day?

MEGAN GARVEY: There were several other stories not included in this entry—and many additional people who deserve credit for getting great information. One piece detailed each of the known victims, who they were, what they did and where they were sitting that day.

How did you deal with the effect the event was having on you personally? How did it help or impede your work?

MEGAN GARVEY: Not being at the scene, I think the emotional impact of the events was a little distant for me. I think, though, that hearing from people who had lived through it gave me a desire to convey how traumatic what had happened was for them. I remember our reporters at the scene being very calm and doing an excellent job interviewing under difficult circumstances—including a cold rain, at least by Southern California standards.

Were any of you pulled away from work on the newspaper story for a period of time to create or update an online version? Or did others handle that? Would the protocols be different now, a year later, as the *Times* and many other papers increase emphasis on online breaking news?

MEGAN GARVEY: We work off of a feeds basket on breaking news stories that the online folks have access to as well. In this case, one of the reasons I started taking feeds from David Pierson at home was so the Web people could grab those takes ASAP. A year later it would likely be about the same.

Can you describe some of the material that ended up on the cutting room floor? Good stuff but secondary, or repetitive?

MEGAN GARVEY: I looked back at the first draft—which I still had because I worked on it in my personal basket before copying it over to a public area—and found one guy who was really compelling and didn't make it into the paper. He was someone who regularly rode that train and worked very close to where it crashed. He had driven to work earlier that morning because rain was forecast and he didn't want to have to bike from the station, his usual routine. When we moved the rescue workers out of the main scene story I guess he got cut.

I think this needed to be boiled down some but here's part of his story from that first draft—complete with notes to self about where he was located:

> Terry McBrien, a manager at a lumber warehouse (Topanga Lumber Warehouse) located (on east side of tracks, opposite side of Costco) about 30 yards from where the trains came to a rest, said he was one of the first people on the scene.
>
> "I easily could have been on that train this morning," said McBrien, standing near the wreckage, tears in his eyes, voice trembling. "Thank God for the rain. I usually take Metrolink into the Glendale station and then ride my bike to work. I didn't want to do that in the rain today."
>
> Shortly after he arrived at work, as he sat at his desk waiting for his computer to boot up, McBrien said he heard a whistle from one of the trains. He thought nothing of it, since trains normally use their whistles as they go through the area. "That's my train," he recalled telling himself. Then came a sudden boom, one of the loudest noises he'd ever heard. He immediately figured a crash or derailment had occurred on the tracks that lay just feet from the back of his warehouse.
>
> In the darkness, McBrien jumped a fence that separates the tracks from the back of the lumber warehouse and saw the devastation: Trains sliced open and scattered across the tracks, and injured people crawling and stumbling out of the twisted train cars. "They were in a daze, trembling, in shock. I saw one woman, she was shaking like a leaf, saying, 'Oh my god, where am I? Where am I?' Another woman, she was sitting down pointing to her husband. She said, 'Please help my husband, please.' I could see blood coming from his leg."

As he began helping people, taking some of them through an opening of the fence into his warehouse, he recognized a man he usually takes the train with, walking among the wreckage in a daze. "I don't know him but he's a guy I see on the train all of the time," said McBrien. "That's when it really hit me. That could have been me. I could have been on that train."

Anything about the making of this excellent story I have neglected to ask about?

JILL LEOVY: As past awards in breaking-news categories have shown, the *Los Angeles Times* has had success with its mechanism for covering these kinds of stories, particularly when they happen on our time line.

We have a structure for covering these things. First, a swarm of reporters are sent out. They call in feeds to "catchers," other reporters who guide them and rewrite some of their material. The catchers overlap with rewrite reporters who are constructing the stories throughout the day. I performed all three roles on this story, but mostly, I was a rewrite reporter, the last stop.

The system means the story isn't written at the last minute, after all the reporting is done. I credit my editors with developing this system, which is bigger than any reporter or writer. The *Times,* of course, is blessed with a large staff so we can do this. But the division of labor seems to work well.

MEGAN GARVEY: I think the quality of these stories and the others that day that also ran are a testament to the great reporting of the metro staff here—honed on a range of large-scale disasters over the years. If the material is outstanding and detailed, the writing is easy.

The Editing

RICK EDMONDS: How and when did you divide the story into the three separate stories? Any alternative treatments considered and rejected?

SHELBY GRAD (right): When the story broke, it took some time to determine its scope. At first, the reports were that a train had derailed and perhaps two people were dead. Luckily, we were able to flood the zone with reporters right away.

The crash occurred not far from downtown Los Angeles and within a few minutes from where many staffers lived. We knew right away we'd have a mainbar. Mitchell Landsberg is the best rewrite guy in the business as far as I'm concerned, so we quickly got him on board.

We also knew we wanted an investigative piece looking at the safety record of Metrolink, particularly the issues of "push-pull" trains. At first, we planned a single story about the scene on the train and the rescue. But eventually, we decided to go with two separate stories: one, the tale of passengers caught in the wreck and getting out; the second focusing on the rescue efforts. The examination of the truck driver who caused the crash came together late. We got his name late in the game and launched a team of reporters to focus specifically on his story. In the end, we felt our strongest pieces were the mainbar, the passengers and the suspect (meaning we pushed the safety record piece inside).

Talk about coordinating and synthesizing the work of the six bylined reporters and other contributors through the day.

Los Angeles is such an insane news town that the *Times* has a lot of experience in dealing with mega-breaking news stories involving dozens of reporters. Our system worked here.

We sent probably 20 or so reporters to the scene. David Pierson was the first there and by around 7:30, we knew he was getting strong material. We then brought into the newsroom about five reporters to serve as "catchers." We generally pick veteran reporters as catchers because we want them not just to take dictation, but to essentially interview the field reporters and make sure the feeds are clear and complete.

We try to make sure all feeds provide times of when events occurred so we can develop a narrative timeline. All feeds are filed into a public basket with clear labels. This allows editors and writers to see the reporting as it comes in and see how the stories should be shaped. It also helps us get a sense of what holes there might be.

We also lined up our rewrite team—people with experience culling through feeds and getting stories together. For this story, we had a rewrite person assigned to each of our stories. Ultimately, we assigned one editor to each story.

How was the story revised, refined or expanded after first-edition deadline?

All the stories were reworked after the first deadline. We moved some more color into the mainbar. We divided the color story into two: one focusing on the passengers, the other on the rescuers. We raced against the clock on the suspect story, getting new details about him in until the last minute.

Does the *Los Angeles Times* have a "disaster game plan"? Do you prepare and practice for huge stories of this kind? How?

Our basic plan on breaking news, as I mentioned above, is to get a good group of reporters out to the scene as soon as possible. Then, we quickly identify catchers who can talk to field reporters and produce feeds.

These catchers are key because they are basically the first writers of these stories, and they must press for key details and make sure the facts add up. The catchers need to be strong reporters, because their "interviews" with the field reporters are key. Two key catchers that day were among our best feature writers: Bob Pool and Carla Hall.

Then we line up writers to put together the stories. Of course, the stories change through the day. Often, one story seems good on paper but either doesn't come together or is trumped by a more compelling tale that develops later. In this case, we pushed hard on the issue of the safety record of Metrolink, assigning several of our top investigative reporters as well as the transportation beat reporters to it. We assumed that would be a front pager. In the end, while the story was excellent, it didn't trump the three stories that got on the front page.

How is the consistency of tone and use of vivid detail achieved?

Our big push with reporters in the field is to really mine sources and the scene. We even had a newsroom seminar on the subject, in which our rewrite team talked about how to produce a good feed and what makes up a bad feed. The seminar included writers who had pulled together major stories over the decades—O. J. Simpson, earthquakes, Patty Hearst and Charles Manson. They agreed that even with improved technology—cell phones, BlackBerrys, e-mail—the basics of a feed haven't changed very much. As veteran *Times* reporter Eric Malnic told reporters: "They talk, you write, we print."

Writers' Workshop

Talking Points

1. Mitchell Landsberg says that his story "simply stops and pivots" from time to time but has few formal transitions. Are transitions necessary or helpful in a story like this? Or do logical links and pacing in presenting the material take care of that?

2. Megan Garvey says that late in the process a segment on the experience of rescuers was cut from her story and made a separate sidebar—a decision she regrets. As a reader, do you miss it? Are there any notable gaps or unanswered questions in the three stories chosen for the front page?

3. How many parts of the *Los Angeles Times* "swarm" system could be adapted to a smaller, or even campus, newspaper? Which would be impractical?

4. Jill Leovy comments that having "catchers" file feeds in polished form rather than as notes throughout the day "means the story isn't written at the last minute after all the reporting is done." Is this good practice? Or do you see potential problems?

5. The writers are disciplined about not using emotive adjectives like "horrific" or "tragic," except sparingly in direct quotations from those involved in the wreck. Is this always a good practice? Landsberg says the aim is for writing that is lean and "muscular." Does the power of detail speak for itself or do you find the stories dry or unemotional?

Assignment Desk

1. Write a disaster coverage plan you could use in various circumstances. How would you organize your reporting if sent to the scene of a disaster on little or no notice? What are some questions you would ask to elicit detail? What practical problems would you expect to encounter talking to witnesses? How would you solve them?

2. David Pierson and Erika Hayasaki seem to have a level of comfort when talking to the injured and their families. Would you find this difficult? How would you prepare?

3. A car plows into a sidewalk crowded with students, killing several and injuring many more. As an editor directing coverage, what would be your objective for the final story or package of stories? How would you communicate with reporters and writers to be sure you get the right building blocks?

4. If you were faced with the reporting problems the *Times* team encountered, where would you go for background information on railroad safety or for details on how intentionally derailing a train is treated as a crime?

John Simerman

Individual Deadline Writing

CONTRA COSTA TIMES

Don't bother asking John Simerman his opinion of the death penalty. He won't tell. He doesn't believe it is important. He wants his editors and readers to trust that he wrote his story from solid ground, not a soapbox.

He knew the controversy surrounding the execution he witnessed. He knew the man, having covered the Stanley "Tookie" Williams story for several years leading up to his execution. But he says he came to the story without an angle, determined to simply report what he saw. That explains why his story unfolds in meticulous detail.

Simerman chronicled considerable death in 2005. Just prior to the Williams execution, he spent six weeks in New Orleans as part of a Knight Ridder investigative team, gathering data on those killed by the storm. He says he "banged on a lot of doors" amid the devastation. He catalogued the people who succumbed to the hurricane, where they died, why and how.

Such morbid duty might be tough on some journalists, but Simerman says, "I don't get emotionally involved in stories." He jokingly refers to himself as a "cold fish." His rationale is that emotion might cloud his judgment. That's why his method is straightforward—dig for the details.

Simerman earned a bachelor's degree from Pomona College in 1990, followed by a master's in print journalism from New York University in 1994. He has worked for the *Contra Costa Times* for 10 years. Prior to that, he worked at the *Press Democrat* in Santa Rosa, Calif.

When he served a stint as an editor at the *Contra Costa Times* from 1999–2001, he became restless. "When I started overworking people's copy," he says, he knew it was time to get back to his real love—general assignment reporting. He enjoys being a go-to guy, jumping into breaking news or big stories. He did so for his paper's coverage of the Scott Peterson case, the 9/11 attacks, and Flight 93. He also covers Indian gaming issues, but adds, "I'll do anything."

What advice does Simerman have for reporters facing a big story on deadline? "Prepare with the time you have. Do whatever you can to know your surroundings. It is all about the detail." He also suggests they follow the advice of one of his professors: "You always have to think you can write the story better than others—even if you can't."

Simerman is married to Tiffany Graham, an artist. Their daughter, Ariela, is 14. The family plans to celebrate the Laventhol Prize by taking a trip to Italy.

—Jill Geisler

The Jesse Laventhol Prize for Deadline News Reporting by an individual is funded by a gift from David Laventhol, a former Times Mirror *executive, in honor of his father.*

4. Watching Williams Die

DEC. 13, 2005

By John Simerman

SAN QUENTIN STATE PRISON—Stanley "Tookie" Williams walked in chains and cuffs through the oval door of the execution chamber. Four uniformed men entered with him. Midnight remained a minute away.

Around the mint-green octagon, 50 people sat in a semi-circle of risers and chairs, peering through thick glass as the guards laid the Crips gang co-founder on the table.

They strapped him down at the shins, knees, waist, chest and wrists. His stomach rapidly rose and fell. Williams lifted his head and peered to his left. Barbara Becnel, his longtime advocate and the editor of his books, stood atop a riser with the four others chosen by Williams to witness his death.

Williams held his gaze. Becnel raised her fist. Later, she would cover her mouth, then her eyes. Seated in front of the chamber, Lora Owens sat motionless, her eyes trained on the man convicted of shooting to death her stepson, Albert Owens, 26 years ago on a February morning inside the 7-Eleven where he worked.

A technician inserted the first IV needle into Williams' right arm with relative ease; but the woman who worked on his left arm struggled to find a vein. Ten minutes passed. She wiped the back of a gloved hand across her forehead.

Williams, wearing glasses, grimaced. He heaved an exasperated sigh. It was 12:17 a.m. now, and witnesses watched and waited in uneasy silence.

Williams lifted his head and spoke. He offered suggestions, the warden would say later. Prison officials reported that he had been cooperative all day. In his final moments, he appeared the same.

The needle finally stuck, two members of the execution staff left the chamber. The two others strapped Williams' hands down with white tape, from wrists to fingers. They rotated the table. One staff member spoke a last word to Williams before latching the door.

Now alone, Williams breathed deeply and moved his sock-clad feet.

A rolled sheet of paper appeared through a small round portal in a door. A proclamation. The female guard unfurled it and broke the silence.

"The execution shall now proceed," she announced.

As the drugs began to course through his veins, Williams lifted his head. He held it there, tilted slightly left. It fell back and he raised it again, refusing to [lie] still. His breathing hitched. His stomach convulsed, lurching upward. Light shone across his damp temples.

His stomach rose again. Then his breathing slowed. By 12:25 a.m., Williams lay motionless. Minutes passed. John Monaghan, the Los Angeles prosecutor who argued against clemency at a meeting last week with Gov. Arnold Schwarzenegger, sat a few feet from the chamber, staring ahead.

A hundred eyes stared at the still body of the man convicted of murdering four people in 1979, the man whose claims of redemption and innocence failed to sway the governor and the courts, the man who refused a last meal and declined to offer the warden any last words.

The man who spurred a massive campaign for mercy and drew a crowd estimated at nearly 2,000 people outside the prison's East Gate.

That man now lay there as lifeless as another sheet of paper shot through the portal, announcing the time of death: 12:35 a.m. Williams was dead at age 51, having spent nearly half his life on death row.

A guard pulled the curtain across the chamber windows.

"The state of California just killed an innocent man!" Becnel and two others shouted as they walked out of the witness area. Becnel, who championed Williams' cause over a decade, later vowed to prove it.

Lora Owens remained seated and she began to weep.

Contra Costa Times *reporter John Simerman was one of 17 media representatives selected to witness the execution of Stanley "Tookie" Williams.*

The writer uses a powerful form: an eyewitness narrative in mostly chronological order.

Watching Williams Die

SAN QUENTIN STATE PRISON— Stanley "Tookie" Williams walked in chains and cuffs through the oval door of the execution chamber. Four uniformed men entered with him. Midnight remained a minute away.

begins with place and personal names

clock starts ticking

Around the mint-green octagon, 50 people sat in a semi-circle of risers and chairs, peering through thick glass as the guards laid the Crips gang cofounder on the table.

description of setting helps transport us there

another useful name

They strapped him down at the shins, knees, waist, chest and wrists. His stomach rapidly rose and fell. Williams lifted his head and peered to his left. Barbara Becnel, his longtime advocate and the editor of his books, stood atop a riser with the four others chosen by Williams to witness his death.

action conveyed by active verbs

point of view shifts from convict to witness

Williams held his gaze. Becnel raised her fist. Later, she would cover her mouth, then her eyes. Seated in front of the chamber, Lora Owens sat

tension established between supporters and victims

motionless, her eyes trained on the man convicted of shooting to death her stepson, Albert Owens, 26 years ago on a February morning inside the 7-Eleven where he worked.

quick reminder of "why"

A technician inserted the first IV needle into Williams' right arm with relative ease; but the woman who worked on his left arm struggled to find a vein. Ten minutes passed. She wiped the back of a gloved hand across her forehead.

another reference to time builds suspense

Williams, wearing glasses, grimaced. He heaved an exasperated sigh. It was 12:17 a.m. now, and witnesses watched and waited in uneasy silence.

more good verbs

more time

Williams lifted his head and spoke. He offered suggestions, the warden would say later. Prison officials reported that he had been cooperative all day. In his final moments, he appeared the same.

series of short sentences make the reader move slowly—building suspense

The needle finally stuck, two members of the execution staff left the chamber. The two others strapped Williams' hands down with white tape, from wrists to fingers. They rotated the table. One staff member spoke a last word to Williams before latching the door.

Now alone, Williams breathed deeply and moved his sock-clad feet.

this is the language of ritual (see also top of next page)

the ordinary detail contrasts with the extraordinary purpose of this event

A rolled sheet of paper appeared through a small round

portal in a door. A proclamation. The female guard unfurled it and broke the silence.

this is the language of ritual

"The execution shall now proceed," she announced.

not a quote, but a monologue— a form of action

As the drugs began to course through his veins, Williams lifted his head. He held it there, tilted slightly left. It fell back and he raised it again, refusing to [lie] still. His breathing hitched. His stomach convulsed, lurching upward. Light shone across his damp temples.

perhaps overly dramatic

verbs, verbs, verbs

His stomach rose again. Then his breathing slowed. By 12:25 a.m., Williams lay motionless. Minutes passed. John Monaghan, the Los Angeles prosecutor who argued against clemency at a meeting last week with Gov. Arnold Schwarzenegger, sat a few feet from the chamber, staring ahead.

tick-tock

A hundred eyes stared at the still body of the man convicted of murdering four people in 1979, the man whose claims of redemption and innocence failed to sway the governor and the courts, the man who refused a last meal and declined to offer the warden any last words.

ancient rhetorical device—the part represents the whole

The man who spurred a massive campaign for mercy and drew a crowd estimated at nearly 2,000 people outside the prison's East Gate.

That man now lay there as lifeless as another sheet of

repetition links paragraphs— with contrasting visions

"doing time"

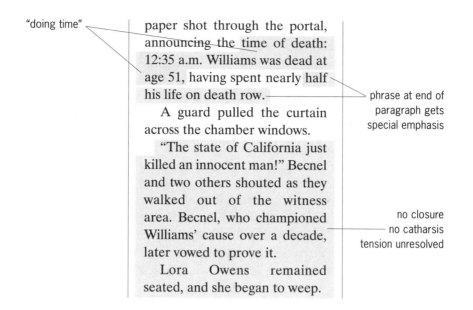

paper shot through the portal, announcing the time of death: 12:35 a.m. Williams was dead at age 51, having spent nearly half his life on death row.

phrase at end of paragraph gets special emphasis

A guard pulled the curtain across the chamber windows.

"The state of California just killed an innocent man!" Becnel and two others shouted as they walked out of the witness area. Becnel, who championed Williams' cause over a decade, later vowed to prove it.

no closure
no catharsis
tension unresolved

Lora Owens remained seated, and she began to weep.

Roy Peter Clark is senior scholar and vice president of The Poynter Institute.

A conversation with
John Simerman

An edited e-mail interview conducted by Poynter Institute faculty member Jill Geisler with John Simerman, winner of the ASNE individual deadline award.

JILL GEISLER: You knew you would be seeing the same sight as all other journalists present. You knew you had precious little time to write. How did you prepare yourself?

JOHN SIMERMAN: I didn't worry much about what other reporters would write. There was no competition for information. The story, I felt, was in this 30-odd minutes of execution theater. The rest of it—context, history, news of the day—we handled in the main news story.

Some of the other media witnesses had seen previous executions. This was my first. I think that was an advantage.

I remember riding on the media bus to the chamber and hearing a veteran of a large newspaper tell another reporter he didn't quite know how he could write another execution story that would be compelling. At that point I kind of resolved to take a naive, wide-eyed approach to reporting—just record everything that moved, or made a sound.

I did worry about trying to do too much, overwriting it. So I set out with a pretty modest approach, just to describe the mechanics of the process and any interaction between the watchers and the watched. I didn't plan the shape of the story until afterward, but I knew what I didn't want to do.

There was brief talk of a first-person account, which I quashed. The last thing I wanted was to inject myself in the story. I wanted to bring readers into the chamber without ever questioning the view. I had written about Stanley Williams over the course of several years, so I felt prepared. My main concern in the hours before the execution was knowing who among Williams' supporters and the victims' family members would be there to watch so I could spot them easily. Those names were not released, but I had a source who helped me.

I also read a few accounts of other executions, just to get an idea of what seemed to work. And I made sure that my watch was correct.

How did you collect information as you witnessed the event?

Prison rules allow no personal items in the execution area, save a watch. No notebooks, pens or recording devices. They gave us each a No. 2 pencil and four sheets of scratch paper. I asked for, and received, a second pencil in case the first one broke. It didn't.

You witnessed the execution, served on a media panel afterward, conducted an audio interview for your Web site, and wrote your story—all within hours of the execution. When did you actually start organizing the final story mentally—and then begin writing?

I left San Quentin maybe a little before 2 a.m. and organized the story in my head on the drive back to the office. Actually, I started earlier while sitting on the media panel right after the execution. The TV footage, I'm told, shows me fairly distracted and jotting down notes, and rambling incoherently when given the chance.

My first thought was to lead with the delay in getting the second IV needle into Williams' arm—as a kind of insult-to-injury moment for both sides—and then back up and go forward with the chronology of the execution. I was a bit bleary, I admit.

It didn't take long to realize how many problems this structure would create, shifting time and vantage, etc. under a very tight deadline. It would have demanded too much wrangling and probably would have failed to draw in readers very well. I decided on something more direct and started writing a little before 3 a.m., I think.

Your account of the execution is rich with detail. Your sentences are often spare. They build upon each other, almost like ticks of a clock, as you recount the step-by-step process. You take the reader there without taking an editorial position other than eyewitness. How did you decide upon this approach, and why?

It seemed to me that, in all of the debate over the death penalty, the execution process itself remains a bit of a mystery for most people. It was for me. So I assumed, rightly or wrongly, that the point of my being there was to bear witness. I just thought it was enough to give a tight-lens look at it, particularly since this was an execution that drew intense national interest. The scene itself was plenty dramatic, so there was no need for histrionics.

I just tried to strip it down and give it a slow and steady pace, panning between the death chamber and the witnesses. I wanted to stay in the execution area at all times and not pull back for context. A sort of ticking clock approach seemed only natural, given what was unfolding.

Once I chose that approach, and having that much material, it was really just a matter of writing good, tight sentences that pushed the story forward.

What role, before or after the execution and your story development, did your editor play?

My editor, Carolyn McMillan, saved me from myself, as usual. She helped me to settle on a straightforward chronological account.

How many drafts did you do?

What's a draft? It was one shot for the Web and a few tweaks the next day for the print version.

Please share your thoughts about bearing witness to an execution—thoughts that might help other journalists.

It's not enjoyable, and it was a challenge to maintain a clear head and do strong reporting at that late hour and under those conditions. You just kind of lean on the skills you bring. I did feel a strong responsibility to exercise, and not abuse, a right that media organizations have fought hard to win and retain.

It was one of those assignments that makes you ask yourself, more than usual, why you're there, and what you could bring to the story that makes it worthwhile.

A conversation about
CONVERGENCE with John Simerman,
Chris Lopez and Ari Soglin

An edited e-mail interview conducted by The Poynter Institute's faculty member Bill Mitchell with John Simerman, winner of the ASNE individual deadline award, and two of his Contra Costa Times *colleagues, executive editor Chris Lopez and online editor Ari Soglin.*

The *Contra Costa Times* had a problem.

Stanley "Tookie" Williams was scheduled for execution just before the paper's final deadline of the night. This high-profile occupant of San Quentin's death row had been convicted of murder in 1979 in the deaths of four people.

With material prepared in advance, the staff would be able to report the basic facts of his death in time to make the final edition for Dec. 13. But an important dimension of the paper's coverage—an eyewitness account of the execution by reporter John Simerman—would not be available until after the presses started rolling at 1:15 a.m.

So the paper turned to its Web site and published an online version of Simerman's story—along with an audio interview with him—by 4:30 that morning. The paper published the story, with just a few changes, on the front page of the Dec. 14 print edition.

Poynter Online editor Bill Mitchell explored some of the convergence issues raised by the story with Simerman and two of his colleagues: Chris Lopez, who is executive editor of the newspaper, and Ari Soglin, who is the paper's editor for online news and citizen media.

BILL MITCHELL: When and how did you decide to write "Watching Williams Die" as a story that would be published first on the Web (www.poynter.org/simerman1) Dec. 13 and then, on Dec. 14, in print? What were the considerations in deciding against filing it for the 1:15 a.m. deadline—or in deciding not to push back the final press start?

CHRIS LOPEZ: We decided in our pre-planning meetings in the days leading up to the execution to have John come back and write for the Web site immediately, or as quickly as possible. We did not have the time on our press runs for the edition of Dec. 13 to get John's "Watching Williams Die" story in that edition. We were pushing past our deadlines as it was to get the main bar story on the execution in our edition of the 13th. Also, John was required to debrief other reporters on witnessing the execution, and the debriefing lasted longer than we anticipated.

How did you alert readers to look online for the story?

CHRIS LOPEZ: We alerted readers to our Web site coverage, including John's eyewitness account, in the newspapers leading up to the execution. We advanced our coverage both in the Sunday and Monday newspapers, and each newspaper included promos that ContraCostaTimes.com would carry up-to-the-minute coverage of the execution. We consistently updated our coverage throughout the evening of the execution.

Please describe the collaboration between the print and online staffs on this story.

CHRIS LOPEZ: We operate under the mindset that our online and print staffs are one team, working for a common goal of providing our readers both in print and online with the most complete coverage we could provide on the execution. Because our producers sit in our newsroom, the producers had a clear idea of the game plan and were able to execute exactly how we planned it. We staffed our producers that day so that we would have a producer in the newsroom during the period of time we knew John would be writing for the Web site. That required reworking the schedule of one of our producers that day. The cooperation by our producers is testimony to the collaboration that exists in the *Contra Costa Times* newsroom when it comes to the online and print editions of the newspaper. Our editor for online reports directly to the executive editor of the newspaper. That reporting relationship makes for a seamless team effort.

How many readers viewed the Web version of the story on Dec. 13? And since then?

ARI SOGLIN: We had about 24,000 page views for "Watching Williams Die" on Dec. 13 and another 2,000 page views since then. On Dec. 12, the day leading up to the execution, ContraCostaTimes.com had what was then its second-highest page view total going back to April 1, when a new Web traffic system was implemented. Then, on Dec. 13, we had our highest page view total for the year (again dating back to April 1).

What changes did you make in the story as it appeared in print on Dec. 14? Why did you make the changes?

JOHN SIMERMAN: Very little was changed, as you can see—a few missing or clarifying words and fixes in sentence structure—but it did make a difference. I recall the Web version had people sitting on chairs and risers. In print, they were sitting on chairs and standing on risers. I was standing on a riser. It was good not to sit.

CHRIS LOPEZ: ...We actually were disappointed in how we displayed John's story in the Dec. 14 edition. In hindsight, we would have done a better job of setting that story apart on our front page for the Dec. 14 edition.

How did you prepare for the audio interview (www.poynter.org/simerman2) that appeared on the Web?

CHRIS LOPEZ: The audio interview was done by Carolyn McMillan, our metro editor. She interviewed John for the audio segment.

How did the reader forum (www.poynter.org/simerman3) fit into your coverage plans? Did it present story ideas or leads? How did you handle moderation of the forum? Roughly how many violations of your guidelines were reported? Roughly how many posts did you delete and why?

CHRIS LOPEZ: We've become accustomed to attaching discussion boards on most of our stories so readers can instantly sound off on the subject of the story or on the reporting of the story.

ARI SOGLIN: ...We don't do active moderation of our discussion boards. Instead, we respond to reader reports of violations. We don't recall receiving any such reports about this thread. (Readers have the ability to delete their own posts, so you may see some deletions in this thread that were done by the authors.)

How would you characterize reaction to your multimedia approach to "Watching Williams Die"? Among readers? Among colleagues? Overall lessons learned?

CHRIS LOPEZ: Our readers and colleagues found a lot of value in the multimedia approach. The lesson we learned was to do more of our journalism this way, which we have since this story. We've become comfortable creating audio segments and photo slideshows that are narrated with our journalism.

Writers' Workshop

Talking Points

1. Time plays an important role in this story. We learn that as Stanley "Tookie" Williams enters the execution chamber, "[m]idnight remained a minute away." We later learn that as a technician tries to insert a needle into his vein, "ten minutes passed." When Williams sighs, "[i]t was 12:17 a.m. now." His breathing slowed, and "[b]y 12:25, Williams lay motionless." Then, "the time of death: 12:35 a.m." Why do the time citations keep readers engaged in the story, even though they already know how it is going to end?

2. During a telephone interview about writing "Watching Williams Die," John Simerman was asked what mental image of the event remains prominent in his mind, months later. He said, "I think it is him lifting his head up, refusing to lie down, fighting to stay up." There are "visual icons" like this in many stories, although no photographer may be there to capture them. There was no photographer with Simerman for the execution, but his carefully chosen words crafted the image. What are some of the challenges of capturing powerful sights with words alone?

3. Capital punishment is controversial. John Simerman was determined to approach his story with no agenda, other than to document the event. Reread the story, first as a staunch proponent of the death penalty who believed Williams should be executed. Then read it as an opponent of capital punishment who believed Williams had turned his life around. As you read the story through each of these biases, how well did you feel Simerman met his own goal of providing a straightforward, fair account of the event? What reporting and, in particular, what *writing* techniques are important for reporters to employ when they are determined to write in a way that clearly takes no side in a controversy?

Assignment Desk

1. Every one of the 17 media witnesses to the Williams execution saw the same event, in the same room, with the same people taking part. Each took his, or her, own approach to telling the story. To appreciate the challenge of writing in such a circumstance, team up with two

other writers. Find an event that takes place in one limited location. It might be a meeting, or a play or a speech. You might even choose something as simple as a 30-minute cooking show on TV. Each of you should write an account of it. Assume you have only an hour after the event to craft a story about what you witnessed. Write—and then compare your approaches to collecting information, framing, organizing and writing your stories.

2. The media witnesses could not bring recording devices or notebooks into the execution area. According to Simerman, they were given a pencil and four sheets of scratch paper. How do you think such restrictions would affect your ability to capture both the sights and the quotes from an event that is unfolding before your eyes—and for which you are not able to say, "Could you repeat that?" Observe a 10-minute conversation between two people. Using a pencil and four sheets of scratch paper (any size), see how well you capture the details—and important quotes—for a story.

3. John Simerman was determined to develop a story about a controversial event in an even-handed, fair way. He didn't want his story to give even the appearance of taking sides. How might this story have differed if he wished to influence readers to support or oppose the execution? Taking what he has written and modifying it only slightly, how might you undo Simerman's efforts to keep it fair and unbiased?

MILWAUKEE
JOURNAL SENTINEL

Finalist

Rick Romell
Team Deadline Writing

5. Quiet Man Gave No Hint of Violence

MARCH 13, 2005

He was the type of person you'd scarcely notice in a crowd—quiet, a bit on the tall side, brownish hair, glasses.

"Not in shape but not overweight—Joe Average," said his neighbor, Shane Colwell.

But Terry Ratzmann, the man believed to have opened fire on members of his congregation as they worshiped, slaying seven and wounding four before killing himself, turned out to be anything but average.

That wasn't clear, however, until Saturday afternoon.

"He was the quietest guy in the world, the nicest," said Robert Blasczyk, another resident of Ratzmann's modest New Berlin neighborhood. "...I would have never believed this in a million years."

Ratzmann, according to Colwell, who talked with him regularly, was a devout churchgoer, an avid gardener and an ingenious tinkerer.

He "just never came off as a person with any kind of an aggressive attitude," Colwell said. "So calm and so mellow of a person, you know. Not somebody with a huge sense of humor but not somebody who was down and dark."

Ratzmann, who an aunt said was 44, lived with his mother and sister in a small, 75-year-old frame house at the north edge of New Berlin. Another neighbor, who asked not to be named, said Ratzmann had lived there since she and her husband moved in 35 years ago.

During that time, the neighbor said, she probably spoke with Ratzmann only twice.

"He just wasn't very communicative, and I'm a very private person myself," she said.

An investigator enters the home of Terry Ratzmann in New Berlin. (Photograph courtesy of Benny Sieu/ *Milwaukee Journal Sentinel*)

But Ratzmann and Colwell clicked. Colwell, 36, is a millwright, and he found in his neighbor across the alley someone who appreciated and was curious about intricate mechanical work.

The two frequently swapped tools when working on one project or another.

"I just helped him fix his clutch the other day because the clutch pedal stuck to the floor; a spring rotted out on him," Colwell said.

That was the clutch on the pickup truck that Colwell saw being hauled away on television Saturday, and when he saw it, he knew Ratzmann was involved somehow.

"I happen to spend a lot of time out in my garage, and it happens to face his garage," Colwell said. "... You end up just helping each other out."

He said Ratzmann built his own garage, as well as a greenhouse where he raised tropical plants, Venus flytraps and vegetables that he transferred to an outdoor garden when the weather warmed.

"He brought me over a zucchini that was about a foot-and-a-half long," Colwell said. "We ate it for a week."

He said Ratzmann raised trout, starting them in his basement, then moving them outside.

"By the end of the season, he'd have about 20 good trout that he could fry up," Colwell said.

He said Ratzmann designed a system in which he used trout waste to fertilize his greenhouse plants, then recycled the water back to the fish tank.

Blasczyk said Ratzmann, quiet as he typically was, occasionally would get rowdy. Blasczyk, though, wouldn't say what his neighbor did. "I know he was a drinker," he said.

But that's not the man Colwell knew. The two would talk to each other while shoveling snow or burning leaves. Colwell said he sometimes offered Ratzmann a beer, but that he never took one. He'd usually drink bottled water instead, Colwell said.

He recalled Ratzmann shooting off a homemade roman candle once and showing him how to produce spectacular colors by burning part of a garden hose inside copper tubing.

He said he never saw Ratzmann with a gun and noticed nothing unusual about his attitude in recent days.

"No change in demeanor whatsoever," said Colwell, who last saw Ratzmann during Thursday's snowfall.

Friends seldom stopped by Ratzmann's house, Colwell said. And when Ratzmann traveled—to Australia last fall and out West in his pickup truck every spring—he traveled alone, Colwell said.

"He was never one for having a partner," Colwell said. "I never really saw him with any guy friends or female companionship."

Ratzmann was tightly knit to his religion, Colwell said.

"Matter of fact we invited him and his mother to our wedding, and he said he couldn't make it, he had to go to church on Saturday," he said.

That was several years ago. When Ratzmann went to church yesterday, he had something else in mind.

Lessons Learned

BY RICK ROMELL

I don't think there are great secrets here. Covering a big, unexpected, breaking story is sort of like rebounding in basketball: You send as many bodies as you can to the boards and hope things bounce your way.

When word got out on a Saturday afternoon that someone had opened fire at a church service in a suburban hotel and killed an as-yet-unknown number of people, several off-duty reporters assembled at the *Milwaukee Journal Sentinel* newsroom. By the time I got in, nearly a dozen reporters already were in the field, feeding notes to Crocker Stephenson on rewrite. Two other colleagues, Dave Umhoefer and Marie Rohde, were digging into the background of the religious group that the killer and victims belonged to.

Meanwhile, several staffers were trying to get the suspect's name. Reporters Meg Kissinger and Reid Epstein, who were at the hotel, found out his first name was Terry. They also identified his pick-up truck from behind police lines. Photographer Mary Jo Walicki got most of the license number standing on top of a car and using a telephoto lens from about 50 yards away.

Because it was Saturday, we couldn't telephone the state motor vehicle department with the partial license number. But reporter Lisa Sink had a police source from another department in the county who was willing to run the number and others from the scene. Lisa's source also told her who the suspect was, but misspelled his last name.

But between the source's tip, the correct first name and the partial license number, we had enough to pinpoint the suspect as Terry Ratzmann.

I called all four Ratzmanns with listed numbers. But the one relative among them was an aunt who hadn't seen her nephew in years. Meanwhile, we didn't have immediate access to fellow church members because the congregation was small and geographically scattered and met in a hotel.

For the moment, that left neighbors. We got their names and numbers from a database, or a regular criss-cross directory—I can't remember which. But most knew next to nothing about Terry Ratzmann, even though he had lived in the same house for more than 30 years.

There was one exception. Luckily, he was one of the first people I called. He described how Ratzmann stuck close to his church, gardened, put up his own garage, built a greenhouse where he tended Venus flytraps, raised trout in his basement and concocted spectacular fireworks using garden hosing and copper tubing. He also said Ratzmann regularly vacationed alone and never had friends, or girlfriends, over—all in all, a sketch of a smart but lonely man.

I got along well with the neighbor during our first interview. I think that helped later in the evening as I called to check on new information as it emerged. In the end, I was convinced the man was the only person in the neighborhood who actually knew Ratzmann. I had no problem relying heavily on him for a necessarily quick profile.

Back at the hotel, a media scrum developed around the one departing church member who would say anything. She gave her name only as "Miss Frazier." But she did give reporters her telephone number. When a cop came to usher her away, he called her something that sounded like "Shonda" or "Shondra."

Nahal "Halley" Toosi called the metro desk with the information she had. Armed with the phone number, last name and a phonetic first name, editors used a database to track down the woman's address in another suburb.

Halley drove to the home and scored an interview that gave us our first eyewitness account of the carnage inside the church service.

Rick Romell, a reporter for 30 years at the Milwaukee Sentinel *and the* Milwaukee Journal Sentinel, *is now a business writer. He has covered courts, police, suburban government, general assignment, features, travel and has done project work. He was a member of a* Journal Sentinel *team that was a finalist for the Pulitzer Prize for explanatory reporting in 2003.*

The Oregonian

Finalist

Anne Saker
Individual Deadline Writing

6. Overweight Trucker Tests Tipping Point for Scales of Justice

NOV. 6, 2005

As the video played in the Multnomah County courtroom, John McDuffy searched the jurors' faces, looking for some reaction to the sight before them: a morbidly obese man, belly swaying, moving around a large truck.

The jurors gave nothing away. But those five long minutes left McDuffy feeling humiliated, as if he were on display.

Yet the truck driver from Molalla knew the jury had to see all 550 pounds of him at work. The video was important evidence in his lawsuit against his employer, a discrimination claim that now is a landmark in Oregon and one of only a few cases involving obesity to go to trial any-where in the country.

So the video played, and McDuffy endured it.

"I didn't really think something like this would ever happen to me because I could always do my job," he said. "I thought people could over-look my size because I could prove to them I could do the job, and every-thing would be fine. But it's not true. It doesn't matter. What they think is what they're going to think."

Even in his own family, McDuffy, 39, did not set precedent: His 6-foot-6 father once weighed 700 pounds. In adulthood, McDuffy daily navigated the innocent questions of children and steeled himself against the open disgust of adults.

"Mostly, it's not really what I hear, it's what I see," he said. "People will pull their kids away from me and go in an opposite direction. I think I'm a decent-looking person. I'm not some horrifying monster."

"I'd always done my job"

A commercial truck driver since 1987, he worked as many as a dozen companies. The money was good, but a life of bad food, no exercise and a sedentary job made it difficult for McDuffy to fight his genes.

He moved his wife and three young children from Ohio to Oregon and in April 2003, he landed a job in Portland with Interstate Distributor Co., a family-owned company with headquarters in Tacoma and 3,000 employees and contractors.

The job went well, McDuffy said, except for the one time he went out on workers' compensation for two days to rest a sprained knee.

In mid-May 2004, his supervisors assigned McDuffy to a truck that was smaller than usual. Plus, the adjusting mechanism for the steering wheel was broken, and he could not fit in the cab. He reported the problem to the supervisors.

The next day, the supervisors told McDuffy he was suspended without pay until further notice. The news stunned McDuffy.

"I could see them suspending me if I did something wrong, or if I couldn't do my job," he said. "But I'd been there 14 months. I'd always done my job. I did whatever I was asked to do."

He was summoned to a meeting with Lani Dalich, Interstate's human resources director. McDuffy said she told him that the company was concerned for his health. She did not talk about how he did his job.

At the end of May, the supervisors found McDuffy a bigger truck. But 10 days later, Dalich suspended McDuffy again until a doctor pronounced him fit to work.

Dr. Timothy Craven determined that McDuffy was morbidly obese at twice the ideal weight for his height of 6 feet. In a report to Interstate, Craven wrote that although McDuffy probably could not operate a forklift, climb up and down from a trailer or handle freight, he could drive a truck.

Interstate's lawyer in Portland, Alan Lee, then asked Craven whether McDuffy posed "a direct threat" to himself or others. The doctor said again that McDuffy's abilities were limited, but he could drive.

Still, Dalich told McDuffy that he would remain suspended. McDuffy opened the telephone directory and picked a lawyer, Michael J. Ross in downtown Portland.

McDuffy hoped that one sharply worded letter from Ross would quickly put everything right. But the company did not respond for weeks. Finally, McDuffy applied for work at another company. Just before his job interview, Interstate told him to report to Craven's office for a physical capabilities test.

With Ross and Lee present, McDuffy performed a series of tasks: lifting an 80-pound box and placing it on progressively higher shelves, getting in and out of the back of the trailer and climbing into the driver's seat then dismounting. When he hit the ground and released his grip on the door, the cab shook.

A video camera caught it all.

Once more, Craven said McDuffy should not handle freight but could do "all the essential duties of his job as a truck driver."

Interstate reinstated McDuffy as a truck driver. But the company also required him to unload freight almost every day.

The company also would not pay the $8,500 in wages McDuffy figured he would have earned if the company had not suspended him.

McDuffy sued.

Company's Concerns

He still did not understand the company's behavior. But in the pretrial process known as discovery, he got a hint: Interstate was worried about another obese employee.

His lawyer, Ross, obtained a May 2004, e-mail to Dalich from Tammy Warn, Interstate's director of risk management, about her observations of the obese driver at a company safety meeting. Warn wrote that the man's "excessive girth" was a problem because "the steering wheel must have free mobility to safely turn the vehicle. His protruding belly gets in the way of the steering wheel."

"In conclusion," she wrote, "he is simply too obese to operate a commercial motor vehicle safely." Six days later, McDuffy was suspended.

While the lawsuit moved forward, McDuffy did his job. One day in January, he bent to pick something off the trailer floor and felt a pull in his back.

The painful muscle strain put him out on workers' compensation for months. Later, the company informed him he was no longer an employee, but his lawyer promised he would work to get his job back after the trial.

The workers' compensation ended, but McDuffy still could not work. With no money coming in, the family relied on the generosity of friends and neighbors in Molalla.

In late September, his trial began in Courtroom 410 with the Circuit Court jury watching the video of McDuffy moving around the large truck. The embarrassment overwhelmed him.

"On the way home," he said, "I pretty much lost it."

His lawyer introduced the Warn e-mail and argued the document led

Interstate to discriminate against McDuffy even though he was not the driver Warn had observed. The lawyer asked for McDuffy's back wages and $100,000 in noneconomic damages.

Interstate's lawyer, Lee, said the company acted out of concern for public safety. At the end, Lee replayed the video and froze the action on a shot of McDuffy's belly, leaving it clearly visible to the jury during his closing argument.

The jury deliberated for less than four hours and brought in its verdict Oct. 5. McDuffy remembered hearing that he had won but he did not know what that meant until Ross leaned over and whispered, "They've given us everything."

The total award: $109,000.

McDuffy and Ross stuck around the courtroom, still amazed. Then 11 of the 12 jurors stopped to talk.

"They were proud of themselves," Ross said. "They were appalled at the way (Interstate) treated John. They told us, 'We wanted to send a message that you can't do this to people.'"

Each juror shook McDuffy's hand and wished him well. More than one said he was courageous.

"I was petrified the whole trial," McDuffy said. "I don't consider myself brave. I don't know what that means. I just did what I had to do, I guess."

Lessons Learned

One fall morning, an extremely large man entered the Multnomah County Courthouse and went to Courtroom 410. I followed him. I learned that he was suing his company for back pay.

But he also had come to court for something more than money.

That was the story to tell.

A county courthouse is the best possible place for a newspaper writer on the journey of a story. No other assignment presents such a rainbow of human behavior. Nowhere else offers such abundance of character and plot. In a courthouse, a writer is a correspondent to a world that to readers is scarily foreign yet bizarrely familiar, and they only want more, more, more.

It's easy to be intimidated by the black robes and the Latin. In part, that's on purpose. Happily, law dictionaries are cheap and easy to use. The rest of it comes from the writer constantly reminding herself: I'm not an advocate. I'm an observer. So…observe.

The obese man in court that fall morning was John McDuffy of Molalla, Ore. He had won his lawsuit, and he was willing to talk. His experience clearly was bigger than a civil case. It sliced open one of the unpleasant realities that for increasing millions of people is obesity.

As I started reporting McDuffy's story, I realized that I needed to dump some assumptions, a lesson that I must relearn with every story. I figured the fat guy had to have done something to merit a suspension without pay. But the company would have played that card at trial. In fact, McDuffy was an exemplary employee. He simply got into a truck one day and couldn't get around a steering wheel with a broken shift mechanism. He asked for another truck. For the company, that was grounds for suspension.

To convey the legal importance of the case, I learned a little employment discrimination law. In covering many courthouses, I have found that lawyers and judges are happy to explain things; the trick is to keep asking, "But what does that mean?" until it's clear. I called a few employment lawyers not connected with McDuffy's case. They talked me through the weeds. It was such interesting stuff that I wrote a short sidebar.

I interviewed McDuffy, his lawyers and the judge. Company officials and outside attorneys did not return 15 phone calls. On the Friday before publication, I tried the company once more. To my surprise, an executive took the call. I'm sure the executive did so by mistake, and said "no comment."

The interview with McDuffy taught me something else. I hate to ask delicate questions. But then I hate myself later if I don't. So I asked McDuffy how much he weighed. He told me without embarrassment. The answer then led him to talking about life in general as an obese man. The afternoon proved again that most people are not as afraid of answering questions as I am of asking them.

Sometimes, I spend days reporting a story as a dodge, to avoid the truly hard work of writing: figuring out what the story is saying. In McDuffy's case, I was fixated for a long time on the legal precedent. But deep down, I knew that wasn't the most important thing. Yet that essence eluded me for weeks.

There's always a moment in writing when I despair that I will never be out of the dark. That's when I need to give my mind room to roam. It needs some place away from the notes and the phone and the computer and the dog. A place to think. Some writers listen to music. Others nap. I swim laps.

John McDuffy stood for something more than obesity.

But what?

One morning, I suddenly saw it.

He wasn't a fat guy.

He was just a guy.

He did not want anything special.

He wanted to do his job.

He wanted fairness.

He wanted ... dignity.

What a story.

In a courthouse, every day brings a story. And every story starts a journey.

Anne Saker is a staff writer for The Oregonian. *She worked previously for United Press International in Norfolk, Va., and Washington, D.C.; Gannett News Service in Washington, D.C. and* The News & Observer *in Raleigh, N.C. In Raleigh, she won the statewide Thomas Wolfe Prize for writing and two first-place awards from the North Carolina Press Association.*

PART 2

Narrative Writing

Jim Sheeler
Non-Deadline Writing

Jim Sheeler, 37, is a general assignment reporter at the *Rocky Mountain News* in Denver, where he has worked since 2002. Since the first Colorado casualty of the war in Iraq, he has specialized in covering the impact of the war at home.

By now, he knows many of the gravediggers at Fort Logan National Cemetery by name. Before joining the *News,* he worked as a freelance writer, primarily for the *Denver Post,* where he started a Sunday long-form feature obituary column called "A Colorado Life." He previously worked for the *Daily Camera* of Boulder and the weekly *Boulder Planet.*

Born in Houston, Texas, he graduated from Colorado State University in 1990, and lives near Boulder with his wife, Annick Sauvageot, and son, James. Past awards include the Colorado Society of Professional Journalists' "Best of Colorado" (Best of Show) for newspaper writing in 1996 and 1997, and second place in the regional "Best of the West" competition—along with dozens of local writing awards. He also won "Community Educator of the Year" from the Boulder Developmental Disabilities Center in 1999 for writing about the developmentally disabled, and the American Legion's "Large Community Newspaper Media Award" for coverage of veterans in 2000.

Rocky Mountain News

A collection of his obituaries, tentatively titled, "The Woman Who Outlived Her Tombstone: Obituaries of Ordinary People Who Led Extraordinary Lives," will be published later this year by Pruett Publishing.

In "Final Salute," Sheeler focuses on another angle of the Iraq War, the heart-wrenching work of Marines with the unenviable task of informing families that their loved ones are coming home in flag-draped caskets. Over the course of a year, Sheeler immersed himself in this world of pain, one tempered by military rituals that have no politics, only devotion to duty. His reporting, bolstered by an uncommon collaboration with photographer Todd Heisler, enables him to construct a narrative built on intimate and painful scenes. Those scenes enable us to witness the cost of war, and the courage and compassion that bind soldiers and the families they leave behind.

—Christopher Scanlan

7. Final Salute

NOV. 11, 2005

By Jim Sheeler

Inside a limousine parked on the airport tarmac, Katherine Cathey looked out at the clear night sky and felt a kick.

"He's moving," she said. "Come feel him. He's moving."

Her two best friends leaned forward on the soft leather seats and put their hands on her stomach.

"I felt it," one of them said. "I felt it."

Outside, the whine of jet engines swelled.

"Oh, sweetie," her friend said. "I think this is his plane."

As the three young women peered through the tinted windows, Katherine squeezed a set of dog tags stamped with the same name as her unborn son:

James J. Cathey.

"He wasn't supposed to come home this way," she said, tightening her grip on the tags, which were linked by a necklace to her husband's wedding ring.

The women looked through the back window. Then the 23-year-old placed her hand on her pregnant belly.

"Everything that made me happy is on that plane," she said.

They watched as airport workers rolled a conveyor belt to the rear of the plane, followed by six solemn Marines.

Katherine turned from the window and closed her eyes.

"I don't want it to be dark right now. I wish it was daytime," she said. "I wish it was daytime for the rest of my life. The night is just too hard."

Suddenly, the car door opened. A white-gloved hand reached into the limousine from outside—the same hand that had knocked on Katherine's door in Brighton five days earlier.

The man in the deep blue uniform knelt down to meet her eyes, speaking in a soft, steady voice.

"Katherine," said Maj. Steve Beck, "it's time."

* * *

The American Airlines 757 couldn't have landed much farther from the war.

The plane arrived in Reno on a Friday evening, the beginning of the 2005 "Hot August Nights" festival—one of the city's biggest—filled with flashing lights, fireworks, carefree music and plenty of gambling.

When a young Marine in dress uniform had boarded the plane to Reno, the passengers smiled and nodded politely. None knew he had just come from the plane's cargo hold, after watching his best friend's casket loaded onboard.

At 24 years old, Sgt. Gavin Conley was only seven days younger than the man in the coffin. The two had met as 17-year-olds on another plane—the one to boot camp in California. They had slept in adjoining top bunks, the two youngest recruits in the barracks.

All Marines call each other brother. Conley and Jim Cathey could have been. They finished each other's sentences, had matching infantry tattoos etched on their shoulders, and cracked on each other as if they had grown up together—which, in some ways, they had.

When the airline crew found out about Conley's mission, they bumped him to first-class. He had never flown there before. Neither had Jim Cathey.

On the flight, the woman sitting next to him nodded toward his uniform and asked if he was coming or going. To the war, she meant.

He fell back on the words the military had told him to say: "I'm escorting a fallen Marine home to his family from the situation in Iraq."

The woman quietly said she was sorry, Conley said.

Then she began to cry.

When the plane landed in Nevada, the pilot asked the passengers to remain seated while Conley disembarked alone. Then the pilot told them why.

The passengers pressed their faces against the windows. Outside, a procession walked toward the plane. Passengers in window seats leaned back to give others a better view. One held a child up to watch.

From their seats in the plane, they saw a hearse and a Marine extending a white-gloved hand into a limousine, helping a pregnant woman out of the car.

On the tarmac, Katherine Cathey wrapped her arm around the major's, steadying herself. Then her eyes locked on the cargo hold and the flag-draped casket.

Inside the plane, they couldn't hear the screams.

* * *

Each door is different.

Some are ornately carved hardwood, some are hollow aluminum. Some are protected by elaborate security systems, some by loose screen doors.

During the past year, the 40-year-old Marine major in the white gloves has stood at the front doors of homes in three states, preparing to deliver the message no family wants to hear.

It is a job he never asked for and one for which he received no training. There are no set rules, only impersonal guidelines. It is a mission without weapons.

Steve Beck trained to fight as a Marine, winning accolades as the most accomplished marksman of his class—a man who later earned two master's degrees in a quest to become a leader on the battlefield. He had hoped to deploy during the Persian Gulf War and definitely thought he would get his chance this time.

Instead, he found himself faced with an assignment that starts with a long walk to a stranger's porch and an outstretched hand. It continues with a promise steeped in the history of the Corps that most people associate only with the battlefield:

Never leave a Marine behind.

In combat, men have been killed while retrieving their comrades' bodies, knowing that the dead Marine would have done the same for them. It's a tradition instilled in boot camp, where Marines are steeped in 230 years of history and the sacrifices of tens of thousands of lives.

For Beck, that promise holds long after the dead return home.

In the past 12 months, he has seen inside the caskets, learned each Marine's name and nickname, touched the toys they grew up with and read the letters they wrote home. He has held grieving mothers in long embraces, absorbing their muffled cries into the dark blue shoulder of his uniform.

Sometimes he's gone home to his own family and found himself crying in the dark.

When he first donned the Marine uniform, Beck had never heard the term "casualty assistance calls officer." He certainly never expected to serve as one.

As it turned out, it would become the most important mission of his life.

Each door is different. But once they're open, Beck said, some of the scenes inside are inevitably the same.

"The curtains pull away. They come to the door. And they know. They always know," he said.

"You can almost see the blood run out of their body and their heart hit the floor. It's not the blood as much as their soul. Something sinks. I've never seen that except when someone dies. And I've seen a lot of death.

"They're falling—either literally or figuratively—and you have to catch them.

"In this business, I can't save his life. All I can do is catch the family while they're falling."

* * *

Hours before Beck's first call, a homemade bomb exploded.

Somewhere in the Iraqi desert, in the midst of the rubble, lay the body of a Marine from Colorado.

The information from his dog tags was checked. Double-checked. And then the name began its journey home.

During World War I, World War II and the Korean War, the message arrived in sparse sympathy letters or in the terse language of telegrams, leaving relatives alone to soak in the words. Near the end of the Vietnam War, the military changed the process, saddling stateside troops with the knock at the door.

On that day in October 2004, inside an office at Buckley Air Force Base in Aurora, Beck's phone rang.

"We have a casualty in your area," the voice said.

At the time, Beck wasn't sure what came next. He did know that he didn't have much time. Once the call is received, the goal for notification is four hours.

Troops in the field now often have access to e-mail and satellite telephones. So when a service member dies, his commander is directed to shut off communications back home to keep rumors from reaching the family before the notification officers.

Still, the pressure is palpable. The call often comes in the middle of the night. Officers must retrieve vital information from headquarters—the Marine's next of kin, the basic circumstances surrounding the death, addresses and phone numbers—and there is no room for error.

With each step, they get closer to the door.

* * *

Beck looks like the job: hard and soft. His white cotton gloves cover calloused hands. They lead to thick, regular-guy arms shaped by work instead of weightlifting, and a round, pale face with big cheeks that turn red when he hasn't had enough sleep, which is most of the time.

Beck's bookshelf is packed with titles ranging from the *History of the Peloponnesian War* to the *9/11 Commission Report*. He can quote Clausewitz and Sun Tsu in regular conversation.

But he never strays far from his roots.

Born in Sand Springs, Okla., he still pronounces his home state "O-koma." He'll describe another Marine's muscles as "hard as a woodpecker's lips," and when he wants something done with precision, he'll require his troops to get it "down to the gnat's ass."

His car radio is eternally tuned to country stations because, he insists, "a day without country music is like a day without sunshine."

It's an Everyman quality that can't be faked, one that has become a crucial component in helping the families of fallen Marines.

After receiving that first call last fall, Beck grabbed for a thick, acronym-studded manual, *The Casualty Assistance Calls Officer's (CACO) Guide.* It offered only the basics:

"In cases of death, the following is suggested and may be modified as follows," it reads in part.

"The Commandant of the Marine Corps has entrusted me to express his deep regret that your (relationship), (name), (died/was killed in action) in (place of incident), (city/state or country) on (date). (State the circumstances). The Commandant extends his deepest sympathy to you and your family in your loss."

When he began the job as site commander at Marine Air Control Squadron 23, Beck knew that death notification was a possibility. The previous commander already had supervised three funerals in the region that includes Colorado and parts of Wyoming, Kansas, South Dakota and Nebraska.

Until that first call, however, Beck had plenty of other worries.

From their base among the top-secret radar installations at Buckley, Beck and his Marines are highly trained to support aircraft and missile operations. They also are continually training Marine Reservists and sending them to Iraq.

Since the beginning of the war, the Marines stationed at Buckley have made 19 notifications following the deaths of active-duty Marines. Fifteen of those were killed in action in Iraq and four died in stateside traffic accidents.

Beck personally has notified five families, but even when he isn't the one who delivers the message, he is involved.

Before leaving on his first notification, Beck asked for advice from two men in another branch of the service.

"One of the first things they said was, 'Don't embrace them. If they embrace you, keep your distance,'" he said, shaking his head.

"I didn't have much use for them."

* * *

Different services have different guidelines for notification. In the Army, one officer is responsible for the knock, while another steps in to handle the aftercare.

In the Marines, the same person who knocks on the door is the family's primary contact for the next year or more.

There is no group of Marines whose primary task is death notification. Just as every Marine is a rifleman—expected to be able to handle a weapon and head to the front, if tapped—any officer also may be called to make the walk to the door.

For Beck, that door is the "LOD"—the line of departure. The point of no return.

After all of the racing, all of the frantic scramble, it's the point where time freezes.

"Once I get to the porch, I stand there and take a deep breath. At that point, you can wait 10 seconds, wait 30 seconds, wait an hour—it's not going to go away," he said.

"There's no option. There's no fork in the road. You just stare down that straight path. You step up because there is no fork.

"I pick myself up, gather my thoughts and ring the bell."

* * *

There were no footprints in the snow.

That struck Beck as he sat across the street in his government SUV that night, outside a house in Laramie blanketed by cold and quiet.

In his briefcase was a sheet of paper: "INITIAL CASUALTY REPORT," it read. "LCPL. KYLE W. BURNS."

Every second he waited would be one more second that, for those in the house, everything was still all right. He stared at the front door, at the drifting snow, then looked at his watch.

When he left Denver, it was still Nov. 11; now it was well past midnight. Veterans Day was over.

Inside the house, the lights were still on.

All during the drive to Laramie, Beck imagined what would happen at the door and what he would say once it opened. This was his second notification. He had easily memorized the words in the manual. There was no script for the rest.

He talked it out with his passenger, Gunnery Sgt. Shane Scarpino. In the truck, the two men played out scenarios the same way they would if headed into battle. What if the parents aren't home? What if they become aggressive? What if they break down? What if, what if, what if.

Two Marines are required for every visit, not just for emotional support, but for each other's protection. While most parents eventually grow close to their casualty assistance officer, the initial meeting tests all emotions. One of the Buckley Marines had been slapped by a mother. Last year, a group of Marines in Florida had their van set on fire by a distraught father.

Amid sheets of blowing snow just outside Laramie, Beck had pulled the truck into a gas station and the two Marines grabbed their garment bags.

When they emerged from the restroom, their spit-shined black shoes clicked on the floor. Their dark blue pants, lined with a red stripe signifying past bloodshed, fell straight. Their jackets wrapped their necks with a high collar that dates back to the Revolutionary War, when Marines wore leather neckstraps to protect them from enemy swords.

As they walked out of the gas station, Beck felt the eyes of the clerk.

He knows, Beck thought.

Once they drove into the family's neighborhood, the modest white house found them first, beckoning with the brightest porch lights and biggest house numbers on the block.

Beck pulled to the curb and cut his headlights. He looked at Scarpino.

Then the two men climbed out of the truck and walked into the pristine snow.

From then on, every step would leave footprints.

☩ ☩ ☩

Down in the basement of their home in Laramie, Kyle Burns' parents didn't hear the doorbell.

The couple had spent most of the snowy night trying to hook up a new television. It was nearly 1 a.m. when the dog leapt into a barking frenzy.

Jo Burns looked out the window and saw the two Marines.

"I thought, 'Go away! Get the hell away from here!' " she said. "Then I just started screaming."

Down in the basement, Bob Burns assumed that someone was trying to break in. He grabbed a flashlight and flew up the stairs.

"When I got up there, I saw Major Beck and the (gunnery) sergeant," he said. "I'll never forget Major Beck's profile."

It was a silhouette their son had warned them about.

"When Kyle left, he sat us down and told us that if he didn't come back, the Marines would come," Jo said. "So when I saw them standing there..."

Beck and Scarpino spent hours with the family, telling them the little information they knew, promising they would take care of everything they could.

Over the next few weeks, Beck found a way to bring home two Marines who had enlisted alongside Kyle. He helped organize a memorial service and Kyle's burial at Fort Logan National Cemetery in Denver. He helped the Burnses navigate the piles of paperwork dealing with insurance and benefits.

The whole time, Marines from Buckley watched over Kyle's body.

That first night, as the two men prepared to leave, Jo Burns gave each a hug. Bob Burns shook their hands.

"I don't know why, but even then I felt compassion for them," Bob Burns said. "I've done a lot of reflecting on that first night and that's what comes back: compassion."

"I don't know how Major Beck does this," Jo Burns said. "Because nobody wants to see him.

"You know, he feels every one of these like they were his own. He does. I tried to talk to him about that once, but he just put his hand up and turned around to face the wall.

"He had tears in his eyes. And he just said, 'I know.' "

* * *

Although Beck had no training as a casualty assistance officer, in a way he had trained for it all of his life.

His earliest memory begins with a needle.

As a toddler, he learned to hold a syringe to inject his diabetic mother with insulin. His parents had divorced when he was 1. Sometimes, he was the only one there to help.

As he grew up, the family scraped by. Some days he wore Salvation Army clothes to school. Things got harder from there.

When he was 13, Beck and his mother watched his 3-year-old brother die after being hit by a car. Months earlier, young Steve had taught the little boy to play catch.

Before the funeral, Beck stood at the open casket and placed his brother's baseball glove inside.

It took years for Beck and his mother to recover. She retreated and he rebelled, leaving home early.

Eventually, Beck channeled his anger into books, even planning to go to medical school, where he hoped to find a cure for his mother's diabetes.

But the stirrings of the Persian Gulf War shook him as he prepared to take his medical school entrance exams. His father had been a Marine and Beck had long thought of joining. He figured this would be the war of his generation and he didn't want to miss it.

His mother died while he was attending officer training school. When he lost her, he also lost his reason for studying medicine. He never went back.

Though his relationship with his father—a cop and former Drug Enforcement Administration agent—wasn't as close as that with his mother, they eventually reconciled. Then his father was diagnosed with cancer.

"On my last trip out to see him, I took a drive with him and asked him if there was anything I could do," Beck said.

"He asked me if I could get a color guard at his funeral. That's all he asked for: a Marine color guard.

"I said, 'Dad, that's easy.'

"I didn't get to talk to him again."

* * *

On a winter night, Beck pulled his SUV into Denver International Airport and looked into the sky, staring at all the lights that were not stars.

A limousine pulled in behind him, followed by an empty hearse.

It was early December, nine months before he would stand on the tarmac in Reno alongside a 23-year-old widow.

There is no rule requiring airports to allow a family into a secure area to receive the body of a fallen service member, and some airports around the country have refused, Beck said, shaking his head.

"In my mind, this is the first time that a Marine is back on Colorado soil, and (the family) deserves to be there," Beck said. "If I had my way, they'd know which frickin' light in the sky is him, which plane is bringing him in all the way."

Inside the SUV, his phone rang. He looked at the number and smiled.

"Hi, babe," he said. "We're at the airport, getting ready to bring one of our guys home. How are the kids?"

For Beck's wife, Julie, and their three young children, his job has sometimes meant his absence on birthdays and anniversaries. He spent last Thanksgiving at a funeral.

Still, when he wakes up in the middle of the night to an ominous call, Julie wakes with him and remains nearby until he heads off to knock on another door. He talks about her the way the families he cares for talk about him: She's his rock.

"Hang in there," he said into the phone. "I'll be home late."

Then another call. Again, he recognized the number: another one of his families.

The contact list on Beck's cell phone is programmed with the numbers of grieving parents and spouses from Rapid City to Reno.

But he's not the only one, he insists, over and over. He said he takes his cues from his Marines, the men and women who get involved to the point where many of their families say they might as well have been deployed overseas.

"This job is all about sacrifice," Beck said. "We sacrifice our family stability. Many of us sacrifice income. We sacrifice our bodies. We break things. We're hard on ourselves. We break each other. And we're asked to make the ultimate sacrifice."

Outside the car, a Denver police officer's walkie-talkie crackled and he motioned to Beck.

The cortege pulled behind the police escort, heading toward the tarmac.

"There are moments in this experience that energize you, and there are moments that suck you dry," Beck said. "Those moments are short, but they're so defining.

"And you're about to see one of them."

As jet engines roared around him, Beck looked at the plane. The Marines marched to the cargo hold, toward the casket.

"See the people in the windows? They'll sit right there in the plane, watching those Marines," Beck said. "You gotta wonder what's going through their minds, knowing that they're on the plane that brought him home."

Commercial airplanes transport caskets every day—including service members killed in action. For the most part, the passengers have no idea what lies below.

Most people will never see the Transportation Security Administration officials standing on the tarmac with their hands over their hearts as a body is unloaded. They won't see the airport police and firefighters lined up alongside their cars and engines, lights flashing, saluting the hearse on its way out.

Occasionally, a planeload of passengers is briefly exposed to the hard reality outside the cabin.

"They're going to remember being on that plane for the rest of their lives," Beck said, looking back at the passengers. "They're going to remember bringing that Marine home.

"And they should."

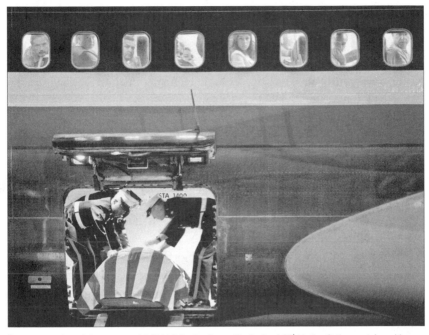

Passengers aboard the commercial flight bringing home the body of 2nd Lt. Jim Cathey watch as his casket is unloaded by a Marine honor guard at Reno-Tahoe International Airport. Maj. Steve Beck, site commander of Marine Air Control Squadron 23 at Buckley Air Force Base, described a similar scene last year at Denver International Airport on the arrival of another fallen Marine: "See the people in the windows? They're going to remember being on that plane for the rest of their lives. They're going to remember bringing that Marine home." (Photograph courtesy of Todd Heisler/*Rocky Mountain News*)

* * *

Before graduating from boot camp, every Marine masters the blank stare: the focused-but-distant look that glares down from recruiting posters, the one meant to strike fear in enemies, the one intended to convey more than two centuries of tradition.

Marines are taught to hold the stare no matter what. If a fly crawls on their face, or in their ear, they are ordered to remain steady.

No training could prepare them for the funerals.

According to protocol—an extension of their sacred "never leave a Marine behind" mandate—a fallen Marine's body must be guarded by another Marine whenever it is accessible by a member of the public.

During the past year, the 60 active-duty Marines stationed at Buckley have taken turns standing guard over the caskets. Inevitably, they get to know the person inside.

Underneath their formal white caps, or "covers," many of the Buckley Marines keep the funeral brochures of every Marine they have watched over.

"Now they're watching over us," said Sgt. Andrea Fitzgerald, as she turned over her cap, revealing a photo tucked inside. "I call them my angels."

At the visitation, Marines hear the families talk to the body. At the memorial services, they hear the eulogies. During the burials, they see the flag presented to the grieving mother or widow.

Through it all, they try to hold the stare.

"They can stand there for hours," Beck said. "Their feet fall asleep up to their knees. The pain we're feeling drives us. It drives us for the family because the pride is bigger than the pain. But the pain—you gotta eat it, you gotta live with it, you gotta take it home and cry in the dark. What else are you going to do?"

For Sgt. Kevin Thomas, of Aurora, it starts when the Marines first meet the casket at the airport.

"You always hear all these statements like 'freedom isn't free.' You hear the president talking about all these people making sacrifices," he said.

"But you never really know until you carry one of them in the casket. When you feel their body weight. When you feel them, that's when you know. That's when you understand."

Thomas said he would rather be in Iraq—or anyplace he doesn't feel so helpless.

Still, he said, he has learned lessons from funeral duty that he knows combat can't teach.

"I'll be sitting in front of the computer and I'll see the news: Another service member killed. It's enough to choke me up, tighten my chest. That's another hundred people that are about to be affected," Thomas said.

"It's almost enough to wish that you could take his place, so these people wouldn't hurt so much.

"There's no way that doing one of these funerals can't make you a better person. I think everyone in the military should have to do at least one."

Still, it doesn't end at the cemetery.

"People think that after the funeral, we're finished," Beck said. "It's not over. It's not over at all. We have to keep taking care of the families."

* * *

The sound of strapping tape ripped through the living room in Laramie.

"Now for the hard part," Jo Burns said, after opening one of the cardboard boxes from Iraq filled with her son's possessions.

Then she corrected herself.

"It's all hard."

It had been more than a month since Beck's midnight drive to the white house with the biggest numbers on the block. Beck wasn't required to personally deliver the boxes to Laramie. He didn't have to stay with the family for two hours more as they sifted through them, either.

But actually, Beck said, he had no choice.

"I know that Kyle Burns is looking at me, making sure I'm squared away—with his family and with him," he said during the drive to Wyoming. "I know I'm going to have to answer the mail on that one day— not with God, but with Kyle."

Inside the living room, Bob Burns began lifting Ziploc bags from the box, cataloging the contents in a shaky voice.

"Here's his wallet," he said, as he looked inside. "A fishing license. A hunting license. A Subway Club card? Good grief."

"They're things that reminded him of home," Jo Burns said.

A few minutes later, she pulled out a list in her son's handwriting and started to cry.

"What is it, Jo?" Bob Burns asked.

"It's everyone he wanted to call. And write."

"Well," Bob said, "now we've got a list, don't we, Jo?"

They found more. A camouflage Bible. A giant clothespin. Pens with their tops chewed up.

Corporal's stripes.

"He already bought them," Bob said. "He only had a couple more tests to take."

Kyle's older brother, Kris, pulled out a book, *Battlefield Okinawa,* and feathered the pages, then placed his finger at a wrinkle on the spine.

"Looks like he only got to about here," he said. "He only got halfway through."

Jo Burns never wanted Kyle to be a Marine. When he invited a recruiter over to meet her, she was openly hostile.

"I have to be honest," she said later. "I didn't believe all that brother-hood bull——. I thought it was just a bunch of little boys saying things that boys say.

"I never believed it until after he died."

In the midst of it all, they found a little snow globe with a typical Wyoming scene: trees, an elk, a bear and a coyote.

Jo Burns shook it up and watched the flakes fall.

She then grasped Beck's hand.

"He told us several times, 'You won't be alone through this—we'll be here,' " she said.

"I guess I didn't understand what that meant."

* * *

Throngs of raucous, face-painted fanatics filled the Stevens High School gymnasium in Rapid City, S.D., preparing for the biggest basketball game of the season.

As the time for tipoff neared, some of the kids cheered and others stomped their feet on the stands. But when the lights dimmed, the teams didn't take the court.

"Good evening, ladies and gentlemen," said a uniformed Marine major, as the gym fell to murmurs, then silence.

Eight Marines from Buckley marched to the front of the gym floor, along with a dozen members of the Stevens High School football team and the family of Lance Cpl. Joe Welke.

"For some of you, this is a surprise," Beck said. "For others, you knew we had something special. For everyone, I promise you, this will be a memorable night."

In the gym rafters hung the retired jerseys of former Stevens High football players who later turned pro. On Feb. 5, the crowd's attention was drawn to a special display case for three more uniforms, all worn by the same man.

"Keep Joseph Welke long in your memories, for his sacrifice and that of others should never be forgotten," Beck said. "For if it is, none of us deserve our freedom."

The spotlight swept across the line of football players as they passed the jersey of No. 36 from player to player, across the gym, until it rested with Joe Welke's mother.

Then the light shone on the Marines. Many of them had been the last to carry Welke's body, the last to feel the weight.

This night, they carried his empty uniforms.

"The Marine dress blue uniform is the only uniform in use today that is comprised of all the colors of the American flag," Beck said to the crowd, as the suit was passed along, through white-gloved hands, until it also rested with Betty Welke.

A Marine then held up a desert camouflage uniform—one that had arrived in the U.S. only a few days earlier.

"The Marine combat utility uniform has seen duty around the globe in the toughest of environments," Beck said. "Joe's combat uniform is with us tonight and comes directly from the deserts of Iraq."

The Marines passed the uniform along until it reached Beck. He turned, cradling it with the same reverence he showed months earlier at the funeral when he presented Betty Welke with the folded American flag that had covered her son's casket.

The lance corporal's mother buried her face in the uniform. Her sobbing lifted into the silence of the gym.

In the stands, the face paint smeared into tears. Beck whispered in Betty Welke's ear.

"I said, 'Do you want to hold that for a little while?' And she said, 'Yes.'"

"She was crying into it pretty good. And for me, that was kind of perfect. Because his combat uniform from Iraq has her tears in it. Her tears are in those threads. Forever."

* * *

The day after the ceremony in the gym, the Welke home in Rapid City filled with Marines Joe Welke never knew. Around the country, as people prepared for Super Bowl Sunday, the Marines prepared for a birthday party.

"Today he would be 21," said Joe Welke's older brother, Nick. "He'd be back in town now. His battalion just got back."

"Twenty-one," he said. "The one you look forward to."

When the Colorado Marines arrived, they were met the way Joe Welke would have welcomed them—with backslaps and beer.

"The Marines were so adamant about coming up here with me on this," Beck said. "They were the ones who carried Joe. That funeral touched them so deeply."

After the start of the football game, the Marines and Joe Welke's high school buddies headed for the big-screen TV in the basement. Betty Welke remained upstairs, looking through photo albums as Beck hovered nearby.

When they were alone, she pressed an album closed and looked up at the major.

"I want to know what's really happening over there," she said.

For the next hour, Beck spoke passionately about the scenes he said not enough people see: the Iraqi elections, the small, successful everyday missions, and the positive days he saw ahead for Iraq—turning points he said her son helped make possible.

He then explained how he believes it could take more than a decade until the sacrifices made by the military pay off. The American public, he said, would have to learn to be patient.

She remained quiet, soaking it all in.

"But is it worth it?" she asked him finally. "Was it worth his life?"

He looked her in the eyes.

"Betty, with all you've been through, that's not something I can answer for you," Beck said.

"That's something for you to decide."

* * *

Casualty notification isn't always conducted with the same care.

In May, the parents of an Army private first class were stunned when their son's casket was delivered to them on a forklift in a cargo area of a St. Louis airport, where employees on break smoked nearby. They also thought it insensitive that, when informing them of their son's death, the casualty assistance officer literally read from a script.

Others have watched their casualty officers "drop off the radar," or end up in Iraq, with no replacement provided. In some cases, the military has taken months to pay for a funeral or left families alone to navigate the morass of paperwork that follows the death of a loved one.

Recently, the governor of Illinois met with Army officials to voice the concerns of military families in his state. Other cases surfaced in February, during congressional testimony by war widows.

"Successful casualty assistance is not the rule, it is quite the exception," one Marine widow told the congressional committee. "This is certainly not the military taking care of its own."

Some branches now offer daylong courses on casualty notification. Next week, the Marine Corps is holding a large symposium in Quantico, Va., where casualty assistance calls officers—including Beck—will convene to share stories and advice.

Many problems could be solved, Beck said, if everyone followed a simple principle:

"To do this right, to do it properly, you have to look at these women as if they were your mother or your wife, and these men as if they were your father or your brother. And you have to ask, 'What would I want someone to do if it were me?' "

* * *

Inside a ballroom at an Aurora hotel in April, Beck adjusted a line of medals on a banquet table, struggling with all they reflected.

"When you think about what these guys did, it's not easy to look at these medals," he said. "What's the trade-off? What's the exchange? How do you say (holding up a medal), 'This is for your son?' "

At the beginning of the year, Beck realized there were a number of medals due the Marines whose families he watched over. Instead of mailing the medals to them, which often occurs, he decided to hold a formal ceremony to present them to the families personally.

He called the ceremony "Remembering the Brave."

Beck considered the medals again, feeling their weight.

"It's not a trade, but in the minds of the mothers, I wonder if they think it is a trade, and that they're thinking, 'I don't want this medal. I want my son,' " he said.

"The only way I can dispel that is through something like this. By showing them the honor. By honoring their son."

After the lights dimmed in the ballroom, more than 500 people fell silent.

"You are about to hear the descriptions of individual acts of courage," Beck said. "Listen closely.

"Listen closely."

For nearly an hour, they heard detailed accounts of rocket-propelled grenade attacks and improvised explosive devices, of ambushes and assaults—each with the same ending.

Slowly, methodically, the Marines brought out the medals and citations and kneeled before a mother or father they had first met on a doorstep. For each family, the Marines also presented a vase of yellow roses, one rose for every year of the Marine's life.

After it was over, Beck sat back and took another deep breath.

"Even some of our Marines say, 'Why are we doing this to the families? Why do you have to keep reminding them? ' "

Beck shook his head.

"This isn't about reminding them—they don't need reminding. These families think about this every day of their lives."

He looked up, addressing every person who hasn't felt what those families have.

"This isn't about reminding them," he said.

"This is about reminding *you.*"

* * *

On the tarmac in Reno, the white glove reached into the limousine, but Katherine Cathey couldn't move.

"Katherine," Beck said, "it's time."

"I'm not ready for this," she said. "I'll never be ready."

Her mother leaned into the car and spoke to her daughter.

Beck supports Katherine Cathey after she breaks into tears at the sight of her husband's casket at the Reno airport. (Photograph courtesy of Todd Heisler/*Rocky Mountain News*)

"Katherine," she said. "Jim would want you to see this."

Katherine looked at her mother, then at Beck, and took his hand. After climbing from the car, she steadied herself, her arm intertwined with Beck's. Then she looked toward the plane.

At the sight of the flag-draped casket, Katherine let loose a shrill, full-body wail that gave way to moans of distilled, contagious grief.

"NO! NO! Noooooo! Not him! Noooooo!"

She screamed as the casket moved slowly down the conveyor belt. She screamed until she nearly collapsed, clutching Beck around the neck, her legs almost giving way.

At the base of the luggage ramp, the screams hit the pallbearers.

Of all the Marines they had met or trained with, Jim Cathey was the one they considered invincible, built with steel-cable arms and endless endurance—a kid who had made sergeant at 19 and seemed destined to leapfrog through the ranks.

Most of the Marines who would serve as pallbearers had first met "Cat" at the University of Colorado, while enrolled in an elite scholarship program for enlisted infantrymen taking the difficult path to becoming officers. They partied with him, occasionally got into trouble with him, then watched him graduate with honors in anthropology and history in only three years.

When they lifted his casket, they struggled visibly with the weight, their eyes filling with tears as they shuffled to the white hearse.

After they placed the flag-draped coffin inside, Katherine fell onto one corner, pressing her face into the blue field of stars.

Beck put a hand on her back as she held the casket tight. By then, he was close enough to her to know that she wouldn't let go. He kept his hand on her back until he found a solution.

"Would you like to ride with him?" he finally asked. She looked up, dazed, and replied with a sniffling nod. She took his hand again as he guided her to the front seat of the hearse, where the surprised funeral directors quickly moved papers to make room for her.

Jim Cathey's mother, father and sister took their own time with the casket, caressing the flag, remembering.

His mother, Caroline, thought of the baby who used to reach out to her from the crib. His father, Jeff, saw the boy he watched grow into a man on long hunting trips through the barren landscape nearby.

His sister, Joyce, saw the kid who became her protector. The day after she learned of his death, she had his face tattooed on the back of her neck, so "he will always be watching my back."

Last of all, the young Marine who had escorted his friend home walked up to the casket and came to attention.

Only a few months before, Gavin Conley had stood before his best friend at the formal commissioning ceremony in Boulder, where Cathey received his brass lieutenant's bars.

For Cathey, it was one of the most important days of his life, and Conley knew the best way to share his pride.

At the end of the ceremony, Conley walked up to the new lieutenant and snapped his arm to his brow, giving the new officer his first salute.

In front of the casket on the tarmac, Conley again brought his hand to his face, this time in one slow, sweeping movement. As the family wept, his hand fell to his side.

His job as escort was officially over.

Before climbing into the hearse with Katherine, Beck took one last look at the scene, fixing on the plane. By then, the passengers had moved on, leaving the Marines and the family alone with the casket—and everything that was about to follow.

* * *

Five days before Jim Cathey returned home, two uniformed men sat in a government SUV, several blocks from Katherine Cathey's home in Brighton, and bowed their heads.

Beck and Navy chaplain Jim Chapman closed their eyes in prayer as the chaplain asked for "words that will bring the family peace."

This time, Beck was dressed in a drab green uniform in accordance with a controversial new mandate from the top brass not to wear dress blue uniforms to notifications, based on concerns that the distinctive blues had become too associated with tragedy.

It was a warm, blue-sky Sunday afternoon. Nearby, a neighbor mowed his lawn.

When the knock came, Katherine Cathey was taking a nap. Her stepfather saw the Marines first and opened the door.

"We're here for Katherine," Beck said quietly.

"Oh, no," Vic Leonard said.

At first, Katherine's mother thought it was someone trying to sell something. Then she saw her husband walking backward and the two men in uniform.

"Oh, no," she said.

"She's pregnant!"

Leonard suggested to his wife that she wake up Katherine. Vicki Leonard shook her head. She couldn't speak.

When her stepfather opened the door to her bedroom, Katherine could hear her mother crying. She thought something had happened to someone in her mother's family. She had never heard her mother cry like that.

"What's going on?" Katherine asked her stepfather.

"It's not good," he told her. "Come with me."

Her own screams began as soon as she saw the uniforms.

Katherine ran to the back of the living room and collapsed on the floor, holding her stomach, thinking of the man who would never see their baby. Finally she stood, but still couldn't speak.

As Beck and the chaplain remained on their feet, she glared at them. She ran to the back of the house and drew a hot bath. For the next hour, she sat in the tub, dissolving.

Shortly after their arrival, Beck had ducked back outside to make a quick phone call.

Inside a government SUV in Reno, just around the corner from the home where Jim Cathey grew up, another phone rang.

* * *

The toolbox was a mess.

Jim Cathey's mother stood in the garage, trying to find the right wrench to fix a sprinkler head in her front yard.

What a frustrating morning, she thought.

As she prepared to leave for the hardware store, the family dog started to howl—a howl like she had never heard before. She put the dog in the house and drove off.

When the silver SUV pulled up, the Marines inside assumed someone was home. A lawn mower sat outside and it looked as if someone was doing yardwork.

No one answered the door.

A neighbor drove up, looked at them and pulled into an adjacent driveway. The Marines started to get nervous. The neighbor looked out a window at them. Their orders were to remain parked at the house until the parents returned.

When Caroline Cathey drove up, she saw the strange government vehicle, then fixed her eyes on the man in the driver's seat.

"She saw me; she pulled in," Capt. Winston Tierney said. "And I hate this, but I think she might have suspected when she saw me. She got out of her vehicle and I told my guys, 'Time to go.' "

Caroline Cathey's hands went to her face.

"As I made my way up the driveway, we didn't say anything," Tierney said. "I wanted to wait until I was there. She looked at me and it looked like she was going to collapse. I supported her and tried to give her a hug."

He recounted the conversation from there:

"Please don't let it be," she said.

"I'm sorry to have to be here today. Can we go inside and sit down? There are some things we need to confirm."

"Please tell me it's not Jimmy, please tell me it's not my son."

The Marines stayed with the Catheys for the next 10 hours. With Caroline's help, they contacted Jim Cathey's 9-year-old daughter, Casey, who was born while he was still in high school. Casey, along with Katherine, had pinned the lieutenant's bars on her father only a few months before.

Casey's mother and stepfather drove the little girl from Carson City, Nev., to Reno, where another one of the Marines—an operations chief who had children of his own—told her that her daddy had been hurt in the war and wouldn't be able to come back. He asked her if she understood. She answered with tears.

The Marines held fast until Jim Cathey's father, Jeff, returned from a trip he had taken to his son's favorite hunting grounds, where he was scouting for game birds.

When it was all over, the Marines climbed back into the silver SUV. A staff sergeant looked at Tierney.

"Sir," he said. "Please don't take me on another one of these."

* * *

The flag never left Jim Cathey.

From the moment his body departed Iraq, the sturdy, heavyweight cotton flag remained nearby, following him from the desert to Dover Air Force Base, Del., where a mortuary affairs team received his body.

According to the Department of Defense, Cathey was killed in Al Karmah, Iraq, on Aug. 21. Members of his unit later told family members that Cathey was leading the search of an abandoned building when a booby-trapped door exploded. The explosion was so fierce it blew off an arm and leg of the Marine directly behind Cathey. That man, now in recovery, credits his lieutenant with saving his life.

Once Cathey's remains arrived at Dover, the mortuary affairs team began the delicate task of readying his body for the final trip home. When possible, military morticians prepare a body for viewing by the family. In Cathey's case, that wasn't an option.

Specialists at Dover wrapped his body in a white shroud and covered it with a satin body-length pillow and his dress blue uniform before closing the casket lid and securing the flag nearby.

When the plane landed in Reno, the same flag was draped over the casket, which was loaded into the hearse to continue its journey to the funeral home.

After all the noise at the airport—the screaming, the crying, the whining of jet engines—inside the funeral home each footstep echoed.

The pallbearers carried their friend's body to the front of an enormous empty room, then faded into the background. Beck posted himself at the head of the casket, his face frozen in the Marine stare.

His eyes trained forward, he still saw everything.

Inside the room, Cathey's mother, Caroline, bent down to hug Katherine. They squeezed each other for a long time.

"You give me strength," the young widow said.

Other family members sat on couches and some sat on the floor—hugging, holding hands, their eyes locked on the casket, for nearly half an hour.

Finally, Beck broke the silence.

"I'm sorry," he said, excusing the family from the room. "There are some things I need to do."

* * *

Beck motioned to the pallbearers and began the instructions that would hold for the next three days.

Although the Marines are required to stand watch over a comrade's body, once the casket is safely inside a locked mortuary or church, they usually leave at night and return when the mortuary reopens.

This time, however, the watch would not end.

"Katherine and Caroline have both expressed concerns about Jim being left alone," Beck told the Marines. "So we won't leave him alone."

He then explained how to guard the casket. They all had posted watch before. They had stood at attention for hours as part of basic training, but nothing like this.

They were to take shifts of about an hour at a time, Beck instructed, standing watch 24 hours a day. When changing the guard, they were to salute Cathey's casket first, then relieve the other Marine the same way.

He showed them the slow salute—the one they aren't taught in basic training—three seconds up, hold for three seconds and three seconds down.

"A salute to your fallen comrade should take time," he said.

For Beck, that salute embodies more than the movement itself. Earlier in the day, someone had asked him about the arrival of "the body." He held up his hand with a firm correction.

" 'The body' has a name," he said. "His name is Jim."

In the room, he walked up to the casket and paused.

"Now, this is important, too," he said. "If a family member wants you to break, you can break. They may want to hug you or kiss you. That's OK. Hug them. If someone wants to shake your hand, shake their hand. I'll take my glove off when I shake their hand—you don't have to, it's up to you. But then go back to position.

"Everyone understand?"

"Yes, sir," they responded. "Roger that."

"This is a serious business," he said. "Jim is watching you."

As the other Marines filed into the hallway, closing the door behind them, Beck walked back to the casket. For the first time, he and Jim Cathey were alone.

It was time for the final inspection.

* * *

Beck walked up to the casket and lifted the flag back, tucking it into neat pleats and leaving just enough room to open the heavy wooden lid. He walked around the flag several times, making sure each stripe lined up straight, smoothing the thick stitching with his soft white gloves.

Then he lifted the lid.

For the past five days, Beck had spent hours looking at pictures of Jim Cathey, listening to the family's stories, dabbing their tears. When he looked inside, they were no longer strangers.

For the next 10 minutes, Beck leaned over the open casket, checking the empty uniform that lay atop the tightly-shrouded body, making sure every ribbon and medal was in place. Occasionally, he pulled off a piece of lint or a stray thread and flicked it away.

Although casualty assistance officers receive an advisory from military morticians about whether a body is "viewable," some families insist on looking. The casualty assistance officer is often the one to make last-minute recommendations, since by then he knows the family and—after the final inspection—knows exactly what the family will see.

Whether or not the family decides on a viewing, Beck said, the procedure is no less meticulous.

In Cathey's case, the family decided not to look under the shroud. But Katherine wanted a few minutes alone with the open casket, to give her husband a few of the things they had shared—and one he never got to see.

Beck ran his hand alongside the shroud, taking one last look at the uniform.

He closed the lid and turned toward the door.

* * *

Katherine draped her body over the smooth wood, pressing her pregnant belly to the casket, as close to a hug as she could get.

Beck placed a hand on her back.

"Tell me when you're ready," he said. "Take your time."

He stepped back.

The air conditioner clicked on, filling the room with a low hum. Ten minutes passed. It clicked off, leaving the room to her soft moans.

She moved only to adjust her feet, continuing to rub her belly against the wood. She closed her eyes and whispered something.

Then she looked up at Beck.

"OK," she said.

As she stood at his arm, he opened the casket.

She didn't cry. She didn't speak. He gave her a few seconds, then took her hand and brought it to the middle of the empty uniform. He held her hand there and pressed down.

"He's here," he told her. "Feel right here."

She held her hand on the spot, pressing the uniform into the shrouded body beneath. She dragged her hand the length of all that was there.

Beck walked back to get the personal belongings Katherine had brought with her from Colorado.

"Where do you want to start?" he asked.

"With the picture of us kissing," she said.

She placed the picture at the top of the casket, above the neck of the uniform. She bent down and pressed her lips to it.

"I'm always kissing you, baby," she whispered.

She took several other photos of their lives together and placed them around the uniform. She gently added a bottle of her perfume, then picked up the dried, fragile flowers of her wedding bouquet.

Before Jim Cathey had left for officer training, they were married by a justice of the peace in Denver, planning a big wedding on his return from Iraq. Her wedding dress still hangs in her closet at home, unworn.

She placed the flowers alongside the uniform, then turned again to the major.

"The ultrasound," she said.

The fuzzy image was taken two days after her husband's death. Katherine had scheduled the appointment for a day when Jim was supposed to call, so they could both learn the baby's gender together. He had a feeling it was a boy, he had told her. If it was, she suggested they name the child after him.

She stood cradling the ultrasound, then moved forward and placed it on the pillow at the head of the casket. She stood there, watching for several minutes, then removed it.

She walked the length of the casket, then stepped back, still holding the only image of James J. Cathey Jr.

She leaned in and placed it over her husband's heart.

* * *

In the house where Jim Cathey grew up, a tattered stuffed animal still peers from a heavy wooden chest.

"This is Floppy Floyd," his mother said. "The last time he was here he said he wanted to take Floyd back, for the baby."

She held the stuffed animal to her face. Elsewhere in the house, she still has all of Jim's baby teeth and every award he ever won.

On his bookshelf, encyclopedias are shelved near the Louis L'Amour novels she used to read to him, next to a collection of Thucydides' writings.

"These are the things that made him who he is today," she said, then caught herself in present tense.

"Who he *was* today," she corrected herself softly.

Later, in the kitchen, she paused at a note that has hung on the refrigerator since the day Jim left home.

"See you all later. You know I love you and will be thinking about you every minute of every day. I miss you. Don't worry about me too much. I'll be back May 8th as a Marine! Write as much as you can. I will look forward to the letters. With all my love, J.C."

She looked away from the note and at the things that made Jim Cathey who he was.

"Maybe now I know why my son was always in a hurry," she said.

* * *

Jeff Cathey almost didn't make it to his son's funeral. From the moment he saw the Marines at the door, he was thinking of his own.

Jeff, who suffers from clinical depression, spiraled deeper the day the Marines came to the house, to the point where his family worried more about him than their own grief. His wife hid all of his guns. Even so, the day after he found out about his son's death, he insisted on going back to the hunting grounds where he and Jim had spent their best times together.

"Before he left, I made him swear on his son's life that he would come back to me," Caroline said.

"I thought about doing it. Ending it," Jeff said, breaking into tears. "I really did. I want to be with him."

As he sat on the couch, he tried to compose himself.

"Good thoughts," he told himself. "Good thoughts."

And then found plenty.

"One of my finest memories was when we were hunting and he came back to the car, overturned a pail, sat down and started doing his homework.

"I wish I had a picture of that."

"You do," his wife said, rubbing his back, pointing to his head. "Right up here."

* * *

Inside the mortuary the night before Cathey's funeral, two Marines stood near the casket, unfurling sheets on a makeshift bed.

"Make it look nice, dude, make it look nice," one of them said.

"Who are you, Martha Stewart?" the other shot back with a grin.

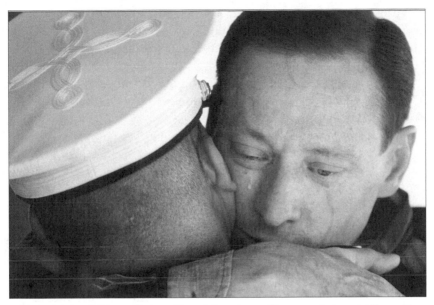

Jim Cathey's father, Jeff, hugs a Marine as his son's funeral nears. "Someone asked me what I learned from my son," he said. "He taught me you need more than one friend." (Photograph courtesy of Todd Heisler/ *Rocky Mountain News*)

Another looked at the blanket.

"If you're pregnant, do you get hot or cold?"

One of the Marines who has a child of his own looked at the bed.

"She's going to need another pillow," he said. "Since she's pregnant, she'll need to put a pillow between her legs."

Then they saw car lights outside and took their positions.

Earlier that day, Katherine had told them she couldn't bear to spend the last night away from her husband. She said she would sleep on a pew if she had to. The Marines found her an air mattress instead and promised to be ready.

Arriving exhausted, she almost immediately crawled onto the bed they had made for her. Her stepfather helped tuck her in.

"Do you have another pillow?" she asked. "I need one to put between my legs."

One of the Marines crouched down and asked if they should continue to post guard in the room.

"We can do whatever you want," he said. "We can stay or we can give you some privacy."

"I think it would be kind of nice if you kept doing it," she said. "I think that's what he would have wanted."

After one of the Marines dimmed the lights, Katherine opened a laptop computer on the floor. In the blue glow of the screen, she listened to the songs they would have played at the wedding they never held.

She swayed, then closed her eyes.

As drowsiness set in, she picked up an old T-shirt—the last shirt Jim Cathey wore before changing into his cammies to leave for Iraq. She hadn't washed it. It still smelled like him.

She held the shirt to her face and breathed in.

* * *

Just past midnight, Staff Sgt. Andrew Price walked to the back of the room and, like a watchful parent, dimmed the lights further. Then he closed Katherine's computer.

For the next hour he stood, barely illuminated by the light behind the altar, until another Marine approached from the shadows, paused before the makeshift bed and raised his hand in slow salute.

As each man was relieved, he walked into a spare room next to the chapel. In the darkness, one by one they spoke:

1:37 a.m. Staff Sgt. Andrew Price

The lanky Marine had stood watch at dozens of funerals at Arlington National Cemetery, but none prepared him for this.

"We would have stayed as long as Katherine wanted us there tonight. Even if she wanted us to go, I would have stayed there for her. I would have walked around in the shadows. Some way or another, we're always going to try to take care of her."

Of all the hours he has walked sentry, the last hour and a half was the hardest.

"It's almost selfish of us to die. James won't have to see her like that. They train us as warriors. They don't teach us how to take the pain away."

2:28 a.m. 2nd Lt. Charlie Loya Jr.

They call him the joker of the group: a massive man with a massive laugh.

"(After Cathey got killed), people would ask me how I'm doing and I'd say, 'I'm fine.' And I was. Then (at the airport)…we picked the casket up off the conveyor belt and all I heard was Katherine screaming. I thought, 'My wife would be doing the same thing.' Then all I could think about was my son."

When he heard about Cathey's death, he was scheduled to leave for Iraq in two weeks. Inside the room, he realized there were only eight days left.

"(Before Cathey died) people would ask how I felt about going over there. I'd say, 'I'm confident, I'm prepared and my boys are ready.'

"Now I'm f—ing scared."

3:19 a.m. Staff Sgt. David Rubio

"Cat" would have wanted them to laugh, he said, so he did.

"He was the smartest dumb guy I knew. I used to always tell him that. He was just a big oaf. I keep seeing that face, that big cheesy face."

He got up, paced the floor, holding the grin, the way the big oaf would have wanted.

"I got a call from him a couple months ago…The last thing he said was, 'Mark time, dude. Mark time. I'll see you in the fleet.'

"It just basically means, 'I'll be waiting for you.' "

4:23 a.m. 2nd Lt. Jon Mueller

He looked at the dark wall and thought of the casket on the other side.

"I'm still going to go when they ask me to go. But I also want people to know what I am doing. I'm not a very emotional guy. I don't show emotion, but I know that it's important for people to know how much you care for them. I'm not the kind of guy who can say, 'I love you.' It's not easy for me.

"I'll make it so that my loved ones know that I love them."

5:19 a.m. 2nd Lt. Jason Lindauer

"Cat was doing what he loved. I suppose that makes it a little easier, but…I called my (4-year-old) son on the phone, and he said, 'Daddy, my friend Cat got killed.' (My wife had told him.)

"I said, 'Yeah, I know buddy. Cat's in heaven.' "

The Marine began to cry.

"(My son) said, 'Well, when's he coming back? ' "

He lowered his head.

"I said, 'He's not, buddy.' "

* * *

As the sun rose in Reno, the casinos continued to chime. Diners began to fill. In the newspapers that hit the porches, Iraq had been pushed to the back pages again.

While the city churned, the sun found the building where Katherine Cathey awoke.

"It's the best night of sleep I've had," she said, surprised. "I really slept."

As she sat, wrapped in a blanket, her eyes bleary, she looked at the casket.

"You take for granted the last night you spend with them," she said. "I think I took it for granted. This was the last night I'll have to sleep next to him."

Behind her, the next Marine approached, preparing to take over the watch.

"I feel like they're my angels looking over me," Katherine said.

She placed her hand on her belly.

"Looking over us," she said.

* * *

It starts in slow motion.

At a windswept cemetery near 2nd Lt. Jim Cathey's favorite hunting grounds, the Marines moved as if underwater, a precision slowness, allowing everyone in the cemetery to study each move, each frame, holding it as long as possible until it's gone.

Beck stood back and started the ritual again.

"Present military honors," he commanded.

In the distance, seven members of the rifle guard from Reno readied their weapons. Because the Reno unit was so small—with many of its members in Iraq—they called in recruiters and other Marines from across the state to help with the duty.

"Ready. Aim. Fire."

With each volley, almost everyone in the shelter flinched.

"Ready. Aim. Fire."

The Marines at the casket held steady.

"Ready. Aim. Fire."

They knew the hard part was still to come: Taps.

As the bugler played, the Marines held onto the flag. Second Lt. Loya blinked almost continuously, trying to hold back the tears.

After the last note, they began to fold.

The afternoon before, the pallbearers spent more than an hour with Beck as he instructed them on how to fold the flag. For such a seemingly simple task, there are hundreds of ways to get it wrong. Especially when you're folding it for your friend's pregnant wife—especially when you're folding his flag for the last time.

The Marines took their time, stretching one fold after another, until the flag strained, a permanent triangle. A sergeant walked up and slipped the still-hot shells from the rifle salute into the folded flag.

Beck took the flag, cradling it with one hand on top, one hand below, and carried it to Katherine.

He bent down on one knee, looking at his hands, at the flag, his eyes reddening.

Before his tears could spill, his face snapped up and he looked her in the eyes.

"Katherine," he said.

Then he said the words meant only for her—words he had composed. When he was done, he stepped back, into the blank stare.

Capt. Winston Tierney walked forward, carrying another flag for Caroline Cathey. The night before, the Marines had used the flag to practice, draping it over the casket—not only for themselves, but also so that Jim Cathey's mother would know that it had covered her son.

The captain bent down on one knee, passed the flag into Caroline Cathey's hands, then faded into the background.

For a group of Cathey's friends, there was one more task.

The Marines, many of whom had flown in from Okinawa the night before, walked up to the casket. One by one, they removed their white gloves and placed them on the smooth wood. Then they reached into a bag of sand the same dark gray shade as gunpowder.

A few years ago, while stationed in the infantry in Hawaii, Jim Cathey and his friends had taken a trip to Iwo Jima, where nearly 6,000 Marines had lost their lives almost 60 years before. They slept on the beach, thinking about all that had happened there. The day before they left, they each collected a bag of sand.

Those bags of sand sat in their rooms for years. Girlfriends questioned them. Wives wondered what they would ever do with them.

One by one, the young Marines poured a handful of sand onto the gloves atop the casket, then stepped back.

Sgt. Gavin Conley, who had escorted his friend's body to Reno, reached into the bag, made a fist and drizzled the grains onto the casket.

Once again, he slowly brought his bare hand to his brow.

A final salute.

"(The day after sleeping on the beach), we all did a hike up Mount Suribachi, where our battalion commander spoke, and we rendered honors to all the fallen on Iwo Jima," Conley said.

He looked over at the sand.

"Now they can be part of him, too."

* * *

Minutes after the ceremony ended, a windstorm blew into the cemetery, swirling the high desert dust.

Beck was one of the last to leave, giving his final commands to the cemetery caretakers in the funeral shelter: Make sure the sand on the casket doesn't blow away.

"It's important," he told them.

As he drove away from the cemetery, Beck replayed the last few hours in his mind, looking for lessons for the next time, hoping there wouldn't be one, but knowing there would.

He thought back to the latest funeral—from the moment he rang the doorbell in Brighton until he handed the flag to Katherine and said those words that usually begin, "On behalf of a grateful nation…"

…."You know, everyone always wants to know what the words are, what it is that I say," he said. "I don't say it loud enough for everyone to hear."

There are scripted words written for the Marines to follow. Beck has long since learned that he doesn't always have to follow a script.

"I'm basically looking into that mother, father or spouse's eyes and letting them know that everyone cares about them," he said. "But the words are nothing compared to the flag."

He then drove several miles without speaking.

In his mind, the subject had not changed.

"You think about the field of cotton somewhere in Mississippi, and out of all of it comes this thread that becomes this flag that covers our brave. Think about it.

"I had a cotton field right behind the house when I was going to command and staff college. Imagine being that farmer who owned the cotton field. Imagine if one of these parents was able to take a flag back to him and say, 'That flag came out of your field and escorted my son home.' "

He shook his head.

"The things you think about," he said.

It's usually on these long drives that he allows himself to step back from it all, or at least tries to. He still hasn't learned how to step back far enough.

"One morning after burying a lance corporal, all I wanted to do was come home and play with my children. Just take them into a corner with all their things and play with them," he said. "But you know, all I was thinking about while I was playing with them were all those guys out there in harm's way, making all that possible.

"Here we are, while they're out there. Someone could be under attack right now. Someone could be calling for an airstrike…"

Someone could be standing at a door, preparing to knock.

"This experience has changed me in fundamental ways," Beck said. "I would not wish it on anyone, but at the same time, I think that it's important that it happened to me. I know it's going to have an impact on someone's life that I'm going to meet years from now."

In a year, he said, so many scenes return. The doors—and doorbells. The first time he completed a final inspection. Sand on a casket.

The scene he sees the most, however, is not of a single moment but the entire journey, viewed through someone else's eyes.

"One thing keeps coming back to me," he said. "It was during the memorial service for Kyle Burns."

The service came only a week after Beck first parked in front of that little white house in Laramie, watching the perfect snow, preparing to walk through it all.

During that memorial service, Kyle Burns's uncle, George Elsom, recounted the call from his devastated sister, who phoned him after she first saw the Marines at the door.

"At Kyle's memorial service, his uncle talked about all they had learned since that night." Beck said. "Then he looked at us and said something I'll never forget."

"He said, 'If these men ever come to your door, don't turn them away.'

"He said, 'If these men come to your door…

" 'Let them in.' "

ABOUT THIS STORY

Almost everyone has heard of "the knock at the door"—the knock that all military families dread. Once the door opens, though, the story has barely begun.

Rocky Mountain News reporter Jim Sheeler and photographer Todd Heisler spent the past year with the Marines stationed at Buckley Air Force Base in Aurora who have found themselves called upon to notify families of the deaths of their sons in Iraq. In each case in this story, the families agreed to let Sheeler and Heisler chronicle their loss and grief. They wanted people to know their sons, the men and women who brought them home, and the bond of traditions more than 200 years old that unite them.

Though readers are led through the story by the white-gloved hand of Maj. Steve Beck, he remains a reluctant hero. He is, he insists, only a small part of the massive mosaic that is the Marine Corps.

With the families' permission, he agreed to take us inside.

A conversation with
Jim Sheeler

An edited e-mail interview conducted by Poynter Institute faculty member Christopher Scanlan with Jim Sheeler, winner of the ASNE non-deadline writing award.

CHRISTOPHER SCANLAN: Where did the idea for "Final Salute" come from?

JIM SHEELER: The story actually began in the cemetery in March 2003, as the dirt fell onto the casket of the first Coloradoan killed in the war with Iraq. The gravedigger at Fort Logan National Cemetery was a Marine, as was the man in the casket. I spent a few hours before the burial with the gravedigger, and then—after all the other reporters and family members had left the cemetery—stayed with him until he tamped the dirt down on Lance Cpl. Tommy Slocum's grave.

He talked a lot about what he thought it meant to be a Marine and to bury one. I didn't know that the Marines guarded the bodies until they were buried, or many of the other rituals. While speaking with one of the mothers during another funeral, she told me how the Marines were at her house, guarding the empty home while the family attended the viewing. I told her I didn't know they did that. She told me there were a lot of things I didn't know.

What was your goal for the story?

Part of the Marines' dress uniform includes a pair of white cotton dress gloves. The gloves feel rough when one of the Marines shakes your hand, but when they take them off, they're actually soft. After one funeral, I noticed that one of the Marines—the one who fires the shots in the rifle salute at the end of every funeral—had a hole at the fingertip of one of his gloves. I asked him about it, and he took the glove off. "We do so many funerals that sometimes they blow out," he said. Then he handed me the glove and said, "Keep it."

For me, that glove was the key to the story. At one point in the article, Maj. Beck tells the Marines that when a family member comes up to shake his hand at the funeral, he'll often take the glove off. To me, that was the goal of the story: to show that moment, the bare hand underneath the glove.

I still have that white glove with the hole in the fingertip—I kept it with me as I wrote the story, and it still rests on the top of my computer.

What stories, if any, did you draw on as models for your story?

I think this story owes a lot to Jimmy Breslin's JFK burial story, where he told most of the story from the gravedigger's point of view. After several funerals in a national cemetery, you see so much that nobody else does— the woman in the red coat who comes to every funeral, the old veterans who stand off in the distance, the gravediggers on the hill, pausing as "Taps" is played. Breslin's story, more than anything else, taught me that when everyone's looking one way, try looking the other. In this case, it led me not just to the guy in the casket, but the ones holding it.

How much time did you spend reporting the story?

We worked on the story on and off for nine months, while reporting other daily stories and projects. Actually, though, I think I was reporting this story for the past three years, since the first death in Iraq.

In a way, all the other stories at home prepared me for this one. There are scenes I witnessed from the home front that I think remain in the shadows of this story—the little boy who took the rose boutonniere off his grandfather's lapel, then walked to the casket and placed the flower on his dead father's chest; the teenage girl who wrote her cry for help—"What do you do when your mom's in Iraq?"—in lipstick on the high school bathroom mirror; the little girl dressed as a princess and her brother dressed as a soldier as they said goodbye to their father for another year; the young war widow who read her husband's last letters to me, and her son who kissed the television good night after watching a tape of his dead father reading a bedtime story.

That same little boy later asked me, "Can you be my Daddy?" Those scenes still tear at me. None of them are in this story, but in a way they all are.

Where did the reporting take you geographically?

Colorado, Wyoming, South Dakota, Nevada.

How did you get access to the Marines?

Before Maj. Beck allowed me into his office, he grilled me over the phone about what I wanted to do with the story. I told him about what I had seen—all the scenes I just mentioned—and what I had not—the troops at home behind the scenes. I think he found out that we'd been in some similar places. If I hadn't done all those stories before, I don't think I would have been ready for this one—and I don't believe he would have let me in. Once he felt comfortable with us, he understood that the more we saw, the better the story would be.

"They have reporters embedded in Iraq," he said. "You should be embedded with us."

How were you able to get such phenomenal access, for instance, spending the night in the mortuary with the widow of Lt. Cathey?

Part of it was regular beat reporting. Most of it was taking the time to care. I first met Katherine Cathey for a daily story on the death of her husband. We came to her home after the television cameras left, and spent the next three hours there, until nearly midnight, listening.

At one point she told a story about the night before Jim left for Iraq. At that point, they knew Katherine was pregnant, and he decided to sleep with a baby blanket that Katherine had knitted. He knew he would be deployed when the baby was born, and he wanted the baby to know how he smelled. She showed us the blanket and the shirt she slept in every night, the last shirt her husband wore—it also still smelled like him.

Spending that time, having a chance to touch the blanket, was crucial for us. Before we left, she told us, "This may sound strange, but I'm glad you were here. You guys made my night."

Two days later, I had to ask her the question that the past nine months had led up to: I had to ask her permission to watch everything that was about to come. At that point, we had seen many of the scenes with Maj. Beck, but it was always from the outside. A few hours before Jim Cathey's body arrived, I sat down with Katherine and told her what we wanted to do.

At that point, I knew more about what was going to happen than she did. I told her that I wanted to ride in the limousine with her to the airport, and that we needed to be there for the final inspection. I promised her we would stay out of her way as much as possible, and I also told her that it was a decision she could revoke at any time. I told her all she had to do was wave her hand if things got too intense, and we would leave immediately. I think that helped cement a mutual trust that we built that first night, and continued as she realized how involved we already were. She never waved us off.

How many of the scenes in the story did you personally witness?

I saw all but the actual death notifications and the scenes inside the airplane carrying Jim Cathey's body. Most of those notifications had already happened before I started reporting the story. Though we spent several hours with Maj. Beck just before a notification was made, we never saw the actual knock on the door.

How do you report for story: taking notes or tape recording?

All by notes only. I carry a cheap microcassette tape recorder (cheap because I'm always dropping them on the ground and smashing them) for backup just in case someone talks too fast for my pen, but in this case I didn't need it. After my first meeting with Maj. Beck I realized he was something special, and wanted to get him on digital tape, possibly to give to the online production staff, but realized it was a big hassle. I was so engrossed with what he was saying I couldn't remember to keep track of the equipment. At that point, I had enough trouble keeping track of my notebooks.

What kinds of things go into your notebook?

One of the few positive things about emotional stories like this is that people take a lot of time to talk and it's usually very quiet. I use the time to retreat behind my notepad, scribbling details.

How long did you spend with Maj. Beck?

I was never really out of touch with him for the entire nine months. Some of the best conversations came on the long drives. He likes to talk through his thoughts, but he also asked a lot of questions, constantly forcing me to think about where the story was headed. During funerals, we mainly just tried to stay out of his way and observe. I also spent hours with him at his home, just talking over a beer.

This story teaches so much about the protocol the Marines rely on—from the slow, final salute to the hot shells in the flag. How did you learn these details?

The mother of the first Marine killed in action continues to attend every funeral at Fort Logan, because she says the first one was such a blur. She says she sees something new at every funeral. I do, too.

How did you crack the Marine reserve you describe? Was there a key to unlocking the hearts of people that appear in the story?

Simply being there. Coming into this, I knew nothing about the Marine Corps—I didn't even know there was a difference between calling someone a Marine or a soldier (a mistake you only make once). Still, there were many from the unit who refused to speak with me—Marines who believed that the ritual was so sacred that nobody should know what went on behind the scenes or in their minds. Beck took grief from some of them, but I think he also knew that the families wanted their stories told as well as the stories of the Marines, and the families' wishes were always the most important.

Touching moments abound in "Final Salute," ones that bring tears to readers' eyes. Was that your intent and if so, how did you make it happen?

I cried a lot during the reporting—and the writing—but I never write with the intent of making someone else cry. All I had to do was write down what I saw.

What is the theme of "Final Salute" and where is it expressed?

I'll have to quote Maj. Beck on that one. There's a point where a grieving mother asks him whether her son's death in Iraq was worth it. For me, it was a pivotal point in the story. Despite his complete belief in the war effort, he also understood that he could never presume to speak for a grieving mother.

"With all you've been through, that's not something I can answer for you," he said. "That's something for you to decide."

When and how did you decide what the focus of the story was? You must have had a lot of notes. So when and how did you decide what it was really about?

It all came together when I realized the importance of the ragged white glove.

The story suggests that the Army's protocol for casualty assistance isn't as meticulous as the Marines. How did you choose the Marines as your subject?

The history of the Marines and the ritual of guarding of the bodies were fascinating to me, but it was mainly that I had covered more Marine funerals. Also, there seemed to be more media focus on Fort Carson (the Army base in Colorado Springs), so that meant more bureaucracy, and less of a chance of finding someone to let us inside. As for the process, the Army's protocol is different—most notably that the person who knocks on the door is not the same one to stay with the family. I think all the services will admit they were caught off guard by the number of casualties, and as a result, all of the services are re-evaluating how best to make the notifications in the future.

How did you decide on the structure?

Originally, the story began with the knock at the door, with the sentence: "There were no footprints in the snow." That was about eight months into the reporting. I thought I could write the story with all I had already reported, and started the story where I thought it logically began, with Maj. Beck standing on the porch. Then Jim Cathey was killed, and everything changed.

When and why did you decide on the beginning of your story?

I started the story the night we returned from the airport on the night Jim Cathey's body was flown to Reno, when we rode with Katherine in the limousine. It was one of those leads that poured out in only a few minutes, and never really changed. I think the only part I changed was "black sky" to "night sky."

Did the structure change after you started writing? If so, how?

For a while, I wasn't sure if the story should be in two parts: part one beginning with the knock at the door, the start of the year's journey, and the second part the realization of that journey played out with Jim Cathey's funeral. The lead at the airport was so compelling, almost cinematic, we realized that it made sense to begin there, and even though I wouldn't return to the scene for 100 inches, the reader would remain involved.

When and why did you decide how it would end?

When Maj. Beck recounted the quote from Kyle Burns' uncle, it seemed to sum up all we'd been through in the same simple language I tried to use throughout the story, but cleaner than any words I could have used: "Let them in."

When did you know you would use the mortuary interviews when each sentry was relieved?

The night that Jim Cathey's body arrived, after Katherine had looked inside the casket and Maj. Beck made the final inspection, I was back in the hotel room when I thought of what must be going on in the mortuary, and started kicking myself for missing it. I realized I should have stayed there with the Marines as they watched over the casket all night. But by then it was too late—it was around 1 a.m. and I didn't feel comfortable going back to the funeral home alone—neither Katherine nor Maj. Beck was there, and I didn't really know the Marines.

I didn't sleep much that night, wondering what was going on in the home, and what I was missing. As it turned out, it was good that I didn't go back. Two nights later, when Katherine decided to sleep in the mortuary, I had a chance to answer the questions I had from that first sleepless night. We met with the Marines before Katherine arrived, and I asked them if it was all right if I interviewed them when they came off their post. We sat in a dark family room at the mortuary, lit only by the glow of my computer, and these guys sat on the couch, really pouring out their hearts. After only a few hours' sleep in three days, we were all in a very raw place at that point—during those interviews, it was impossible not to feel what was going on in the room next door, as Katherine spent the last night with the casket. One by one, they took off the glove.

Were any of the scenes reconstructed? If so what did you rely on to write those scenes?

We never actually saw a Marine knock on a family's door on a notification. So those scenes were reconstructed from interviews with the casualty assistance call officers and the families. The scenes on the plane were recounted by the escort.

In one scene, Capt. Tierney recounts a conversation with Caroline Cathey that appears within quotes. What's your paper's policy on reconstructing dialogue?

I spoke to Caroline Cathey and Capt. Tierney independently and their recollections matched, so we were comfortable using the dialogue.

How do you write a story like this? In bursts? Drafts? Graf by graf?

Some scenes—most of the scenes from Jim Cathey's funeral, for instance—poured out hours after I watched them. Others evolved over the six weeks I had to write it.

How did you describe your story to your sources?

I tried to give them a sense of what I had seen during other funerals and interviews with families, and how much I knew I hadn't seen. I had been covering the war for two years, yet I knew there was still so much that was missing. I told them that if I didn't know by now, the public still had no clue. In many ways, I don't think the public wanted to see them.

How long did you spend on this story?

Nearly a year.

Did the story change from its initial conception? How much revision did you go through?

Countless drafts, continuously. I worked on the story almost nonstop for those six weeks, and it never stopped changing.

What role did editors play in this story?

I can't say enough about the support that the newspaper gave the story—from the time required to write and report it, to the commitment to a 24-page all-color special section with no ads.

It started with city editor Tonia Twichell, who first realized that the story wasn't just a weekend package—that there was something else worth waiting for. It was then overseen by assistant managing editor Jim Trotter, who kept my mind open by making sure the story included something he called "the sweep," the larger scope of the story, the journey he'd seen me take over the past year.

I sent it through several staffers—from reporters to copy editors—but worked the most with columnist Mike Littwin, who helped me understand Maj. Beck's crucial role in the story, and how to bring him out.

When publisher John Temple gathered the design and production staff in the room, he made sure that each one of them understood the weight of the story. He told them, "There's a point in this story where Sheeler describes the care the Marines take when folding the flag for the last time. I want you to treat this story with the same care."

That's when I was comfortable knowing that he got it. Temple also helped with the writing and structure, calling up on weekends, asking if one section shouldn't be switched for another, even faxing and BlackBerry messaging me with suggestions when he was out of town at corporate meetings. It was one of those stories that wouldn't let go of any of us.

What was the range of reactions to the story from readers?

We received nearly 1,000 e-mails from around the world. They came from current and former veterans from all branches of the military. They came from war supporters thanking us for what they saw as the personal side of the military and from war detractors saying the story illustrated the cost of war.

We received letters from casualty assistance officers who served during the Vietnam War—one of whom wrote that he always wondered what happened when the body bags left the field, and was heartened to learn the rest of the story. We received a letter from a casualty evacuation pilot who flew many of the bodies out of the combat zone in Al Anbar province:

> We took great pride in knowing that Americans would welcome their sons home alive, in part because of our efforts. However my strongest memories—and worst recurring dreams—are the ones where my cabin contained a fallen Marine . . . I knew Marines like Steve Beck were out there, but I never really thought about their own challenges and heroism.

One letter from a reader said the article was "neither pro-war or anti-war but absolutely pro-people." We also received letters from troops in Iraq.

Some of the most touching were from families who had been through the same situation—in this war, and in others.

"It's a hard story to hear but everyone should know there's a family attached to the name scrolling across the screen as the most recent casualty," wrote a woman who, like Katherine, was pregnant when her husband was killed.

"This article will be very useful when my young children start asking questions that will be very difficult for me to answer," wrote another young war widow. "I am now left to raise my 4-year-old and 18-month-old. Someday I will be able to tell them all that I went through when we got the knock that fateful day."

What in your career prepared you for this?

I'm a terrible telephone interviewer, which ended up working to my advantage—for the most part, I do almost everything in person. When I started writing obituaries, I did nearly every interview with families in person, and, when possible, attended the funeral of the person I was writing about. I think it gave me a better ability to feel comfortable in a home where nothing is comfortable. Once the family realizes that you really want to know the story of the person's life, the awkwardness almost always disappears.

How emotionally difficult was it for you?

It hurt. It had to. Otherwise I don't think I would have been able to tell the story.

What is the most important lesson you learned from reporting and writing this story?

I think it underlined what I learned while obituary writing—people can tell when you care.

What was the hardest part of this assignment?

Coming home to my family after leaving homes that were so empty.

How did you overcome it?

A lot of long hugs with my family. I couldn't have written it without them.

What advice would you give another reporter attempting a story as sensitive as this one?

Same as above—people can tell when you care.

What role did photographer Todd Heisler play in the process?

It was a true partnership. We really could tell what each other's next move would be—I stayed out of his pictures, he stayed out of my story, but in many ways we're in both of them. In a different way, Todd also helped me with the writing—not necessarily in words choice, but in helping contextualize the story, and work through my own emotions. I sent drafts through him, and he brainstormed with me in late night coffee shops. With his help, I realized that I really needed to take the reader on the same journey that both of us had taken during the last year.

I think Todd's time in Iraq also helped in earning the trust of the Marines—he embedded with troops three times, and during the last time was in a Humvee blown up by a roadside bomb. By understanding the terminology and going through experiences that many of the Marines were about to, he was able to relate to them in a way I couldn't, while I was able to relate to the families by watching so much of the war from their side. The story wouldn't have been the same if Todd hadn't been there.

How did the collaboration between you work?

We're both looking for the same thing—scenes—so both of us knew when to grab the other one when something was about to happen. When the reporting was over, I kept some of his pictures with me as I wrote. After I was finished, I had tons of material I had cut out of the story, so I was able to use a lot of that material in writing captions. We knew that people would likely look at all the pictures first, read the captions, then go to the story. So they were also key.

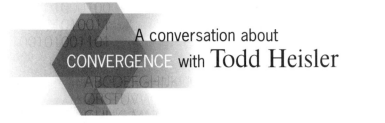

A conversation about
CONVERGENCE with Todd Heisler

*An edited e-mail interview conducted by Poynter Institute faculty member
Kenny Irby with Todd Heisler, winner of the ASNE community service photojournalism award for "Final Salute."*

**KENNY IRBY: When did you first start talking to the Web staff about the on-
line presentation of "Final Salute" (http://denver.rockymountainnews.com/
news/finalSalute/)?**

TODD HEISLER: We started talking to the Web staff just over two
months before our publication date.

What were their goals for the online storytelling?

One of the main goals of our Web production was to reach a larger audience and to have something that would have more of a lasting impact than
a newspaper usually does. We knew there was a very strong possibility this
piece would resonate throughout the military community and that the
Internet would be a way for them to see it.

The Web staff's goals were to make it interactive and dynamic, with
sound and video, not just a simple slideshow, and to incorporate reader
feedback. They also wanted the entire story available, which we did by
posting PDFs of all the pages as they appeared in the newspaper.

What were your goals?

We had the same basic goals for the online section. I wanted something
dynamic that would reach a larger audience. We differed in that I wanted
it to be as respectful and spare as the printed piece. I did not want a lot of
bells and whistles that would distract from the experience, because I felt
the photographs were very powerful on their own, and that the viewer
needed a chance to experience them. I agreed the sound enhanced it, but
I truly felt video would break down the fourth wall and take away from the
experience.

Projects editor Sonya Doctorian understood my position and did an
amazing job editing the sound. Jim Sheeler and I were also adamant about

not being a big part of the piece, such as with narration and interviews. We did not want it to be "look what we did"; rather, we wanted to step back and let the story tell itself.

How did you work together to accomplish what you envisioned?

I started editing different chapters with Sonya Doctorian, which were looser edits that would be more cinematic, while our Web designer, Forrest Stewart, started working on overall design and usability. Doctorian then used a video camera to capture sound and made some rough edits. Stewart put the sound and photos together to follow the same basic arc of the printed storyline.

Writers' Workshop

Talking Points

1. Read Jim Sheeler's description of reader reactions to "Final Salute." What about the story resonated so powerfully for both supporters and critics of the war?

2. Jim Sheeler says his plan for organizing "Final Salute" emerged after eight months of reporting, but he reorganized it after Lt. Cathey was killed. What is the lesson for reporters and editors about Sheeler's willingness to change his mind?

3. "Final Salute" begins with the arrival of Lt. Cathey's body at the Reno, Nev., airport, but as Sheeler says in his interview, the story doesn't return to that scene for 100 inches, approximately 4,000 words. He was convinced "the reader would remain involved." Do you think that organizational gambit paid off? Why or why not?

4. Sheeler says, "We never actually saw a Marine knock on a family's door on a notification." Instead, he reconstructed those scenes from interviews with the casualty assistance call officers and the families. Did you assume the reporter was actually there? Do you believe readers would make that assumption? Discuss the ethics of recreating scenes. What pitfalls face the reporters who rely on narrative reconstruction to show a scene they haven't witnessed?

Assignment Desk

1. Jim Sheeler says he discovered the focus of "Final Salute" when he realized the importance of a "ragged white glove" that a Marine had given him. Look back over your last five stories for a single detail that encapsulates what your story was about. In your next story, look for a tangible object—what Tom Wolfe called a "status detail"—that contains your story's theme.

2. Sheeler credits assistant managing editor Jim Trotter with keeping his mind open by making sure the story included something Trotter called "the sweep"—"the larger scope of the story, the journey he'd seen me take over the past year." Scope is also one of six elements writing coach Bill Blundell relied on during his award-winning

career at *The Wall Street Journal.* The other five are history, central reasons, impacts, gathering and action of contrary forces, and the future. Read more about it at www.poynter.org/blundellbook, or in Blundell's book, "The Art and Craft of Feature Writing." Let those six building blocks guide your reporting and writing.

3. "A scene is a point in time," says Stuart Warner, who edits and coaches narrative writing at *The Plain Dealer* in Cleveland. "Summary carries you between points in time." Put another way, scenes show, summary tells. Using two different highlighter pens, separate scenes from summaries in "Final Salute."

4. Sheeler recognized a truth about reading newspapers—"we knew that people would likely look at all the pictures first, read the captions, then go to the story." In future stories, follow his suggestion of using prose cut from the story as material for photo captions.

St. Petersburg Times

Finalist

Lane DeGregory
Non-Deadline Writing

8. Broadway Calls

DEC. 4, 2005

When the call came, Michelle Dowdy was rushing through New York's JFK Airport, trying to catch a plane home to Florida. She had to be back in St. Petersburg in a few hours for her high school commencement.

She flipped open her cell phone. "Hey!" she said, expecting someone she knew. Then she stopped walking, straining to hear above the airline announcements.

"Yeah...," she said. "Yes...this is Michelle." Her friends call her Dowdy, so whoever this was didn't know her.

Michelle listened, frozen by what she heard.

"You're kidding!" she gasped into the phone. She started screaming, right there in the airport, bouncing up and down in her scuffed Keds.

"Omigod! Really?" she squealed. "Okay, thank you! ...Omigod!"

Racing onto the plane, throwing herself into her seat, she had time to make just one call. "Mom!" she breathed into her cell phone. "Omigod, Mom, this is crazy!"

At 18, with no professional acting experience, and just shy of getting her high school diploma, Michelle Dowdy was going to Broadway.

* * *

She had auditioned on a lark.

In January she had come to New York with her mom, Karla Harris, to visit colleges. A friend had phoned to tell Michelle about an open casting call for *Hairspray.* They needed someone to be the understudy to the lead character.

Michelle and her mom had stayed up past midnight, trying to piece together a resume. But what to say? Michelle had never studied with a private acting coach, never had a voice lesson. She had performed only in school productions, and never as the lead. A boisterous size 14, she had always played the sidekicks and nameless others: Rizzo in *Grease,* Woodstock in *You're a Good Man, Charlie Brown.* In *Alice in Wonderland,* she was only a card.

Michelle was a dynamo onstage: funny, brassy and pitch-perfect. Her teachers marveled at her ability to lose herself in a part, to completely fill a role. But in the tiny world of high school theater, lots of kids seem talented.

Michelle didn't even have a glossy professional portrait. She had never needed one.

Her mom always carried a school picture in her wallet, so Michelle had stapled it to her makeshift bio and hoped the producers wouldn't laugh.

The morning of the audition, she and her mom had walked into the casting agency, dragging their borrowed suitcase behind them, wading through the first snow Michelle had ever seen. The rehearsal hall had been packed—dancers stretching on the wooden floor, singers squeezed against the mirrored walls.

"Every fat chick in New York must be here," Michelle had said. Of the 300, she had been the youngest, the only one who had brought her mom.

"Just be yourself, Honey," Karla had kept saying. "Have fun, and be yourself."

That was the easy part. From the first time she watched the John Waters film *Hairspray* in elementary school, Michelle had seen herself in the lead character, Tracy Turnblad, a fat girl who loves to sing and dance and yearns to be famous, but doesn't fit in. For her senior project at Gibbs High in the Pinellas County Center for the Arts, Michelle had performed scenes from the Broadway musical.

So when she skipped around the studio that morning in Manhattan, crooning, "I know every step, I know every song," she had really meant it. She *was* Tracy Turnblad: "Oh, oh, oh, don't make me wait one more moment for my life to start…"

They had made her wait. And wait. For three months, she didn't hear anything.

She had finished her senior year with flair, earning an A-plus on her *Hairspray* project and being named best actress in musical theater. She had gone to prom, been rejected from Juilliard and accepted at Marymount Manhattan. Figuring Broadway was a bust, she had started counting on college.

Then, in May, four months after that audition, the casting director had finally called. Michelle was one of 50 finalists. Could she be back in New York by the end of the week?

Karla couldn't afford two plane tickets, so this time Michelle had traveled alone. The callback day had been a whirlwind: a song, a dance, more fat girls, a harried dash to JFK.

And a phone call at the airport.

* * *

By the time Michelle got to St. Petersburg for commencement, everyone knew. Her mom had told the whole world.

Karla steered into the parking lot of the Palladium Theater in St. Petersburg and teenagers swarmed the car like paparazzi. "Omigod! Omigod! You're kidding, right?" her friends asked, crowding around her. They all wanted to hug Michelle, congratulate her, find out if it was really true.

Michelle had come straight from the airport, so she had to go to the bathroom to change out of her sweaty dance pants and into her long black dress and stilettoes. As she made her way through the lobby, teachers stopped to hug her.

Michelle was one of three seniors chosen to speak. She was supposed to be funny, but she didn't feel funny. To introduce her, a fellow student read from a bio she had written months before, back before she ever knew about the audition:

"One day," the student read," she hopes to play Tracy Turnblad, her dream role, on Broadway."

The auditorium erupted. "Broadway!" hundreds of seniors, parents and teachers cheered. They stood up, clapping and whistling. It was her first standing ovation as a Broadway star, and she hadn't even left Florida.

Slowly, carefully, trying to balance on her high heels, Michelle threaded her way toward the podium. Her bare shoulders shook. She was laughing and crying at the same time.

She turned the microphone toward her, beamed and wrinkled her freckled nose. Later, she wouldn't remember a word she had said. All she would remember was seeing her mom about halfway back in the crowd, still standing, still clapping.

In *Hairspray*, Tracy Turnblad asserts her independence, crying, "Mama, I'm a big girl now!" She wins a role on her favorite TV show, convinces everyone fat girls can dance, and drags her reluctant mom into the spotlight. Of course, the play has a happy ending.

But what about Michelle's story? At 18, she didn't know how to drive, had never had a bank account or done laundry, had never even had a job. She depended on Karla for just about everything.

Could she tear herself away from her mom and make it on her own in New York?

Michelle didn't know it then, but she had to leave in three days.

9. Goodbye, Mom

DEC. 5, 2005

By Lane DeGregory

ST. PETERSBURG—Brighter lips. The photographer said Michelle needed brighter lips.

"Don't you have anything stronger?" she asked, turning to Michelle's mom.

On the last Friday in May, Michelle Dowdy and her mom were at a photography studio, getting Michelle's head shots made. The pictures had to be printed and mailed to New York by 4 p.m. to make the deadline for the Playbill.

Then Michelle had to buy new dance shoes and a suitcase, pack, get her hair cut, visit her friends and, oh yeah, find somewhere to live in New York—where, magically, at 18, she had landed a role in the Broadway musical *Hairspray.*

Before she could go be a star, though, she would also have to figure out how to wash clothes and make grilled cheese and do all the other things her mom had always done for her.

She'd have to hurry. At first, Michelle was told she had a month to get to New York. Then the stage manager called and said the lead actress was having vocal problems. They needed Michelle in three days. As the understudy, she would rehearse for six weeks and make her Broadway debut as early as July.

Michelle's mom, Karla Harris, pulled a tube of lipstick from her purse. "Clinique, gingerbread," she told the photographer, thrusting it toward Michelle.

As Michelle took the lipstick, her blue eyes widened in alarm.

"Mom!" she asked, "You okay?"

Karla's face was flushed and puffy, her black eyeliner smeared.

She dropped her head, shook it yes, then no. "It's just, I've been crying all day today," Karla said. "I can't help it."

Michelle slid her arm around her shoulder and squeezed. "I wrote my bio for the playbill this morning," she said. "You're in it."

Michelle and her mom lived in a 500-square-foot apartment overlooking a parking lot in Treasure Island. Michelle slept in a single bed in the only bedroom, where posters from school plays papered the walls. Her mom slept on a couch in the living room with framed photos of her only child smiling down on her.

Michelle's parents divorced when she was 2, and it had been her and her mom ever since. Karla runs the before-school and after-school programs at Gulf Beaches Elementary. She always wanted a job where she could bring her daughter to work with her.

When Michelle was 7, Karla started driving her to dance lessons, gymnastics and acting camps. Later, Karla chauffeured her to high school play rehearsals, often waiting past midnight to drive her home.

They always said they were like sisters, but it was more complicated than that. Michelle was everything to Karla: her daughter, her buddy, her reason to get up in the morning and to come home at night. And even as a teenager, Michelle liked having her mom around. She hung out with Karla at cast parties, as if she were just another one of the kids.

They even look alike. Michelle has always been heavy, like her mom. But Karla never plagued her with diet pills or shipped her to fat camps, as her own mother did. She taught Michelle to accept herself.

At 5 feet 2 and 172 pounds, Michelle seems comfortable in her body—something few teenage girls can say. She wears tight jeans or long, gauzy skirts with low-cut blouses and doesn't try to hide her curves. She jokes about herself so others don't have to: "Fat girl's gotta eat!" she'll say, chomping into an inch-thick cheeseburger.

The only thing that ever bugged her about being big was that she seldom got to play the lead.

* * *

At the portrait studio, Michelle wore black boots, jeans and a clingy black blouse. The V-neck was lined with thick rows of silver sparkles. Karla had on her signature flip-flops, shorts and oversize T-shirt.

The photographer had Michelle sit on a stool, stand in front of a screen, prop her foot on a fake rock. "Give me a natural smile. Cut those eyes at me," she ordered. "Now how about a naughty smile…"

Karla frowned. Michelle was much too young to show the world her naughty smile.

After the shoot, they looked at the pictures on the photographer's computer. Everyone liked the one where Michelle sat with her hair draped across her right shoulder.

As they raced to the post office, Karla asked Michelle about her travel plans. Where would she stay? Who would look after her? She desperately wanted to go to New York with Michelle, but couldn't afford it.

Before leaving for New York, Michelle Dowdy and her mother, Karla Harris, look at Michelle's head shot for Playbill on a computer screen. (Photograph courtesy of Cherie Diez/*St. Petersburg Times*)

"It's crazy," Michelle told her mom. "They're putting me up at this swanky hotel and sending a car and driver to pick me up."

Karla smiled. She kept forgetting: Her little girl had hit the big time.

* * *

The next two days were filled with packing and saying goodbye. Michelle was going to miss all the graduation parties. And she had to leave her boyfriend.

R. J. Hunt, a 10th-grader and a theater rat like Michelle, told her he was worried that she'd find somebody else. "But I told him, 'Hey, I'm just the fat girl,' " Michelle said to her mom.

The night before Michelle left, she and her mom couldn't sleep. Well after midnight, they cuddled on the couch, watching videos of Michelle's school plays. Michelle kept laughing. Her mom kept choking back sobs.

For 18 years, Karla had tucked Michelle into bed every night. Tomorrow, there wouldn't be anyone for her to tell, "Sweet dreams."

* * *

Karla didn't even bother putting on her trademark black eyeliner in the morning. She knew she'd only cry it off.

"I called the cell-phone people, and you can keep your number so we don't have to go on roaming to talk," she said on the drive to the airport. "I told the operator all about you and Broadway."

Michelle grabbed her mom's hand. "I'll call you every night."

Inside the terminal, Karla didn't want to let go. She stood there hugging Michelle, wetting her hair with tears. Finally, Michelle pulled away and walked toward security.

Then she turned, raised her fingers to her lips and blew her mom a kiss.

* * *

Michelle slept all the way to New York. She arrived at baggage claim to find a man in a suit and tie holding a sign with black letters.

"MICHELLE DOWDY," the sign read. She had never seen her name so big.

"That's me," she told the man. He lowered the sign. "Wait, wait!" she said. "I have to get a picture of that to show my mom."

10. Turning Into Tracy

DEC. 6, 2005

By Lane DeGregory

Somewhere in the darkness, her cell phone was ringing. Michelle Dowdy rolled over in a too-big bed, wondering where she was. Lamps with painted faces stared at her from the end tables. Her purple suitcase was propped against the wall.

In Michelle's sleepy haze it dawned on her: New York! It was May 31 and she was waking up in the Hudson Hotel, a few blocks from Broadway...where, just out of high school, she would start work that day.

She answered the phone ("Yes, Mom, I'm fine. Sorry I forgot to call."), caught some more sleep, then enjoyed a long soak in the tub. After a stop for a burger, a Coke and a slice of cheesecake ($26!), she made her way to the Neil Simon Theatre at the corner of Broadway and 52nd.

Hairspray, the marquee read. A giant, glittering, purple can towered above the building.

Michelle stared up at it. She had always wanted to be here. But now that she was, she couldn't help wondering whether she belonged.

As she stood there, star-struck, a thin, dark-haired woman approached with her hand extended. "Welcome!" she said. "Welcome to Broadway!"

* * *

Margo Lion, the show's lead producer, is the one who cast Michelle as the understudy for the role of Tracy Turnblad. She escorted Michelle into the old theater and introduced her to *Hairspray*'s publicist.

"She's got a great voice. She's a wonderful dancer," Lion enthused as the publicist nodded. "She has an authenticity about her, and a genuine warmth."

Blushing beneath her freckles, Michelle shuffled her feet.

Through a thick gray door, up a narrow flight of stairs, Lion led Michelle to a cramped corner office. Stage manager Frank Lombardi got up to greet her.

"You'll be watching the show tonight, and probably for a while, from the audience," he said. "We'll rehearse you two or three times a week, until you're ready to go on."

Michelle nodded, and they were off again. Lombardi guided her up another winding staircase, past head shots of former cast members.

Dowdy, left, meets actress Shannon Durig outside the stage door. Durig was starring as Tracy, the lead in *Hairspray*. Dowdy had come to New York to be her understudy. She longed to play the part "for real." (Photograph courtesy of Cherie Diez/*St. Petersburg Times*)

She recognized some: that woman was on *One Life to Live;* that man had been on *Too Close for Comfort*. She was part of this now, one of them.

Lombardi said they were going to meet the person who would do her hair.

"I'll have my own hairdresser?" she asked.

"And a dresser ... and a makeup artist ... and a wardrobe supervisor ..."

"That's awesome. This is awesome," Michelle said. Her face hurt from smiling.

She learned she would have three wigs, six dresses and four pairs of shoes, each custom-made.

"Now, you'll want to come meet your mother," Lombardi said. "He's right in here."

A huge man with frizzy hair hurtled out of his dressing room. He was wearing a flowered housedress. She knew him immediately: Bruce Vilanch from *Hollywood Squares*. He crushed her in a bear hug.

"Oh," he bubbled, "you're cute as a peach."

* * *

She sat that evening in the center of the seventh row, beneath the gilded dragons circling the domed ceiling. At a minute past 7, the lights dimmed and the fluted curtain rose. A huge bed was balanced vertically at center stage.

On it, a chubby girl in a big wig was stretching and yawning.

As Tracy sang *Good Morning, Baltimore,* Michelle felt she was watching someone playing her. Through the whole show, perched on the edge of her crushed velvet seat, she mouthed the words, swaying and clapping, laughing louder than anyone at jokes she already knew.

Afterward, outside the stage door, she met more of the cast while they signed autographs. Michelle had never signed an autograph. She couldn't imagine anyone wanting hers. "Did you find a place to live yet?" an actor asked.

"No," she answered. "I haven't even started looking."

The stage manager came out, bearing a black three-ring binder. "Your script," he said. "Tomorrow, 10 a.m., we need you here to learn the music. Bring a tape recorder and a blank tape."

"Thank you! I will."

Michelle turned and walked up Broadway, her feet throbbing in the stilettos her mom had bought her for graduation, wondering where she could buy a tape recorder at 11 p.m. and how to hail a cab.

* * *

The musical director's office is a cluttered cubby with green walls, the windows painted shut and an air conditioner held in place with duct tape. It's far from glamorous, backstage at Broadway.

"Okay, so we'll run through the whole thing," Len Hoyt said. Michelle hadn't found a tape recorder, so Hoyt let her borrow one.

She sang the opening number sitting down, right on time, right on key. Hoyt noticed she didn't look at the score. "You did your homework!" he said. "How long have you been listening to the cast album?"

Michelle wrinkled her nose. "Ever since it came out."

Her character, Tracy, sings 10 songs. During the first half of the show, she leaves the stage only for a 20-second costume change.

"So what you need to work on," Hoyt said, "is stamina. Practice singing on a treadmill."

Michelle laughed.

"I'm serious," he said.

* * *

"All right, we're going to torture you into playing Tracy, are we?" asked a white-haired woman with a lilting British accent. It was the next day and Michelle was standing in a fitting room at Euro Co. Costumes, chewing gum.

"I'm going to ask you a few questions here," said the woman, Janet Bloor.

Height? 5 feet 2. Weight? 172. Dress size? 14. Hose? Large. Allergies? Pollen.

Bloor laughed. That one had been a joke.

"We'll be making you a bum pad to hide the mike, and they'll probably want me to do other padding," she said. "There's a specific silhouette they're looking for."

Her bum sufficiently sized up, Michelle had to go to a custom shoe-fitter, blocks away. She stepped off the curb and thrust her right hand into the air, toward traffic. Three days in the city and she was hailing taxis.

At T.O. Dey Custom Fitted Shoes, the owner ushered Michelle into a side room. "Sit on the bench, take your shoes off," Gino Bifulco said. She handed him an order sheet.

"Ahh, you're going to be Tracy."

He traced her foot on a piece of paper, measured its width, length and height. Bifulco has made shoes for Mariah Carey, Jerry Seinfeld and Julie Andrews. He would make Michelle buckled black dance shoes, checkered Keds with custom arches and hot pink pumps for the grand finale.

"When are you going on?" he asked.

When? Well…

They told her she would start rehearsal that week. They said she could go on as the understudy—her Broadway debut!—within a month.

They didn't tell her everything.

11. Are You Happy, Honey?

DEC. 8, 2005

By Lane DeGregory

Mornings were miserable. Now that her baby had gone to Broadway, Karla Harris had no one to wish "Good morning" to, no one to drive to school.

Afternoons were worse. Karla had always looked forward to catching up on Michelle's day, taking her to play practice, making her dinner. Now she didn't even feel like coming home.

"The other day, I started bawling so hard I couldn't see," Karla said when asked how Michelle was doing. "We've never been apart this long."

Three weeks had passed since Michelle Dowdy had left for New York. At 18, she had won the part of understudy to the lead in the musical *Hairspray*. Karla worried constantly about where her daughter was sleeping, what she was eating. She couldn't imagine Michelle's new life.

At night Karla curled up on the sofa in her Treasure Island apartment, just as she always had. She couldn't move into the only bedroom. That was still Michelle's room. Alone in the dark, Karla watched videos of Michelle's high school plays.

It was the only way she could fall asleep: listening to her daughter sing.

* * *

The only place Michelle was performing was on her mom's TV.

The directors had told her she would be ready to go on by July. The lead actress would take a night off and she would get her chance.

But now it was late June and Michelle hadn't even run through the entire show. She had rehearsed her songs exactly once and practiced her dance steps a few times, but that was it. The director told her to watch the show from the audience, so she did.

Twenty-seven times.

"They put me on the back burner," she complained to her mom. The directors hadn't told Michelle, but they had been negotiating to bring in a new lead actress, pushing Michelle down to second understudy. There was no need to rehearse her yet.

"I'm not even running lines," Michelle said.

She was still excited about New York, but she was overwhelmed, too. She had run out of money for hotels, so for two weeks she had been hauling her suitcase around, crashing with friends who had moved to New York for college. And even though she had spent her college savings—$3,000—on an apartment hunter, he still hadn't found anything she could afford.

Over the phone, Karla asked Michelle about her laundry. Michelle had never done laundry. "Baby, you don't have a funky pile, do you?"

She did indeed. She kept recycling the same four outfits. Finally, she took her clothes to this "groovy little dry cleaner," but when they were done she didn't have the $15 to pick them up.

Karla wanted to help, but her last long-distance bill had been $402. So she borrowed money from her own mother and mailed a check to the theater, the only address Michelle had.

Michelle had always longed for the glitter of Broadway, and Karla had always hoped she would get whatever she wanted. But now that Michelle had made it, Karla wasn't so sure she was okay.

One night she asked, "Are you happy, Honey?"

It wasn't that simple.

* * *

The broker finally found an apartment on the East Side, a two-bedroom with a rusty fire escape. Michelle moved in the last day of June, with a friend from high school. The apartment leased for $2,000 a month—four times as much as Karla's place in Treasure Island.

"You should see it!" Michelle told her mom.

Part of Karla—the part that had once been a teenage girl—knew Michelle didn't really want her mom around all the time.

The rest of her was going to New York.

"I'll be there next weekend," Karla said.

* * *

When Karla landed, she took a cab straight to the theater, where Michelle was watching the show again. She stood outside the stage door, waiting.

Karla had never seen a Broadway show. The theater looked old and important, even from the outside. And her baby was working here. Soon, people from all over the world would see Michelle onstage.

A crowd had gathered outside the door: 70 autograph seekers wielding cameras, posters and programs. Karla couldn't believe how dressed up everyone was. She tugged at her long, faded T-shirt, the one with cats on it, and wished she had brought shoes instead of flip-flops.

Just after 10:30 p.m., the stage door cracked and Michelle emerged, smiling and waving.

She looked so thin. That was the first thing Karla noticed. Michelle, who had been hired to play a fat girl, had lost 10 pounds because she wasn't eating.

"C'mon!" Michelle called, pulling Karla toward the stage door. "I told everyone you were coming. They all want to meet you. And guess what? I met Jeff Goldblum today!"

Backstage, Michelle introduced her to the cast. The actor who dresses in drag to play Tracy Turnblad's mother insisted on having his picture taken with Michelle's real mom.

"I can't wait for you to see the show tomorrow," Michelle told Karla as they left the theater.

Karla was dying to see *Hairspray,* but how could she? "Sorry, Honey," she finally said. "I can't afford a ticket."

Michelle pulled an envelope from her purse. Good news: She had started rehearsals, so her pay had shot up. "Look," she said, grinning. She showed her mom the check: $1,579 for one week. "I bought you this," Michelle said, handing her a $100 ticket to the next performance.

The show would have given Karla a ticket in the balcony. But Michelle wanted her mom in the front, right beside her.

* * *

Michelle's apartment was almost empty. The only furniture was a sagging futon and a torn leather armchair. "Can you believe someone was throwing it out?" Michelle asked.

Karla laughed and shook her head. Ah, the life of a diva.

Well after midnight, an old high school friend came by to take Michelle out for ice cream. "I'll meet you downstairs," Michelle told him.

Then she took her mom's hand and led her down the hall. "This is it," she said, showing Karla an inflatable mattress.

Karla still didn't know when she would see her daughter on Broadway, but it felt good to be with her, to know she was okay. She kicked off her flip-flops and lay down. Michelle spread a blanket across her mom and tucked her in.

12. Waiting in the Wings

DEC. 9, 2005

By Lane DeGregory

July dragged by, hot and heavy as a bouffant wig. Michelle Dowdy had been in the cast of *Hairspray* for two months, but she had rehearsed her part only eight times, mostly with the other understudies.

She was dying to show what she could do.

Finally, the stage manager told her she could do a "put-in." The next day, she would run through the entire show with the regular cast. The producer, director, choreographer and musical director would be watching. When they saw things she needed to change, they would stop the rehearsal.

Suddenly Michelle had doubts. "Some of these people won Tonys!" she told her mom on the phone that night. "I'm nervous." Karla had never heard her say that before.

The next day, she was relaxed and ran through the whole show: 14 scenes and 14 songs. She danced the "Madison," the "monkey," the mating dance called "Peyton Place After Midnight." No one stopped her. Not once.

Afterward, the directors gave her notes:

Keep pitch on "Oh's" during *Good Morning Baltimore*. Hold hair spray can in left hand during detention scene. Remember arms in *Big Girl*. Don't spin lollipop.

Breathe!

Pretty minor stuff for a first put-in, the cast told her. You were the talk of the theater! the understudies said. In a pinch, the stage manager told Michelle, we could put you on now.

But they didn't.

* * *

At least she could stay backstage during performances now.

After watching *Hairspray* from the audience more than 40 times, Michelle was glad to hang out in the dressing room. She and two other understudies shared a space the size of a walk-in closet. A speaker in the wall broadcast what was happening onstage. If something happened, the actresses could get dressed and be onstage in minutes.

Michelle spent most evenings watching *Golden Girls* DVDs with the other understudies or sleeping on the floor, under the makeup counter. She devoured the latest Harry Potter book backstage.

At first she understood, sort of, why she had to wait. The directors had brought back Marissa Jaret Winokur, the actress who had originated the role of Tracy in *Hairspray*. Of course, Michelle had to take a backseat to her—and her understudy.

But then Marissa had landed a part on Pamela Anderson's new TV show, *Stacked,* and her understudy had started playing Tracy. For the past few weeks, Michelle had been the understudy to Shannon Durig.

She would have to wait in the wings until Shannon got a night off. And nobody was saying when that would be.

* * *

She needed a break. She needed to go home.

One Sunday in mid August, Michelle hopped a midnight flight to Florida. Karla picked her up, all hugs and tears.

The next morning, Michelle went back to Gibbs High, where she had graduated just three months earlier. She wanted to see her teachers and theater friends who were still there. This was where she had learned to act and dance and sing. If not for this school, she felt, she never would have made it to Broadway.

"Dowdy!" "Girl!" "Look at you!"

Teenagers pounced on Michelle outside the drama department. All her friends call her Dowdy. "We've missed you sooo much!" "Oooh, your hair!"

Michelle had let the Broadway stylist cut off her waist-length hair. Now the ends brushed her shoulders. He had highlighted it too, with wide caramel streaks. Michelle had always wanted highlights, but could never afford them.

One of her friends made her a name tag: "Michelle—the best person ever."

In high school, she and her many theater friends combed thrift stores for costumes, built sets together and sang show tunes. Michelle was the one they all called when they needed help with their characters; she was never too busy to help others run their lines.

And, incredibly, she had made it. She was where they all wanted to be.

"We want to know what your life is like," drama teacher Keven Renken told Michelle, cupping her hand in both of his. "Tell us stories."

So Michelle pulled up a stool in Mr. Renken's classroom, under the poster from her *Hairspray* senior project. She looked out at the 18 students. Suddenly it felt weird, being back here. Like she was playing this person who was supposed to be her.

She didn't know what to say. Everyone thought she was a star—and she hadn't even gone onstage.

"Ask me questions," she said.

* * *

"Tell us about the clubs."

"Well, I've only really been to one, and it was a gay drag club. It was crazy."

"Have you been mugged?"

"No, not yet. I'm tough."

"Tell us about your regular day. What's it like?"

"Well, I get to the show, like, 30 minutes before it starts. That's all it takes to get ready, if they need us. And I mostly just go to the dressing room and hang out and watch movies with the other swings."

"What's a swing?"

"They basically cover all the other parts. They're like the understudies to all the other actors."

"What about costumes?"

"I don't have mine yet. But they built me a fat suit. It's weird. They built me a new butt, it's like an inch thick. It's like a fat leotard, but with shorts."

"Do you have a crush on anyone?"

"There are five straight guys in the cast, but they're all married. The guy who plays Seaweed is really cute. But we just flirt a lot."

"Are you still with R. J.?"

They all knew R. J., a junior in Gibbs' theater department. But no one had wanted to ask R. J. directly.

Michelle shook her head no. They were worlds apart now.

"Have you met any famous people?"

"Well, I got free tickets to go see *Lennon* and I met Jeff Goldblum. Okay, who else? Well, I didn't really meet them, but I was walking past the theater where they do *Spamalot* and I saw Hank Azaria and David Hyde Pierce and they sort of just smiled. And I was like, 'Wow!'"

When the bell rang, everyone mobbed her.

"You'll have to let us know when you go on. We all want to come see you."

"When I come, can I crash on your couch?"

"When's it going to happen? Why's it taking so long?"

* * *

The rest of August crawled by, then September. For six weeks, she didn't rehearse at all.

In October, Michelle had to buy her first coat. She had been in New York since May. Five months!

One Sunday night, the stage manager called her into his office.

13. Showtime

DEC. 11, 2005

By Lane DeGregory

The stage manager wanted to see her.

Michelle climbed the stairs to his office, wondering what was up. Maybe he needed her to perform at a charity event or do a promotional appearance at a shopping center. As an understudy, she did lots of those. Maybe he wanted her to do another run-through.

"Are you ready?" he asked, when she stepped through the door.

Ready? What? To do the real show?

"You'll go on Thursday," he told her. Four days from now.

She couldn't believe it. After six months of waiting, of rehearsing and hoping, of listening to the show in the dressing room, Michelle Dowdy finally was going to make her debut on Broadway.

* * *

As she left the theater, she called her mom in Florida. Karla screamed and cried, and called JetBlue.

She got to Michelle's apartment the night before the show. They ordered pizza and sat on the rusty fire escape, watching the New York skyline, their arms around each other. Holding on.

At 1:30 a.m., Michelle made herself lie down. She had to be at the theater in 12 hours. She kept imagining herself on that enormous stage, wearing that hot pink dress and bouffant wig, doing all the scenes perfectly, but in the wrong order.

* * *

On any other day, Michelle would have had to climb five flights of stairs to the cramped dressing room she shared with two other understudies. But on Thursday, Oct. 27, the stage manager told her to get ready on the second floor—in the lead's dressing room.

Someone had penciled her name on a purple card and taped it to the door.

Michelle smiled. This was so cool!

Then she opened the door and gasped.

Flowers filled the room: daisies and lilies, red and yellow roses, sunflowers and tulips and chrysanthemums. A high school friend had shipped a box of chocolate-covered cherries. Darlene Love, the '60s singer who plays Motormouth Maybelle in *Hairspray,* had sent a basket, 4 feet tall, filled with candy. In one corner, a giant purple balloon bobbed "Congratulations!"

"This is crazy," Michelle said out loud. "Crazy!"

After rehearsal, back in the dressing room, her cell phone rang. "Oh, the flowers are gorgeous." Her high school drama teacher had sent a spray of roses. "Of course, I'm nervous. All the bigwigs are going to be here." The producer, the director, the choreographer—they all wanted to see what she could do. That's why they were putting her on now.

"So," she told her drama teacher, "I better not suck."

* * *

Outside the Neil Simon Theatre, 15 of her friends were waiting. They had flown up from Florida and were shivering in the New York cold. They ambushed Michelle, circled her on the sidewalk.

"I'm so glad to see you guys," she said.

She hadn't eaten all day, so she went across the street to the Cosmic Diner and ordered a cheese omelet and fries.

She was worried about her hairpiece. It kept falling off during the detention scene.

She was thinking about *I Can Hear the Bells,* her fourth song and the longest by far. If she could remember to breathe and pace herself, as the music director had suggested, then she thought she'd be fine.

Michelle stared at her food. She didn't feel like eating.

* * *

Back in her dressing room, she arranged her good luck charms on the makeup counter: a penguin in a top hat, 2 inches tall; a rock with the word *Believe* etched into the top; a yellow rose from her mom.

She dropped a fizzy vitamin C tablet into a glass of water. She needed a boost. She was yawning the whole time people were pinning up her hair, tugging on her wig, making up her face.

She stretched to warm up her muscles, sang scales to warm up her voice. Her dresser zipped her into the first costume: a ruffled white blouse and straight skirt, white Keds.

Then Michelle crept downstairs. She opened the door to the stage where Ethel Merman once sang in *Porgy and Bess.* Five minutes before her first call, she stood there, feeling the heat of the lights and the weight of her wig, staring at the back of the crimson and purple curtain, listening to the people shuffling into their seats.

* * *

When the usher handed Karla a Playbill, a small square of paper fluttered out: "At this performance the role of Tracy Turnblad will be played by Michelle Dowdy." Karla picked up the slip of paper and tucked it into her purse. "Can I have a few more of those?" she asked.

Michelle's bio was on Page 29. "MICHELLE DOWDY is making her Broadway debut in *Hairspray*." Nothing about experience or awards, like all the other cast members. "She would like to thank her mother for being the best person she has ever known." Karla wept, her tears splattering the paper.

The house lights went down and the audience fell silent and slowly the fluted curtain began to rise.

* * *

"Oh, oh, oh, woke up today, feeling the way I always do. Oh, oh, oh, hungry for something that I can't eat. Then I hear the beat…"

Michelle's voice, clear and strong, rang through the theater. She was stretching and yawning, in a bed 8 feet tall, alone onstage, in the spotlight.

She was Tracy Turnblad, a fat girl who loves to sing and dance, who has a loud, loving mom, who starts out as an outsider but winds up in the center of everything.

She remembered to breathe during *I Can Hear the Bells*…maybe too often. But she got through it smiling. And when her hairpiece flipped up during the detention scene, she just kept on dancing.

All she could think was: This is where I belong.

Before the last song ended, 1,350 people were on their feet. In the front row, Michelle's high school friends whooped and cheered. In the sixth row, Karla clapped her hands above her head while black eyeliner trickled down her cheeks.

Michelle couldn't see her mom in the glare of the lights, so she squinted into the theater and blew a kiss in hopes it would find her.

* * *

A crowd was waiting outside her dressing room. The producer, director, stage manager, dance captain. They came to her, gushing.

"You were fantastic! So comfortable," the producer said. "There was no sense at all this was your first time on Broadway. I'm just bowled over. A triumph, really."

"Like you were shot out of a cannon," the musical director said.

Michelle kept smiling outside the dressing room that wasn't really hers, nodding and not quite hearing everything. She couldn't believe she was

Dowdy, as Tracy Turnblad, leads the ensemble during the final scene of *Hairspray*. Dowdy had been waiting five months to make her Broadway debut. (Photograph courtesy of Cherie Diez/*St. Petersburg Times*)

here, that this was happening. She felt like she was outside herself, watching herself. Those two hours onstage had been the most fun ever.

Forget the cast party. Never mind the friends who were waiting, or the people with the posters and programs who were out on the sidewalk, eager to get her autograph. Michelle wanted, more than anything, to go back onstage right then and do it all again.

Karla waited until the show people left, then ducked into Michelle's dressing room and crushed her in a hug. Michelle squirmed back to look up at her.

"So, Mom," she said, wrinkling her nose. "Did you like it?"

Where's Michelle Now?

Six weeks after making her Broadway debut, Michelle Dowdy is still understudy to the lead in *Hairspray*. She has performed the part several times onstage since then. But she spends most evenings waiting in the dressing room with the other understudies.

There is talk of a *Hairspray* show opening in Las Vegas. A new movie of the musical, produced by New Line Cinema, is in the making. John Travolta, Billy Crystal and Aretha Franklin have been mentioned as possible cast members.

No one is saying who might play Tracy Turnblad in either production.

To read more about this series or to hear audio of Michelle Dowdy, click on www.sptimes.com/big-girl-now.

ABOUT THIS SERIES

This series is based on six months of reporting. *St. Petersburg Times* writer Lane DeGregory and photographer Cherie Diez met Michelle Dowdy and Karla Harris in May 2005. They interviewed Michelle and her mom, as well as Michelle's teachers, friends and relatives in Florida. They also made three trips to New York City, where they interviewed the producer, stage manager and musical director of *Hairspray* and watched Michelle at work on Broadway. Most of the scenes described were witnessed by the reporters. Others are based on people's recollections.

Lessons Learned

BY LANE DeGREGORY

All the teenagers were talking about it: Michelle Dowdy, a senior at a Florida high school, a chubby actress who had never played the lead, had landed a role on Broadway. A few days after graduation, she was heading to New York to be understudy to the lead in the musical *Hairspray*. Everyone said the part was perfect for her. The show itself seemed to mirror Michelle's life and dreams.

But what would happen when this 18-year-old girl, who lived in a one-bedroom apartment with her mom, who had never done her own laundry, learned to drive or had a job, left home and tried to make it on her own in New York?

That was the question I set out to answer when I started reporting this story. I thought I would follow Michelle for a few weeks, write a Sunday lead.

I wound up spending six months with her and her mom and writing my first serial narrative. I ran into a lot of walls, and figured out a few things along the way...

Step back and listen. Michelle was wonderfully kind and open, excited to have me along—at first. But after a few days of tolerating my shadow and constant questions, it became obvious that I was in her way.

I had to make myself retreat, learn to watch instead of interfere. When you remove yourself from the action, you start to see scenes unfold and can write down dialogue instead of just quotes.

Sell yourself. I should have worked harder pitching my story to the PR people. The Manhattan firm that handled publicity for *Hairspray* was used to the press coming in on preview night, snapping a few posed shots after the show. But the public relations staff—and, especially, the Broadway directors and stage managers—couldn't understand why the photographer and I wanted to watch Michelle getting her shoes fitted, having her hair done, rehearsing in sweatpants. The toughest battles we fought were trying to get access to the smallest backstage moments. After writing countless certified letters and e-mails, getting yelled at and hung up on, we had to lower our expectations. Instead of getting access to the half-dozen two-hour rehearsals, we wound up being grateful for just 20 minutes. If you take the time to explain, up front, what you want and why, it saves a lot of hassles.

Ask mom. It was hard being in Florida when Michelle was in New York. After I was bounced from backstage on Broadway, my editor was reluctant to keep sending me back to the Big Apple. I called Michelle every few days, but she was so busy, weeks often went by before she called back.

Thank goodness her mom, Karla, lived close by and always answered my calls. Karla was more than willing to meet me for lunch, dinner, drinks … any excuse to talk about Michelle. When you can't get to the main character, get close to the person she's closest to.

Follow the story. Originally, this was going to be a fairy tale about a little girl chasing her big dream. But as the months went by, and I began to see Karla's saga as well as Michelle's, I realized the story was really more about a daughter-mother relationship: growing up and letting go. Once I dropped the diva angle, the tale became more universal, more real. Don't be afraid to let the story take you places you hadn't imagined.

Think small. By the time Michelle finally got to perform the lead role on stage, I had been to New York four times, filled 15 notebooks, interviewed at least 50 people. "Let's try a serial," my editor suggested. Then he dropped the ax: Each installment had to be short.

Really short. "We don't want to intimidate anyone," he said. He made me make a timeline, then split the action into scenes. Each segment had to have a single theme, a beginning that would draw readers in, a cliffhanger that would leave them wondering. I learned to pick only moments that meant something, only details that showed insight or furthered the action. I had to chop huge blocks of great stuff to whittle each day's installment down to its core. In the end, that's what readers liked best about the series: You could read each story over a cup of coffee.

Lane DeGregory is a features writer at the St. Petersburg Times. *Her stories have appeared in* Best Newspaper Writing 2000 *and* 2004. *She has won many awards, including: second place, 2005 National Headliner award for feature writing; finalist, 2004 American Society of Newspaper Editors award for non-deadline writing; and second place, 2004 American Association of Sunday and Features Editors for short feature writing.*

The Washington Post

Finalist

Mark Leibovich
Non-Deadline Writing

14. Pressure Cooker

JAN. 5, 2005

Andrew Card is talking about his kitchen. "I know my kitchen really well, as evidenced by my rotund being," Card says, patting his belly. "I know where the oven is and I know where the microwave is and I know where the sink is and I know where the refrigerator is and the freezer and the cupboards and the table and the chairs."

Card, 57, is sprawled on the couch of his West Wing office, describing the kitchen from his mind's eye. It is from here that the White House chief of staff organizes the nation's most potent workplace and man-hours. Like his boss, Card is an aggressively lowfalutin character. He is the longest-serving chief of staff in 46 years, yet he reminds people that he toiled many years at a McDonald's and spent one summer as a garbage collector.

"I'm not a very smart person," Card says. "I have to work really hard at remembering things." Which explains the deceptively prosaic tour of Card's Arlington kitchen. Card rarely takes notes. He does not make to-do lists or scrawl reminders to himself on Post-its. Instead, he keeps much of the Bush White House in his head, or in his kitchen. This is where it gets eccentric for everyman Andy Card.

Card is a student of memory. He practices a technique pioneered by Matteo Ricci, a 16th-century Italian Jesuit. Ricci, who did missionary work in China, introduced the notion of a "memory palace" to Confucian scholars. The "memory palace" is a structure of the mind, to be furnished with mnemonic devices. Ricci might construct an imaginary palace room for each of his students—filled with furniture and shelves to represent aspects of that student (a painting to express his appearance, a shelf on which to array his scholastic record).

Memory is central to a chief of staff's job. He must possess enough instant knowledge to execute the president's minute-to-minute pursuits, be it macro (his agenda) or micro (when he's due for a haircut).

Brad Blakeman, a former White House scheduler, says it's not uncommon to have someone ask where the president will be on a certain date three months in the future and have Card answer precisely. "He knew the president's schedule a lot better than me," Blakeman says, "and I was the scheduler."

While Ricci used a palace, castle or other elaborate edifice, Card's palace is his mental kitchen. Every Monday morning when he arrives at the White House, Card performs the ritual of "cleaning my kitchen."

"I view my job as being responsible for the president to have everything he needs to do his job," Card says. "So when I clean my kitchen, it's really about anticipating what it is the president will have to do, what kind of help he will need to do it, and when it has to be done."

When tackling matters of top priority, Card stands at the stove, working his "front and back burners." Intelligence reform is cooking this morning. He needs to call several people: 9/11 Commission Chairmen Tom Kean and Lee Hamilton, Reps. Duncan Hunter and James Sensenbrenner, and House Speaker Dennis Hastert. They are "on my right front burner," he says.

"Then I shift gears to my left front burner, which is second most important," Card says. He will help the president hire a Cabinet secretary, then move to his right rear burner (hiring White House staff for the second term). "I do that all in my kitchen," Card says.

"Now the things I want to put off for a long time, I put in the freezer. But then I can go to my freezer and generally remember things that I put there a long time ago." He will store matters that were resolved or tabled yesterday in a cupboard.

"If you go see Andy at his desk, it looks like he's not doing anything," says Andrew Natsios, a close friend of Card's who is head of the Agency for International Development. "It's almost empty, there's no paper anywhere. But he's created this whole system in his head with this mind discipline of his."

So much institutional history and memory of both Bush administrations is stored in Andy Card's kitchen. He has been as entrenched in Bushworld as the family furniture. He is chronically there—as in *there* in the room, in the meeting, in the photo, on the Sunday shows. Card was *there,* next to Bush One when he vomited on the Japanese prime minister, *there* in the Oval when Bushes One and Two choked up together on

Inauguration Day 2001, and *there*, in Bush Two's ear as he read "My Pet Goat" on 9/11.

He wakes at 4:20 each morning, commonly stays at work until 10 p.m. and spends most weekends at his office or at Camp David with the POTUS.

He wears his fatigue proudly, advertises his minimal sleep regimen, mentions what bad shape he's in, how he drinks too much coffee and that he needs to spend more time with family—three grown children, four grandchildren and wife Kathleene, a Methodist minister, whom he met when both were in the fifth grade. In 2003, he passed out during a three-mile run with the president in Crawford, Tex.

Does his fatigue make it harder for Card to remember things? He shakes his head: "My kitchen is in order," Card says, "though I may not be."

Card loves to doodle, a rare indulgence of paper for him. "I am almost always doodling," he says. He can look at old doodles and recall where he was when he drew them, what meeting he was in and what was decided. They are his de facto notes.

Card pulls out a doodle from the top drawer of his desk: It is a pencil sketch of a Canadian flag, which Card drew in a meeting during the president's recent visit to Canada. Beneath the flag is a network of circles, jots, lines and warped squares. It is the driveway of his summer house in Poland, Maine: "Here's the house," he says, leading a tour of the doodle. Here's the rock garden, the drainage scheme and a tool shed that he's thinking about building.

"Doodling helps my thinking," Card says, a corollary to creating pictures in his mind. "It helps me to visualize that which I'm listening to."

A Range of Options

As Card describes his "kitchen," he is cagey about his front-burner items. "I'm not gonna show you everything I have in my kitchen," Card says. But when less pressing topics arise, Card offers a window into the size and complexity of his kitchen.

An eager storyteller, Card can take a long time with his explanations and descriptions. He is at times compelled to show you every crumb in his cupboard.

Ask Card, for instance, how he chose the exact words he whispered to President Bush on the morning of Sept. 11, 2001: "A second plane hit the second tower. America is under attack."

"Very carefully," Card says, noting that he wanted to give the president maximum information without giving him a chance to respond, avoiding a public conversation. "I wanted to pass on two facts and one editorial comment and then back away."

The rest of his answer—unloaded from Card's 9/11 cupboard—takes 20 minutes.

Card describes the vivid smell of dead fish at the Sarasota golf resort where the president ate dinner on the night of Sept. 10. Walking back to the hotel, Card saw a car parked in a way that blocked a narrow alley. He asked an advance man to remove it.

The next morning, Card became concerned that there was a misspelled word on the blackboard behind the spot where the president would read. The word—Card doesn't say what it was—"was adroitly covered by a book cover," he says, adding that it was written in red, orange and blue chalk.

Bush learned that the first plane had hit the North Tower as he stood at the door of the classroom, just before he was to begin reading. "We're standing at the door, I'm standing to the president's left," Card says. "The president was holding a doorknob in his right hand."

Card first learned the discipline of Matteo Ricci as a high school junior. He was attending a talk given by "some kind of memory expert" at a Rotary Club near his home in Holbrook, Mass., a middle-class suburb south of Boston. The man quizzed the 50 or 60 people in the audience about personal details—their names, where they lived and so forth. Then, without notes, he repeated all the information back to them.

Card approached the speaker afterward and asked if he had a photographic memory. "No, no, no," the man said. "I work really hard at this." He explained the Riccian principle of linking facts to visual mnemonics. "He said, take something that you know really well and then associate something with it," Card says. "And I began doing that over the course of time."

Card studied engineering at the University of South Carolina while working at a McDonald's in Columbia (rising as high as night manager). As he manned counters, Card tried to calculate the total price of an order before the clerk could punch it into the cash register. "It really turned into great sport," Card says.

Another McDonald's episode bears mention: Once, when money went missing from the cash register, Card threatened to fire everyone unless it was returned. The cash reappeared and the crew kept their jobs. But Card was serious about his threat, and the episode reflects the resolve behind Card's soft edges, a combination that has served him in politics.

Card's father, a small-town lawyer and unsuccessful candidate for the state legislature, was active in Holbrook politics. Card was elected to the

Massachusetts legislature in 1974, a Republican moderate who favored abortion and gay rights. "He was always very supportive of the things that the Bush administration has been hostile to, like gay rights," says Rep. Barney Frank (D-Mass.), who served with Card in the legislature.

Card sought the GOP nomination for governor in 1982 but finished third. An early supporter of George H. W. Bush's campaign for president in 1980, Card ran Massachusetts for Bush, who narrowly won the state's Republican primary over John Anderson. "From then on, it became personal for Andy and the Bushes," says Phil Johnston, a former Democratic state House member who worked with Card on a landmark anti-corruption bill.

Through his link to Bush, Card joined the intergovernmental affairs office of the Reagan White House in 1983. He remained close to Vice President Bush, eventually taking a senior position on his presidential campaign in 1987. He worked closely with Bush's sharp-edged political guru, Lee Atwater.

"Lee always thought Andy was his guy," says Ed Rogers, a Republican lobbyist and close Atwater associate. "But everyone thinks that Andy is their guy. That's the beauty of him. He has assumed the role of chief therapist in the Bush camp." Rogers also dubs Card "a human Alka-Seltzer" who offsets the acid of clashing egos, ideologies and agendas in a political enterprise.

He was deputy chief of staff in the Bush administration under John Sununu and gained a reputation for his forthright and pleasant manner, especially when performing unpleasant tasks. "We always said that if we ever got fired, we wanted Andy to do it," said Bush press secretary Marlin Fitzwater. (This reputation endures: "I figure when Andy fires me, I'll probably be slapping him on the back laughing on the way out the door," says Dan Bartlett, the current White House communications director.)

Card's signature firing occurred in 1990 when he had to tell his own boss, Sununu, that it was time to leave. There is a vivid scene in Fitzwater's memoir, "Call the Briefing," in which Card, White House counsel Boyden Gray and Bush family friend Dorrance Smith nervously enter Sununu's office after the president concluded that it was time for him to go. Smith and Gray hold back, leaving Card to deliver the news. "This kind of thing always winds up falling to Andy," Fitzwater says.

"Hearing bad news from Andy is like hearing bad news from Dudley Do-Right," says Rogers. "You can't shoot the messenger with Andy. And this is a town where the messenger gets shot all the time."

After being appointed Bush One's secretary of transportation, Card was given the dirty work of running the president's outgoing transition team. He spent the rest of the '90s lobbying, first for the American Automobile Manufacturers Association, then General Motors.

Card first met George W. Bush in 1979 during his father's first presidential campaign. ("May. Kennebunkport. We were on Ocean Avenue.") When Card was deputy chief of staff, Bush Two would sometimes walk into his office, collapse on the couch and gather intelligence about his father's administration. "I wouldn't call us friends," Card says of that time.

Card was not involved in George W. Bush's primary campaign, not unusual given that few people who worked at a high level for the former president also worked for his son. "There was an aggressive effort to avoid it," says Bush's longtime media adviser, Mark McKinnon. But in the spring of 2000, Bush's team was dissatisfied with the planning for the summer's GOP convention in Philadelphia and needed someone to take over. "It was a difficult situation in that there was an existing structure in place," says Bush political adviser Karl Rove.

The elder Bush suggested to his son that Card's convention performance could be an audition, according to a source familiar with the discussion. If it worked out, and if Bush won the election, Card would be a natural for White House chief of staff. The younger Bush referred to the job as "The Big One."

The Crisper

The story of how Card went from running the 2000 GOP convention to "The Big One" is, frankly, long. At least it is in Card's retelling, which takes 25 minutes.

"This is one of those cupboards you don't open until somebody says, 'Hey, where are those string beans?' " Card says.

Herein, the string beans:

Card tells of discussions he had "that were not very directioned" with Rove, future commerce secretary Don Evans and Bush.

And how, just before he began working on the campaign, Card took his wife to Bermuda after she graduated from divinity school.

And a conversation Card had with Bush on the night of his acceptance speech in Philadelphia, in which Bush told him to "keep your dance card clear."

And the conversation Bush had with Card in Boston on the night of Bush's first debate with Gore ("when Gore had a little too much orange makeup on"). They were on a boat ferrying them from Logan Airport across Boston Harbor (not as polluted as before, "thanks to the good leadership of the former President Bush").

And how, over breakfast, an annoyed Kathleene Card asked her husband, "Are you married to me or George W. Bush?"

And then the phone rang and it was George W. Bush, who told Card to call his gubernatorial chief of staff, Clay Johnson.

And so Card flew to Austin and met with Johnson, who had a bunch of notebooks marked "transition" on his desk, and Card figured they wanted him to run the transition, which Card calls "a pain-in-the-neck job," but one he'd be willing to do.

And then, on his way out of Texas, Card visited the elder Bush in Houston, where he began to believe they were considering him for "The Big One." Card arrived in Houston at 9, and the Bushes were out when he arrived. Barbara Bush arrived home at 11, the former president at midnight. "I woke up early the next day. I made the bed. I showered. I shaved. I got all dressed."

And then Card flew to Tampa to meet the younger Bush, who was holding a rally in Jacksonville. But Card's flight was delayed and he missed Bush before the candidate went to sleep. ("Karen Hughes was there, her son Robert. Got a bite to eat late at night in the hotel.")

Next morning he met with Bush, who mentioned "The Big One," and the rest, as they say, is in another cupboard.

"Sorry I talked so much," Card says.

Counter Strategy

Shortly after Bush took office, Mack McLarty, Bill Clinton's chief of staff, and Ken Duberstein, who held the same post under Reagan, co-hosted a dinner for Card at McLarty's Kalorama home. Several former White House chiefs of staff attended—or, as McLarty puts it, "those of us who have held the office of chief javelin catcher in the White House." Guests included McLarty's neighbor Donald Rumsfeld (chief of staff under Gerald Ford), Donald Regan (Reagan) and Samuel Skinner (Bush One).

In a toast at the dinner, McLarty told of how Reagan chief of staff Howard Baker called him when Clinton took office to say, "Congratulations, you just got the worst job in Washington."

It's a job that Card is neatly suited to do. "He has that intangible ability to anticipate the rhythm of the presidency," says Duberstein. Card is "a comfortable shoe," Duberstein says, someone the president has become accustomed to.

Bush will tease Card in meetings for his long-windedness and tendency to veer off on tangents. People who have watched them together say the president will sometimes order Card around in a tone that suggests he's talking to a servant. In "The Price of Loyalty," former Treasury secretary Paul O'Neill describes a scene in which Bush impatiently demands that Card get him a cheeseburger.

One former Bush administration official compares Card to a little-brother figure to the president, even though Bush is only 10 months older: Bush regards him as a member of the family and would never doubt his loyalty. "But the president can walk on Andy a little bit," says the former official, who asked not to be identified because he doesn't want the White House to be angry with him. "The president talks to him like he's hired help more than he would someone like Cheney or Rumsfeld."

Card loves reminding people that he *is* hired help—that the "of staff" in his title is more important than the "chief," as if he were manning a drive-through window back at McDonald's.

"The president has every right to be selfish with my time," Card says. "That means there are sacrifices I need to make for the president to have what he needs. And those sacrifices usually impact my wife or my kids or my grandkids, or my siblings or my friends. And that is a burden I carry."

The burden wears heavily on chiefs of staff. It is "the ultimate burnout job," Duberstein says. In her memoir "Ten Minutes From Normal," Bush confidante Karen Hughes describes Card telling a prospective White House hire what he expects of his staff. "You don't get home until late at night, you work every weekend," Card said, according to Hughes. He said he didn't have a single day off in several years during the first Bush administration.

Card likes to point out that the average tenure of a White House job is 18 months. And that the chief of staff's job in particular is not suited for the long haul. Yet a few days after his re-election, Bush showed up at Card's morning senior staff meeting to announce that Card would stay on.

"He's under severe stress and I worry about him," says Card's friend Natsios. "I'll call him at his office, at 6 [a.m.], when I know he's there, just to see how he's doing."

Card's name is periodically raised for Cabinet posts—most recently, he was rumored to be the successor to John Snow as Treasury secretary. Card says he places such items "right on top of the garbage disposal." He shakes his head, asks, "What are you gonna do?" He rubs his eyes and says that it's been another long week.

He was in the office at 5:10 this morning. And he was out at a function at the Kennedy Center two nights earlier. He went to bed at 11:35, "then got a call at 3:50 a.m. from the Situation Room."

Don't bother asking: The rest of that cupboard is closed.

Lessons Learned

BY MARK LEIBOVICH

The profile of former White House Chief of Staff Andrew Card testifies to the notion that sometimes all you need is a decent break.

Shortly after President Bush's re-election, I was assigned to write a profile of Card for *The Washington Post* Style section. I emphasize, "assigned." It was my editor's idea.

I wasn't terribly compelled by it, or by Card. He'd always struck me as a competent functionary. He was prized for his loyalty, stamina and organizational skills—all noble and valuable traits. But it was certainly not the stuff of a meaty profile subject.

At best, I figured the story would be a passable "Man in the News" profile. Maybe it would be something that focused on Card's longevity in the Bush administration. (He was the longest-tenured White House Chief of Staff since the 1950s.)

But then came the aforementioned break.

I was wrapping up my interviews with Card's friends, colleagues and adversaries before meeting with the chief of staff himself in his office. It's best to interview the subject later in the reporting process, if possible, the better to accumulate knowledge and formulate smarter questions.

My research to that point had revealed about what I expected it to: Card is a workaholic of solid character and integrity who is generally well liked. Again, this was a serviceable if unspectacular notion to build a profile around.

But then a gem fell in my lap in the last minutes of the last interview, before I was scheduled to meet Card. The interview was with someone who has known Card a long time. The individual, at the end of our discussion, informed me that Card was a student of memory: specifically that he was a disciple of a 16th-century Italian Jesuit named Matteo Ricci.

Huh?

I had no idea what this meant. I'd never heard of Matteo Ricci. I needed to learn more. Paging Mr. Google. Ricci, it turns out, had devised an elaborate mnemonic system by which he remembered things. He taught this discipline to Confucian scholars during a mission to China, inventing something called a "memory palace."

Ricci's "memory palace" was an imaginary structure through which he would organize and retain data in his head. For instance, he might visualize a list of his students against the backdrop of an imaginary chair in his imaginary palace.

The result was something akin to a self-taught photographic memory. This was fascinating to me, particularly in the case of Card—a man who'd hitherto struck me as singularly non-eccentric. I made a mental note to ask Card about Matteo Ricci in my interview with him. Early on.

He appeared surprised that I asked. It was not that his devotion to Ricci was any great secret. But few people knew about it, let alone asked him about it, in White House interviews.

But Card was hardly embarrassed. On the contrary, he delighted in describing his own Riccian method—the mental "kitchen" by which he organized the Bush White House in his head and recalled its most vital (and pedestrian) workings.

The concept of "Andy Card's kitchen" framed the whole interview, and ultimately, my story. It turned out to be a lot more interesting than had it been centered on Card's loyalty, or diligence, or (yawn) sheepishness.

One other thing: I recall feeling that I didn't need that last interview, the one with Card's old friend; I believed that I was well-enough informed about Card to start writing (which I was eager to do). I thought about blowing off that last conversation altogether, in fact.

But I forced myself to pick up the phone. Or maybe I'd already placed the call, and the guy called me back. Either way, the maxim holds: When in doubt, have that last conversation. You never know what lucky break it might yield.

Mark Leibovich began writing about national politics for The Washington Post *Style section in February 2002. Before that, Mark spent five years writing about the information technology industries for the* Post's *financial section. He previously wrote for* The San Jose Mercury News *in San Jose, Calif., and, prior to that,* The Phoenix *in Boston. In May 2006, Mark moved to the Washington bureau of* The New York Times, *where he covers national politics.*

Narrative Strategies

BY THOMAS FRENCH

The stories honored in this year's non-deadline category could not be more different. They take the reader from the corridors of power in Washington, D.C., to the cramped dressing room of a teenager fighting for her big break on Broadway, to a hushed funeral home in Reno where a pregnant woman says goodbye to her husband, a fallen Marine. Yet all of these pieces, taken together, reinforce an age-old maxim of storytelling:

Action reveals character.

In the hands of the three reporters whose work is showcased here, the concept of "action" is defined more broadly than what most of us learn in the city room. Action is not just the moment when an important decision achieves critical mass in the Senate or the White House, and then is announced at a press conference. It's more than the instant when the teenager finally steps onstage and fulfills her dream, or when a bomb explodes in the Iraqi desert. In these pieces, action can be smaller, quieter. It's the accumulation of *sotto voce* conversations and personal dynamics that lead to the political victory. It's when the girl, on her own for the first time, learns to hail a cab or figures out how to make her own grilled cheese sandwich. It's the awful silences that take hold once the news of the explosion in Iraq, and its human toll, is delivered to loved ones back home in the United States.

In a series of stunning profiles published in *The Washington Post,* Mark Leibovich takes us deep inside the lives of several of our nation's leaders. In one piece, he lets the reader see Harry Reid, the Senate minority leader, proudly brandishing a scar on his right hand, a reminder of a classroom fight in eighth grade. In another, he shows Rick Santorum, the Republican senator from Pennsylvania, slouching with exhaustion after a public appearance at Bucknell University. In yet another piece—included in this collection—he tells us how Andrew Card, then the White House chief of staff, dislikes taking notes, preferring instead to keep track of the president's agenda and his own schedule through an elaborate memory technique pioneered four centuries ago by a Jesuit missionary. As Leibovich describes it:

> Memory is central to a chief of staff's job. He must possess enough instant knowledge to execute the president's minute-to-minute pursuits, be it macro (his agenda) or micro (when he's due for a haircut).

Brad Blakeman, a former White House scheduler, says it's not uncommon to have someone ask where the president will be on a certain date three months in the future and have Card answer precisely. "He knew the president's schedule a lot better than me," Blakeman says, "and I was the scheduler."

Lane DeGregory, a friend and colleague of mine at the *St. Petersburg Times,* chronicles the life of Michelle Dowdy, a girl who graduates from a theater program at a Florida high school and then, on the day of her commencement, finds herself cast as the understudy for the lead in the Broadway production of *Hairspray.* DeGregory is reporting on someone with no title or power or money—all her subject has going for her is talent and drive and a mom who pays attention—and yet she approaches Michelle with both respect and honesty. DeGregory shows Michelle struggling toward independence, moving directly from her adolescence into an almost dream-like approximation of adulthood. The writer, meanwhile, does not shy away from describing her subject's weight:

> At 5 feet 2 and 172 pounds, Michelle seems comfortable in her body—something few teenage girls can say. She wears tight jeans or long, gauzy skirts with low-cut blouses and doesn't try to hide her curves. She jokes about herself so others don't have to: "Fat girl's gotta eat!" she'll say, chomping into an inch-thick cheeseburger.

In DeGregory's six-part serial narrative, the bite into the cheeseburger—and Michelle's unapologetic description of herself as a "fat girl"—is a crucial moment, a tiny snippet of essential action. As it turns out, the part that Michelle is pursuing specifically calls for a heavy girl, someone who is confident enough to challenge our culture's relentless push for women to adhere to a monolithic physical standard. The fact that Michelle is at ease with herself, in other words, is central to understanding how she winds up performing on Broadway.

Character, action and theme are braided together with almost unbearable power in "Final Salute," the remarkable story from a collection of pieces that won this year's non-deadline award. Jim Sheeler, a reporter with the *Rocky Mountain News,* follows several Marines stationed in the United States who are assigned the terrible duty of informing families when a loved one has been killed in Iraq. In the unforgettable opening scene, set at night at the Reno airport, the body of Lt. James J. Cathey has been brought home in the cargo hold of an American Airlines jetliner. His widow, Katherine Cathey, waits in a limousine on the tarmac. Pregnant, she can feel her unborn baby—a son her husband will never know—kicking inside her.

> "He's moving," she said. "Come feel him. He's moving."
> Her two best friends leaned forward on the soft leather seats and put their hands on her stomach.
> "I felt it," one of them said. "I felt it."
> Outside, the whine of jet engines swelled.
> "Oh, sweetie," her friend said. "I think this is his plane."

* * *

> Katherine turns and closes her eyes.
> "I don't want it to be dark right now. I wish it was daytime," she said. "I wish it was daytime for the rest of my life. The night is just too hard."
> Suddenly, the car door opened. A white-gloved hand reached into the limousine from outside ... The man in the deep blue uniform knelt down to meet her eyes, speaking in a soft, steady voice.
> "Katherine," said Maj. Steve Beck, "it's time."

In the hands of another writer, this scene—and all that follows—could have easily lapsed into melodrama or sentimentality. Sheeler avoids those traps. His story is built on careful, meticulous reporting, and on restrained, understated writing. The effect is all the more devastating.

The spine of Sheeler's story is built around the Cathey family and how they get through the first days of their grief with the assistance of Maj. Beck, an officer with almost superhuman reserves of empathy and strength.

Steve Beck is the kind of subject most of us long for, and Sheeler writes about him with carefully modulated power and grace. He shows us how Beck's childhood prepared him for the duties he would later shoulder. His mother was diabetic; as a toddler, he learned to hold a syringe so he could inject her with insulin. At 13, he saw his younger brother fatally struck by a car. Steve had recently taught the brother to play catch; when it was time for the funeral, Steve stood at the open casket and placed the younger child's baseball glove inside.

In painstaking detail, Sheeler shows us how Beck's firsthand experience with grief now informs the careful attention he gives the families of the Marine casualties. At one point, as Lt. Cathey's body arrives at the funeral home, we hear Beck tutoring other Marines on how to conduct themselves.

In the room, he walked up to the casket and paused.

"Now, this is important, too," he said. "If a family member wants you to break, you can break. They may want to hug you or kiss you. That's OK. Hug them. If someone wants to shake your hand, shake their hand. I'll take my glove off when I shake their hand—you don't have to, it's up to you. But then go back to position."

Near the end of the story, Sheeler allows us to witness the moment when Beck accompanies Katherine Cathey to her husband's casket so she can touch his shrouded body one more time.

Beck placed a hand on her back.
"Tell me when you're ready," he said. "Take your time."
He stepped back.
The air conditioner clicked on, filling the room with a low hum.
Ten minutes passed. It clicked off, leaving the room to her soft moans.

Finally Katherine is ready for the casket to be opened. Beck takes her hand and guides it to her husband's uniform. He helps her gather personal objects to be placed inside. Katherine puts in some photos, a bottle of her perfume, dried flowers from her wedding bouquet. Finally she covers her husband's heart with an ultrasound image of the couple's unborn son.

Sheeler describes all of the above with respect, patience and a depth of understanding that seems to mirror Maj. Beck's sensitivity. The writer and the subject are perfectly matched, and the story that flows forth is both beautiful and searing. It's one of the most memorable portraits in the history of journalism.

PART 3

Diversity Writing

Phuong Ly
Diversity Writing

The Washington Post

Phuong Ly remembers her family's escape from Vietnam—but only in fragments. She recalls people crowded on a small fishing boat, throwing up in plastic bags. She can see the barbed wire around the refugee camp where she stayed for six months. And then there was the chewing gum she tasted when her family arrived in America. She didn't realize she wasn't supposed to swallow it. The year was 1978, and Ly was only four.

Those early memories and everything that came afterward—settling in a small town in North Carolina, serving as her parents' interpreter, discovering the power of the written word—contributed to her approach to journalism.

As a reporter with *The Washington Post*, Ly, 31, brings depth and subtlety to her stories about immigrants' lives. Her goal, she says, is to write stories that are not simply about "the other," but that reveal immigrants as real people, with quirks and flaws, as well as "deep human experiences, emotions and relationships." She is interested in "the gray areas of life, the nuances, and capturing people's decisions and the results of those decisions, how their past influences the present and the future."

Most of all, her roots drive her toward excellence.

"These experiences really pushed me to succeed, to do as much as possible, whether it's to be a journalist or anything else," she says. "So much depends on faith and fate. My mother nearly left me behind at the last minute, in the care of one of my aunts, who was a Buddhist nun. She feared all of us drowning in the ocean."

Ly's family settled in Salisbury, N.C., where she got into journalism by accident. She chose journalism as an elective class in high school. "We got to talk to the principal without having to get in trouble first," she recalls. "And we joked about how to crop photos of the homecoming court. My classmates and I were a bunch of nerds ignored by the popular kids, but when our newspaper was published every few months, everybody read it!"

Then she connected with her hometown newspaper, compiling a school activities list for the teen page of the *Salisbury Post*. Reporters at the paper encouraged her to write and assigned her some stories. By the time she graduated from high school, the reporters and her guidance counselor helped her apply for journalism scholarships. The Knight Ridder Minority Scholars program offered her a $20,000 scholarship and a newspaper internship every year she was in school.

"I doubt I would have become a journalist without the *Salisbury Post* and Knight Ridder," she says. "They showed me a life that I did not know existed."

At the University of North Carolina at Chapel Hill, she studied journalism and history. Her parents would have preferred that she pursue a career that they understood, such as medicine or pharmacy. But they soon understood her calling.

"I think journalism became a home, sort of a safe haven," she says. "I had been shy, but I noticed myself changing gradually. I could go up and talk to people because I had an excuse—I was a reporter... So I think it was a feeling, more than a story, that made me think I was in the right field. I felt I was learning and growing."

She worked at *The Charlotte Observer*, covering police, public housing and general assignments. She worked at *The Washington Post* from 1999 to 2006, covering immigrant communities for the Metro desk. Ly now works as a freelance magazine writer, consultant and journalism lecturer.

"My personal background is one of contrasts, as a Vietnamese and an American, as a Southerner and as a resident inside the Beltway," she says. " ... I think all of that has helped me see issues and stories from different angles and be curious about all sorts of subjects. I appreciate absurdity and contradictions and look for them.

"Initially in my career, I wasn't really interested in writing about immigrants," she says. "But frankly, what got me going was seeing so many inaccurate and stereotypical stories about immigrants in the media."

Recently, she studied religion in Nigeria as a 2006 International Reporting Project fellow at the Johns Hopkins University School of Advanced International Studies. But even as she travels far and wide to educate herself about the world's cultures, she doesn't forget where she came from.

—Thomas Huang

The award for Distinguished Writing on Diversity is funded by the Freedom Forum, which has partnered with ASNE on many diversity efforts.

15. A Wrenching Choice

JAN. 9, 2005

By Phuong Ly

The flag of South Korea hung high above Hannah Kim's head as she sat in her Howard County classroom, listening to the day's lesson on immigration.

Her social studies teacher described how 14 million people have immigrated to this country since 1990, the year before many of these seventh-graders were born.

"Fourteen million," repeated Cliff Bernstein, looking around. "Why do people want to come to the United States so badly?"

Jobs and homes and democracy, one girl offered hesitantly. A couple of students doodled in their notebooks; others stared into space.

Hannah's hand shot up. "They want to learn English and get a better education," she said.

Education has brought Hannah to this classroom and to a white frame townhouse in Ellicott City. But the price of her American education—and her escape from the relentlessly competitive Korean school system—is a fractured family. Hannah's mother, Jungwon Kim, and two younger siblings are here with her. Her father, Keeyeop Kim, an executive in South Korea, stayed behind to finance his family's life abroad.

They have lived this way—children without a father, wife without a husband—for a year. Their plan is to live this way for nine more years.

The Koreans call them *kirogi*, or wild geese. The birds, a traditional symbol at weddings, mate for life. And they travel great distances to bring back food for their young.

Korean officials can't say how many families are kirogi, but they know how many children are leaving the country: 10,000 school-age children left to study overseas in 2002, up from 4,400 in 2000.

Hannah's mother knows at least two other families like hers in their tree-lined subdivision. Several more attend her church. Their numbers swell the ranks of Korean children in Howard County schools: Each year, nearly 400 Korean-speaking students are enrolled in English for Speakers of Other Languages classes, making them the largest ethnic group in the program.

The families also are turning up in other suburbs with well-regarded public schools. The Korean Embassy Web site links to the home pages of the Fairfax and Montgomery counties' school districts.

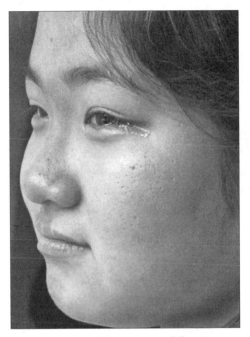

Hannah Kim, 13, wistfully watches her father drive away after a visit. (Photograph courtesy of Hyosub Shin for *The Washington Post*)

In South Korea, a First World country of broadband Internet and skyscraper shopping malls, society still runs on an education system that dates to the age of kings. Jobs, social status, even marriage prospects often are determined by how well someone performs on national school exams. There is little room for creativity or enterprise.

To live successfully in the family's homeland, Hannah, 13, would have to give up her drums and piano unless she expected to make music a career, the Kims said. Eugene, 11, would have to put away his inline skates to attend after-school tutoring sessions. Even Terry, 4, would be doing something practical, such as studying the IQ tests that the bookstores sell packaged in bright cartoon covers.

"I see the big picture in the U.S.," Jungwon Kim, 38, said. "They can go to a nice college and have time to have a good time with their friends."

The Kims are part of a middle-class subset of U.S. immigrants who arrive here not out of financial need but out of a desire to give their children other advantages. For the suburban school districts, the influx of Korean students requires additional resources to teach them English. But many move quickly into regular classes and help raise the school's performance.

Korean society always has placed a premium on an American education, with the English skills and global experience it brings. Keeyeop Kim, Hannah's father, remade his future at age 20 when he went to the University of Nevada at Las Vegas, after failing to score high enough on a foreign service exam and being shut out of South Korea's marquee universities.

With the slots at those universities becoming more precious, many students are leaving well before college. Agencies in Seoul offer to help settle mothers and children in English-speaking countries, and Web sites provide tips on real estate, banking and handling stress. Typically, the mothers enroll in community colleges and apply for student visas, which allow them and their children to immigrate easily.

For the Kims, the details of immigrating were simple: Jungwon Kim, who lived in this country with her parents as a teenager, is a U.S. citizen. So are the three children.

But the details of dividing the family have been far more complex. Eugene struggles with English. Hannah feels guilty about her parents' separation. Jungwon Kim finds herself questioning the choices they made. And Keeyeop Kim senses an odd distance from his children: With just three visits in the past year, his chief connection is a nightly phone call.

When the phone rings in Ellicott City and the caller ID flashes "Out of Area," they become a family again.

"Appa," Eugene will say, grabbing the phone. Daddy.

Best Year Ever

When Hannah thinks about school in Korea, she remembers the afternoon her classmate approached her in tears.

The scores for the year-end exams in their school were announced days earlier, and Hannah had finished first in the class. A perfect 100. Her friend received the second-best score. His parents grounded him. Now he was terrified of the next round of testing.

This was fourth grade.

"I didn't want to live in a place where you get so much pressure," Hannah said, recalling that day.

By Korean standards, the Kims' home town of Taebaek is considered slow-paced. A town of 50,000 tucked in the mountains, it is four hours southeast of Seoul.

Still, Hannah soon would be facing the maxim of "four in, five out," a Korean proverb that means those who settle for four hours of sleep a night will get into the most prestigious universities and those who sleep five hours will not.

Her classmates already were filing out of school every afternoon onto buses taking them to "cram schools" for hours of tutoring. Her parents did not want that type of future for their children.

So in August 2002, before the start of sixth grade, Hannah was sent to live with her grandparents in Howard County. The next summer, her mother and siblings followed, and the Kims bought a townhouse, a Toyota minivan and new furniture.

Here, Hannah's afternoons are filled with band practice, private drum lessons and church youth group. Academically, she has thrived, cycling quickly out of ESOL classes and making the honor roll at Patapsco Middle School.

In many ways, she is a typical teenage girl—she hates wearing her glasses, frets over her baby-fat cheeks and cuts out photos of Korean pop stars and Orlando Bloom. But she exudes a self-confidence uncommon for her age; along with the hearts doodled across her notebooks are her mantras: "I won't be marked as average" and "I will be remembered."

"Patapsco is so much fun. This is the best year of my life. Ever," Hannah declared one evening.

She and her mother—matching images in their jeans, untucked T-shirts and auburn-tinted hair—were lingering over their dinner of Korean barbecue beef.

"What about next year?" Jungwon Kim asked.

"Mom, are you going to kill me if my grades are underwater? You know, 'under C.' Get it?"

Her mother shot her a look of mock threat: "I'll have to think about going back to Korea."

"Then I'll get all F's," Hannah retorted. "I've forgotten most of my Korean."

Kim touched her daughter's hand lightly. "No, I don't care if you don't get straight A's. But I know you probably will. You work hard. You're special and you're smart," she said, and then smirked. "Because your mom's smart."

"I'll say my dad's smart, but you, I don't know," Hannah replied.

Her mother doesn't look offended. She began reminiscing about her husband, whom she met in college.

Hannah said nothing. That night, she was scouring the living room for her drumsticks when she stopped suddenly. The sticks were lying on the end table. So were the framed family snapshots, two pictures taken at Tokyo Disneyland, the family's last big vacation before Hannah left.

"I kind of feel sorry, mostly for my mom," Hannah said, looking at the photo of herself, Eugene and their father sitting on a park bench. "She can't have a husband because of us. If we weren't here, why would she leave her husband?"

She picked up her drumsticks and pounded the couch.

'Don't Need a Husband'

The light in the freezer refused to blink on. Jungwon Kim could still see the ice pops that the children wanted that summer evening, but the burned-out bulb bothered her. She screwed in a 60-watt and watched the freezer light up. "See," she said smiling. "I'm good at these things. Don't need a husband."

She has trouble believing it. In the mornings, she cannot attend the sunrise service at her church—a ritual she observed faithfully in Korea—because she doesn't want to leave the children alone in the house. The maintenance of the minivan, which she calls a "man's job," is her responsibility. When three of her sisters and their husbands took a vacation to Europe this summer, she didn't join them. "Couples only," she said.

She misses the companionship of the man she calls her lifetime friend. "When I get moody, I think about my husband and think, why am I doing this alone?" she said. "I'm sure God has a special purpose for my family. I don't know what it is."

The decision to split the family did not come easily, Kim recalled. She and her husband considered coming here together, as her parents did years ago. But her father had retired from his job as a police officer when he moved. Keeyeop Kim is at the height of his career, director of slot machine operations at South Korea's largest casino.

They talked about opening a business, as many Korean families do. But Jungwon Kim said the pressures of running a seven-day-a-week grocery or dry cleaners would mean the children might be, in a sense, losing both parents.

Ultimately, Keeyeop Kim decided the family should go on without him. Jungwon Kim said she hesitated but finally resolved that she could not ask him to give up his career and the status of his executive position. She experienced something like that herself when they moved back to Korea years ago and she was expected to stay home with the children, despite having a college degree.

She said she now believes her role as a full-time mother is a blessing. But she recognizes that the burden of cultural expectation falls squarely on Korean men. "Being Korean, in that way, I know I can't push my husband too much."

Her pastor in Columbia said he understands the dilemma.

"Biblically, the husband and wife should stay together, rain or shine. But this is not a black-and-white matter," said the Rev. Jonathan Song of the Korean American Church of the Philippi. "In Korea, only one in 10 children can bear the education system. What about the remaining nine?"

He said he knows several kirogi families in his congregation. One man missed his wife and children so much that he joined them, coming on a tourist visa and staying illegally. Now he works at a restaurant, busing tables. In Korea, he had an office. He asked his pastor whether he made the right choice.

Song closed his eyes. "It's almost unthinkable for a man of his stature to do this," he said.

In many ways, Kim said, her husband is making a bigger sacrifice than she is. Here, at least she has the children and her extended family. And increasingly, she has a circle of friends, including other kirogi mothers.

The separation is bearable, Kim said, when she thinks about the advantages they are giving their children. Still she worries about the children, especially Terry, who was just 3, and her father's pet, when the family moved here.

Sometimes, she gives the little girl a test.

"Where's Daddy?" she asks her. Terry always answers that he's in Korea—working to buy her things, such as Barbies and Hello Kitty toys.

Kim said she worries that one day, her youngest child will ask why.

Missing Korea

It was time for dinner, but all Eugene could think about was math homework. He loves math, except for word problems. Numbers are a snap; they look the same in Korean. Words don't. Does "minus" mean the same as "subtract"?

Eugene handed his worksheet to his mother. Hannah jumped in: "When are we going to stop helping Eugene with his homework? We've helped him for nine months already."

Eugene glared at her. Try your best in school, Kim told her son in Korean. No more video games.

Eugene stomped downstairs to the playroom and slammed the door. Unlike Hannah, Eugene was not having the best year of his life.

Twice, Kim had been called up to Hollifield Station Elementary School by Eugene's fourth-grade teacher. Eugene had been involved in shoving arguments after he had trouble expressing himself in English. He would stand up in class and walk to the window, staring outside.

Eugene wasn't the perfect student back home, Kim acknowledged, but this year has been unusually tough. Of the three children, Eugene is most like his father, often shy about speaking to people he doesn't know well. And of the three, Eugene seems to feel his father's absence most acutely.

Eugene has told his mother that he would like to go back to Korea. Because that has not happened, he has made his life here as Korean as possible. All his friends are Korean. When it is "Drop Everything and

Terry Kim was 3 and her father's pet when the family moved to Ellicott City, Md. She now calls the Ellicott City townhouse "our house" and told her father the flat in South Korea is "your house." (Photograph courtesy of Hyosub Shin for *The Washington Post*)

Read" time in school, he pulls out a Korean book. He uses less English than Terry, who is in preschool but already knows the "SpongeBob SquarePants" theme song.

His teachers said Eugene is bright and are puzzled by his struggle with English. A Korean-speaking outreach liaison works at the school. In the afternoons, Eugene spends an hour with an ESOL teacher. On Tuesdays, he attends an after-school "homework club" for immigrant children.

One in eight students at Hollifield Station has limited English skills. Still, the school's standardized test scores top the state average. Even the scores for ESOL students are at the state average. Many teachers have noticed the influx of Koreans and are flattered that these families have traveled so far to reach their classrooms.

Eugene comes from a middle-class background and, in that sense, is like most of Hollifield Station's students. He also has a stay-at-home mother who speaks English, an unusual asset for an immigrant child.

Kim, however, knows she is not enough. "Of course Eugene is missing something...," she said. "He doesn't have his father."

Boys often have the hardest time adjusting to the separations, said Sue Song, a mental health consultant in Howard County who has worked with about 20 kirogi mothers and their teenage sons in the past two years. The boys have failed classes, flown into violent rages and experimented with drugs. One family gave up and went back to Korea.

"They make a decision based on an idealistic situation, not so much based on reality," Song said. "When the years go by, a lot of things can happen."

Kim recognizes that and said she wants to shield her children from additional pressure. "I'll never tell Hannah and Eugene, 'You have to make good grades because Mom and Dad are suffering,' " she said. "I'll never say that. They didn't ask us to do it this way."

By the end of the school year, Eugene began to make some progress. He raised his hand in class, especially during math, in which he excels. He shared with some non-Korean classmates the games on his handheld computer. Still, he didn't like to speak much English. "It not fun," he said.

Fourth grade ended with a project on poetry. Eugene managed to fill a blank book with short rhymes, and his teacher, Jennifer Wilkins, praised him for his cover artwork: an aqua-blue house, red flowers and a big tree with a little cicada on the trunk.

Wilkins told the class to give their books one final touch: a dedication. As usual, most of the students started working right away. As usual, Eugene looked around the room.

Wilkins bent down beside Eugene and tried to explain what a dedication is.

Eugene raised his eyebrows: *"Mwoh?"*

It is a Korean word that Wilkins understood because Eugene said it so often. *"Mwoh?"* What?

She called over Justin, a Korean American boy. "It's like who inspired these poems," she said. "If he was going to give this book to someone, who would he give it to?"

Justin translated. Eugene finally understood.

He took a pencil and, in unsure print, wrote: "This book is for my dad because my dad in Korea."

Hedging His Bets

Halfway around the world in Taeback, Dad was walking outside his high-rise apartment building. Dozens of dragonflies were darting around the deserted parking lot.

It was a gray, drizzly Sunday, the only free time in the six-day Korean workweek. Keeyeop Kim spent the morning in church. Except he missed half the service when someone from the casino called his cell phone. He would spend the rest of the day home alone, with file folders of paperwork. He shrugged. He had nothing else to do.

Across the parking lot, a little girl giggled. She was running, her arms propelling her like wings, and she breezed past Kim. Her mother followed, a bright blue net in hand. They were chasing dragonflies.

"A couple of years ago," Kim said quietly, "Eugene caught hundreds of dragonflies."

In the family's three-bedroom flat, all the children's furniture is gone. Eugene's room, with its sailboat wallpaper, has been turned into his father's office. On the computer, the weather is set to Ellicott City. Hannah's room houses an exercise bike and a weight machine. Snapshots of the children hang on the refrigerator.

Out on the balcony sat two blue American Tourister suitcases. Nearby, there was a new purchase: a set of Ping golf clubs. "There was nothing to do after I sent my family to the States," Kim said of playing the sport.

Of course, the golf—like everything else in his life—is intertwined with work. He was recently elected chairman of the employees' golf club, and his casino is building a world-class golf course. Kangwon Land rises, all glittering glass and marble, amid the low-slung buildings of this coal-mining region.

When Kim strides through the resort's chandelier-lighted halls, employees bow. He is a slight man who commands attention in his Italian suit and Cartier watch.

Inside the cavernous casino, Kim outlined his challenges with the precision of a math professor: where to position the machines to draw the most customers; how to increase slots revenue compared with the table games; which coins people are more likely to use in their wager. Kangwon Land's $300 million annual profit puts it in the ranks of such casinos as the Bellagio in Las Vegas, he said.

Not that it would be possible, he said, to become a top executive at the Bellagio or any other U.S. casino. Every Asian person he knows in U.S. casinos has a job on the marketing side, which he said is not in line with his shy, by-the-numbers personality. He worried about his lack of any network in the United States. And he is 39. It is not an age for starting over, he said.

"I want to be at the top," said Kim, who supervises 101 people. He will retire at 49, he has decided, 10 years without his family.

"It's a sacrifice," he acknowledged. "I don't live with the family. That's what parents do for the kids."

It is also a gamble.

A steady stream of stories in Korean newspapers depicts a shadow society of lonely fathers spiraling into depression. Many move from their empty homes into "officetels," or single rooms with maid service. Some are gaining weight on fast food and frozen dinners. Others are succumbing to what one newspaper delicately called "temptations," or sexual affairs. Several have committed suicide.

Han Jun Sang, a professor of education at Yonsei University in Seoul, said the kirogi phenomenon undermines the strong Korean belief that fathers are the head of the household. Without regular contact, the children will rebel against the father's authority, Han said, and his wife will become more independent. The fathers, Han said, "shrink psychologically."

Keeyeop Kim knows something about gambling. The only card game he plays is blackjack. And only for a half-hour at a time. Because if you play too long, he said, you can lose everything.

A Whirlwind Reunion

Jungwon Kim had a deadline and could not believe what the sales clerk at Sears was telling her: All the store's photographers were booked for the week. Kim insisted; she begged. Her husband was here in Ellicott City, for only a week.

She didn't know when he might be back. Finally, the Kims were squeezed into a Friday slot.

Their family life in Howard County, compressed into a visit of eight days, seven nights, was a whirlwind. They saw friends and relatives in Howard; they watched sports on television; they ate out every night.

There was a day trip to Hagerstown to shop for school clothes at the outlet mall and an open house at Hollifield Station to meet Eugene's teachers. For a wedding anniversary that was months away, Kim ordered his wife a Gucci purse and had it shipped express mail so he could give it to her in person.

One evening, Keeyeop Kim measured the children, as he did during his visit last January, and marked their heights on a piece of tape against the refrigerator. Hannah and Terry had grown about an inch; Eugene had shot up more than two inches.

But Keeyeop Kim's work intruded every day. Phone calls from his colleagues in Korea interrupted dinner. What bothered his wife, though, was that some of his time online—and away from the family—wasn't about work. Once, he was simply checking the CNN Web site.

By the final day of his visit, Jungwon Kim expressed some of the frustration she had been feeling for months. "He doesn't need a wife," she scoffed.

Keeyeop Kim was anxious, too. He felt like a visitor, more like an uncle than a father or husband. Terry has called the Ellicott City townhouse "our house" and told her father the apartment back in South Korea is "your house."

Kim, suddenly unsure of his decision to live this way for a full 10 years, began considering other options: retiring earlier or finding another job.

As he waited for a relative to pick him up, the children were scattered about the house. Eugene was in the living room, watching television with a neighborhood friend. Hannah was updating her Web diary to note that her dad was leaving: "sniff* i'll miss him...church was awesome today...the message was really...meaningful...what i just needed." Terry played games on the Barbie Web site.

At 3 p.m., it was time for Daddy to go, and Terry erupted into tears.

But not for her father. Her mother had shut off the computer. Terry wailed for Barbie. Finally, Keeyeop Kim scooped the little girl into his arms and walked to the front door. He gave her a kiss.

He hugged Eugene and Hannah and told them to be good. Listen to your mother, he said in Korean. Study hard.

He patted his wife on the cheek. Her eyes were red; so were his.

Hannah leaned against the door, weeping. Eugene immersed himself in his Game Boy. Terry forgot about Barbie and began crying for her father.

Outside, a car door slammed.

Two weeks later, Jungwon Kim picked up the family portrait. The large, silver-framed picture of her husband—hand on her shoulder, surrounded by their three beaming children—hangs in the living room.

In Korea, Keeyeop Kim has a smaller copy, tucked in his wallet.

Staff writer Phuong Ly reported this story in Ellicott City and Taebaek, South Korea.

16. 30 Years Later, Immigrants Shed Vietnam War's Burdens

APRIL 24, 2005

By Phuong Ly

On humid Washington days, after thunderstorms churn up the smell of fresh earth, Sandy Hoa Dang remembers the war. When the bombs fell on Hanoi, she was a little girl, cowering with her family in a hole in the ground.

Hundreds of miles away, as victorious North Vietnamese soldiers stormed a beach town near Saigon, 5-year-old Phuong Nguyen's mother stashed her in a concrete cistern. Her fair, freckled face and uplifted nose were evidence: Her father was an American.

Kara Mai Delahunt, an infant then, was buckled into a seat of a 747 on one of the rushed flights that brought more than 2,000 orphans to the United States. Her new parents discovered that their child reacted strangely in their arms. She stiffened. She was not used to being held.

Thirty years have passed since Saigon fell on April 30, 1975, time enough for these three women and a generation of Vietnamese Americans to come of age. Thirty is now the median age of the 1.2 million people of Vietnamese heritage living in the United States. Thirty is young enough to be haunted by Vietnam, old enough to have created new lives.

The war brought the three women to the United States under starkly different circumstances: one as a baby adopted into a Massachusetts home; another as a teenager escaping with her family on a fishing boat; the third as a mother granted a chance to immigrate because of her American blood.

They are connected by the past they left and the lives they lead here: Dang is the founder of a social services organization in Washington for immigrant families, Nguyen is a client there and Delahunt is a volunteer mentor for Nguyen's teenage son.

Yet in their own way, they are defying the war's hold on their identity.

A Sought-Out Heritage

"Lovely with rosy and chubby cheeks," was how the adoption papers described Nguyen Mai Tai Trang, abandoned by her mother two days after her birth in a Saigon hospital.

She is now Kara Mai Delahunt, and the description is still apt. Even after a long day of work at a downtown Washington public relations company, she is poised and polished—hair in a neat bun, makeup fresh and clothes professional. She has recently returned from a seven-month business trip to Madrid. Tucked in her black purse is a travel book on Peru, her next destination.

She sometimes wonders, though, what price was paid for this life.

"My mom would always say, 'Say a prayer for your birth mother,' " said Delahunt, 30. "I was always told that she loved me so much and cared for me so much that she was willing to give me up."

Delahunt arrived as part of Operation Babylift, conducted in the frantic weeks before North Vietnamese tanks rolled into Saigon. The U.S. government commissioned jetliners to ferry hundreds of orphans to new homes here. Some Vietnamese parents, learning of the flights, left children at hospitals and orphanages. Advocates called it a humanitarian effort, and critics decried it as ripping children from their homeland.

Delahunt was adopted by Kati and William D. Delahunt, now a Democratic congressman from Massachusetts. The couple tried to make their new daughter comfortable with her heritage, taking her to Lunar New Year events, buying her Asian dolls, introducing her to another adopted Vietnamese girl, hopeful that the two would become friends.

She resisted. "The Vietnam War to me is exactly that—it's history," she said. "I just wanted to be American."

She learned German—her adoptive mother's native language—and took summer trips to Germany. Her master's degree is in Spanish from Middlebury College in Vermont, her father's alma mater. After school, she moved to Washington and landed a public relations job specializing in Latin American issues.

Only then did she begin thinking about Vietnam.

"As you get older," she explained, "your history becomes more important."

Five years ago, Delahunt accepted an invitation to travel to Vietnam with a group of adoptees and officials from Holt International Children's Services, an Oregon adoption agency that placed many of the children from Operation Babylift.

This trip was dubbed a homecoming. It didn't feel that way.

After mastering two foreign languages, Delahunt thought she could learn a few Vietnamese phrases, but the unfamiliar tones overwhelmed her.

Everywhere, she saw young children. Some sold chewing gum; others held out empty plastic bowls.

Delahunt had seen poverty on trips to India and Chile, but this was different. "That could have been me," she said, shaking her head. "I could be in Vietnam on the streets right now."

What Delahunt found on her trip, she said, was a comfort with other Vietnamese Americans. After the trip, she attended a conference with other adoptees, and some became her close friends.

"For the first time in my life," she said, "I was with people who were like me."

A friend introduced her to Asian American LEAD, a nonprofit group in the District's Columbia Heights neighborhood serving disadvantaged immigrant families. Delahunt became a mentor, and eventually, a member of its board of directors.

Almost every week, she meets with 15-year-old Man Pham, who immigrated with his family in 1997. He gives her advice on computers, and she helps him with his Spanish homework.

During the visits, Delahunt sometimes sees his parents, Minh Pham and Phuong Nguyen. Their exchanges are short and awkward because of the language barrier.

She is more comfortable with Man, who like her, thinks of Vietnam as only a part of himself. Once, when Man asked, Delahunt told him that she left as a baby and was adopted. His response: "Cool."

Different but Determined

In this city, Phuong Nguyen is nearly invisible.

At a hotel in downtown Washington, she cleans empty rooms. Customers at the U Street nail salon where she works part-time barely acknowledge her, except to pick their polish. In the international melange of her Columbia Heights neighborhood, Nguyen's looks attract little attention. She doesn't mind.

In Vietnam, she was singled out for her pale skin and faced discrimination for it. Here, she believes her opportunities are limited only by how hard she can work.

"This is nothing," she said, doing laundry in the bathtub after a 12-hour workday. "In Vietnam, life is much harder."

Her ticket out was her face.

The Amerasian Homecoming Act, passed by Congress in 1987 after much debate, allowed children born in Vietnam to American service members to come to the United States with their families. Few people had documents to prove their heritage, so U.S. Embassy officials based their decisions, in part, on whether they looked "American." About 26,000 eventually immigrated.

Nguyen, 35, said she knows little about her father. He left in 1969, before she was born. Her older half-sisters told her that he was a doctor for the military. Her mother never spoke of him.

Early on, Nguyen realized she was different. In a culture that values family background, Amerasians were considered the products of shameful liaisons. Nguyen recalls the taunt from her classmates, *con lai*—half-breed.

"I would beat them," she said, her voice rising at the memory. "Boys, I would beat, too. They called me names. How dare they?"

Still, even a determined girl who towered over her classmates—thanks to her "American" size—could do only so much in Vietnam.

Shortly after the war, the communist government ordered her family from the seaside city of Vung Tau to the remote highland. Accustomed to city life, the family had to pick coffee beans and pepper on collective farms. Nguyen dropped out of school after the fourth grade and settled for what was expected of her: marriage, children and work.

When news of Amerasians being able to emigrate reached the countryside, Nguyen said she didn't hesitate.

"Older people always said, in America, everything is possible," she remembered. "They said people even had fish in cans."

She lives with her husband and three children in a studio apartment that is cramped but spotless. Canned fish is no longer a novelty—they've moved onto bigger things: two televisions, a desktop computer and a sport utility vehicle.

Nguyen has changed, too. When Man, her eldest child, was having trouble in school, she sought help from Asian American LEAD. She has worked with caseworkers to learn more about American schools and how she can help her son and daughters.

A couple of years ago, she accompanied a social worker to a conference in San Diego, leaving her husband to care for the children for the first time.

Nguyen said she has no desire to find or meet her American father— "I don't need him. He left." She only wants his citizenship.

She has struggled to learn English and fears that she cannot pass the citizenship test.

U.S. law usually allows citizenship for children born overseas to Americans, but Amerasians don't qualify. A bill in Congress that would have granted that right to Amerasians living here died last year in committee.

"I want to be an American," Nguyen said. "I don't want to go back to Vietnam to live."

In 2002, Nguyen returned to her homeland for a visit and, as usual, she stood out.

Friends envied her smooth skin and confident walk. They were tanned and worn from farm work.

In the cities, when shopkeepers noted she was a bit taller, paler and plumper than typical Vietnamese, they quickly fingered her as a Vietnamese who lived in the United States, a Vietnamese American.

The strangers, she recalled with a shy grin, never called her *con lai.*

In Community, a Mission Emerges

Sandy Dang keeps the letters of complaint in a white notebook.

They are dated from 1998, after she founded Asian American LEAD, and were written by Vietnamese Americans to officials in the District government.

"Sandy Dang cannot speak Vietnamese correctly," wrote an older woman questioning whether Dang could properly represent the community. Several others accused her of seeking publicity. A few called her a communist, probably the worst epithet among Vietnamese Americans.

"Can you believe this?" said Dang, 37, a petite woman with a loud voice. "I was really disappointed. But I am stubborn."

She persisted, determined to challenge what she said is the patriarchal tradition that dominated Vietnam and immigrant circles here. "We have to rebuild," Dang said. "You can't call yourself a community and just have a group of old men sitting around the table."

Dang was 7 years old when the war ended. She only knew that the bombs had stopped falling and she would never have to hide again.

The conflicts within a community, Dang soon learned, never end.

In Hanoi, her ethnic Chinese family members were never considered "real" Vietnamese. They didn't fight in the war. When fighting later flared between Vietnam and China, they fled north. In China, though, they weren't considered "real" Chinese. The Chinese government sent them to labor on sugar cane plantations.

In 1979, Dang's family bought passage on a fishing boat crammed with more than 300 refugees from Vietnam. The family spent three years in a Hong Kong refugee camp before immigrating, eventually landing in New York.

Her father worked as a janitor, her mother as a seamstress. Dang was the eldest of four children and served as her parents' translator. For 10 years, the family lived in a one-bedroom apartment.

Dang escaped through her studies, excelling in school and winning scholarships to Duke University. She arrived on a Greyhound bus. Her classmates drove luxury cars.

When she came to Washington to earn a master's degree in social work from Catholic University, she found a Vietnamese American community of 50,000 still governed by rules and hierarchy from the old country. Elders have priority, and men are the leaders.

Many families from the elite social circles in South Vietnam—who escaped the country as soon as Saigon fell—had little interaction with the poorer, less educated families who came later. Such as those in the enclave of about 5,000 Vietnamese living in Mount Pleasant and Columbia Heights.

These immigrants, who arrived in the 1990s, were the last significant wave of refugees. Many were Amerasians. Others had been imprisoned for years in communist "re-education" camps and immigrated under political asylum. Social service agencies in the District were ill-equipped to help.

Dang found her mission. "I know this as an extension of my family. I know how difficult it is to be in this country and come here with nothing."

She started Asian American LEAD as an after-school program, and it has grown into a nationally recognized group with a $1.2 million budget. President Bill Clinton invited her to the White House.

The number of Vietnamese immigrants in the District has dwindled to about 2,000, Dang estimates. Many families have moved to the suburbs; Dang jokes that some of them now drive cars fancier than her Honda Civic. Those left, including Phuong Nguyen's family, are planning to follow soon.

Dang, too, is moving her life beyond the organization. For years, she has been so consumed with work that friends worried about her. Last year, she married, and her husband, Sanal Mazvancheryl, has no connection to Vietnam. He was born in India to an upper-class family and is a business professor at Georgetown University

Dang returns to Vietnam every few years. Her Vietnam no longer is bombs falling from the sky. It is fresh, ripe mangoes, she said, firecrackers exploding at Lunar New Year and quiet, green vistas.

17. Setting the Stage

AUG. 7, 2005

By Phuong Ly

His classmates are pointing and giggling, but Charlie Benitez sits still. A white sheet swaddles his shoulders, and his clean, buzz-cut head sticks through like a mannequin's.

Charlie B., as he's called by his teachers and classmates to distinguish him from another boy named Charlie F., usually wells up with tears when it is time for reading or writing. Today, he is beaming.

This October morning, the 25 kids of Mary Ruth McGinn and Ellen Levine's second-grade class at New Hampshire Estates Elementary School in Silver Spring are learning about stage makeup. They are about to start on a year long project that their teachers believe has the power to change the way they see themselves and the world around them. They will write, produce and perform an opera.

Eyes closed, Charlie B. hears a girl wishing she had been chosen to demonstrate why actors need makeup. Cool cream is smeared onto his face. The flat edge of a pencil presses his brows. A brush tickles his cheeks. Soon, another Charlie B. emerges. This 7-year-old boy is ruddier and more defined. The makeup itches, but he keeps his hands folded on his lap.

"He doesn't look all that different," explains music teacher Emily Hines, as she brushes off runaway smudges, "but now everybody will be able to see him under the lights."

McGinn flips on a spotlight. Charlie B. turns his head from side to side, admiring himself in an imaginary mirror. He says nothing—he just grins. He is still smiling when it is time to leave the music room and go to reading.

* * *

Charlie B. and his fellow students do not call themselves a class. Regular second-graders do not learn about makeup and costumes and Mozart, and visit the Kennedy Center. These second-graders call themselves a company. That, they will inform you, is the proper name for a group of people who are making an opera.

In this company, nearly everyone is an immigrant or a child of an immigrant, from Latin America, Africa or Asia. There's Charlie B., whose parents came from El Salvador and are struggling to get by on one income. There's Tigist Tadesse, who cries when another student moves away because she remembers having to leave her grandmother and other relatives behind in Ethiopia. And there's Kathleen Pham, whose Vietnamese father and Salvadoran mother recently divorced and have married new spouses.

Most of the kids at New Hampshire Estates come from poor families, with nearly 80 percent qualifying for free or reduced-price government lunches. About a third, including Charlie B., who speaks Spanish at home, have to be pulled aside every day for extra help with English. But everyone knows how to say "opera" correctly. It was the first word on their spelling list.

This is the fourth year that New Hampshire Estates has had an opera company. The program was the brainchild of Levine, 50, who has taught at New Hampshire Estates for 14 years, except for one year when she was transferred temporarily to Farmland Elementary in Rockville, a school with middle-class kids, high test scores—and an opera program.

Levine didn't teach opera there, but she watched the performances by the fourth-graders and saw how excited the kids got when they learned about acting and music. When she returned to New Hampshire Estates as a reading teacher, she couldn't get the opera out of her mind. She took McGinn, her longtime friend and colleague, to see the year-end performances at Farmland. Both women became convinced that opera could be a way of engaging children who struggle not only with reading and math, but with low self-esteem and limited horizons.

"We're giving them a purpose for learning," says McGinn, 40. "We're helping them see beyond the classroom, that they can do anything."

But the principal then at New Hampshire Estates hesitated to approve the opera program. Usually she advocated creative learning, but she wasn't sure there was time for it anymore, Levine recalls. Test scores at New Hampshire Estates were—and still are—among the worst in Montgomery County, and there was increasing pressure to raise them.

Later that year, in 2001, the principal retired and an interim administrator from New York approved the opera program, with the stipulation that Levine join McGinn in co-teaching a larger class, to take some of the load off the other second-grade teachers. Their class is the only one at New Hampshire Estates involved in the opera program, which is subsidized by private donations. Although just two to three hours a week are set aside for opera, the teachers thread the lessons through the entire second-grade curriculum. Both women have attended summer workshops in New York sponsored by the Metropolitan Opera Guild, where they've learned how to integrate reading and writing into lessons about opera jobs.

McGinn had been staging plays for several years at New Hampshire Estates, but neither teacher knew much about opera. Levine, who minored in music in college and plays the flute, says she's not crazy about some of the music. It doesn't matter. Stripped down, operas are simply stories with interesting characters and exciting plots. Producing one requires teamwork and responsibility—the kind of skills that schools want kids to learn.

Still, the teachers say they have heard doubts from some of their colleagues. Levine knows some teachers at New Hampshire Estates, which teaches children from pre-kindergarten to second grade, initially considered opera "elitist." Others have asked her how a group of kids used to learning through opera will be able to function in an ordinary classroom the next year.

In many ways, it would be easier not to focus on opera at New Hampshire Estates, where the staff was being pushed to "teach to the test" even before President Bush signed the No Child Left Behind Act in 2002, which tied test scores to federal dollars. Seven other county schools with opera programs are in more affluent suburbs such as Potomac and Bethesda, where test scores are high and there's less need to defend unconventional teaching. The program at New Hampshire Estates started at the same time as one at another low-performing school, Greencastle Elementary in Silver Spring.

At New Hampshire Estates, the opera program has proved to be a transforming experience for many second-graders. Levine and McGinn see it happen every year: Bullies learn about working cooperatively. Kids who hate school will stay in during recess to practice their lines. Newly arrived immigrants learn English by writing dialogue and songs.

During the first year of the opera program, McGinn says, a second-grader's father committed suicide. His daughter kept coming to school. She was the opera company's production manager. She told her mother she needed to do her job.

* * *

"This is an exciting day," McGinn announces in her chirpy voice. She is wearing dangly theater-mask earrings, and she and Levine are holding plastic bags filled with different tools. Today, the kids are getting their opera jobs.

Over the past couple of weeks, the children have tried all kinds of theater work. They got a chance to sing and act out emotions. They measured pieces of wood and hammered nails like carpenters and electricians—

Charlie Benitez, along with Yadhira Torres (left) and Nataly Escobar await the announcement of their job assignments in the opera company. (Photograph courtesy of Sora DeVore/*The Washington Post Magazine*)

work that felt familiar to many of them because that's what their dads do. Nobody knew much about public relations officers, so McGinn brought in an old telephone and had the kids pretend to make calls and invite people to the opera.

Each student had to choose three jobs and explain why he or she wanted to do them. Now the children are sitting on the floor of the music room, waiting for Levine to announce who will do what.

"And," she says with a pause to tease them, "Your performers are . . . Milan. Kevin. Emmanuella. Jacob. Nashaia."

Production manager Deborah Moreira, right, with costume designers Jennifer Arana and Jasmine Wilson (peeking). (Photograph courtesy of Sora DeVore/*The Washington Post Magazine*)

Everybody yells and claps. The performers jump up and run to the front of the room. Levine hands them each a different kind of hat, from baseball cap to safari-style topper. They put them on right away and strike poses.

The scriptwriters get packets of multicolored pens. The public relations officers get markers, and the composers get recorders. Costume and makeup artists receive small mirrors, which they promptly make faces into.

The production manager and recipient of a striped notebook is long-haired Deborah Moreira, who is used to responsibilities because she helps take care of her 4-year-old brother.

Danilo Mejia, a tall, sometimes pushy boy who wears oversize T-shirts printed with dragons and monsters, is the stage manager. He will now wield a bright green clipboard, which the teachers hope he will use to write suggestions for the actors.

Charlie B. is an electrician, exactly what he wanted. When he gets his screwdriver—which he has been told firmly is not a toy—he examines it and compares it to those of the other electricians.

They are no longer students, McGinn tells them, because they have jobs. It is time for them to go off to different rooms with their teachers and volunteers, and start making an opera.

When the children write about their first day on the job, Charlie B. has a lot to say. He writes that he learned how to use a screwdriver, met a man named Mr. Fox who is helping them with their work, and can't wait to go to opera class again. He misspells a lot of the words but among the ones he does spell correctly are "happy" and "excited."

* * *

Charlie B. has been fired.

He faces the music room wall. The other boys are stripping electrical wire. Phil Fox, a school volunteer who has professional stage-crew experience and a big belly laugh, jokes with them.

Charlie sneaks peeks.

"Turn around," Fox says.

Charlie B. has to spend opera class in the corner while all the other students do their jobs. When he refuses to do his class work or displays a bad attitude, his teachers tell him he can't take part in opera class. They tell him he's been fired, which basically amounts to a timeout.

Nearly all the kids get fired at least once. Danilo gets fired on the second day for scaring Tigist with a fake spider. Even Deborah, the serious-looking production manager, gets fired once for forgetting the books she borrowed from the classroom book corner. She makes sure she brings her books from then on.

Charlie B. doesn't learn so quickly. Sometimes, he gets fired in the middle of opera class for grabbing tools from the other kids. When Fox tries to give directions, Charlie jumps up and says he already knows how to do it. He wants to cut wood before he takes time to measure it properly.

At the end of each opera class, the kids gather together and report on what they did. Usually, Charlie likes to chime in and speak for the electricians, but not today.

"Today, we stripped wire," Luis Valdez says.

Gilbert Vargas has something to add. "Charlie got fired."

Charlie says later he was embarrassed. When Luis and Gilbert get fired, Charlie makes sure to report it to the company.

Getting fired is not a good legacy, and legacy is the theme of this year's opera.

"It's not about you, it's about all of us working together and leaving a good legacy," McGinn often tells the class.

Ever since Levine and McGinn taught them about legacies, the kids have been looking for examples. Danilo brings in a picture of his grandfather, who took care of him in Honduras and has passed away. Robel

Sentayehu's drum helps him remember his grandfather, who lives in Ethiopia.

Each day, the company adds to its word list. "Script" is what the writers are writing. The performers are going to be "characters" and speak in "dialogue." (They are using the term opera loosely; the story will be told through both dialogue and song.) Making an opera is a long "process."

The teachers often have the different job groups stand up and talk about their work. Tigist and Robel, who receive extra tutoring in English for Speakers of Other Languages, sometimes open their mouths wordlessly, searching for how to say something. Luis and other kids will say that they "do a nail" or are "learning a lot of stuff," but McGinn urges them to use their new words and speak clearly.

Charlie B. is not shy, but words trip him up. He tries to say that a character is tricky but says "turkey." When he wants to explain to the kids who aren't electricians that wire has to be stripped, he says "wire has to be scripted."

McGinn tells him the difference between strip, which is what electricians do with wire, and script, which is what the writers are producing. He practices over and over, so when the electricians report on the progress of their work to the rest of the company, he can say it correctly.

One day, Charlie B. is again facing the wall. This time, however, he doesn't try to play with the drums or talk to the other students as he has during previous firings. He sits quietly, hands on his chin. With about 10 minutes left before the end of opera class, Fox comes over to him.

"Okay, you've learned your lesson," Fox says and motions him back.

Charlie strips a piece of wire—carefully—and then shows it to Fox.

"Is this right?" he asks.

Fox nods. "Good."

Charlie B. is back on the job.

* * *

"*Estos son wire nuts.*" These are wire nuts.

"*Estos son plugs.*" These are plugs.

Charlie B. is teaching his mother about the tools that he and the other electricians are using to make lights for the stage. Maria Benitez has made special arrangements for a neighbor to baby-sit her toddler daughter this February morning so she can see what her son is learning in opera class. She is suspicious.

Late last fall, Benitez had approached Levine in the parking lot after school. She brought along her daughter Jacqueline, 11, to help translate.

Levine recalls Benitez crossing her arms over her chest.

"I don't agree," Benitez said, in a halting but firm English, "with the way you teach."

Jacqueline explained: Charlie told his family he hates opera. He hates his job, he hates his teachers and he hates school. He does not want to do his homework.

Jacqueline, at her mother's direction, has tried to help Charlie with his work, but when he writes, he circles words that he knows are misspelled rather than try to spell them correctly. He says that this is what his teachers told him to do. His mother wants him to write the words over. Evenings end in screams and tears.

Levine remembers being surprised by what she was hearing. She thought Charlie B. loved opera class.

"I asked [his mother] to please think of it as an experiment," Levine recalls. "We will teach the kids how to spell, but this is not the focus of the assignment. It's to try to get their ideas on paper." She asked Benitez to refrain from asking Charlie to correct his spelling and let him write. She invited her to come to a class and see Charlie do his job. Give us a chance, she said.

The Benitezes live in a squat brick house a few blocks from New Hampshire Estates, but Charlie is not allowed to walk home from school without an adult. Not even his older sister can venture out by herself. Too many men, some reeking of alcohol, loiter around the neighborhood. Benitez says she feels like she has already lost one child. She fears losing another.

In 1987, she left El Salvador to escape the country's civil war and grinding poverty. She also left behind a baby girl. To support her daughter, mother and other relatives, Benitez worked as a live-in nanny for a Navy couple and their two little boys. It would be 13 years before she could return to El Salvador for a visit.

Her daughter, now 19, immigrated two years ago and lives in Northern Virginia. Benitez purses her lips when she discusses her oldest child. They talk, she says, but "not like mother and daughter."

These days, Benitez, 38, is a full-time mother. Jose Benitez, the "good, good man" she married in 1991, works 14-hour days as a self-employed contractor, building decks and painting houses. Money is tight on one income, and the children barely see their father during the week, but Jose Benitez prefers that his wife be home. He, too, left behind his first child— a son—when he immigrated here.

In their house, Christian books and videotapes of Bible stories line the shelves of the entertainment center. The children are not allowed to watch much else. Saturday nights and Sunday afternoons are spent at the Spring of Life Apostolic Church in Hyattsville.

Maria Benitez, a sober-looking woman, wears long skirts and a lace headscarf required by her church. Daughter Jacqueline is an image of her mother, sans scarf.

Jacqueline "never has trouble," Benitez says. This coming year, Jacqueline will be in sixth grade, the point at which her mother had to quit school and help take care of her younger siblings after her father abandoned the family. Jacqueline's school certificates, for honor roll and perfect attendance, hang on a living room wall.

"But Charlie," Benitez says, taking a deep breath. Last year, Charlie learned bad words from a classmate and insisted on wearing baggy jeans. His best friend was a boy whose parents worked all the time and "was like a grown-up already," says Benitez, who went to the principal to get the two separated in class. Sometimes, Charlie gets so angry, she says. "It was terrible. He break things in the room."

"Liar!" Charlie says as he walks by, holding a pair of binoculars to watch birds from the living room window.

"Charlie, that's not true," she scolds, ordering him with her eyes to be quiet. He goes to the window. She sighs.

At a parents meeting in December, Levine and McGinn had explained the concept of legacy—the theme of the opera—by asking everyone to write about what gift they wanted to leave their children.

Benitez sat, watching the other parents write. A Spanish interpreter at the meeting came over and prodded her. Finally, with the help of the interpreter, she composed a few sentences in Spanish: Her legacy to Charlie is that he will study. She doesn't have a specific career in mind for Charlie, who wavers between being a carpenter and a police officer. She just wants him to grow up to be a good, honest man.

For the rest of the meeting, Benitez crossed her arms over her chest. She thought the teachers were wasting her time. She already knew what she wants for her children. She needed to see the teachers helping.

When Benitez visits opera class, the teachers are scattered with other children. It is Charlie B. who leads her by the hand to the electricians' corner and tells her about their project. He points to the cans that they are cutting in half with clippers so they can be used to hold light bulbs.

"They're reflectors," he says. "We have to make lots of them."

Benitez doesn't understand everything that he is talking about, but his enthusiasm makes her smile. He doesn't act like a boy who hates school.

Charlie B. puts on fuchsia gloves, an old pair found in the storage room, so his hands will be protected from any jagged pieces of metal. Luis giggles, "Pink, like a girl!"

Charlie B. doesn't pay attention to him. "This is hard work," he says, struggling to clip the heavy metal. His mother holds the can.

"You can do it, but it's a process," Fox says. "You have to keep your fingers away from the metal."

"I'm getting there," Charlie B. says, several clips later.

He grunts. Finally, the can snaps into two halves. "I can't believe I actually did this."

"*Fuerte,*" Fox tells Charlie B.'s mother, using the little Spanish he knows. Strong.

She laughs and whispers in Spanish to Charlie. He looks up and shouts to Fox: "My mama says she's going to buy me gloves!"

* * *

Charlie B. keeps raising his hand.

It is early March, almost time for the state standardized tests. This morning, the kids are hovered over their math worksheets. They are getting ready for the assessment tests that all second-graders must take.

"Can I go to the bathroom?" Charlie B. asks. A teacher's aide shakes her head and tells him to finish his work first.

Charlie has completed the addition and subtraction, but he can't understand the word problems. "Can you read me this?" he pleads. But the teachers and the aide are busy with other students.

Charlie puts his head down: "I'm going to take a nap."

Levine and McGinn have been worried about Charlie B. They know he is a bright boy and has improved so much from the fall, but he still reads below grade level. Sometimes, he won't try to sound out words. He simply shuts down.

At the teachers' request, Charlie's mother and father come in for a conference. Levine and McGinn later recall telling them that Charlie doesn't recognize words that an average second-grader should. The teachers want him examined to find out whether he is learning disabled. The principal and a counselor give the Benitezes forms to sign, with the help of a Spanish interpreter.

The Benitezes do not say much. It is the first time Charlie's father, 35, has come to the school this year, and he took off work so he could be here. He wears his button-down shirt tucked in, and his dark brown hair and moustache are neatly trimmed.

When they finish with the forms, Jose Benitez starts to thank the teachers, but he is unable to finish the sentence. He breaks into sobs. He is afraid for Charlie, the teachers remember him saying.

"This was me," he says. He had problems in school, too. In fragmented English, he tells them that he was placed in a special program in El Salvador. He never finished his education. Here, in the United States, his clients appreciate his work and urge him to go to community college and get a degree.

"I know I can't," he tells the teachers.

Levine and McGinn jump in to reassure him. Charlie is no longer crying when he has to read, they say, and they can tell that he's trying. The tests will show the teachers if he needs special help. He will not be labeled "stupid" and sent away.

Jose Benitez looks embarrassed about his outburst; his wife sits quietly, expressionless. The meeting ends. There is no more time for the teachers and principal to talk with the Benitezes. Parent conferences are scheduled back-to-back, and so many other students at New Hampshire Estates need extra help.

The upcoming state tests put every school under scrutiny, and the pressure is especially intense in the so-called red zone, the cluster of Montgomery County schools that includes New Hampshire Estates and others with low-income students.

At the beginning of March, county schools Superintendent Jerry Weast uses New Hampshire Estates as the backdrop for a news conference touting gains in reading scores during the previous year, but says more needs to be done. Weast and the school system are spending $60 million on the red zone to cut class size, offer full-day kindergarten and boost teacher training. They want to do everything they can to make sure these schools perform well, but schools outside the red zone are clamoring for funds, too. The test scores need to prove that the money is justified, and No Child Left Behind has put the jobs of school officials on the line.

Levine and McGinn say that so much is riding on test scores that they wonder if they will be able to do the opera program in coming years. Not even kindergartners have been spared from testing pressures: Art, music and playtime have been reduced to make room for more reading and writing, and the 5-year-olds get summer homework packets or attend summer classes before they start school.

Jane Litchko, the current principal at New Hampshire Estates, says she appreciates the way the opera program helps children with skills the tests can't measure, like self-esteem, and introduces them to sophisticated vocabulary words. At the same time, she says, the kids in the opera program do not score significantly higher on the standardized tests than the other second-graders. She says she supports the opera lessons, but "who knows what the future may hold for the testing."

In March, afternoons that were previously devoted to "buddy reading"— when the students are allowed to pick a storybook and read with a friend—have been dedicated to drills from a test prep manual called "Scoring High." The picture on the book shows smiling kids giving a thumbs up. Charlie B. likes to toss his manual on the floor. Several kids keep asking for buddy reading.

One afternoon, McGinn says she wants to share something special with the class. It is a Robert Frost poem, "The Road Not Taken." She discovered the poem when she was in middle school and has loved Frost's work ever since. Each year, she reads the poem to her second-graders before test time.

"He left a legacy for the world with his poetry," McGinn says. "See, everything comes back to legacy."

She reads the poem once, twice, and again. The kids hear about a traveler standing where "two roads diverged in a yellow wood." He took the one less traveled and "that has made all the difference."

Several kids are whispering to one another. A couple are more interested in the imaginary spots on the carpet. Charlie B., who is usually one of those, is looking straight at McGinn.

"I love the way Charlie B. is sitting, thinking about this," she says. "Why can't other people be like that?"

When the class is asked to draw a picture of Robert Frost's two roads, Charlie B. draws a boy in the middle of two two-lane roads with his finger to his head, and explains: "He's thinking."

As the teachers walk around the room to look at the children's work, Charlie B. makes a request. "Miss McGinn, Miss McGinn," he says waving her over, "can we write about it?"

Charlie writes that a boy is deciding between two roads, and the sun is shining on the woods to make them look yellow. On the margins of his paper, he prints, "I can do it. I can do it."

If only, McGinn thinks to herself, the county could give Charlie a score for this.

* * *

The lights work. They flash all around the stage, in the tin-can reflectors that Charlie B. and his fellow electricians have spent weeks cutting.

Onstage, the carpenters have erected a wooden eagle cage. The story is about four kids who see an eagle at the National Zoo, which the opera company visited in February. One boy, a bully, secretly lets the eagle out of its cage and the eaglets are left without a mother.

Kathleen and the other carpenters are responsible for moving the silhouettes of the animals between the acts. In the fall, Kathleen had been distracted, and withdrew into her own world with worries about her parents' divorce and remarriages. She hid her face behind her long, brown hair. Today, she is listening to the actors rehearse, ready for her cues.

"I hardly recognize her," says Levine.

It is early May, a week before the performances, and the teachers wish they had more time. Not because they are behind schedule on the script, sets or costumes. But because each week, more second-graders redefine themselves.

In late March, Tigist, who spoke no English last year, began raising her hand. She wanted to share news about the script, which she had been working through recess to complete. One day, Tigist and her fellow writer, Judy Kindo, sing to the class the song that they wrote for Ozzie the bully, who realizes that he acts out of anger and sadness for his own dead mother.

Tigist raises her voice with each verse. "I'm tired of being shy," Tigist says later, flashing a dimpled grin.

By now, the performers are learning to project their voices and stay quiet if it isn't their turn to speak. The public relations officers have made invitations and sent out press releases explaining the opera. The composers will play their glockenspiels with a pianist accompanying their music. Deborah the production manager wrote a speech to introduce the opera, "Endangered Legacy."

Danilo, the stage manager, spent several nights drawing diagrams of where the performers should stand. Being in charge is hard work, he says. "Poor Miss McGinn," says Danilo, who now relies on persuasion rather than pushing to get his classmates to do what he wants. "How can she take care of all of us?"

* * *

Standing tall on a chair, Danilo motions across the room to Charlie B., cuing him to switch off the lights. A few seconds pass. Charlie B. doesn't see his cue. He is looking toward the back of the auditorium, where his mother and two sisters are sitting. His father, who arrived late because of work, stands near a doorway.

When Charlie B. looks back to see Danilo, he ducks his head in embarrassment. He pulls the plug on the house lights and the auditorium goes dark. The show has begun.

It's a humid May evening, made even hotter inside the auditorium by the presence of about 150 parents, relatives, teachers, former school staff members, and performers and artists who have visited the opera class during the year.

The kids are clearly nervous performing in front of this crowd. Deborah, who wears a frothy pink dress her mother bought for the occasion, freezes and forgets to recite the Spanish translation of her opening speech. Between scenes, there is a drawn-out lull and loud thumps behind the stage as the carpenters change the set. The actors forget some of their lines as they speak and sing.

But, unlike in some of the rehearsals, actors Kevin Ventura and Jacob Dweh remember to stay away from each other and not laugh inappropriately. Danilo follows the script and reminds Luis when to turn on the back and front stage lights. Without their teachers to prompt them, Kathleen and the carpenters remember their cues.

Levine, wearing an ivory pantsuit, and McGinn, in a black dress, couldn't be prouder. They stand to one side, watching their students go through the entire half-hour performance on their own.

The opera concludes with Ozzie the bully, played by blond-haired Milan Moreau, regretting that he let the eagle out of her cage and hurt the eaglets. He tells the other kids that he doesn't want to leave a bad legacy.

The actors break into song, and this time Charlie B. is ready. He dashes up to the stage. This is his favorite part of the performance. Deborah introduces all the job groups and the entire company joins in the chorus:

Listen to the stories,
learn the lessons,
keep them in your heart
or in your mind,
and pass it on, pass it on.

The audience is on its feet, applauding. The principal presents bouquets of flowers to Levine, McGinn and the volunteers.

In the days to come, reading assessments will show that nearly every child involved in the opera is reading at or above grade level. Charlie B.

is just a few points shy of grade level, and the teachers call the improvement remarkable. On a critical-thinking test with puzzles to identify gifted and talented children, Charlie B. gets two-thirds of the problems right. The tests to detect learning disabilities uncover weaknesses but no serious problems. Charlie B. just needed more confidence in himself, his teachers conclude. And now he's got it.

After the show, Jose Benitez wraps his son into a hug. "He did a good job," Charlie's father says.

Later, he quietly drops a $5 bill into a jar for donations to the opera program. Charlie and his family walk home, hand in hand. Charlie hums the opera's theme song. It's a legacy. Pass it on.

18. Vietnam Buffs Bring Jungle to Va.

AUG. 8, 2005

By Phuong Ly

Leaves rustled, and Robby Gouge, sweating in his jungle boots and Army fatigues, clutched his semiautomatic rifle tighter. He walked slightly crouched and listened intently, just as he thought his father might have done.

The 30-year-old son had come to the oak forests of central Virginia to relive his old man's war in Vietnam.

Walking behind Gouge on this hazy summer morning were a dozen men, toting gear culled from military surplus stores. Another team had fanned across the other side of the woods. A few men and women, dressed in the black pajamas of enemy fighters, waited in ambush.

Most war reenactments are staged to make history come alive for generations who know it only dimly from books. Vietnam, though, isn't quite history. To many people, it's a painfully current event.

Presidential candidates still have to explain what they did during the war, and every military action since 1975, including the conflict in Iraq, risks being compared to the failures there. Even those who stage battles from other wars question whether it is too soon to reenact Vietnam.

Most of the men and women at the Virginia event were in their thirties and forties—too young to have experienced the action firsthand but too old to escape the war's grip. Their fathers, like Gouge's, served in Vietnam, or they grew up watching it on the news.

As the 90-degree heat and his 50-pound rucksack weighed on him, Gouge conceded that spending a few weekends a summer pretending to be a U.S. soldier in the jungles was crazy. He missed his wife and two kids and wondered why he wasn't at home enjoying the air conditioning.

But this feeling of misery was what he was after. Too much war talk is wrapped up in theory and politics.

"It gives a mental picture of what our dads did," said Gouge, who teaches history at a middle school in Asheville, N.C. "I was blessed. I never had to really do this."

Road to the Past

To get to Vietnam, follow Interstate 64 to Louisa, Va., where signs point out Civil War sites. In 1864, field hospitals were set up around town as

Tony Bean patrols in his role as a North Vietnamese fighter behind Viet Cong reenactors. (Photograph courtesy of Tracy A. Woodward/*The Washington Post*)

more than 1,600 men were killed or wounded when Union forces tried to shut down the Virginia Central Railroad.

Past the fast-food joints that make up the business district, the paved roads turn into gravel lanes and, finally, into dirt. Signs show the way: "To the Nam," "Phou Bai—2 km."

By mid afternoon Friday of a reenactment weekend, a clearing on 50 acres of private property was filled with tents and cots. Water in plastic jugs was transferred to green military containers. Participants carried their ammunition in plastic bags, making it easier for others to check that they were blanks.

The communists hung their hammocks a half-mile away, past several scorched acres of forestland leveled after a neighbor sold the timber. The burned stumps added a nice touch. "Looks like it's been napalmed," one guy said.

Gouge began unpacking his gear, including replicas of his father's dog tags and patches from other veterans. His reenactment unit is named in honor of the Army's 199th Light Infantry Brigade, the one his father served in, the one Gouge has written two books about.

"A lot of the [veterans] that I know, their own kids don't really care or don't take the time to talk to them about this," said Gouge, who sported a military buzz cut for the weekend. "I guess I'm the person for that."

On this weekend, about 20 people from North Carolina, Virginia and Georgia were doing "impressions" of Americans who fought in Vietnam. Several have military experience, including one Gulf War veteran. There are police officers, firefighters, a sheriff's deputy and a district attorney. A pediatric therapist came to play medic along with his wife. One man, a chemist, cooked meals in an antique field kitchen.

This is a fledgling endeavor, with the first units starting about five years ago. Several hundred people reenact the Vietnam War, with about a dozen units listed on the Internet. Their events generally are private affairs, and some participants say they're reluctant to tell too many outsiders for fear of stirring up the war's raw emotions.

In contrast, many Civil War reenactments are public; Gettysburg draws as many as 20,000 participants and spectators.

Most at the Virginia event know one another from other historical gatherings, chiefly for the Civil War and World War II. About four years ago, they started doing Vietnam.

They don't concern themselves with the politics of the war that still divides the United States 30 years after Saigon fell. They come as history buffs.

To them, this is a hobby, like golf or collecting model trains, but more educational. What some of them don't understand are "Star Trek" and "Star Wars" fans. If they're going to dress up, one reenactor asked, why not pick a real time period?

"People, they're so weird," Patrick Hubble said. "Unlike us."

Hubble, an affable mortician and former Navy sailor from Lynchburg, Va., plays a North Vietnamese soldier because he figures somebody has to do it. This time, he was leading a band of six enemy fighters. It's always hard to find people to be the bad guys, so the U.S. soldiers say that the enemy is so elusive that most are hidden in the forest.

Hubble, who gave his age as "born in 1968, year of the Tet Offensive," is always on the lookout for new recruits. Several times, he visited a Vietnamese-owned grocery store to ask if he could borrow the family's elder sons for a weekend. He showed them photos of himself dressed up as a communist.

Hubble said the family always told him their sons were busy. This remark would be followed by laughter and chatter in Vietnamese. "They were probably thinking, 'What a weirdo,'" Hubble said. "But I just wanted things to be more authentic."

The enemy ranks included his only child, Meagan, a quiet 15-year-old who said she considered this quality time with her dad, and a University of Delaware history major who was as interested in Vietnamese culture as in the war.

The newest recruit was Caitlin Parker, a soft-spoken New Yorker.

Parker started looking into reenacting after she heard someone making fun of the participants. She was offended. Her father, whom she described as a sensitive intellectual, served in Vietnam as a Marine. He mentions the war occasionally, but she has never probed further, assuming the subject was taboo.

"This is kind of a way to understand him better," said Parker, 29, a producer for an audiobook company. "Maybe this will open up a conversation."

Hubble, the first person to e-mail her back, was so encouraging and empathetic that Parker decided to come for a weekend with her boyfriend, David Markowitz. They would be Viet Cong recruits to beef up the enemy forces.

The pair were among the last to arrive, driving up in a cranberry Subaru wagon, their hammocks stuffed in a Whole Foods Market grocery bag. On the way down, they worried about whether they would fit in. Neither had ever fired a gun.

In the Heat of Battle

Loud booms echoed out of the trees. Vietnamese fighters took aim at two men from Gouge's squad; the Americans fell to the ground. Gouge flopped onto his belly, firing back.

It was the second day of reenactment weekend, and Parker, crouching behind a pile of sandbags, was still rattled from the previous night's fiery battle. She knew everyone was firing blanks, but she couldn't get over how real the scenario seemed. She wondered whether her father felt this way.

After a burst of gunfire, one of her comrades collapsed. Another popped up from behind the sandbags.

"You, you in the bunker!" Gouge shouted. "You're down."

Seconds later, the man resurfaced.

"You in the bunker, with your back to me," Gouge said, raising his voice. "You're out."

It was Hubble, and he yelled back that he knew he was dead: "I've been out for the last 10 minutes!"

The reenactors try to recapture the war's fear and danger, but the biggest risk is turning the war into a game or parody. Because they rely on the honor code to determine "kills," sometimes there's a dispute over whether someone is dead. Battles often come to an abrupt end when people get tired or when weapons jam. The commanders carry walkie-talkies to tell one another where their teams are—there's nothing worse than walking around and not finding an ambush.

Gouge admitted that it sometimes feels fun—and he hates that. He wants to feel scared and somber. "You're remembering what they did," he said.

At his middle school, Gouge has only a few days to teach the Vietnam War at the end of the required state curriculum. At first, his students can't locate Vietnam on a map. It is as unknown to them as it was to Americans before the 1960s.

At home, Gouge keeps a "war room." Once crowded with Civil War memorabilia, the basement shelves are now filled with items that Vietnam veterans have given him: leftover C-rations, field manuals, pictures, radios and letters from home. A full dress uniform hangs in one corner.

His father lives next door, but when he visits, he avoids this room.

Jack Gouge was drafted in 1968 soon after getting married. For nine months, he drove a jeep, ferrying supplies to satellite support bases in the jungles. When he left Vietnam, he was so jumpy from memories of sniper fire, he avoided turning his back on anybody.

"When I came back, I tried to forget," said Gouge, 58, a retired phone company manager. "Can't recall it. Don't want to."

When his son wanted to join friends enlisting in the Army after high school, Gouge and his wife said no. They told him to go to college first.

They remain puzzled over his interest in the Vietnam War. Eloise Gouge wishes he had stuck with the Civil War. "Vietnam," she said, "we lived through that."

"I think he's gone too far," Jack Gouge said. Although he said he was proud to serve his country, he didn't attend reunions of his unit. He finally went to one only because his son, well known among the veterans because of his books, was asked to give a speech.

Maybe, he conceded, all this was good for his son: "It's history."

Looking the Part

The midmorning battle ended quickly. After 10 minutes, the popcorn gunfire from the Americans' semiautomatics didn't get an answer from the communist rifles.

"Well, I think it's time to resurrect," someone called out to a downed U.S. fighter.

Markowitz grumbled that he could have done more damage if his gun hadn't jammed. Parker turned out to be tougher than her delicate features suggested. She became an expert at loading her rifle. Sprawled on the ground as "dead," she looked relaxed and managed a laugh at her boyfriend's boasts.

Gouge also allowed himself a smile. He went to an enemy bunker to check on Hubble and his daughter.

"You guys all right?" Gouge asked. "You need water?"

The battles here end nice and neat. No hard feelings.

Besides, reenacting is about more than fighting. It's about the clothes.

From the moment they arrived, they were exchanging tips on their "impressions." Several talked about losing weight so they could fit into real Army fatigues rather than reproductions. They swapped and sold gear like boys trading baseball cards.

At communist headquarters, one guy gave Parker's feet a long stare.

"Are they actually PAVN boots?" asked Rob Williams, the Delaware student, using the abbreviation for the North Vietnamese army.

Williams motioned Hubble over: "They have the actual PAVN boots in her size."

Most reenactors, Williams explained, can't fit into the smaller Vietnamese sizes. They have to settle for the model worn by French soldiers during their war in Vietnam and later adapted by the North Vietnamese. "This is the French Indochina boot," Williams said, showing Parker his footwear.

Parker didn't know what to say. But her worries about feeling out of place were fading. The group's shock that she and her boyfriend had never handled guns quickly turned into gentle ribbing.

Being one of three women wasn't a big deal, either, as Parker had feared. It was authentic: Women fought with the Viet Cong.

The guys cursed and used racial slurs about the enemy, but a couple of them apologized later. Again, it's a "period" thing.

"They're just geeks," Parker said. "They're a lot less macho than I thought. It's kind of sweet."

For her, Vietnam often had been defined by stereotypes rather than reality. She knew the war traumatized her father. He once told her he couldn't bear to attend a welcome-home party thrown by his mother. Parker said she figured it was best not to bring it up.

Gerard Parker, a retired trade show coordinator in San Francisco, said he never consciously avoided discussing Vietnam. He just thought it was something his daughter didn't care about.

When she first told him about reenacting, he worried that the war would be trivialized. But he said he's glad Vietnam is finally being treated like other wars—and that his daughter has taken an interest.

"In the 1970s, if you said you had been in Vietnam, people would stay away from you," the 65-year-old said. "Things have gotten a bit more realistic and balanced. With the passage of time, that divisiveness is fading into history."

At the reenactment site, there was a range of opinions about the politics of war, in both Vietnam and Iraq. But most conversation steered clear. "That's not what we're here for," Robby Gouge said.

Like real soldiers, they sat around and talked about life "back home," about job promotions and families. One guy showed off photos of his two little girls. Others took turns cradling a grenade launcher. "Great toy," someone said.

The cook fretted over dinner plans. The vintage oven wasn't working, so he had to use a modern gas grill. Reality often spoils a good reenactment.

By Saturday night, 24 hours of Vietnam had become enough. Period music, the Rolling Stones, blared through the woods. But it came from the CD player in a sports car.

Parker and Markowitz left early for the long drive back to New York. Parker said she got what she came for.

"I know these people aren't actually going to kill me, but I had this very strong fear out there," she said. "My father had to deal with it for real, and I just got a vague, vague, removed idea of it."

She intends to visit her father at the end of the summer and talk with him about the war.

Gouge skipped the evening battle because he wanted to go to bed early. He had called his wife earlier; the family was at the beach, and his 4-year-old son, Jackson, saw his first crab. Gouge couldn't wait to join them.

But his sacrifice had been worth it. "You've got to think, if you've got 365 days of this and it gets worse," he said. A taste of grunt life every summer "humbles your thinking."

On Sunday, the reenactors dismantled their tents and packed up Vietnam. Just the shell casings were left, glittering on the ground.

19. Washing Their Hands of the Last Frontier

OCT. 8, 2005

By Phuong Ly

A couple of months ago, in the privacy of his Reston townhouse, Alan Chien made a final break from cultural tradition, a guilt-filled decision he has yet to share with his parents.

He used his dishwasher. He knows his parents will not understand.

"They don't believe in it," said Chien, 35, an engineer who emigrated with his family from Taiwan when he was a toddler. "Just because they never used it, I never used it, so it was just a mysterious thing to me."

In many immigrant homes, the automatic dishwasher is the last frontier. Long after new arrivals pick up football, learn the intricacies of the multiplex and the DMV and develop a taste for pizza, they resist the dishwasher. Some joke that not using the appliance is one of the truest signs of immigrant heritage, whether they hail from Africa, Latin America, Asia or Eastern Europe.

If they have a dishwasher—and many do, because it is standard equipment in most homes—it becomes a glorified dish rack, a Tupperware storage cabinet or a snack-food bin. It's never turned on.

Officials at appliance companies have noticed: Sears doesn't even highlight the appliances in its ads in Spanish-language media.

It's a quirk in the assimilation process that baffles social scientists. "It's really striking," said Donna Gabaccia, who studies immigration and culinary history at the University of Minnesota. In the home, "technology is generally embraced by women. Certainly in terms of technology, their homes don't look that much different from Middle American homes."

Gabaccia said one explanation could be that immigrants can absorb only so much change. The dishwasher is a U.S. invention that is rare in most countries, even among the upper-middle class.

Chien, too, has a hard time explaining dishwasher guilt. Chien, whose younger sister goaded him into breaking his "mental block" on the matter, marvels over how the appliance scrubs off caked-on food. But he isn't sure whether he will keep using it.

"I still have the sense that it's kind of a waste of electricity," he said. "It's odd. We buy American clothes; we use the oven; we use the stove; but, somehow, that appliance…"

Graciela Andres laments that her daughter, son-in-law and three grandchildren have abandoned washing by hand. "They do it the American way—they put everything in the wash machine, no matter if it's a little spoon," said Andres, who emigrated from Bolivia in 1981.

She does not disdain her family's washer and dryer, microwave, heavy-duty mixer, DVD player or computers. But the dishwasher?

"I think if I wash by my hands, I do a better job," said Andres, 65, of Germantown. "We have to fill up the dishwasher. If you do it by hand, it gets clean right away."

Her daughter, Grace Rivera-Oven, says she cannot afford not to use it. Her five-cycle, stainless-steel Kenmore allows her to spend more time shuttling her children to baseball and soccer, serving on community boards and freelance writing.

As a teenager, she got a friend to teach her how to operate the dishwasher—"She was white; I figured she knew how." Before her mother got home from work, she would run a load.

These days, she can use the dishwasher anytime she wants. Even so, she feels as if she's missing something. That's why, every Saturday morning, she does the breakfast dishes by hand with her 10-year-old daughter, Amalia.

"We just gossip, gossip," said Rivera-Oven, 35. "I just wash them, and she dries. It just reminds me of when I was her age. I did them with my mother. Oh, I loved the drying."

Her mother chimes in, stirred by the memory. "Oh, yes, I remember when she would dry and I would check," Andres said, pretending to rub a glass between her fingers. "Squeak, squeak, squeak."

Kitchen historians speculate that the dishwasher lies at the heart of what it means to be a family. Dishwashers began appearing in many middle-class American households in the late 1960s and 1970s, about the time that many women began entering the workforce. A decade later, the microwave came along. The family dinner hour disappeared. It's been downhill from there.

"When people ate dinner together, they also cleaned up together," said Vicki Matranga, a kitchen historian and designer for the Illinois-based International Housewares Association. "Americans now want convenience. The kitchen is a showplace where you heat up your food in the microwave."

Outside the United States, Canada and Western Europe, dishwashers are uncommon. In most countries, people cannot afford them; if they could, then they already have maids, who can do the dishes by hand.

A 2004 economics report from the government of India noted that a growing middle class had pushed up sales of clothes washers, refrigerators and small appliances by 20 percent a year. Dishwashers, however, were a "negligible market."

In tech-crazed South Korea, many families boast refrigerators with built-in TV screens and a cooler that regulates the temperature especially for jars of kimchi, the spicy pickled cabbage—but no dishwasher.

At Sears, officials do not make much of an effort to market dishwashers to immigrants. The company's Kenmore Elite TurboZone was touted in mainstream media, but Spanish-language newspapers and magazines ran only general ads about appliances.

Anecdotal evidence from Sears associates and customers suggests that Latinos care far more about cooktops than dishwashers, said Tina Settecase, vice president of home appliances.

"We're very careful about not changing our Hispanic customers," she said. "We're just trying to identify what the Hispanic customer wants and supply it."

But Mike McDermott, general manager of merchandising at General Electric, wonders whether more information about dishwashers might make a difference.

Like other appliance-makers, GE extols the dishwashers' energy efficiency. The U.S. Department of Energy agrees, citing findings that dishwashers, with a full load, use half as much water as washing by hand. Statistics from the D.C.-based Association of Home Appliance Manufacturers show that using the dishwasher six times a week costs $49 a year, a little more than the refrigerator.

"Where there isn't a dishwasher in a home, we need to understand why it's not there," McDermott said, "and what are some of the tools we can use to educate the consumer."

He will not have any luck with Douglas Lee's family. His American roots stretch back to 1963, when his grandparents emigrated from China. In three generations, nobody has used a dishwasher.

Lee, 22, of Springfield said he does not understand the appeal.

"Do you have to wash it beforehand to rinse it off? And if you wash it beforehand, why do you even need to use it?" asked Lee, a program manager for the Washington-based Organization of Chinese Americans. "I see a lot of my white friends doing it. I'm like: 'Oh, well, whatever. I guess I can't judge them on how they clean their dishes.' "

Bernie Fischer, a self-described "typical white guy" who grew up in Baltimore, knows all the benefits of the dishwasher. His parents had been so attached to theirs that they used it even though the wash cycle caused the lights to dim in their aging house.

But these days, his dishwasher is simply a drying rack. It was his wife's idea. Mary Ngo is a Vietnamese American.

"Mary's kind of set in her ways," said Fischer, 29, a soft-spoken Columbia psychiatrist.

"I just don't see the practicality of using the dishwasher," explained Ngo, 28, a job trainer born and raised in Montgomery County.

But she does let her husband turn on the appliance every two weeks— to clean it, not the dishes.

A conversation with
Phuong Ly

An edited e-mail interview conducted by Thomas Huang, an editor at The Dallas Morning News *and a Poynter Institute ethics fellow, with Phuong Ly, winner of the ASNE Award for Distinguished Writing on Diversity.*

THOMAS HUANG: Where did your ideas come from?

PHUONG LY: I find ideas from a variety of sources. I'm a voracious reader, so I'm always online looking through ethnic media Web sites, blogs and academic journals. I'm also always having lunch or coffee with someone, or asking people to take me through their neighborhoods.

Some ideas result from personal experiences, like dishwashers and the Vietnam War anniversary. For the *kirogi* story, I relied on sources in the Korean community of Howard County, in particular, an immigrant outreach coordinator for the school system and a Korean newspaper reporter.

The war reenactors story was the result of two photos I saw in an art gallery in New York City several years ago. The photos were of woods in South Carolina and the captions said that the woods were used by Vietnam War reenactors. There was no other information. I was completely intrigued by the idea, but it wasn't until this year that I finally found an e-mail for a reenactors' group, thanks to Google.

Where and how did you collect the information for your stories?

Right after I talk to a few sources, I turn immediately to NEXIS and Google. For every story I do, I collect a huge file folder full of information taken from ethnic media Web sites, blogs, foreign media and chat rooms. Those types of sources help connect me with more "real people" and organizations. I also use NEXIS as a way to gauge whether I'm onto a new trend or type of story. My editors know that I'm likely to kill a story idea if it's been done before by another mainstream media organization.

I'm relentless at interviewing and will try to talk to as many people as possible. I prefer personal visits. People need to see you face to face, to decide whether to trust you. I've been reporting in the Washington region since 1999, so I've also developed a cadre of "introducers"—ethnic media reporters, social workers and the like, who can give me an introduction to ordinary folks who aren't used to being interviewed by a reporter.

I also will read novels or listen to music from the cultures I'm writing about. When I was working on the *kirogi* story, I read several books written by Korean Americans. It helps me get the mood and feel for the characters' language.

How did you decide what the focus would be for each of your stories?

I don't want people to see my stories and think that they're about "the others." Many stories about immigrants tend to treat their subjects as scientific oddities being examined by white America. I'm not interested in writing Ripley's "Believe It or Not" pieces.

My stories deal with universal themes—loss, identity, growing up, etc. I take the theme and then develop it with a character. Their ethnicity or culture may be relevant and add to the theme, but it is not the focus of the story.

For the *kirogi* story, I have to give credit to a good friend for helping me focus. He said, "People should read this story and ask themselves, 'Would you do this for your child?'" That helped me realize that the Kims were similar to many suburban American families who switch school districts to give their children a better education, except the Kims moved to another continent.

As for the Vietnam War reenactors, the more time I spent with them, the more I realized they were a lot like the women I had written about in the Vietnam War anniversary piece. They were in their 30s and trying to make their own peace with a war that they only knew as a memory. These guys weren't total freaks; their experiences said something about war and memory and identity.

The same with the "dishwashers" story. The sociologists and kitchen historians gave context to this quirk in cultural adaptation. They explained that the use of dishwashers said just as much about American culture as the non-use of it says about immigrants.

The opera story was about these second graders and the big changes they experienced during their nine months in that class.

How did you organize your stories?

I organize by scenes. I write down all the major scenes I've witnessed and then decide whether they illuminate a point I want to make in the story.

As I'm reporting, I'm always rereading through my material—I type up my notes frequently and print them out—and making outlines. I do a lot of free writing and post notes to myself weeks before I'm ready to tackle the real thing.

How many drafts did you do for each of your stories?

Countless. I keep all the drafts on my personal computer, and I'm really embarrassed by some of the first attempts! I'll also e-mail bits and pieces to a few good friends who are brilliant writers and extremely patient and generous teachers.

What revisions did you make to your stories before publishing?

Loads. When I'm writing a long story, I'll usually write in pieces, and send the bits to my editor to either trash or approve. I sometimes write out of order, depending on what scenes grab me first and demand to be written. For the children's opera story, I wrote the entire story except for the last section. My editor had nearly finished editing everything else, but I was struggling with the last section for a week later.

What role did your editor play?

My immediate supervisor, Phyllis Jordan, really helped encourage me. Before the *kirogi* story, I had never really written anything longer than 30 inches. My life completely changed when she was assigned to me in 2003. She actually listened to my story ideas!

This means more to a reporter than anything. Often, editors are pressed for time and will cut you off and ask you: "What do you have for tomorrow's paper?" One editor once said that I spent too much time dreaming up my own story ideas rather than taking direction from editors.

Say things like that enough times to a reporter and you kill off any creativity that newspapers need to survive the Internet age. Phyllis recognized that I had a different way of seeing neglected communities and told me to put those ideas in the paper.

And she really LISTENED. When I was in South Korea, I sent her a memo every few days about my reporting. She saved the e-mails, and a few sentences from them ended up nearly verbatim in the final version of the story. Thank God she was paying attention because I had forgotten about those e-mails.

For organizing stories, Mary Hadar, our writing coach, and Lynda Robinson, an assistant magazine editor, were great. They taught me how to write in scenes and how to pace a story.

Tell me a little bit about your own personal history and how that drives your passions and interests in the subjects you report on.

My personal background is one of contrasts, as a Vietnamese and an American, as a Southerner and as resident inside the Beltway. I was a kid who qualified for free school lunches and rarely left central North Carolina. These days, I have full passports. I think all that has helped me see issues and stories from different angles and be curious about all sorts of subjects. I appreciate absurdity and contradictions and look for them.

Initially in my career, I wasn't really interested in writing about immigrants. I didn't want to be pigeonholed. But frankly, what got me going was seeing so many inaccurate and stereotypical stories about immigrants in the media.

It reminded me of when I was growing up and people would assume certain things about me, and my family. My parents don't speak English, so I've served as their interpreter since age five. As I got older, I noticed how my parents would be treated with disrespect, as if they were toddlers, or mentally disabled. I think those experiences gave me a passion for reporting on topics and people outside the mainstream.

I didn't realize this until recently, but my parents were probably my first editors. They always asked me, "Why?"—"Why does the government do this? Why do I have to fill out this form? Why do Americans do this?" I had to constantly go and search for explanations to satisfy them. Of course, all this drove me crazy as a kid. But now I'm very grateful for these experiences. My parents helped me see the world in a different way, as both an insider and outsider.

How does your personal background affect your reporting? Does it help you get access? Does it sometimes hinder that access?

An editor once said to me, "I'm not sure you should cover immigrants full-time. Because well, you're an immigrant yourself." This person worried that I would write mainly "cheerleading" stories.

This was said to me after I had produced a portfolio of work that included a controversial story about a homicide at a Vietnamese shopping center. (A few Vietnamese-language newspapers called me a communist for writing about the incident.) I know for some people, my work will be viewed suspiciously because of my ethnicity and personal background. I'm sorry they are so narrow-minded.

My background is both a hindrance and a help, just as it is for every reporter. The fact that I'm Vietnamese can help because I can speak the language. But at the same time, Vietnamese-language newspapers have called me a traitor because I air the dirty laundry that they think should stay "in the family."

I'm not a Christian, but I've written many stories about Christianity and most of my immigrant characters are evangelicals. I'm not Hispanic or Korean but I can read as much as I can about the cultures and have other people help me.

Being a Southerner sometimes gives me a better rapport with fellow Southerners, like the Vietnam War reenactors. But other people think that my Southern accent means that I just fell off the turnip truck.

If you simply show genuine interest in a subject or a person, your background becomes more irrelevant.

You seem to have a strong affinity for children. Many of your stories seem to focus on their experience. Can you tell me more about why you're drawn to them and what you see in them?

Children are honest. They haven't learned how to "spin." They often have original, fun ways of describing things, especially when they speak half in English and half in their parents' language. And they very much want to help dumb reporters like me understand the world!

You have to report on children to find out anything about the great demographic changes in our country.

They're also one of the best entry points into a family when you're doing immersion journalism. Parents can be reluctant, but if their kids take a shine to you, then the grown-ups figure you can't be that evil. This happened in both the *kirogi* story and *The Washington Post Magazine* "opera story." I played countless "Barbie" computer games with Terry, the toddler in the Korean family. She once tangled up my hair when playing hairdresser. But I think the Kims just felt that if I was willing to put up with that stuff, I could stick around and follow them all I wanted.

Charlie B., of the opera story, begged his mother to let me come to their house for an interview. His mother did not want to be part of the story. But Charlie was excited about having a grown-up visitor and helped convince his mother.

Another overarching theme to your stories seems to be cultural identity, and how that changes over the generations, from grandparents to parents to children. What are you discovering about these identity changes?

Some identity issues are the same as during the turn of the twentieth century—the grandparents tsk-tsking over the younger generation losing their traditions, the parents upset about their kids marrying a non-Chinese or a non-Mexican.

But cultural identity is not always that straightforward these days. Boundaries have changed. There's no longer a typical assimilation process, thanks to globalization, attitudes about diversity and a critical mass presence of immigrants.

In the *kirogi* story, Hannah was as devoted to Orlando Bloom as to Korean pop stars. In the dishwasher story, there were second- and third-generation Americans, young professionals, who were still doing the dishes by hand, just as their parents taught them. If I had written the dishwasher story simply about young people converting to dishwasher use and their parents lamenting this fact, it would not have been as interesting—or accurate.

The Dishwasher Story

THOMAS HUANG: How did you sniff out a story that was under all of our noses, yet had gone unnoticed?

PHUONG LY: Some of my friends and I have had a running joke over the years about "You Know You Grew Up Immigrant If ..." We keep adding to the list. I never really thought about writing a story until this year.

At dinner parties, when I brought up the topic, everybody seemed to latch onto the dishwasher part of my list. The immigrants would talk about their families' resistance to it and the non-immigrants would talk about how they had to put up with a weird roommate's kitchen habits. A couple of my friends—non-journalists—said to me, "This would be a great story."

How did you go about finding the immigrants for the story?

I subscribe to a lot of listservs, so I sent out a bunch of queries. I also just sent e-mails to people from different immigrant groups whose business cards I had collected over the years. I spent about three weeks reporting it off and on, in between other duties. I am a real stickler about anecdotes. Each anecdote I use in a story has to mean something or reveal a different angle. I didn't want a bunch of anecdotes saying the same thing. I would send out e-mails or call people saying, "Do you know an interracial couple with dishwasher issues?" or "Know of a recent convert to dishwashers?" I talked to dozens of people. I tend to overreport.

What is the symbolism of the dishwasher for you? What larger issues did its use or non-use reveal to you?

The dishwasher was just a great vehicle to tell a cultural story.

How did you find the expert sources for the story?

I did NEXIS and Google searches for stories about dishwashers and appliances in general and came up with some names. I'm a huge fan of NEXIS and Google!

How did you discover the trends going on in India and South Korea?

I had visited South Korea for the *kirogi* story and noticed the great appliances in the department store. Except for the dishwasher, of course. The Kims, the family I wrote about, were middle-class, but they didn't use the dishwasher. Mrs. Kim nearly screamed at me when I tried to help out in the kitchen one night and piled all the dirty dishes in the dishwasher.

As for India, I did a NEXIS search on India and dishwashers and I found that funny report from the Indian government on appliance use. I think it's very important to read widely and find out if a trend is occurring in other cultures. Often, people report on a trend and say it's a Hispanic thing or an Asian thing. Sometimes, it is. But more so than not, a trend can cut across several cultures.

Was it difficult for you to discern how a specific behavior could be linked to culture?

It started when I was in college and living with white roommates and discovering, "oh, they keep their kitchens differently," and, "oh, they make their beds like this." Since then, I've tended to observe little things like that as cultural cues. I've developed a diverse group of friends, many of them non-journalists, who generously give their opinions about my observations and story ideas. Traveling widely has also helped me see similarities and differences.

When I'm visiting a family, I tend to point to things in their kitchen or living rooms and say, "Tell me about this." It helps the family relax and let down their guard and I get to learn about all these quirks in a culture.

The *Kirogi* Families Story

THOMAS HUANG: How did you come upon the *"kirogi"* families? Did you first see the school numbers reflecting the children's presence? What are your different discovery points or entry points for stories like these?

PHUONG LY: When I came to Howard County, I had expected a typical, predominantly white suburb. Most of the *Post*'s reporting from Howard County had characterized it as such. I was shocked when I saw all these Korean immigrants and Korean-owned businesses. I kept wondering what was driving people there.

At first, Koreans and non-Koreans just told me it was the county's good education system. This is what had been mentioned in a few previous stories we had written about Koreans in this county. But I knew enough about South Korea to know that it was a pretty developed, high-tech country. Middle-class people don't usually leave a first-world country. You don't get Germans immigrating here en masse to go to the public schools.

During my second meeting with an immigrant outreach coordinator for Howard County schools, who is Korean American, I kept insisting to her that the idea of middle-class Koreans coming to the United States didn't make sense. She said, "Well, you know these families don't come with the fathers—the fathers have good jobs in Korea and can't leave." Bingo. I knew I had a great story.

I did NEXIS and Google searches and found stories in the Korean press about these *kirogi* families and the pressures in the Korean schools. I also talked to reporters from the two major Korean dailies based here. From there, I started looking for a family willing to talk.

How do you help the reader care about and identify with the immigrant families? What specific steps did you take to achieve this?

As I said before, I'm not interested in writing about people as freaks. My stories are focused on universal themes. The theme here was sacrifice, what would you—as a parent—do for your child?

I don't set out to intentionally have a reader like or dislike a family. I just want to get to know my subjects, report in as much detail as possible, and let those details paint the portrait.

What reporting techniques do you use to gain access to these families and get them to open up to you?

It took me nearly a year after I heard the word *kirogi* to find a family willing to be interviewed extensively and to have their names in the paper. In fact, some of my Korean American friends and community sources told me they doubted I would ever find a family. Most Koreans don't want strangers to know about their personal life, particularly on such a controversial subject as immigration and family break-up. I got very discouraged, but my editor kept saying, "All it takes is one family to talk."

So during that year, I wrote smaller stories about the Howard County Korean community. A few stories ended up on the front page, but the majority was written for our weekly community section. I just wanted to get my name and face out in the community and widen my net of sources.

I wrote about Korean churches, a Korean retirement home, Korean newspapers, etc. Along the way, I was learning a great deal about the culture.

Finally, the immigrant outreach coordinator who had first given me the tip found a family. And by that time, I already knew a lot of people in their world. I knew where they shopped. I had visited the church where they worshipped and knew the pastor. I knew one of the kids' counselors because I met her on another story.

How do you get the broader context from overseas cultures? For example, you cited the agencies and Web sites in South Korea.

The information came from many long nights of sifting through Google and NEXIS searches. Koreans are very high-tech, and so there's a lot of good stuff on the Web. When I was in South Korea, my translator/fixer helped confirm a lot of the information.

How did you identify and select Hannah's family? Were there other candidates? What qualities do you look for in selecting a family?

The Kims were the only ones willing to have their names in the paper. I had talked to other families but they wanted anonymity. I just got lucky with the Kims.

Let's talk about immersion reporting. How much time did you spend with Hannah's family and how did you immerse yourself in their lives?

I met the family in March and followed them intensively through the spring and summer. I saw the father in South Korea in July but I had been e-mailing him previously.

During that time, I had to write other stories, but I spent a lot of my nights and weekends with the Kims. I was around so often, Mrs. Kim would automatically set out an extra dinner plate for me. A few times, she left me in the house alone with the kids when she went over to a neighbor's home.

I typed up my notes every week and reviewed them. I knew so much about them that I would correct Hannah on some things. She said she had given her mother a book for Mother's Day, and I said, "No, you gave it to her for her birthday."

Hannah kept a blog, so, with her permission, I looked on it occasionally to keep up with her life. She was really key, because she was so articulate. I also interviewed all their teachers, their grandparents, their pastor, other people in their church, their friends, etc. Most of it never made it into the story, but all the interviews helped inform me about their characters and their lives.

The Vietnamese Immigrants Story

THOMAS HUANG: How did this idea develop? Did you start by looking for a story pegged to the 30th anniversary of the fall of Saigon?

PHUONG LY: Initially, I thought I was going to write the reenactors story as the anniversary piece. However, the reenactors don't hold events until the summer, so it would have been too late for the anniversary. I had to search around for another story. It was pretty easy to find another idea because I've been writing about Vietnamese immigrants since I arrived at the *Post*. I follow a lot of the films, novels and academic journals about Vietnamese immigrants, so I'm very well versed in what's been written and what's new.

In recent years, a big theme has been about the children of war coming of age.

I happen to be 31, almost same age as the war anniversary, so I thought it would be neat to write about how this war affected people who were just children when Saigon fell.

How did you find the three women, with their lives so intertwined?

I sent out dozens of queries to sources, asking if anybody knew three people who were connected to each other, yet had different Vietnam experiences. The Vietnam story has been told so often, that one character wouldn't be interesting enough to make it a front-page story. Three intertwined people would.

When I got a press release about a reunion of Operation Baby Lift organizers and the orphans, I called up the group and asked if there was anyone living in the Washington region. There was just one person—Kara Delahunt. She happened to be a mentor to the kid of an Amerasian. And the organization happened to be run by a former "boat person." Bingo. I got lucky.

What were some of the issues you were trying to show through the three women?

So much about the Vietnam War and its aftermath has been told from the American perspective, particularly white Americans. I wanted to do an anniversary story told from a Vietnamese perspective. But I didn't want to do the clichéd, "oh, the Vietnamese immigrants have done so well in America" story.

There are a lot of nuances to the immigrant story. There's a sort of caste system in the community about how you came to the States and what year. Most non-Vietnamese don't know about this bit of dirty laundry. This is changing, though, with the younger people, and the women's stories illustrate this.

I was also intrigued by the idea of one historic event directly impacting a child. We've done so many stories about how the war has affected veterans, peace activists, politicians, etc. The three women are very different, yet their fates were sealed on that single day.

The Vietnam Reenactors Story

THOMAS HUANG: What techniques did you use to remain neutral and fair—nonjudgmental—on a pretty controversial subject?

PHUONG LY: Simple. I was just damn interested in what these guys had to say. If I was going to act judgmental, they would have stopped talking to me. Also, these guys were extremely nice. I didn't feel threatened or disrespected, so why would I have been judgmental toward them?

How did you gain the reenactors' trust?

Again, I was just interested in them. The reenactors were tickled to talk about their hobbies with a captive audience. Most of their wives and girlfriends were pretty sick of hearing about the Battle of Khe Sanh and the like.

I also think being a Southerner helped. Many of the guys at the reenactment were from North Carolina, my home state. Several of them said they expected some fancy pants, big-city reporter from *The Washington Post,* not someone who knew the location of small towns like Statesville, N.C.

How did your own ethnic background affect your ability to get the story?

Well, the leader of the communist forces wanted me to join in. They never have enough communists at these events. I had to keep saying, "No, the *Post* won't let me."

Then, he wanted to see if I could teach them Vietnamese words to use in battle. I had to break the bad news to him that my parents didn't teach me dirty words or battle terms.

And all the reenactors quickly realized that I was just ignorant, and didn't know much about the war in terms of battles and military history. After a while, they just treated me as an observer, and someone to whom they had to very patiently explain all the military jargon.

Because I'm part of the younger generation of Vietnamese Americans, I have pretty neutral feelings about whether the war was right or wrong.

Because Saigon fell, I am an American and have all the opportunities I can dream of. But if the communists hadn't won, my parents would have never had to leave their family and homeland. Many people expect me to feel one way or the other about the war. I wasn't even alive during most of it. I end up telling people, "I just don't know."

The Children's Opera Story

THOMAS HUANG: How did you hear about the story? How did you pitch it as a magazine piece?

PHUONG LY: This is actually one of the few enterprise stories that was not my idea. Lynda Robinson, a magazine editor, approached me with the idea. She had seen the *kirogi* story and wanted me to do more long stories about immigrant children.

How long did you follow the company?

I followed them from October to May, off and on. I tried to spend at least two hours a week in the classroom.

Did you feel pressure, either from yourself or your editor to find out whether the opera program was truly effective for kids' learning?

Of course. I wanted to write about the program and the kids' development, warts and all.

How did you select Charlie B. as your main character?

I was really stressed out about who would be my central character. I initially narrowed it down to four kids and Charlie B. wasn't one of them. I had reams of notes and was worried that I was going to pick a kid whose family would move by the end of the year, or a kid whose parents would refuse later to participate in the story.

It wasn't until March that I decided on Charlie B. All of sudden, he became a class leader. When I asked the teachers, they told me that Charlie's parents had been skeptical about the program but were changing their minds. I looked through my notes and realized that on the very first day that I attended, I had taken notes on this kid with a big smile. That was Charlie.

Writers' Workshop

Talking Points

1. Phuong Ly describes her personal background as both a help and a hindrance in reporting her stories. What do you think she means by that? How does her background as an immigrant help her on these stories? How could her background get in the way? Think about your own personal history. What communities can you get access to and what unusual pressures might you face?

2. Identify three scenes in the South Korean *kirogi* families story that focus on the relationships in the Kim family. What do we learn about Jungwon and Keeyeop's marriage? How do Hannah, Eugene and Terry get along with their parents? Discuss how Ly uses details and movement in these scenes to show us the family dynamics.

3. Ly says she doesn't want her stories about immigrants to be about "the others." What do you think she means by that? Search for a story about immigrants in a national publication or your local newspaper. Were the immigrants portrayed as "the others"? If so, how? If not, how was the reporter able to help readers find some connection with the immigrants?

4. Ly focuses her stories by developing a universal theme for each of them. She is often able to narrow the theme down to a few words: loss, identity, growing up. What are the universal themes in each of Ly's stories? Can you describe these themes in just a few words?

Assignment Desk

1. Ly says that she was inspired to do the dishwasher story after she and her friends developed a running joke about "You Know You Grew Up Immigrant If…" Not using the dishwasher made it onto the list—and that often drew the most interest at dinner parties. Think about an ordinary thing that you use on a daily basis, and brainstorm five feature story ideas dealing with the object. Or, alternatively, the next time you attend a party, pay attention to the topics that come up in conversation. What story ideas are prompted by these topics?

2. In the story about the South Korean *kirogi* families and the story about the children's opera, Ly sheds light on the lives of immigrant

children. To do that, she spent a lot of time with them and gained their trust, as well as that of their families. As an exercise, get permission to spend a day in a classroom or at a community center. Observe the children and talk with them. What stories can you draw out of them?

3. Ly gets many of her story ideas from community publications, Web sites, blogs, academic journals and listservs. Find a newspaper or Web site that covers an ethnic community in your city. Then read your city's daily newspaper for a week. Is the ethnic community reflected in any of the daily newspaper's coverage? If so, how do the stories compare to the stories in the ethnic publication or Web site? Brainstorm five story ideas based on what you read from the ethnic community sources.

4. As a follow-up exercise, identify a leader or interesting person in the ethnic community above. Contact the person and request an opportunity to talk about the issues that are most pressing for the community. Write a page-long essay about your experience.

The Boston Globe

Don Aucoin

Diversity Writing

20. The Discomfort Zone

JUNE 22, 2005

Before Tiffany Dufu moved from Seattle to Boston last August, some of her friends and co-workers were eager to assure her how much she would love her new city. Only in retrospect did she note that all of those singing Boston's praises were white.

There are aspects of Boston that Dufu has indeed come to love. The city's physical beauty lifts her spirits as she runs along the Charles River. She is intrigued by the way Boston's idiosyncratic neighborhoods make her feel that she is "being absorbed by something larger than myself." On a personal level, she has liked many of the Bostonians she has met; on a professional level, she feels she has grown.

But as an African-American woman, Dufu is also troubled by some of what she has seen and heard in the Boston area. So troubled, in fact, that she is far from sure she will stay here when she and her husband, Kojo, start a family. "I'll be really candid and say that as long as it was just Kojo and I, I'd be fine with it," she says. "But I have concerns about raising my black children in Boston. This would be a tough place for me to have a family."

In many respects, Tiffany Dufu is exactly the sort of young professional Boston should want to attract. She is 31, smart, friendly and so intent on broadening her horizons that she spends several nights a week at lectures and cultural events. In her role as a fund-raiser for Simmons College, Dufu is plugged in to the vital academic heart of the city. With her zest for networking and her civic-mindedness (she periodically volunteers at a homeless shelter), Dufu could be a role model for the upwardly mobile women at Simmons who may eventually make their own contributions to Boston's future.

Tiffany Dufu (left) talks with Tad Heuer, who is also new to Boston, outside the pub Solas. (Photograph courtesy of Jonathan Wiggs/*The Boston Globe*)

So why is she so uncertain that her own future lies in Boston? The answers are complex. Dufu readily admits that she has not personally experienced overt racial discrimination in Boston. But she nonetheless feels a persistent unease about the city's racial climate. It stems from her day-to-day observations and interactions, a mosaic of moments and events—some small, some not so small—that, to her, add up to a worrisome portrait.

"Boston is just so ..." Dufu pauses. "Under the surface," she finishes. Another pause. "And yet it's so blatant, so obvious."

Dufu has a nuanced take on Boston race relations that is delivered not with anger, but with honest perplexity. Her views echo the findings of a report released in April by the Civil Rights Project at Harvard University, which found there are "high levels of perceived discrimination among minority groups" in the Boston area and that racial intolerance and inequality have "taken new forms." That report cited a poll conducted last October in which 80 percent of African-American respondents and half of Hispanics called racial discrimination in the Boston area a "somewhat or very serious problem." The report also noted that "Perceptions of racial discrimination can affect the decisions of talented minorities within the region to stay or to leave."

Those words could describe Dufu (who did not participate in the poll). As a newcomer, she can't help comparing Boston with Seattle, where she lived for a decade. Why, she wonders, are interracial couples so much more scarce in Boston, where nearly one-quarter of the population is black, whereas in Seattle, such couples were "a dime a dozen," even though the black population is only 8 percent? "It's quite a mixed city, and I did not think of it that way till I came to Boston," she says.

So many questions swirl around her new life in this new city. Why is she so often the only black woman in the room when she attends a networking event? Why do so few Bostonians seem to have friends across racial lines, in sharp contrast to Seattle? Why did so many people warn her against living in certain Boston neighborhoods (accentuating their "danger") that all turned out to comprise mostly black residents?

"The places where they didn't want me to live were probably the places where people like me lived," she says. "I'm not afraid of those people. Those are my cousins. Those are my aunties." (She and her husband rented an apartment in Cambridge to be close to MIT's Sloan School of Management, where he is working toward an MBA.) Or, conversely, why have some Bostonians warned her against going to certain white neighborhoods? And why are Boston neighborhoods always identified in terms of race, anyway? "In Seattle, there are distinct communities, but it's not necessarily based on race," says Dufu.

Dufu found it jarring that a white woman whom she had just met felt comfortable confiding, "Oh, I just love bald black men," without seeing the objectification inherent in that remark.

She was flat-out stunned when a list of "The 100 People Who Run This Town" in last month's issue of *Boston* magazine contained only one black person. (It was the Rev. Eugene Rivers, listed at No. 97.) "I'm looking at the list and I'm going, come on, you've got to be kidding me," says Dufu. "Either this can't be true, or this *is* true and this place is in big trouble. How can the civic leadership tolerate that?"

Perhaps most troubling of all to Dufu was the Pop Warner controversy this month that exposed yet another racial gulf in the Boston area. Citing the hard-hitting approach to football practiced by urban players, "intimidating" rap music featured at some Boston fields, and what they say are safety issues at some city fields, five suburban Pop Warner teams opted to leave a youth football conference that includes players from Roxbury, Dorchester, and Mattapan. To Dufu, it confirmed her growing sense that this region, or at least the adults in this region, tend to build walls between black and white.

"That is heavy. That is so loaded," she says, her voice rising. "I wanted to say to them: 'Did it occur to you that that is someone else's child, and if that place is not safe for your child, it may not be safe for their child, and they have to live there? Can't you see that your child could learn something from that child?' How could they just say no?"

The Pop Warner episode reverberated deep within Dufu because it got her thinking about what her children's lives would be like in the Boston area. Would she want to raise them in a mostly black neighborhood, gaining the benefits of a strong racial identity but possibly being shortchanged in terms of resources? Or would she want to raise them in the suburbs, thereby gaining access to more resources but possibly encountering people who, in her words, "may reflect their stereotypes onto my children"? Seeing Boston-area race relations through the eyes of her prospective children added a disconcerting new layer to her experience in this city.

This question is crucial, because family is of utmost importance to her. She grew up in Tacoma, Wash., the older of two children, both girls. Her father became a minister and an elementary school counselor after a stint in the Army; her mother was a homemaker for many years before becoming a social worker. The family had little money, but her parents instilled in both girls a deep sense of racial pride and reach-for-the-skies ambition. "If you believe it, you can achieve it," her father used to say to her.

Dufu achieved quite a bit. A stellar student in high school, she was accepted at Spelman College in Atlanta, a historically black women's college. After one enjoyable year there, though, she switched to the University of Washington to ease the financial strain on her parents (who had divorced when she was 16). She majored in English and reveled in reading Shakespeare, Faulkner, Baldwin, Bellow, and Sonia Sanchez. She joined a black sorority and participated in efforts to pressure the college administration to hire more black faculty.

One day, a classmate introduced her to Kojo Dufu, an engineering major from Ghana who was working as a residential assistant in her dorm. The two would marry two years after she graduated.

Intent on becoming a high school teacher, Dufu received a master's degree in English from the University of Washington. But she started to chafe at graduate school life; she wanted to get out in the world and work for causes that were important to her. So she began working for a nonprofit foundation, honing her marketing and public-relations skills. She was offered a job as a fund-raiser for a girls' middle school that sought to do battle against all the "isms" (racism, sexism, ageism) except idealism. Though she had never done any fund-raising, Dufu said yes. It was just the kind of mission she was looking for.

"I know that my life's work is advancing women and girls in the world," she says. She went on to spearhead a drive that raised nearly $2 million for the school in 18 months. The same ambition prompted her last year to cross the country to come to Simmons, a women's college.

During her year in Atlanta and her decade in Seattle, she grew used to seeing a lot of casual interactions among people from all ethnic groups and income levels. It disappoints her that she does not see many of those kinds of interactions in Boston. Fundamentally, she does not believe that Boston is honest about race, instead preferring to submerge tensions beneath a veneer of niceties and pieties.

"When you talk about diversity, they tend to tense up here," says Dufu. In Seattle, she says, people of other ethnic groups would challenge her in an argument, whereas "Here, people are too afraid of being perceived as racist, so they close up."

Dufu also discerns a more subtle level in which race seemingly comes into play in Boston: namely in the city's obsession with class. She is startled by how often people ask her not just what she does for a living, but what her parents do for a living. "I had never experienced class the way I experienced it in Boston," she says.

One episode was simultaneously baffling, wounding, amusing, and revealing. At a professional networking event, a woman regaled Dufu with a tale of a childhood friend who had five children and lived near her mother. The woman's tone of voice implied there was something wrong with both those facts. Then the woman bitingly observed that despite her early promise, the friend "ended up going to a state school." As a graduate of the University of Washington, Dufu was jolted by that strange locution—"ended up."

"That was the first time it dawned on me that I am not part of some upper echelon, because I didn't go to Harvard or Yale or MIT," says Dufu. Back home, she had felt like a success, having received both a bachelor's and a master's degree in English. "Then I come here, and I find there's a crop that's creamier," she says with a bemused laugh.

Her education in the byzantine ways of Boston continues, both good and bad. She worries that the region's stratospheric real estate costs amount to a kind of invisible racial barrier. She wonders why the media don't find more room amid copious crime coverage for stories on the "heroes" of the black community. She is surprised that some Bostonians still seem bitter about the court-ordered busing to achieve desegregation in the 1970s.

But she greatly enjoyed Black History Month in February because she got to absorb firsthand how much significant black history was made in

Boston. "Here, I don't have to just read about Crispus Attucks," she says, referring to the black man who was the first victim of the Boston Massacre. "I can go to the place where Crispus Attucks fell."

On a daily basis, Tiffany Dufu wrestles with the paradoxes of this city that she wants to understand, wants to learn to love, to call home. She has many good days on that score. But then she will walk down the street and notice how segregated the city seems on so many levels. And she will wonder again if her future lies in Boston.

"It's just so deeply rooted that it's almost paralyzing," she says. "At the same time that Boston represents liberty, represents democracy, it also represents the sore. I think it's a tough thing to deal with. And I don't know if people are prepared to do the work to make it better."

Lessons Learned

BY DON AUCOIN

Except for a few years in Connecticut, I have lived in the Boston area my entire life (and I have the thick-as-clam-chowdah accent to prove it).

It's no secret that race and class are entwined in Boston. That became painfully and inescapably clear in the mid-1970s, when the city was convulsed by violent protests over court-ordered busing to desegregate the public schools.

Still, when I sat down with Tiffany Dufu to discuss her view of Boston's racial climate, I was struck by how frequently our conversations detoured into the subject of class.

Thirty years after the busing crisis, a young African-American newcomer to Boston was telling me that her perception of the city's racial climate was not necessarily shaped by large, wrenching events like that. That it was not necessarily shaped by overt instances of discrimination. But rather, it was shaped by small, snapshot moments that, on the surface, did not seem to be about race at all.

Why, Tiffany asked me with a puzzled expression on her face, did so many Bostonians ask her what her parents did for a living? Why did they seem so intent on learning where she went to college? And why, once they learned she had gone to a "state school," did they sometimes react with ill-concealed disdain?

I might have been tempted to dismiss such attitudes as mere elitism, as half-amusing, half-annoying relics of the city's Brahmin-dominated past. To Tiffany, though, those insistent questions about her background revealed a troubling dimension of Boston.

To her, such questions grew out of a complacent assumption that the deck was stacked FOR some, and AGAINST others, from an early age. And that it was simply a matter of sorting out the winners and losers.

To her, the questioners were tacitly endorsing an ethos of exclusion that could only hurt African-Americans. Even Boston's insane housing costs struck her not just as a matter of economics, but as a tear in the social fabric. It created a kind of *de facto* segregation that impedes African-American entry into the middle class.

The take-away lesson from my conversations with Tiffany was that the old paradigm for understanding race is no longer sufficient; and that the truest portrait of race in Boston today cannot always be captured in bold strokes.

Sometimes, it requires a carefully constructed miniature, a single story that is a piece of the larger story. So I needed to subtly weave the theme of class through my story to reflect the new, more nuanced reality of race in Boston. Once an open wound, it was now partly submerged within what has been called "the hidden injuries of class."

But there were so many facets of Tiffany's life to cover, and she was so insightful on so many aspects of race relations, that I didn't devote as much space to the issue of class as I wanted to. When I embarked on my second story for the *Globe*'s series on race, I made sure to raise the subject during my interview of Raymond and Idella Johnson, an African-American couple who had left Boston for North Carolina.

Sure enough, their concerns about Boston's class striations had been a factor in their decision to move. They faced the prospect of an unwelcome trade-off: To get their three children a top-notch education, they felt, they would have to move to the suburbs, which meant their children might then feel isolated in an overwhelmingly white environment.

The nut graf of my story noted that "for this African-American couple, there was a hidden cost of living in the Boston area that had nothing to do with housing, or taxes, or insurance. That hidden cost had to do with Boston's most intractable problem: race. And it was further inflamed by Boston's enduring obsession: class."

Thanks to the online afterlife that newspaper stories have nowadays, I was able to learn another indelible lesson from my work on the race series: Namely, that readers care more deeply about this issue, and respond more personally to it, than almost any other.

The *Globe*'s Web site, Boston.com, had set up a message board where readers could post responses to our stories. The Tiffany Dufu story triggered an absolute avalanche of reader reaction. Hundreds of readers went online to put in their two cents worth on the message board. I've been told that it was the largest outpouring on Boston.com for any story that wasn't related to the Red Sox. In addition, I personally received more than 100 emails that constituted some of the best reader reaction I've ever had—and some of the worst.

There were some ugly e-mails and postings that attacked Tiffany with thinly veiled (or not veiled at all) racism. I took some predictable heat as well, with some emailers accusing me of pursuing an agenda driven by "political correctness." But there were also critics who made thoughtful arguments that my story was going to saddle Boston with a reputation it no longer deserves.

Most touching to me were e-mailers and letter-writers who responded with personal stories rather than polemics. Some African-American Bostonians told me that by tracing the long but elusive shadow cast by racism, my story had put into words the truth of their own lives. Some white Bostonians told me that the story had made them determined to examine their own behavior, and their own hearts.

That's when I knew my story had made a difference, which is what it's all about.

Don Aucoin is a reporter for The Boston Globe's *Living/Arts section. He was a Nieman Fellow at Harvard University in 2000–2001. In 2003, Aucoin shared in a Taylor Family Award for Fairness in Newspapers for a series (co-authored with Bella English) about a Catholic parish's attempts to come to grips with the clergy sex abuse crisis. In 1997, he won second place in the profiles category of the Sunday Magazine Editors Association Awards for "An Ordinary Life," a story about a developmentally disabled man's struggle to live independently in the community.*

Argus Leader

▮ Finalist

Steve Young

Diversity Writing

21. Will We Ever Get Along?

DEC. 25, 2005

Two young girls—one white, one black—shuffle across the playground at Sioux Falls' Terry Redlin Elementary their first day of fourth grade and tentatively seek each other out.

Jazzmyn Rolle and Muna Osman are acquaintances but not quite friends, having never shared the same classroom in all their years at the school.

But now surrounded by hundreds of noisy, freshly scrubbed school-children, the two 9-year-olds—different in ways both obvious and subtle—discover that they have a common denominator. They're going to have the same teacher. So they begin to talk. They begin to laugh. They begin to connect as they pass through the shadows of the tether ball poles.

Jazzmyn is the color of northern Europe; Muna, of Africa. Jazzmyn goes to Sunday School. Muna attends a mosque. Jazzmyn's genealogy runs deep into the Dakota prairie. Muna's parents were born in Ethiopia. All of which is irrelevant to two schoolgirls as they chirp beneath a brilliant August sun. They neither know nor seem to care that they represent the hope of a state which, under the prodding of then Gov. George Mickelson, embarked 15 years ago on a century of trying to realize a racial Utopia among its people.

The only thing that matters to them is that they are about to become good friends.

* * *

In Sioux City Falls, the chances that two kids of different skin colors will meet, become friends, go roller-skating together, chat on the phone

Muna Osman (left) and Jazzmyn Rolle play at recess at Terry Redlin Elementary. The two girls' friendship will face challenges as they make the transition to middle school. Growth in the city's minority population has meant challenges in striving for racial harmony. (Photograph courtesy of Stuart Villanueva/*Argus Leader*)

together or sleep at each other's house have increased dramatically since Mickelson's declaration.

In 1992, minority students accounted for 6.3 percent of the Sioux Falls' public school population, according to district statistics. Today—fueled by refugee resettlement and the secondary migration of refugees from other parts of the country—18 percent of the 19,600 students in kindergarten through 12th grade are minorities. That's more than 3,500 children.

It's no surprise then that lanky, blonde-haired Jazzmyn Rolle and shy Muna Osman with her black braids discover one another in a Sioux Falls elementary school where the enrollment is one-third minorities.

"We just started talking one day," Muna explains of how her friendship with Jazzmyn began.

"We knew who each other was, but we were not really friends," Jazzmyn says. "But we were so bored, we just started talking…like at recess."

And what did they talk about?

"About how bored we were, probably," Muna says.

* * *

Becoming friends is easy. Remaining friends in a community relatively new to cultural diversity is the challenge for Jazzmyn and Muna.

A black girl and her white friend shooting baskets together would have been an oddity on most school playgrounds during South Dakota's first century. Except for towns bordering the state's Indian reservations, and places such as Sioux Falls and Rapid City with significant Native American populations, children's faces tended to reflect northern European ancestry.

Of course, every now and then, a child of color ended up in an all-white classroom. It still happens. And maybe they fit in all right. Maybe they are broadly accepted by the majority.

Still there are some, particularly in the counseling profession, who worry about the psychological effect on a child who has to dismiss the color of his or her skin just to fit in.

Will white South Dakota society invite Indian and Hispanic and black kids to its children's birthday parties and sleepovers? And just as important, will that same white society allow them to take its daughters to the prom?

Jazzmyn and Muna are fortunate. Unlike most South Dakotans older than 30, they live in a time and place where their classroom is filled with so many faces of different colors that no one person sticks out.

"I never think about being different," Muna says. "It's good to be different. If everyone was the same, it would be torture."

* * *

What Jazzmyn and Muna understand better than many adults in South Dakota is that culture and ethnicity are not prerequisites for friendship.

In elementary school, it's not nearly that complicated.

Instead, connections are made when two children sit next to each other in class. They start playing at recess. They eat lunch together each day. And when things get really serious, they call each other on the telephone.

That and a basketball are how Jazzmyn and Muna became friends.

"Our sisters played basketball together," Jazzmyn says. "And sometimes we'd shoot hoops. I mean, I like basketball. I've played it since second grade. So I wanted her to play."

"She just wanted to bug me," Muna says. "She bugs me all the time."

"No I don't," Jazzmyn says. "I was just trying to get her to do stuff."

That "stuff"—particularly outside of school—became part of the glue that bound them together. And that's important if friendships are going to last.

When children are bused into a school and live in different neighborhoods, as they often are in Sioux Falls, nurturing a friendship out of school becomes all the more difficult.

If parents are new to the country, are just learning the language and haven't developed the English skills to, say, take a driver's test, they can't transport their fourth-grader to a friend's house to play. If those same parents work odd hours, sleepovers and get-togethers don't happen. And of course, if parents aren't open to the mixing of cultures and religions, then a friendship can wither quickly, too.

Again, Jazzmyn and Muna are lucky. They live within six blocks of each other in their neighborhood near Whittier Middle School. They can ride a bicycle to one another's house. They have siblings who are acquainted with each other.

Becoming friends is going to be easy for them.

* * *

Staying friends is indeed the challenge, especially as they move through fourth and fifth grades, into middle school and beyond.

The tides of change will sweep them in new directions. They will develop other friendships, perhaps join other cliques. Their interests will change. And as they grow older, these two friends of different colors might find themselves bombarded by the forces of racism, of classmates and peers who aren't as accepting of differences in skin tone, accents or beliefs.

The question becomes: If their physical friendship doesn't survive for whatever reason, will they retain for the rest of their lives the lessons learned from having known each other once upon a time? Will their intellect embrace diversity? Will their spirit condemn racism?

On a sunny August morning, on their first day of fourth grade at Terry Redlin Elementary, Jazzmyn Rolle and Muna Osman don't have the foggiest notion about all that. Nor do they care.

They're too busy laughing. They're too busy being silly.

To be honest, they're just too busy becoming friends.

Lessons Learned

BY STEVE YOUNG

One of the greatest tools any journalist can use—at any stage of his or her career—is the good work of others.

So I read good writers whenever I can. I study their use of words. I pick apart their narratives. I marvel at their wonderful turn of a phrase.

That appreciation for good writing led me to a conversation three years ago with an outstanding journalist: Ken Fuson of *The Des Moines Register.*

Ken had written an award-winning story on two fourth-grade girls at a Catholic school in Des Moines. One was white. The other, African. As we talked, I told Ken that it seemed to me that finding such a friendship in Sioux Falls would be a good way to tell our readers about the growing diversity in our community.

With his encouragement, I embarked on an effort not to replicate his efforts. But it took patience to find a friendship that could provide the framework for a larger discussion about a community whose minority population in its public schools had gone from 6 to 18 percent in the last 15 years.

From the day I started, until the last installment of the eight-day series ran, took three years. My first mistake was thinking that school district administrators and principals could help me identify the friendships I sought. I should have started with the teachers and custodians who ultimately helped me find two girls—one white, one black—who became friends as fourth-graders.

It required an understanding that I didn't need to find "best friends," but simply "good friends." I wanted to write about children who talked on the phone, and slept at each other's houses on Friday nights, and shared their most intimate secrets.

But I also came to learn that children's interests change. They can grow apart. That doesn't mean they forget the lessons learned from friendship.

Finally, it needed perspective. It required a broadening of voices to show that even though bigotry may be diminishing in our community because of diverse children growing up together in classrooms and neighborhoods, racism still exists in Sioux Falls. Talking to teachers, parents, counselors, and high school students of various cultures reinforced that reality. And in so doing, it made that single friendship we wrote about a shining example of the possibilities that exist for racial acceptance and harmony in Sioux Falls.

Steve Young, a projects and general assignment reporter for the (Sioux Falls, S.D.) Argus Leader, *began working at the newspaper in 1981. In Sioux Falls, he has covered sports, religion, county government, Native American issues and corrections and has been a city columnist. He won back-to-back year-end awards for outstanding achievement in writing from Gannett in 1999 and 2000 and was recognized in May 2002 as one of 10 Gannett journalists honored for outstanding achievements during 25 years of Best of Gannett contests.*

PART 4

Commentary/
Column Writing

Nicholas D. Kristof
Commentary/Column Writing

Nicholas D. Kristof cares about the international issues that many journalists rarely, if ever, focus on: genocide, sex trafficking, malaria, AIDS and the challenges women face in the developing world.

He uses his position as a columnist for *The New York Times* to cast a spotlight on such topics. He hopes that by doing so he will raise the visibility of those topics on the international agenda—and thereby convince fellow journalists of their newsworthiness.

Getting people to care about these issues would be a journalistic legacy he would be thrilled to leave. He has been hard at work at such a legacy throughout his career at the *Times.* He started there in 1984 as a 25-year-old business and economics reporter. His reportorial stints include business correspondent *Times'* Los Angeles business bureau, Hong Kong bureau chief, Beijing bureau chief and Tokyo bureau chief. He also served as an associate managing editor in charge of Sunday editions.

While Kristof enjoyed reporting and editing, he harbored an interest in becoming a columnist. But he wondered whether he would be able to realize his ambition at the *Times.* He specialized in international issues at a newspaper that already had a columnist, Thomas Friedman, who was addressing foreign affairs.

Then the 9/11 attacks happened, Kristof says, and the *Times* decided it could feature another voice on the opinion page focusing on international issues. They chose him.

His columns, which focus on injustices and struggles against disease and genocide in developing countries, won him the Best Newspaper Writing award for Commentary for 2005. Judges cited his clarity, precision and strength. The award joins a long list of other awards Kristof has amassed, including a Pulitzer Prize, a George Polk award, an Overseas Press Club award, a Michael Kelly award and an Online News Association award.

The transition from reporter to columnist turned out to be harder than Kristof expected. "Being fair is deeply ingrained into any good reporter," Kristof says, "and then I became a columnist and suddenly found that I was expected, in a sense, to be unfair—or at least to take sides and emphasize one side of an argument."

Kristof uses his reporting skills to clarify points he wants to make. He infuses his columns—about issues he feels a passion for—with information he hopes will help readers learn something. "I believe that journalism should be about adding to the pot, not just stirring it," he says.

The ingredients he adds to the pot make a difference to the people he writes about and to the people who read him.

—Aly Colón

22. When Rapists Walk Free

MARCH 5, 2005

By Nicholas D. Kristof

One of the gutsiest people on earth is Mukhtaran Bibi. And after this week, she'll need that courage just to survive.

Mukhtaran, a tall, slim young woman who never attended school as a child, lives in a poor and remote village in the Punjab area of Pakistan. As part of a village dispute in 2002, a tribal council decided to punish her family by sentencing her to be gang-raped. She begged and cried, but four of her neighbors immediately stripped her and carried out the sentence. Then her tormenters made her walk home naked while her father tried to shield her from the eyes of 300 villagers.

Mukhtaran was meant to be so shamed that she would commit suicide. But in a society where women are supposed to be soft and helpless, she proved indescribably tough, and she found the courage to live. She demanded the prosecution of her attackers, and six were sent to death row.

She received $8,300 in compensation and used it to start two schools in the village, one for boys and one for girls, because she feels that education is the best way to change attitudes like those that led to the attack on her. Illiterate herself, she then enrolled in her own elementary school.

I visited Mukhtaran in her village in September and wrote a column about her. Readers responded with an avalanche of mail, including 1,300 donations for Mukhtaran totaling $133,000.

The money arrived just in time, for Mukhtaran's schools had run out of funds. She had sold her family's cow to keep them open because she believes so passionately in the redemptive power of education.

Now that cash from readers has put the schools on a sound financial footing again. And Mercy Corps, a first-rate American aid group already active in Pakistan, has agreed to assist Mukhtaran in spending the money wisely. The next step will be to start an ambulance service for the area so sick or injured villagers can get to a hospital.

Down the road, Mukhtaran says, she will try to start her own aid group to battle honor killings. And even though she lives in a remote village without electricity, she has galvanized her supporters to launch a Web site: www.mukhtarmai.com. (Although her legal name is Mukhtaran Bibi, she is known in the Pakistani press by a variant, Mukhtar Mai.)

Until two days ago, she was thriving. Then—disaster.

A Pakistani court overturned the death sentences of all six men convicted in the attack on her and ordered five of them freed. They are her neighbors and will be living alongside her. Mukhtaran was in the courthouse and collapsed in tears, fearful of the risk this brings to her family.

"Yes, there is danger," she said by telephone afterward. "We are afraid for our lives, but we will face whatever fate brings for us."

Mukhtaran, not the kind of woman to squander money on herself by flying, even when she has access to $133,000, took an exhausting 12-hour bus ride to Islamabad yesterday to appeal to the Supreme Court. Mercy Corps will help keep her in a safe location, and those donations from readers may keep her alive for the time being. But for the long term, Mukhtaran has always said she wants to stay in her village, whatever the risk, because that's where she can make the most difference.

I had planned to be in Pakistan this week to write a follow-up column about Mukhtaran. But after a month's wait, the Pakistani government has refused to give me a visa, presumably out of fear that I would write more about Pakistani nuclear peddling. (Hmm, a good idea...)

Mukhtaran's life illuminates what will be the central moral challenge of this century, the brutality that is the lot of so many women and girls in poor countries. For starters, because of inattention to maternal health, a woman dies in childbirth in the developing world every minute.

In Pakistan, if a woman reports a rape, four Muslim men must generally act as witnesses before she can prove her case. Otherwise, she risks being charged with fornication or adultery—and suffering a public whipping and long imprisonment.

Mukhtaran is a hero. She suffered what in her society was the most extreme shame imaginable—and emerged as a symbol of virtue. She has taken a sordid story of perennial poverty, gang rape and judicial brutality and inspired us with her faith in the power of education—and her hope.

23. A Policy of Rape

JUNE 5, 2005

By Nicholas D. Kristof

NYALA, Sudan—All countries have rapes, of course. But here in the refugee shantytowns of Darfur, the horrific stories that young women whisper are not of random criminality, but of a systematic campaign of rape to terrorize civilians and drive them from "Arab lands"—a policy of rape.

One measure of the international community's hypocrisy is that the world is barely bothering to protest. More than two years after the genocide in Darfur began, the women of Kalma Camp—a teeming squatter's camp of 110,000 people driven from their burned villages—still face the risk of gang rape every single day as they go out looking for firewood.

Nemat, a 21-year-old, told me that she left the camp with three friends to get firewood to cook with. In the early afternoon a group of men in uniforms caught and gang-raped her.

"They said, 'You are black people. We want to wipe you out,' " Nemat recalled. After the attack, Nemat was too injured to walk, but her relatives found her and carried her back to camp on a donkey.

A neighbor, Toma, 34, said she heard similar comments from seven men in police uniforms who raped her. "They said, 'We want to finish you people off,' " she recalled.

Sometimes the women simply vanish. A young mother named Asha cried as she told how she and her four sisters were chased down by a Janjaweed militia; she escaped but all her sisters were caught.

"To this day, I don't know if they are alive or dead," she sobbed. Then she acknowledged that she had another reason for grief: a Janjaweed militia had also murdered her husband 23 days earlier.

Gang rape is terrifying anywhere, but particularly so here. Women who are raped here are often ostracized for life, even forced to build their own huts and live by themselves. In addition, most girls in Darfur undergo an extreme form of genital cutting called infibulation that often ends with a midwife stitching the vagina shut with a thread made of wild thorns. This stitching and the scar tissue make sexual assault a particularly violent act, and the resulting injuries increase the risk of H.I.V. transmission.

Sudan has refused to allow aid groups to bring into Darfur more rape kits that include medication that reduces the risk of infection from H.I.V.

The government has also imprisoned rape victims who became pregnant, for adultery. Even those who simply seek medical help are harassed and humiliated.

On March 26, a 17-year-old student named Hawa went to a French-run clinic in Kalma and reported that she had been raped. A French midwife examined her and confirmed that she was bleeding and had been raped.

But an informer in the clinic alerted the police, who barged in and—over the determined protests of two Frenchwomen—carried Hawa off to a police hospital, where she was chained to a cot by one leg and one arm. A doctor there declared that she had not been raped after all, and Hawa was then imprisoned for a couple of days. The authorities are now proposing that she be charged with submitting false information.

The attacks are sometimes purely about humiliation. Some women are raped with sticks that tear apart their insides, leaving them constantly trickling urine. One Sudanese woman working for a European aid organization was raped with a bayonet.

Doctors Without Borders issued an excellent report in March noting that it alone treated almost 500 rapes in a four-and-a-half-month period. Sudan finally reacted to the report a few days ago—by arresting an Englishman and a Dutchman working for Doctors Without Borders.

Those women who spoke to me risked arrest and lifelong shame by telling their stories. Their courage should be an inspiration to us—and above all, to President Bush—to speak out. Mr. Bush finally let the word Darfur pass his lips on Wednesday, after 142 days of silence, but only during a photo op. Such silence amounts to acquiescence, for this policy of rape flourishes only because it is ignored.

I'm still chilled by the matter-of-fact explanation I received as to why it is women who collect firewood, even though they're the ones who are raped. The reason is an indication of how utterly we are failing the people of Darfur, two years into the first genocide of the 21st century.

"It's simple," one woman here explained. "When the men go out, they're killed. The women are only raped."

24. Mr. Bush, This Is Pro-Life?

OCT. 23, 2005

By Nicholas D. Kristof

ZINDER, Niger—When I walked into the maternity hospital here, I wished that President Bush were with me.

A 37-year-old woman was lying on a stretcher, groaning from labor pains and wracked by convulsions. She was losing her eyesight and seemed about to slip into a coma from eclampsia, a complication of pregnancy that kills 50,000 women a year in the developing world. Beneath her, cockroaches skittered across the floor.

"We're just calling for her husband," said Dr. Obende Kayode, an obstetrician. "When he provides the drugs and surgical materials, we can do the operation," a Caesarean section.

Dr. Kayode explained that before any surgery can begin, the patient or family members must pay $42 for a surgical kit with bandages, surgical thread and antibiotics.

In this case, the woman—a mother of six named Ramatou Issoufou—was lucky. Her husband was able to round up the sum quickly, without having to sell any goats. Moreover, this maternity hospital had been equipped by the U.N. Population Fund—and that's why I wished Mr. Bush were with me. Last month, Mr. Bush again withheld all U.S. funds from the U.N. Population Fund.

The Population Fund promotes modern contraception, which is practiced by only 4 percent of women in Niger, and safe childbirth. But it has the money to assist only a few areas of Niger, and Mrs. Issoufou was blessed to live in one of them.

Nurses wheeled her into the operating theater, scrubbed her belly and administered a spinal anesthetic. Then Dr. Kayode cut open her abdomen and reached inside to pull out a healthy 6-pound, 6-ounce boy....

After removing the placenta, Dr. Kayode stitched up Mrs. Issoufou. Her convulsions passed, and it was clear that she and the baby would survive. For all the criticism heaped on the U.N., these were two more lives saved by the U.N. Population Fund—no thanks to the Bush administration.

Even when they don't die, mothers often suffer horrific childbirth injuries. In the town of Goure, a 20-year-old woman named Fathi Ali was lying listlessly on a cot, leaking urine. After she was in labor for three days, her mother and her aunt had put her on a camel and led her 40 miles across the desert to a clinic—but midway in the journey the baby was stillborn and she suffered a fistula, an internal injury that leaves her incontinent.

Village women are the least powerful people on earth. That's why more than 500,000 women die every year worldwide in pregnancy—and why we in the West should focus more aid on preventing such deaths in poor countries.

Mr. Bush and other conservatives have blocked funds for the U.N. Population Fund because they're concerned about its involvement in China. They're right to be appalled by forced sterilizations and abortions in China, and they have the best of intentions. But they're wrong to blame the Population Fund, which has been pushing China to ease the coercion— and in any case the solution isn't to let African women die. (Two American women have started a wonderful grass-roots organization that seeks to make up for the Bush cuts with private donations; its Web site is www.34millionfriends.org.)

After watching Dr. Kayode save the life of Mrs. Issoufou and her baby, I was ready to drop out of journalism and sign up for medical school. But places like Niger need not just doctors, but resources.

Pregnant women die constantly here because they can't afford treatment costing just a few dollars. Sometimes the doctors and nurses reach into their own pockets to help a patient, but they can't do so every time.

"It depends on the mood," Dr. Kayode said. "If the [staff] feel they can't pay out again, then you just wait and watch. And sometimes she dies."

A few days earlier, a pregnant woman had arrived with a dangerously high blood pressure of 250 over 130; it was her 12th pregnancy. Dr. Kayode prescribed a medicine called Clonidine for the hypertension, but she did not have the $13 to buy it. Nor could she afford $42 for a Caesarean that she needed.

During childbirth, right here in this hospital, she hemorrhaged and bled to death.

Somewhere in the world, a pregnant woman dies like that about once a minute, often leaving a handful of orphans behind. Call me naïve, but I think that if Mr. Bush came here and saw women dying as a consequence of his confused policy, he would relent. This can't be what he wants—or what America stands for.

25. Never Again, Again?

NOV. 20, 2005

By Nicholas D. Kristof

TAMA, Sudan—So who killed 2-year-old Zahra Abdullah for belonging to the Fur tribe?

At one level, the answer is simple: The murderers were members of the janjaweed militia that stormed into this mud-brick village in the South Darfur region at dawn four weeks ago on horses, camels and trucks. Zahra's mother, Fatima Omar Adam, woke to gunfire and smoke, and knew at once what was happening.

She jumped up from her sleeping mat and put Zahra on her back, then grabbed the hands of her two older children and raced out of her thatch-roof hut with her husband.

Some of the marauders were right outside. They yanked Zahra from Ms. Fatima's back and began bludgeoning her on the ground in front of her shrieking mother and sister. Then the men began beating Ms. Fatima and the other two children, so she grabbed them and fled—and the men returned to beating the life out of Zahra.

At another level, responsibility belongs to the Sudanese government, which armed the janjaweed and gave them license to slaughter and rape members of several African tribes, including the Fur.

Then some responsibility attaches to the rebels in Darfur. They claim to be representing the tribes being ethnically cleansed, but they have been fighting each other instead of negotiating a peace with the government that would end the bloodbath.

And finally, responsibility belongs to the international community—to you and me—for acquiescing in yet another genocide.

Tama is just the latest of many hundreds of villages that have been methodically destroyed in the killing fields of Darfur over the last two years. Ms. Fatima sat on the ground and told me her story—which was confirmed by other eyewitnesses—in a dull, choked monotone, as she described her guilt at leaving her child to die.

"Zahra was on the ground, and they were beating her with sticks, but I ran away," she said. Her 4-year-old son, Adam, was also beaten badly but survived. A 9-year-old daughter, Khadija, has only minor injuries but she told me that she had constant nightmares about the janjaweed.

At least Ms. Fatima knows what happened to her daughter. A neighbor, Aisha Yagoub Abdurahman, is beside herself because she says she saw her 10-year-old son Adil carried off by the janjaweed. He is still missing, and everyone knows that the janjaweed regularly enslave children like him, using them as servants or sexual playthings. In all, 37 people were killed in Tama, and another 12 are missing.

The survivors fled five miles to another village that had been abandoned after being attacked by the janjaweed a year earlier. Now the survivors are terrified, and they surrounded me to ask for advice about how to stay alive.

None of them dared accompany me back to Tama, which is an eerie ghost town, doors hanging off hinges and pots and sandals strewn about. The only inhabitants I saw in Tama were camels, which are now using the village as a pasture—and which the villagers say belong to the janjaweed. On the road back, I saw a group of six janjaweed, one displaying his rifle.

Darfur is just the latest chapter in a sorry history of repeated inaction in the face of genocide, from that of Armenians, through the Holocaust, to the slaughter of Cambodians, Bosnians and Rwandans. If we had acted more resolutely last year, then Zahra would probably still be alive.

Attacks on villages like Tama occur regularly. Over the last week, one tribe called the Falata, backed and armed by the Sudanese government, has burned villages belonging to the Masalit tribe south of here. Dozens of bodies are said to be lying unclaimed on the ground.

President Bush, where are you? You emphasize your willingness to speak bluntly about evil, but you barely let the word Darfur pass your lips. The central lesson of the history of genocide is that the essential starting point of any response is to bellow moral outrage—but instead, Mr. President, you're whispering.

In a later column, I'll talk more specifically about actions we should take, and it's true that this is a complex mess without easy solutions. But for starters, we need a dose of moral clarity. For all the myriad complexities of Darfur, what history will remember is that this is where little girls were bashed to death in front of their parents because of their tribe—and because the world couldn't be bothered to notice.

26. What's to Be Done About Darfur? Plenty

NOV. 29, 2005

By Nicholas D. Kristof

In 1915, Woodrow Wilson turned a blind eye to the Armenian genocide. In the 1940's, Franklin Roosevelt refused to bomb the rail lines leading to Auschwitz. In 1994, Bill Clinton turned away from the slaughter in Rwanda. And in 2005, President Bush is acquiescing in the first genocide of the 21st century, in Darfur.

Mr. Bush is paralyzed for the same reasons as his predecessors. There is no great public outcry, there are no neat solutions, we already have our hands full, and it all seems rather distant and hopeless.

But Darfur is not hopeless. Here's what we should do.

First, we must pony up for the African Union security force. The single most disgraceful action the U.S. has taken was Congress's decision, with the complicity of the Bush administration, to cut out all $50 million in the current budget to help pay for the African peacekeepers in Darfur. Shame on Representative Jim Kolbe of Arizona—and the White House—for facilitating genocide.

Mr. Bush needs to find $50 million fast and get it to the peacekeepers.

Second, the U.S. needs to push for an expanded security force in Darfur. The African Union force is a good start, but it lacks sufficient troops and weaponry. The most practical solution is to "blue hat" the force, making it a U.N. peacekeeping force built around the African Union core. It needs more resources and a more robust mandate, plus contributions from NATO or at least from major countries like Canada, Germany and Japan.

Third, we should impose a no-fly zone. The U.S. should warn Sudan that if it bombs civilians, then afterward we will destroy the airplanes involved.

Fourth, the House should pass the Darfur Peace and Accountability Act. This legislation, which would apply targeted sanctions and pressure Sudan to stop the killing, passed the Senate unanimously but now faces an uphill struggle in the House.

Fifth, Mr. Bush should use the bully pulpit. He should talk about Darfur in his speeches and invite survivors to the Oval Office. He should wear a green "Save Darfur" bracelet—or how about getting a Darfur lawn sign for the White House? (Both are available, along with ideas for action, from www.savedarfur.org.) He can call Hosni Mubarak and other Arab and African leaders and ask them to visit Darfur. He can call on China to stop underwriting this genocide.

Sixth, President Bush and Kofi Annan should jointly appoint a special envoy to negotiate with tribal sheiks. Colin Powell or James Baker III would be ideal in working with the sheiks and other parties to hammer out a peace deal. The envoy would choose a Sudanese chief of staff like Dr. Mudawi Ibrahim Adam, a leading Sudanese human rights activist who has been pushing just such a plan with the help of Human Rights First.

So far, peace negotiations have failed because they center on two groups that are partly composed of recalcitrant thugs: the government and the increasingly splintered rebels. But Darfur has a traditional system of conflict resolution based on tribal sheiks, and it's crucial to bring those sheiks into the process.

Ordinary readers can push for all these moves. Before he died, Senator Paul Simon said that if only 100 people in each Congressional district had demanded a stop to the Rwandan genocide, that effort would have generated a determination to stop it. But Americans didn't write such letters to their members of Congress then, and they're not writing them now.

Finding the right policy tools to confront genocide is an excruciating challenge, but it's not the biggest problem. The hardest thing to find is the political will.

For all my criticisms of Mr. Bush, he has sent tons of humanitarian aid, and his deputy secretary of state, Robert Zoellick, has traveled to Darfur four times this year. But far more needs to be done.

As Simon Deng, a Sudanese activist living in the U.S., puts it: "Tell me why we have Milosevic and Saddam Hussein on trial for their crimes, but we do nothing in Sudan. Why not just let all the war criminals go. ...When it comes to black people being slaughtered, do we look the other way?"

Put aside for a moment the question of whether Mr. Bush misled the nation on W.M.D. in Iraq. It's just as important to ask whether he was truthful when he declared in his second inaugural address, "All who live in tyranny and hopelessness can know: the United States will not ignore your oppression, or excuse your oppressors."

Mr. Bush, so far that has been a ringing falsehood—but, please, make it true.

This short column fulfills a number of the moral purposes of journalism: to mobilize citizens; to comfort the afflicted; to act as a watchdog guarding against corruption, cruelty and abuse of power.

When Rapists Walk Free

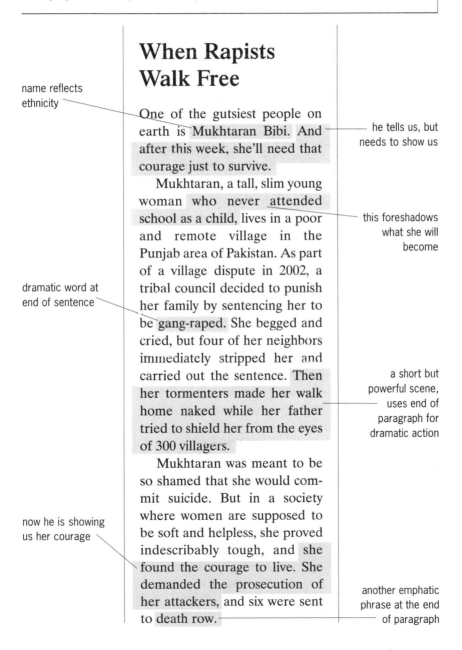

name reflects ethnicity

One of the gutsiest people on earth is Mukhtaran Bibi. And after this week, she'll need that courage just to survive.

he tells us, but needs to show us

Mukhtaran, a tall, slim young woman who never attended school as a child, lives in a poor and remote village in the Punjab area of Pakistan. As part of a village dispute in 2002, a tribal council decided to punish her family by sentencing her to be gang-raped. She begged and cried, but four of her neighbors immediately stripped her and carried out the sentence. Then her tormenters made her walk home naked while her father tried to shield her from the eyes of 300 villagers.

this foreshadows what she will become

dramatic word at end of sentence

a short but powerful scene, uses end of paragraph for dramatic action

Mukhtaran was meant to be so shamed that she would commit suicide. But in a society where women are supposed to be soft and helpless, she proved indescribably tough, and she found the courage to live. She demanded the prosecution of her attackers, and six were sent to death row.

now he is showing us her courage

another emphatic phrase at the end of paragraph

suddenly the columnist becomes a character; offers eyewitness credibility

She received $8,300 in compensation and used it to start two schools in the village, one for boys and one for girls, because she feels that education is the best way to change attitudes like those that led to the attack on her. Illiterate herself, she then enrolled in her own elementary school.

closes a circle of meaning

I visited Mukhtaran in her village in September and wrote a column about her. Readers responded with an avalanche of mail, including 1,300 donations for Mukhtaran totaling $133,000.

reflects power of the press and generosity of the public

The money arrived just in time, for Mukhtaran's schools had run out of funds. She had sold her family's cow to keep them open because she believes so passionately in the redemptive power of education.

author takes us from the bottom of the ladder of abstraction…

…to the top

Now that cash from readers has put the schools on a sound financial footing again. And Mercy Corps, a first-rate American aid group already active in Pakistan, has agreed to assist Mukhtaran in spending the money wisely. The next step will be to start an ambulance service for the area so sick or injured villagers can get to a hospital.

reflects her movement from victim to survivor to advocate

wonderful word pairing— 'galvanized' comes from electrical engineering— look it up!

Down the road, Mukhtaran says, she will try to start her own aid group to battle honor killings. And even though she lives in a remote village without electricity, she has galvanized her supporters to launch a Web site: www.mukhtarmai.com. (Although her legal name is Mukhtaran Bibi, she is known in the Pakistani press by a variant, Mukhtar Mai.)

story complication comes in the middle

Until two days ago, she was thriving. Then—disaster.

A Pakistani court overturned the death sentences of all six men convicted in the attack on her and ordered five of them freed. They are her neighbors and will be living alongside her. Mukhtaran was in the courthouse and collapsed in tears, fearful of the risk this brings to her family.

short sentences in a short paragraph for dramatic effect

quote used to reaffirm her courage

"Yes, there is danger," she said by telephone afterward. "We are afraid for our lives, but we will face whatever fate brings for us."

Mukhtaran, not the kind of woman to squander money on herself by flying, even when she has access to $133,000, took an exhausting 12-hour bus ride to Islamabad yesterday to appeal to the Supreme Court. Mercy Corps will help keep her in a safe location, and those donations from readers may keep her alive for the time being. But for the long term, Mukhtaran has always said she wants to stay in her village, whatever the risk, because that's where she can make the most difference.

nothing comes easy for her

great word— makes me think of exhaust fumes

another expression of the power of the press

I had planned to be in Pakistan this week to write a follow-

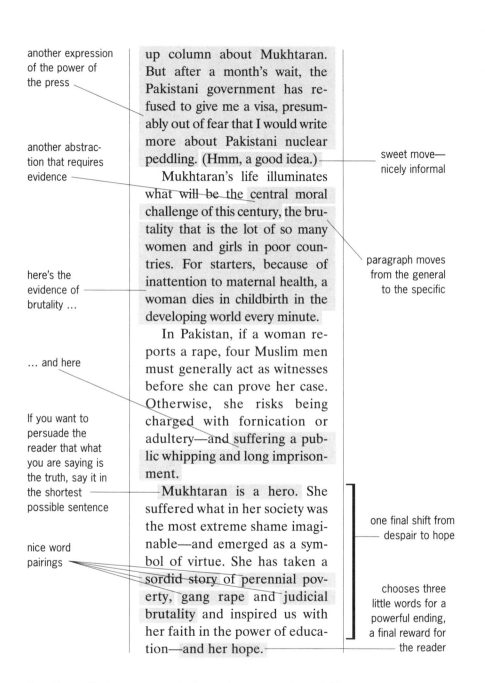

another expression of the power of the press

another abstraction that requires evidence

here's the evidence of brutality ...

... and here

If you want to persuade the reader that what you are saying is the truth, say it in the shortest possible sentence

nice word pairings

up column about Mukhtaran. But after a month's wait, the Pakistani government has refused to give me a visa, presumably out of fear that I would write more about Pakistani nuclear peddling. (Hmm, a good idea.)

Mukhtaran's life illuminates what will be the central moral challenge of this century, the brutality that is the lot of so many women and girls in poor countries. For starters, because of inattention to maternal health, a woman dies in childbirth in the developing world every minute.

In Pakistan, if a woman reports a rape, four Muslim men must generally act as witnesses before she can prove her case. Otherwise, she risks being charged with fornication or adultery—and suffering a public whipping and long imprisonment.

Mukhtaran is a hero. She suffered what in her society was the most extreme shame imaginable—and emerged as a symbol of virtue. She has taken a sordid story of perennial poverty, gang rape and judicial brutality and inspired us with her faith in the power of education—and her hope.

sweet move— nicely informal

paragraph moves from the general to the specific

one final shift from despair to hope

chooses three little words for a powerful ending, a final reward for the reader

Roy Peter Clark is senior scholar and vice president of The Poynter Institute.

A conversation with
Nicholas D. Kristof

An edited e-mail interview conducted by Poynter Institute faculty member Aly Colón with Nicholas D. Kristof, winner of the ASNE commentary/column writing award.

ALY COLÓN: Where do the ideas for your columns come from?

NICHOLAS D. KRISTOF: I read everything, and file away tidbits—both in my head and in file cabinets. I'm looking for areas where I'm not just going to pontificate but where I can add reporting and a perspective to an issue. Ideally, I like to be unpredictable and counterintuitive. But that doesn't always work. I've been hammering away on Darfur for two years now, and on that subject every reader knows exactly what I'm going to say.

What prompted you to write about international issues?

I spent most of my reporting career as a foreign correspondent, so it seemed natural to address issues I knew a little about. And in general, my readers tend to know less about international issues than domestic ones. So I figure a column often has more value added if it's about some international topic.

You travel to places often ignored by the news media. How do you decide where to go?

One of the things that has surprised me since becoming a columnist is how rarely columns seem to change minds. I had assumed that op-eds have an amazing persuasive power, but in general, I think we change few people's minds on any issue that they've thought at all about. When they start out agreeing with a column, they think it's brilliant. And when they start out disagreeing, they think it completely misses the point. So we tend to be far more effective at confirming people's judgments than at making them question them.

On the other hand, I've found that columns can have a real power in putting an issue on the agenda, or forcing readers to wrestle with an issue that they haven't thought about at all.

So increasingly I see the power of a column less in persuasiveness and more as a spotlight to force people to examine an issue or a crisis. That's why I go to places like Darfur. And that's why I write about issues like sex trafficking.

More fundamentally, I think we in the news business already do a great job of covering what happens on any given day. But our weakness tends to be covering things that happen every day, or those that dribble along very slowly. Malaria, for example, kills about 2 million people a year and is a major reason why Africa is so poor—but we tend to see it as the backdrop, rather than as something to write about it. So I try to figure out ways of putting those forgotten issues onto the agenda.

The places you go to are hard to reach, and journalists often may not be welcome there. How do you obtain access to these places, and the people?

I spend a ton of time trying to get visas, and acting smarmy to unpleasant people. Saddam Hussein's Iraq gave me a visa because I made myself a fixture at its embassy at the U.N. Likewise, I hounded the North Koreans for years to get my visa. Iranians gave me a visa when I found the right intermediary, after spending a lot of time with the wrong ones. Now I spend my time figuring out ways into Sudan—and when I can't get a visa, I sneak in illegally from Chad.

Frankly, it's a pain to spend so much time on the logistics of getting to remote places, but that also makes the columns more compelling. There isn't a lot of reporting from places like North Korea, Iran or Darfur, and that makes reports from those places all the more valuable.

I'm also more willing to take risks to cover a story like Darfur, which I don't think is being adequately covered and where my reports can make a real difference, than to cover Iraq, where lots of reporters are already providing great coverage and I'm not so sure that I'll have anything much to add.

What steps do you take in collecting the information you need before you go somewhere and after you arrive?

As a foreign correspondent, I was always suspicious of pundits who bounced into the country in which I was living, without speaking the language or knowing the culture, talked to a small number of people, and then bounced out again with firm ideas about what to do.

Now I find myself in the same position. The Chinese have a saying, *"qing ting dian shui,"* describing how a dragonfly flits across the surface of the water, and that's exactly what columnists do. We're flighty.

To address that problem, I do lots of research ahead of time. I read books, articles, reports and talk to people. I try to figure out ahead of time where in the country I want to go and who I want to talk to—while staying ready to toss all those plans out in a moment if necessary. And the last step is to remember that I'm still a *"qing ting dian shui."*

Your columns uncover injustices, or suggest solutions to injustices. What draws you to such themes?

I sometimes feel a bit of a fraud as an opinion columnist, because I'm not naturally an incredibly opinionated person. At a dinner party, I'm not the one raging about this or that, but usually the person who replies by saying that it's more complicated than that. I like nuance, but unfortunately, nuance and wishy-washy views don't make for strong columns. So I tend to lean to issues I do feel strongly about, which tend to involve injustice and, especially, neglected injustices where attention can make a difference.

How do you organize your columns?

When I first joined the *Times,* as a 25-year-old business/economics reporter, I would take the subway in to work each morning. And I would watch other subway riders read the paper—they would get to my article, scan the headline, and then—if I was lucky—they would read the first paragraph or two.

If that top didn't grab them, they would move on. I'd want to shake them, and say, "Hey, I've got a hell of an anecdote in the 13th graf." But those riders made a great focus group. They taught me that you need to work exceptionally hard on the headline and the first few sentences. I also try to imagine readers who are on a swaying, loud subway and listening for the announcement of the next station—in other words, distracted by a million things.

So I work hard to make columns as reader-friendly as possible. That doesn't mean talking down to readers, but it means working hard to find just the right anecdote or top. And then I try to tell a story, where possible. A thousand years ago, I would have been a minstrel; now I'm a storyteller in a different medium.

How do you decide what your lead will be?

I search desperately hard for something that will captivate the reader and tug him or her along.

How do you determine what your ending will be?

Ideally, I'll have some plot twist, or something that will refer back to the opening and tie it up nicely. But I don't believe in recipes for columns, and so often the ending just writes itself or convinces me that it belongs there. If you've got great reporting, how you shape it matters less.

In "When Rapists Walk Free," you use a narrative approach. In "What's to Be Done about Darfur? Plenty," you use a prescriptive approach. How do you decide the writing technique that works best for each column?

I like narratives. My sense is that readers aren't very interested in 300,000 people suffering from genocide, but that they can be tremendously moved by the story of one person—particularly a person who doesn't just suffer but is also inspiring. So I often try to use one person's story as a window into a larger problem.

The story I've written about that readers have found most compelling is that of Mukhtaran Bibi, a.k.a. Mukhtar Mai, a Pakistani rape victim who has fought back and started schools to fight the chauvinism and brutality that she suffered from.

Mukhtaran is an amazing woman, and I've been privileged to tell her story. Now she's famous, received at the White House, and the subject of several documentaries and movies. But that was all there already. It just took somebody to bring her case to public attention.

On the other hand, prescriptive columns never attract as much interest, but I like to mix the topics up and add variety. And, particularly in Darfur, I have strong feelings about what needs to be done. I don't like to spend my column always complaining and carping. So when I have suggestions that seem practical, I build a column around them.

In some of your columns, you employ a twist in the narrative that surprises the reader and drills deeper. In "Never Again, Again?" you spotlight a woman whose sisters disappeared. Then you add another nugget of information about her husband that drives your point even further. Is this a conscious writing technique to make your point even more strongly? Or is it a function of following the narrative you're writing about as you witness it?

It's both. I try to surprise readers, and that means that column writing is sometimes more like magazine writing—telling a narrative—than like an inverted-pyramid news story. And, frankly, I like layers and nuances, even if readers don't always.

Some of your columns contain very vivid, graphic descriptions. In "A Policy of Rape," you write: "Some women are raped with sticks that tear apart their insides, leaving them constantly trickling urine." How do you decide how graphic the writing needs to be to convey the message you want in your column?

I'm not a believer in euphemisms. When horrible things happen, I believe in generally writing about those horrible things. And when the problem is that Americans are tuning out a problem like genocide in Darfur, then I'm willing to be pretty graphic in an attempt to grab their attention and get them to act on it.

In general, American newspapers are still pretty timid about matters of sex, much more so than other media out there. And I think that we're right not to be gratuitously salacious. But frankly there are a lot of important policy topics that have to do with sex, and I'm impatient with the idea that we should pull back from some areas because of their content.

Beginning in 2002, I began writing about obstetric fistulas, a routine problem in the third world, but one that is pretty graphic. In the past, they never got much attention because it's hard to have a tasteful discussion of fistulas, but it's much better to be tasteless and graphic than to ignore an issue. The same applies to condoms and AIDS, to sex trafficking, and to rape and violence as they fit into genocide.

Details play a role in how you craft your column. In "Mr. Bush, This Is Pro-Life?" you give the readers information about the ages of people, the number of people affected, and even the weight of a newborn. But you go even further. You focus on one specific woman. You tell us her blood pressure, the name and price of the medicine she needs and the cost of the operation that could save her life. Why do you gather such details and how do you think they help the story?

Readers don't care about issues or classes of people, unless they can visualize a particular person. And the way to build empathy and to help readers visualize an individual is to provide that detail. I'm also a big believer in photos for the same reason. But I can't get them on to the op-ed page that often.

How do you go about deciding who the sources will be for a story?

I talk to everyone, with a special bias toward people in the field. When I go to a country, I'm wary of just talking to officials in the capital. I strongly believe in getting out to the countryside and talking to young people and uneducated people as well. I also try to talk to people who take an opposite view to make sure I understand the counter-arguments of what I'm urging.

In "A Policy of Rape," you mention some women by first name only. One woman was not named. What do you take into account when it comes to identifying, or not identifying, your sources?

I try to use names whenever possible. In that case, though, the women who spoke to me were at risk of being arrested for defamation and for adultery, since they acknowledged having sex but could not provide four eyewitnesses to the rape.

So I agonized over what to do. In the end, I chose to use first names but not mention hometowns, or other identifying information. In a camp of 80,000 people, I figured that would protect them. I was right. None got into trouble.

So I believe in full names and detail to make a better column. But there's one thing more important than having a good column, and that is not getting sources in trouble.

How many drafts do you do when you write your column?

I write and rewrite and rewrite. I spend much longer rewriting than writing.

Do you make revisions after you've sent the column to your editor but before it's finally published?

Yes, but not many. At that point, most of the changes are to make the column fit the space.

What role does your editor play in your column writing?

At the *Times,* there's not much editing of columns. There's a strong belief that the columns should have their own voice and should be the author's own product. So my columns are read by a copy editor who makes sure the column fits the space and raises any grammatical issues and the like, but there's not much formal editing. As a result, I tend to seek a lot of informal editing. I show drafts to my wife, Sheryl WuDunn, and to my researcher, and to my parents, and to others, and get their feedback.

What role do you believe a columnist plays in a newspaper?

A columnist should help readers wrap their minds around policy questions and offer some guidance about what's important. There's so much noise out there, so ideally columnists can help readers focus on what's important.

Tone plays a crucial role in how a columnist communicates with the reader. How do you craft your writing so it's strong but not a screed?

I wrestle with that question, and I'm not sure I've figured it out. When I began the column, Tom Friedman told me that he sees *Times* columnists as being in the lighting business, not the heating business, and I sure agree with that. But I also see that columns that are all interpretation and nuance, frankly, often aren't as interesting as table-thumpers. I'm still learning how to navigate the question of tone.

Your columns deal with complicated topics. What do you do to keep your writing clear, simple and precise?

This is another challenge that I haven't quite figured out. I believe in wrestling with serious and complicated topics—in science, for example—and it can be tough to tell these stories in ways that aren't boring. Recently, I did a column on positive feedback loops in climate change. Now that's immensely important, but it's not going to sell papers.

When I do write about a topic that is intrinsically complicated, I search extra hard for a vehicle or anecdote that can lure the reader along. Unfortunately, it doesn't always work.

What columnists, or writers, do you admire and what have you learned from them?

Years ago, when I was a university student in Britain, the *Guardian* had a columnist named Victor Zorza who wrote about India through the prism of one little village. It was masterful, and it sure taught me the importance of microcosms to tell a larger story.

At the *Times,* I've also had the benefit of watching some real pros in action, like Clyde Haberman and Tom Friedman, and to be edited by the best in the business, like Joe Lelyveld and Bill Keller—not to mention my wife.

How would you advise a journalist who wants to be columnist? What kind of skill, talent, drive and disposition does such a job require?

The hard part isn't coming up with opinions. It's coming up with reporting that sustains opinions that are fresh and well-informed. So I think persevering in the essential journalism skills—reporting and writing, all accurately—is the best background.

A conversation about CONVERGENCE with Nicholas D. Kristof and Naka Nathaniel

Two edited interviews conducted by The Poynter Institute's Bill Mitchell: the first, an e-mail interview with Nicholas D. Kristof, winner of the ASNE commentary/column writing award; the second, a telephone interview with Kristof's New York Times *collaborator, multimedia producer Naka Nathaniel.*

The heart of Nicholas D. Kristof's column on the op-ed page of *The New York Times* beats far more visibly in his reporting than in his opinions. A master of showing rather than telling, Kristof relies heavily on the converged tools of multimedia to move readers beyond the printed page to the spot on the globe reflected in the datelines atop his columns. His main collaborator in that initiative is multimedia producer Naka Nathaniel, who is based in Paris for the *Times*.

Poynter Online editor Bill Mitchell e-mailed questions to both journalists about their converged work. Kristof responded by e-mail "while bouncing over a road in rural Pakistan." Nathaniel spoke by telephone from his Paris apartment, shortly after he returned from his trip to Pakistan with Kristof.

The impact of their converged efforts is reflected in an e-mail sent to the *Times* by Joan Blanusa, a student at Harvard's Graduate School of Education:

> I regularly read Kristof's columns, and am particularly interested in his reports from Darfur. The columns themselves get to me, emotionally and intellectually, and inspired my work. The videos combined with his essays, however, are even more powerful by bringing 'to life' the very issues and horrors he describes. Thank you for this combination.

What follows is an edited transcript of Mitchell's e-mail exchange with Kristof.

BILL MITCHELL: What were some of the turning points in your development as a Web-enabled journalist?

NICHOLAS D. KRISTOF: My interest in Web reporting grew out of two concerns. First, as a foreign correspondent, I had long noticed that articles with photos had much more impact than those without. But in the column, I normally was stuck just with print, and I missed the bond that photos can make with readers. So I've experimented with occasionally using photos in the column, but I also saw that Web features were another way of making that link.

Secondly, newspapers generally have an aging audience, and so I thought Web features would be the best avenue for cultivating younger readers and luring them into the world of my column and the issues I care about.

Can you point us to some of your earliest uses of e-mail or the Web in your reporting? What interested you about the results?

With the Iraq war, I began to collaborate with Naka Nathaniel on Web reports. Then we decided to travel together in the fall of 2003 to do a Web feature from the Arctic National Wildlife Refuge. That had a huge audience, because lots of people had firm views on the refuge—without necessarily having a clear idea of what it looked like on the ground.

The other thing I've done periodically is to invite readers to contribute. For example, I had a "Name That War Contest," in which I asked readers to send in suggestions for a name for the Iraq War. And I had a poetry contest, in which readers sent in poems about the war. They were a fair amount of work, because so many entries came in, and I wanted to verify everything that I used. But I also think they're useful for building a two-way street with readers.

What's surprised you about your recent work on the Web? What are some of the problems, or challenges, that you and your colleagues are facing with your work on the Web?

The main tradeoff is that it takes longer if we're shooting video and taking pictures. I believe in traveling very nimbly and lightly and covering ground fast. And it definitely slows us down when we need to stop and record things.

The other tradeoff is the presence of a camera. In Iran, for example, we got detained a couple of times in part because our video camera stood out and was so visible.

Can you tell us a bit about the transition from *Kristof Responds,* your former home on www.nytimes.com, to *On the Ground*? What are the key changes?

The main change is simply that now it's behind the (subscription) wall so fewer people see it. I don't know the traffic numbers...Clearly many fewer people see the multimedia work since the introduction of TimesSelect. That's particularly true in places like China or Pakistan, and among university students. So that does mean somewhat less impact now than before.

How did you and your colleagues arrive at your current approach to reader comments?

I try to put questions of general interest on *On the Ground.* But it varies a good deal with how busy I am during a particular week. I'd be open to posting comments—in general it's good to be more interactive—but there was a sense that our old forums were not terribly successful.

What Web work of yours generates the most reader response?

Darfur stuff has generated a fair amount of reaction, but I'd say that anything about politics, or Bush, still generates the most.

Your online discussion about Ann Curry of NBC and Bill O'Reilly of FOX departs from some of the journalistic traditions of ignoring competitors and critics. What prompts you to get into such topics? What's the reaction been like from readers and colleagues?

I raised the issue of TV coverage in July '05 because it seemed to me that one of the main reasons for the world's failure in addressing Darfur was that TV had missed the story. And that if we in the media claim certain privilege, we also have to show certain responsibilities—and covering genocide is one of them. That led me to hound the TV networks to cover Darfur, and then to hound Bill O'Reilly. The reaction has been varied, but I don't have any doubts that it's a fair topic. The media are part of the world we need to cover, and it would be odd to cover business and science and culture but not the TV networks.

Can you discuss the role that online interactivity plays in linking your roles as a journalist and an activist? What lessons learned might you share with local columnists just beginning to incorporate online interactivity into their work?

One lesson is that it's not as easy as it looks. It does take extra time. And I'm always concerned that the extra time I devote to multimedia doesn't come at the expense of my printed column. But another is that especially for stories with some emotional resonance, or about people whom readers can't quite visualize, photos and video make issues come alive. My columns about Cambodian sex slaves were hard-hitting, but they never came close to the emotional impact of watching those girls on video as they told their own stories.

And if the aim of journalism is to inform and give readers a feel of a place, then video does that better than print. It's one thing to try to explain the Arctic, another to show it.

* * *

What follows are edited excerpts of a telephone conversation with Naka Nathaniel, based on the notes Mitchell typed during their interview.

BILL MITCHELL: What's the response been like to your multimedia work with Nick Kristof?

NAKA NATHANIEL: It's been tremendous. I just spoke with a bunch of students from Northwestern. I showed them my computer and they loved going through my (e-mail) inbox. It provides total validation of why I would hope most people become journalists—making a difference with the audience. It's so easily reflected whenever Nick does a piece. People tell us that they are emotionally moved by it. Other people are moved to take action.

What are some of the key lessons learned that you think might have relevance for journalists just beginning to add audio, video and interactivity to their work?

Be prepared to tell a smaller story to make a bigger point. Be prepared to zero in on one person's story...We would like to tell winding, half-hour stories, but we have to be realistic and produce stories with short chapters. We have to come up with a way to get people in and out of the story within three or four minutes.

How has your work changed now that Nick's columns and your multimedia work are accessible only to subscribers to TimesSelect?

We are dealing with a much different audience, meaning a smaller audience, and we're trying to find ways to connect. We're doing more to engage people at a one-to-one level.

Did you see the inclusion of the NBC "Dateline" crew on your latest trip as one way to compensate for some of your lost audience?

Yes. We're looking at different and creative ways to expand the audience. I've been doing shared blogs with universities—I take a class along (virtually, via online correspondence) and I blog about what Nick and I are doing.

How do you bring readers into the story?

I think about a reader with a nice warm cup of coffee next to the computer, sitting in a nice comfortable chair. Sometimes readers need to be jostled free from the comfortable life that so many *Times* readers are able to lead. Nick is excellent at doing that. This is a different sort of journalism from 20 or 30 years ago when a foreign correspondent would visit the prime minister for the official view instead of talking with people and getting a much deeper understanding of what's going on around you.

* * *

Nathaniel followed up by e-mail with a description of the tools he carries and how he puts them to use.

NAKA NATHANIEL: The nice thing about the gear is that it's getting lighter and easier to use.

The hardware is toted around in a Lowe photo backpack that was last weighed at 13 kilos (about 29 pounds). Inside the back pocket is a 15-inch Mac G4 Powerbook. The biggest item in the main cabin of the bag is a Sony PD150 MiniDV cam. In the surrounding compartments are a wireless microphone system, a wide-angle lens for the camera, a shotgun microphone, batteries, tapes, 40-gig external hard drive and cables of all sizes and shapes. The top flap holds notebooks.

If the trip is to a developing country, then out comes the Pelican case with the RBGAN satellite hook-up, a minidisc recorder with a Sennheiser mic, a small, small light kit, a power strip, blank DVDs and the chargers. I carry an ugly green duffel bag from the Gap that my wife, Meredith, bought when she was in high school. That's where I'll stash my clothes, the tripod and a sleeping bag (if needed).

I use a half-dozen applications to create the features. All the video is constructed in Final Cut Pro, the audio is edited in Audacity and the stills are edited in Photoshop after being cataloged in iPhoto. Oftentimes, the project calls for a lot of interactivity, so out comes Flash 8. Then it's all sent to the servers in New York via an FTP program called Transmit.

After that, I use a bunch of Web-based tools to get the features on to the site. Then I check to see if the podcast feed is working by using iTunes.

What Nathaniel Carried	What Nathaniel Uses

• Lowe photo backpack
• 15-inch Mac G4 Powerbook
• Sony PD150 MiniDV cam
• wireless microphone system
• shotgun microphone
• batteries
• tapes
• 40-gig external hard drive
• cables of all sizes and
    shapes
• notebooks
• RBGAN satellite hook-up
• minidisc recorder with a
    Sennheiser mic
• small light kit
• power strip
• blank DVDs
• chargers
• tripod
	• Final Cut Pro
	• Audacity
	• Photoshop
	• iPhoto
	• Flash 8
	• Transmit
	• iTunes

Writers' Workshop

Talking Points

1. Nicholas D. Kristof engages in research and first-hand reporting before he writes a column. Review some of his columns in this book. Identify those parts that show the reader that Kristof knows what he's talking about. Discuss how the information he provides helps you understand the issues more clearly.

2. In the interview for this book, Kristof says he's a *"qing ting dian shui."* What does he mean by this? What does this imply about the work of a columnist and how a reader should read columnists?

3. Compare Kristof's writing approach in "Never Again, Again?" to that in "What's to Be Done about Darfur? Plenty." How do the writing techniques differ? Is one more effective than the other? Why?

4. Pick a local, or syndicated columnist who seems popular. Compare her, or his, column-writing approach to Kristof's approach. How are they similar? How are they different?

Assignment Desk

1. Nicholas D. Kristof makes a point of traveling to places that are off the beaten track for many journalists: Darfur, rural Pakistan, Niger. You may or may not be able to travel to such places, but think about "off-the-beaten-track" places you could visit locally or regionally. Do some research and find out if there is an unreported issue. Travel there and gather information. Report and write a passionate, opinionated column about what you find.

2. Kristof likes using a narrative approach in his columns. Write a column that uses a narrative approach to convey your point.

3. Columnists often deal with complicated topics. Kristof is known for his clarity and precision. What techniques does he use to clarify complicated issues? Find a complicated issue on your campus or in your community. Write a column that explains clearly and precisely what is going on and what you think needs to be done.

4. Vivid writing sometimes requires graphic descriptions. Find an example in Kristof's writing in which he uses graphic descriptions to help readers see the issue in a compelling manner. Describe the details that Kristof uses to create a vivid picture in the reader's mind without being offensive or obscene.

Hartford Courant.

Finalist

Helen Ubiñas
Commentary/Column Writing

27. Cowards: Look into the Eyes of Yet Another Life You've Erased

FEB. 25, 2005

You cowards who shot into that crowd of kids on Tuesday night. You should know what you did.

The kids piled into the hospital to say goodbye to Lorenzo "Morgan" Rowe because of you. Friends, girlfriends, his boys. They were sitting in the waiting room, hanging outside, crying and laughing and then going silent until finally one of them cried out. "Why?"

Why, they asked the adults around them, should we be good? You tell us to do the right thing, to stay in school and out of trouble and things will work out. But then, Morgan was good; good grades, good kid, all he was doing was walking down the street after a Weaver High School basketball game Tuesday night. And now he was dead. Why?

How do you cowards answer that? What do you say?

The mothers looked frozen in the waiting room Thursday, panicked as they talked about how it could have been any of their kids that night, about how it still could. "They're angry," one mother said, watching the teenagers in the other room. She hears them talking in corners when they think no one is listening about retribution. "Yours is coming," they say.

The problem, said another mother, is not that they're angry, but that they're not afraid. Not afraid of walking into Morgan's room. Not afraid of staring into his swollen face, at the tubes inserted into his mouth. Not afraid of dying.

That's why even after Morgan's father, Lorenzo Rowe, knew that his son was gone, that the only thing keeping his son's chest moving were the machines he was connected to, that he had to make a decision about donating his son's organs, he let the kids keep going into the room. There was a line at one point. They sat and stared as though they expected him to wake up any minute.

"It looks like he might, right?" one girl said.

But last rites had been given to him hours ago and doctors were just waiting until after midnight Thursday to wheel him into the operating room to give someone else a chance at a life you took—if his father could just sit still long enough to sign the papers.

"Five minutes, just five minutes," Lorenzo Rowe said. He wanted to drink some tea, grab a cigarette. He had been like this all day, his girlfriend, Robin Abrams, said, looking for an excuse not to have to deal with it.

"It's not fair," she said. "He was shortchanged, the world was short-changed."

In the parking garage, Rowe kept saying he was fine, but you should have been there to see the way his hands shook when he described his son, that smile he had, the one girls didn't stand a chance around. His love affair with X-Box and 50 Cent. He's thinking about playing something by him at the funeral. The quick way he picked up chess.

"He even beat me a few times," he said, laughing.

That's why the first night when doctors asked him about donating Morgan's organs, he thought they were crazy. Morgan was going to wake up. "He was going to snap out of it."

He still believed that the next day, too, when he went to see his mother, Morgan's grandmother, and she told him in that quiet way that maybe, just maybe, he should think about it. "Maybe Morgan can live through someone else."

But the swelling was down, he thought. He looked like himself, not like he had the day your bullet traveled from your gun and into the middle of his head. The bullet is still there.

And so he took one last shot, put his lips up to his son's ear and whispered, "I got your X-Box, come and get it."

But Morgan wasn't going to come and get it. And he's not going to University High School for Science & Engineering like he planned. He won't be that engineer he dreamed about being. And sometime around 7 p.m. Thursday, his father had to admit that to himself and sign the papers. "To give someone else a chance," he said, his hands still shaking.

And you, you cowards, need to know that.

Lessons Learned

BY HELEN UBIÑAS

By the time I walked into the hospital room that morning, my work as a metro columnist had already acquainted me with death.

I knew the primal screams of a mother who had just learned her son was dead. I had been ushered into the cold, dark basement of a funeral home to view the charred body of a young man who had died in a fire. I had been to so many funerals of young people who died violently in the city that I was pretty certain I had become hardened to it all.

It wasn't that I was no longer moved. It was, in fact, the theme I returned to most often in my writing. I was looking for an answer, I suppose; a way to make sense of it all. But I had been in these situations too often. So often, that I sometimes wondered if there was anything else I could offer, if any of the words I wrote could move anyone else, to anger, to horror, to action.

What, I remember thinking, am I supposed to say about a 14-year-old boy who was shot while walking home from a basketball game? He had heeded all the advice, the warnings so many parents in the city offer their kids: Go to school. Stay out of trouble. Dream.

Lorenzo "Morgan" Rowe was an honors student, a good kid. He had enough dreams for ten kids. His only mistake was walking home with the wrong friend. I can still see Lorenzo's father chain-smoking in the hospital garage, laughing when he recalled teaching his son how to play chess, crying when he realized those teaching moments were likely gone. The doctors were telling him it was time to decide if the family wanted to donate his organs.

And then, suddenly it seemed, we were in Lorenzo's hospital room and I was witnessing a father say goodbye to his son. But first, Lorenzo's father took one more try at trying to wake him up. He took one more chance at telling his boy: Listen to his Daddy. Wake up.

On the way back to the office, I found myself searching the faces of the young kids hanging out on the street corners, wondering if any of them were responsible, wishing I could drag the cowards who had killed this little boy back into that hospital room. Even if the police caught whoever did this, I remember thinking, they would never really know the destruction their actions caused. They'd never see how their bullet swelled Lorenzo's face. Or hear the way his father's voice cracked as he begged his son to come back to him. They'd never see the anguished look in his eyes when he realized his son was gone for good.

That's the problem with this kind of destruction; the people who should see it never do. So when I sat at my computer, I decided to tell them. Emotion can be a dangerous thing when you're writing—it can cloud the message, it can turn people off. But when the reality of whatever you are writing about sparks anger or sadness or, on those much too rare occasions, joy, you have to surrender to it.

So, I did.

"Do you really think those cowards read your column?" a reader challenged me. Of all the responses the column received, I remember that one best. Fact is, I'll never know if the two young men arrested for Lorenzo's death ever read my column. I've learned and come to accept that when you write, you have no control over the effect. You can only write and hope.

Helen Ubiñas is a columnist for the Hartford Courant *in Hartford, Conn. She has won many awards, including Columbia Graduate School of Journalism's "Let's Do It Better" program for outstanding newspaper storytelling on race and ethnicity. She was on the team that won the 1999 Pulitzer Prize for breaking news, and shared the 2004 Scripps Howard Foundation National Journalism Award for Public Service.*

PART 5

Editorial Writing

Mike Trimble
Editorial Writing

Mike Trimble honed his writing voice in the presence of two giants of Arkansas journalism. But when he sums up the path that led to Denton, Texas, and an award-winning seat among the men he admires, it's with a characteristically self-deprecating tone.

"I started out . . . at a daily newspaper with a circulation of 30,000," says Trimble, opinion page editor of the *Denton Record-Chronicle.* "And after 43 years of unremitting effort, I've worked my way to a 17,000-circulation paper."

His winning editorials are flavored with that sort of dry wit. When it's unleashed on scoundrels and fools—or whipped cream—it resonates with the edge you'd find in the editorials of the late Harry S. Ashmore of the *Arkansas Gazette* and the *Arkansas Democrat-Gazette*'s Paul Greenberg. And though Trimble insists he hasn't had to summon the same courage that earned Ashmore and Greenberg Pulitzer Prizes in the days of desegregation and civil rights, he does not shrink from an opinion.

Trimble was born in Bauxite, Ark., a small mining town southwest of Little Rock. He studied for two years at the University of Arkansas, joined the Army National Guard, and began his journalism career at the *Texarkana Gazette* as a reporter. Three years later, he launched an 18-year stretch with the *Arkansas Gazette,* serving as a copy editor, news reporter and columnist. He worked for seven years at the *Arkansas Times*, where he wrote an award-winning personal story about "being the worst player [on] the worst high-school football team in the history of the game."

After Trimble's seven-year stretch with the magazine, editor Jane Ramos hired him to be a reporter, then city editor of the *Pine Bluff* (Ark.) *Commercial.* He started in 1991, overlapping Greenberg there, and was gone in a year. His next two career moves are best explained in his words: "You fall in love, you follow the wife."

He married Ramos, and office rules being what they were, Trimble says, "She had to fire me." So he went to work as a state desk reporter at the *Democrat-Gazette* for the next three years. Then he followed the wife to Texas in 1994 when she got a publishing job in the small town of Weatherford. At the *Record-Chronicle,* he started as a copy editor and moved up to city editor, writing editorials on the side. After about six years, "it was decided that I wasn't fit for anything else," Trimble says. So he became a one-man editorial department, writing opinion pieces seven days a week, e-mailing the weekend pieces from home.

He writes for selfish reasons. "You write to please yourself," Trimble says. "The only judge I have is me." Maybe so. But his editorials brim with a celebration of language and common sense sure to please the reader, too.

—Keith Woods

28. Big Brother Moves in Just Down the Street

MAY 8, 2005

By Mike Trimble

We probably shouldn't worry about the Code Rangers, but we do, a little bit. The Code Rangers, if you didn't see the paper the other day, are a corps of volunteers who are going to keep their eyes on how often we cut our grass and how high we stack our garbage.

When we don't measure up, the Code Rangers will send us a little reminder in the mail. If we don't straighten up and fly right after that warning, our friendly neighborhood Code Ranger calls in the heavy artillery, the "city code officers."

We shudder to think what that might mean: the knock on the door in the dead of night; the endless interrogations ("Are you saying this isn't your rotten two-by-four, MIS-ter Anderson?"), landscaping miscreants being herded into the backs of city trucks, which will take them for "re-education" at Frenchy's Lawn Care and Gulag, or, if the offense is particularly heinous, to a device hidden in the city Service Center on Texas Street, a device known only as "The Big Chipper."

You see? We're working ourselves into a lather over this for no reason at all. All the City Council has asked residents to do is what good citizens do anyway: Keep an eye on things and drop a dime—er, a reminder—on a neighbor if something isn't quite up to snuff. The council came up with the idea last year when it approved some stricter requirements concerning grass cutting, tree trimming, junk-car displaying and the like. Because we assume the council acts only with the best of motives, we assume it believed it was simply tapping Denton's renowned well of volunteer spirit in recruiting residents to keep an eye out in their neighbors' Johnson grass and garbage piles.

We wish we could think of it in the same way, but we can't.

At best, we think of it as an amusing annoyance, in which the neighborhood Barney Fifes patrol the streets, secretly yearning for a uniform and a whistle, on the lookout for high grass and old washing-machine parts. Gotta nip it, nip it, nip it in the bud, Andy.

At worst, we can see neighborhood grudges escalating into blizzards of warning letters and the use of official power to settle personal business. We can see suspicion blooming with the azaleas, ill feeling piling up along with the old newspapers.

We think it is revealing that the city's two existing Code Rangers declined to comment on their activities for the story in the paper the other day. What would they say? What *could* they say? Would they have to appear wearing a ski mask?

Yes, we all have a stake in clean, healthy neighborhoods, and there needs to be a way to help an overtaxed code enforcement staff find out about the most egregious violations.

But it seems to us there already is a way. Anyone who sees an overgrown lawn or a clapped-out Henry J in somebody's front yard already has the power—and, we believe, the obligation—to report them to the proper city officials.

Of course, the possibility of abuse exists with individuals just as it does with the Code Rangers, but a complaint that comes from a private resident is just that—a complaint to be looked [upon] with no prejudgment of guilt or innocence. A complaint from a Code Ranger has the imprimatur of the city government right from the get-go. If the Code Ranger says your back yard's a mess, it's up to you to prove that it isn't.

If it's all the same to the City Council, we like our neighbors just fine like they are, and would rather not see any of them turned into the lawn Gestapo. We had just as soon skip this side trip to the brave new world.

29. The Governor Closes the Borders

JUNE 10, 2005

By Mike Trimble

Gov. Rick Perry has invited homosexual war veterans from Texas to move elsewhere, a statement so breathtaking in its bigotry that we thought at first that reports of it had to be incorrect.

Sadly, they were not. A quick check in newspapers and wire service Web sites confirmed that the governor had uttered the 21st-century equivalent of "Send 'em all back to Africa," and, even sadder, that he did it before an approving audience at a private Christian academy in Forth Worth.

There are a couple of circumstances that might tend to mitigate the governor's vile pronouncement:

1. It was in response to an obviously hostile question, and,

2. Perry may simply be too dumb to realize just how vile his answer sounded.

Perry had orchestrated a big campaign photo op at the Calvary Christian Academy in Fort Worth over the weekend to watch him sign legislation requiring minors to get parental permission for abortions and a proclamation putting a constitutional amendment banning gay marriage on the Texas ballot. There were several protesters on hand who objected to one or both of the measures Perry was signing, and to what they perceived as an unhealthy melding of church and state. At some point in the proceedings, someone asked Perry what he would say to a returning veteran of the Iraq war who wished to marry someone of the same sex, the unfriendly but not unreasonable implication being that a Texan who has fought for his or her country has pretty much earned the right to marry whomever he or she damn well pleases.

Perry answered thus:

"Texans have made a decision about marriage, and if there is some other state that has a more lenient view than Texas, then maybe that's a better place for them to live."

Setting aside for a moment the technicality that the people of Texas have not yet voted on this proposed amendment, let us examine the malign prejudice that is implicit in Perry's words.

There are plenty of intellectual arguments to be made for and against constitutionally defining marriage as a union between one man and one woman. They involve custom, sociology, child welfare, economics, individual liberty and a raft of other issues. Perry addressed none of them; he simply implied—strongly, in our opinion—that gay and lesbian people are not welcome in "his" Texas. Because the question was couched in terms of returning war veterans, that's the way he answered it, but his "invitation" seemed pretty general in nature: If you're gay or lesbian, don't let the door hit you on the way out.

There are some people in Texas, and everywhere else, who believe that way, and Perry seemed to be pandering to that constituency. He may well win their votes with such statements, but they do him no credit among people of good will, no matter how they feel about same-sex marriage.

We do not want our governor to be a bigot. We fervently hope he just said something stupid again. We can live with stupid.

30. Bye Bye, American Pie; Hello Whipped Topping

JULY 6, 2005

By Mike Trimble

These are the times that try men's souls. The summer soldier and the sunshine patriot will, in this crisis, shrink from the service of their country; but he that stands by it now, deserves the thanks of man and woman.
—Thomas Paine, "The Crisis," 1776

Here I stand; I can do no other. God help me. Amen.
—Martin Luther, 95 Theses of Contention, 1517

The pie-eating contest, really a whipped topping-eating contest, was the biggest dish served up in the city's rain-soaked Fourth of July Jubilee.
—Cliff Despres, *Denton Record-Chronicle,* 2005

These are indeed trying times. When a city government can plop a dollop of whipped "topping" on a paper plate and call it a "pie;" when these "pies" are then used in a "pie"-eating "contest" in which no one eats more than one "pie;" and when this "contest" is held on the Fourth of July, a day revered by all as being as American as "apple pie," well, our endurance is exhausted, as are our typing fingers and our supply of quotation marks.

For those who missed the account in Tuesday's newspaper, here is the grave situation:

As is the custom in this good town, the city government scheduled a wingding on Monday to celebrate Independence Day. It rained, forcing cancellation of the big parade and the horseshoe-pitching tournament, but spirits were still high for the pie-eating contest.

Imagine our shock upon reading our correspondent's account of the contest in Tuesday's paper and learning that contestants were asked to eat only one pie, and that the winners were determined by timing the contestants, shortest time winning.

Worst of all was what passed for pie.

Let us ponder for a moment the entire concept of a pie-eating contest: It must involve pie. A fruit pie is best, and cherry is the best of all, given its arresting, attractive color. Banana cream is OK, too, but meringue pies should be avoided, as they contain too much air, and lead to falsely impressive eating totals.

At its very least, a competition-worthy pie includes a metal pie tin, crust and a substantial filling that requires some chewing. That is to say, the pies in a pie-eating contest must be pies, not "pies."

The "pies" used Monday in the city of Denton's Fourth of July pie-eating contest were not pies at all; they were plain old plates onto which were splashed some kind of whipped "topping" that we can only assume was suitable for human consumption.

And what, may we ask, is the idea behind timing the eating of just one pie? For children, maybe this is the way to go, but a Fourth of July pie-eating contest for grownups should be an exercise in good old American gluttony, with moaning and eye-rolling and the threat of projectile vomiting. It is the American way!

This newspaper has never avoided controversial editorial positions before, and it doesn't intend to begin now. It is with faith in the right, as we see the right, that we hereby declare that if the city of Denton is going to throw a pie-eating contest, it should supply the contestants with real, honest-to-God pies. Moreover, the winners should be determined by the amount of pie they eat, not the time in which they eat it.

If the city cannot afford to buy pies, it should encourage someone to donate them. We nominate Ken Willis, the proprietor of Ruby's Diner on the Square. Willis would no doubt be more than happy to donate a couple of hundred pies to avoid being branded a cheapskate.

That is our position. Here we stand; we can do no other. God help us. Amen.

We modestly await the thanks of man and woman.

31. Ernest Wayne Dallas Jr.: Two Pictures, One Life

JULY 29, 2005

By Mike Trimble

That picture of Ernie Dallas Jr. in Thursday's paper, the one that shows him as a child in his baseball uniform, is what being an American boy is all about.

In that picture, replicated a million times each summer across this land, you can tell the young Ernie Dallas is already rehearsing how he'll pose for his rookie baseball card. He's got the stance down pat, and his uniform is perfect, from the gentle major-league roll on the bill of his cap to the batting glove on his left hand.

One senses that he is doing his best to affect a menacing batsman's stare for the camera, but he can't quite pull it off. The moment is just too perfect: The sun is shining, school is out and Ernie Dallas is playing baseball. A smile threatens to break out at any moment.

You can see that threat of a smile in the other picture of Ernie Dallas that appeared in Thursday's paper. In that one, he is in desert camo and the black beret of a United States infantryman. He is a man now, there is no doubt of that, but the young baseball player is in that picture, too—in the clear eyes and the determined set of the jaw. Just as he had been in that earlier photo, Ernie Dallas was at home in the uniform. We know that about him if we know nothing else.

It is a source of both pride and sadness in this country that children in baseball uniforms grow up to be young men and women in military uniforms, and the physical stamina, enthusiasm and team spirit they learned on the playing field is spent on battlefields and carrier decks, and cockpits and control rooms in lonely outposts the rest of us cannot pronounce.

When any of these young men and women falls in battle, we are overcome by both the sadness and the pride. When it is one of our own, the loss and the pride are doubly strong.

The fog of war still surrounds his death, but we do know that Ernie Dallas died Sunday in Baghdad when the Bradley fighting vehicle he was riding in struck an explosive device. He was one of ours, the first of Denton's sons and daughters to die in that far place, and suddenly this war is brought home to us as it has not been before.

We have all formed our opinions about this war—the politics of it, or the economics—but this is not about politics or economics today; this is about one of our sons.

When members of his family spoke of him in Thursday's paper, we all became a part of that family. We went with them to baseball games, and to activities at Fred Moore High School.

We shared his parents' pride, and, we would guess, their quiet, unspoken fears, when he announced in high school that he wanted to be a police officer, and enrolled in the Denton Police Department's Citizen Youth Academy.

We shared both emotions again upon reading of how he joined the Army in 2003, itching to help avenge the terrorist attacks on the United States in September of 2001. His anger made us proud again, and afraid again, afraid for him and all the young men and women whose anger, skill, strength and confidence are necessary to survive the deadly business of war.

And on Thursday, when we read that he had died, our fear became ineffable sadness, though our pride was undiminished.

Ernie Dallas Jr. had dreamed of a life in uniform, his family said, a life of service. He fulfilled that dream, and it is our prayer that knowing this brings a measure of peace to those who loved him, and who miss him so today.

32. The Manchurian Televangelist

NOV. 14, 2005

By Mike Trimble

The public pronouncements of the Rev. Pat Robertson have become so bizarre that responsible conservatives don't even bother to defend them anymore. Instead, they chide the press for paying any attention whatsoever to anything Robertson says, and we are forced to concede they have just about convinced us.

Robertson's latest outrage was to warn the people of Dover, Pa., that they had best not expect any help from the Almighty should they be beset in the future by fires, floods, pestilences or any other disasters of an apocalyptic nature. Should they do so, Robertson predicted, God would simply tell them to go fish.

The sin of the Doverines, a sin that surely ranks up there with those of the Sodomites and the Gomorons, was to vote from office a school board that had approved the inclusion of Intelligent Design in their schools' curricula.

Spake Robertson on his television show, *The 700 Club*: "I'd like to say to the good citizens of Dover, if there is a disaster in your area, don't turn to God. You just rejected him in your city."

This, you will remember, is the man who twice claimed to have prayed hurricanes away from the Virginia coastline and nodded like a bobble-head doll at fellow parson Jerry Falwell's assertion that Sept. 11 was God's retribution against an apostate United States, a view that happened to coincide perfectly with that of al-Qaida.

Robertson has also suggested in the past that an atomic bomb be dropped on the American State Department, that the U.S. government assassinate a leftist South American dictator and that feminism urges women to "kill their children, practice witchcraft, destroy capitalism and become lesbians."

Let us leave aside the merits of the Intelligent Design theory, which, simply put, argues that the universe is just too complicated a structure to have come about by chance. There are arguments to be made about it pro and con, but that is not our purpose today.

Our purpose is to (1) ask who made Pat Robertson the arbiter of whom God will save and whom he will condemn, and (2) point out that he shot the Intelligent Design argument square in the knee with his pronouncement.

Second point first: The proponents of Intelligent Design know that they must present their theory on a purely secular basis. Intelligent Design, they argue over and over, *is not about God.* It is *about science!* Now comes the Rev. Robertson to proclaim that God Himself is supremely cheesed off at the people of Dover, Pa., for rejecting this allegedly secular educational approach.

Does God take sides in these secular matters? What ever happened to rendering unto Caesar? How does God feel about cold fusion? How about the Designated Hitter Rule? Surely there should be some divine retribution for *that.*

First point: Pat Robertson's insistence that he speaks for God has at long last ceased to enrage us and has put him firmly in the tinfoil-hat section of the Peanut Gallery.

We knew it as soon as we heard clear-headed conservative commentators horse-laughing his Intelligent Design dithyramb along with everyone else. Some conservatives even speculated facetiously that he might be under the diabolical control of the lefties, a Manchurian preacher programmed to spout crazy stuff that makes the right look bad.

When your own side brands you a crackpot, you have pretty well slipped into the slough of irrelevance for good and all, and we don't envision commenting much about Pat Robertson in the future. He has passed into the realm of the truly whacked-out, where space flight is faked and pro wrestling is real.

Out there be dragons.

Because the editorial covers a trivial issue, the author feels free to use exaggerated language—as if it were important.

Bye Bye, American Pie; Hello Whipped Topping

"These are the times that try men's souls. The summer soldier and the sunshine patriot will, in this crisis, shrink from the service of their country; but he that stands by it now, deserves the thanks of man and woman."

—Thomas Paine, "The Crisis," 1776

the writer uses an old trick: use three items, but vary the third for effect

"Here I stand; I can do no other. God help me. Amen."

—Martin Luther, 95 Theses of Contention, 1517

"The pie-eating contest, really a whipped topping-eating contest, was the biggest dish served up in the city's rain-soaked Fourth of July Jubilee."

—Cliff Despres, *Denton Record-Chronicle*, 2005

picks up rhetoric of Thomas Paine

lots of "p" words leading to repetition of "pie"

These are indeed trying times. When a city government can plop a dollop of whipped "topping" on a paper plate and call it a "pie;" when these "pies" are then used in a "pie"-eating

quote marks used for editorial comment = "so-called"

quote marks
used for editorial
comment =
"so-called"

"contest" in which no one eats
more than one "pie;" and when
this "contest" is held on the
Fourth of July, a day revered
by all as being as American as
"apple pie," well, our endurance
is exhausted, as are our typing
fingers and our supply of quotation marks.

evocation of
patriotic themes

the writer is in
on the joke

hyperbole

For those who missed the account in Tuesday's newspaper,
here is the grave situation:

whiz-bang word

As is the custom in this good
town, the city government scheduled a wingding on Monday to
celebrate Independence Day. It
rained, forcing cancellation of the
big parade and the horseshoe-
pitching tournament, but spirits
were still high for the pie-eating
contest.

see "grave" above

Imagine our shock upon
reading our correspondent's
account of the contest in Tuesday's paper and learning that
contestants were asked to eat
only one pie, and that the winners were determined by timing
the contestants, shortest time
winning.

writer varies
length of
paragraphs—
short ones used
for emphasis

Worst of all was what passed
for pie.

Let us ponder for a moment
the entire concept of a pie-eating
contest: It must involve pie. A
fruit pie is best, and cherry is the
best of all, given its arresting,
attractive color. Banana cream
is OK, too, but meringue pies
should be avoided, as they con-

appeals to two
senses: color
and taste

tain too much air, and lead to falsely impressive eating totals.

At its very least, a competition-worthy pie includes a metal pie tin, crust and a substantial filling that requires some chewing. That is to say, the pies in a pie-eating contest must be pies, not "pies."

more sarcastic quote marks

The "pies" used Monday in the city of Denton's Fourth of July pie-eating contest were not pies at all; they were plain old plates onto which were splashed some kind of whipped "topping" that we can only assume was suitable for human consumption.

And what, may we ask, is the idea behind timing the eating of just one pie? For children, maybe this is the way to go, but a Fourth of July pie-eating contest for grownups should be an exercise in good old American gluttony, with moaning and eye-rolling and the threat of projectile vomiting. It is the American way!

abstraction, followed by three specific acts

satiric juxtaposition

This newspaper has never avoided controversial editorial positions before, and it doesn't intend to begin now. It is with faith in the right, as we see the right, that we hereby declare that if the city of Denton is going to throw a pie-eating contest, it should supply the contestants with real, honest-to-God pies. Moreover, the winners

more hype

we like diners with
vintage names

short sentences
to hammer home
the satire

should be determined by the amount of pie they eat, not the time in which they eat it.

If the city cannot afford to buy pies, it should encourage someone to donate them. We nominate Ken Willis, the proprietor of Ruby's Diner on the Square. Willis would no doubt be more than happy to donate a couple of hundred pies to avoid being branded a cheapskate.

That is our position. Here we stand; we can do no other. God help us. Amen.

We modestly await the thanks of man and woman.

calling on a higher
power to solve a
trivial problem

Roy Peter Clark is senior scholar and vice president of The Poynter Institute.

A conversation with
Mike Trimble

An edited e-mail interview conducted by Poynter Institute faculty member Keith Woods with Mike Trimble, winner of the ASNE editorial writing award.

KEITH WOODS: Your editorials carry a distinct tone that has two consistent qualities: You speak in the collective voice of "we" and "us," and you prefer folksy to formal. Over the years, how did you land on those choices?

MIKE TRIMBLE: Many papers now eschew the editorial "we," and I can see their point. It can be seen as an archaic affectation, and just a little pompous. I cling to it, though, for a couple of reasons. First, it reinforces the idea that this is the opinion, not just of a person, but of an institution—the community's newspaper. (That's the reason I also prefer unsigned editorials.) It also gives me a way to gently remind folks that what we're offering up is just an opinion ("We feel that's ridiculous.") and not a pronouncement from on high ("That's ridiculous!").

As for the style of the pieces, I guess it's like my Arkansas accent—undetectable to me but apparent to everyone else.

It's interesting to see the down-home phrase "horse-laughing" juxtaposed against a swanky word like "dithyramb," which you whip out in "The Manchurian Televangelist." What effect are you after when you do that?

Just looking for the right word. Sometimes I find it; sometimes I don't.

In "The Governor Closes the Borders," you devote a sizeable portion of the piece to background. How do you determine how much context the reader needs for each editorial?

I always try to give enough background that a reader who missed the news story will still have a pretty good idea of what I'm talking about. I also assume that our readers get their news from our paper, not from other papers or television. That's an inaccurate conceit, of course, but I don't feel guilty about indulging it.

How do you generate ideas each day?

My desk is out in the newsroom, so I'm privy to all the crosstalk that goes on during the making of the next day's newspaper. I seldom write a "spot" editorial, though, preferring to comment on stuff that has been in the paper the day before (sometimes two or three). I read the *Denton Record-Chronicle* before leaving for work every morning, looking for an editorial topic. I also read *The Wall Street Journal, The Dallas Morning News* and the Fort Worth *Star-Telegram* when I get to the office, and check out the *Austin American-Statesman* online when the legislature's in session.

As you're searching for ideas, what sorts of subjects or issues tend to capture your attention?

Anything local is grist for the mill. I am a giver of praise when I think it's due (particularly to kids who excel—or even strive—intellectually or artistically), a scold when I think a person or an institution needs it. I'm also interested in the odd and the funny.

How long does it take to write each editorial?

It varies with the amount of research I have to do and the amount of background I need to include in the piece. If I'm allowed to count research and cogitation time (please!), I'd put it at about four hours. The actual writing varies with the length of the piece and how well the juice is flowing—as little as an hour and a half; as much as three hours. (The editorials range from 360 words to about 750, with the average being about 600, I would guess.) I generally open up a blank Word document when I get in from lunch. If I'm not done by 5 p.m., I am in trouble. I certainly don't write steadily all that time; I also spend time with visitors, phone calls and consultations with reporters and editors. (Mornings are spent reading papers, editing syndicated columns and verifying and editing letters to the editor.) On weekends I write from home, and without office distractions, the editorials don't take quite as long, unless I get sucked into a digital hearts game.

How much rewriting do you do on each piece?

I "rewrite" as I go, if that counts, and I think it should. I will rewrite a sentence or a paragraph five or six times if I need to before going on to the next one. This can result in some bumps between paragraphs, so I give it a final look before sending it on.

How do you know when you've transformed a sentence or paragraph from bad to good or good to really good?

It either looks right on the screen or sounds right when I read it silently to myself.

As you're writing and rewriting, do you read aloud? If so, why?

I read aloud silently, if that makes any sense. I checked this today to make sure, and yes, I soundlessly mouth the words as I type, and again at the end of a phrase, a sentence or a paragraph that has been giving me fits. I can usually check on the rhythm of a sentence by reading it, but sometimes it takes saying it.

How does the editing process work?

Our editorial page is a one-man shop, but I get as many eyes on my pieces as I can. The publisher gets a copy, and while he doesn't line-edit it, he gives it his thumbs-up or -down. (He hasn't bounced one yet, but you never know.) The managing editor edits it closely. She leaves the editorial positions to me, but is a stickler for fairness, and she doesn't hesitate to let me know if she thinks I'm going off half-cocked. It's then read for style, accuracy and spelling by an editor on the rim of the universal desk and by the person in the slot. I've been saved from humiliation many times by an alert copy editor.

Describe the image you have of your readers.

I can't say I have an "image" of our readers, but I keep them in mind all the time. I'm not out to impress them with flowery language, but I don't want to condescend to them with simplistic statements, either.

What do you hope they'll get out of your editorials?

I hope they'll think about the issues involved. On a selfish level, I also hope they'll think it's well written and thoughtfully presented, even if they disagree with it.

Your imagery in "Big Brother Moves in Just Down the Street" is striking. It's captured in this passage: "At worst, we can see neighborhoods escalating into blizzards of warning letters. . . We can see suspicion blooming with the azaleas, ill feeling piling up along with the old newspapers." How did you come up with the verb and analogy choices you make there?

I simply visualized front yards I have known, and there they were.

The peril in imagery often lies in over-doing it with the details or missing the mark with an analogy. How does one avoid those pitfalls?

I don't know. Maybe I fall in them more often than I think.

How much original reporting do you typically do for your editorials?

None. I realize that this is the new frontier of editorial writing, but it is not what I grew up reading or writing, and I will leave it to those who can do it well. I will be dead soon, and they will inherit the earth.

In "Bye Bye, American Pie; Hello Whipped Topping," there's a punch line in nearly every sentence. How do you know when you've tried too few, just enough or too many zingers?

Once a man has made the conscious decision to write an editorial about a pie-eating contest, he is already off the high board and heading fast for a belly-buster. He might as well make as big a splash as he can.

Some writers say they know the structure of a piece like "American Pie" before they start writing, others say they discover the plot as they write. What's your method?

On some editorials, usually the more serious ones, I do know the points I want to make—sometimes even the order in which I want to make them. With a piece of editorial tap-dancing like the "Pie" opus, however, I generally just turn on the tap and see what comes out. This doesn't make it easier; it often means that a lot of backing and filling has to be done while writing the piece.

In the humor pieces, there's a fair amount of pointed—and not always gentle—sarcasm to be found ("We're working ourselves into a lather over this for no reason at all." "Out there be dragons." "We can live with stupid.") How does that tool serve you as an opinion writer?

I'm glad you brought up sarcasm and the Rick Perry piece; that's one I might want to take back for some reworking. I don't regret for a second saying that what he said was stupid, or that "we can live with stupid." What he said WAS stupid, and anyone, editorial writers included, can say something stupid. But I called him "dumb" in an earlier sentence, and I think that went over the line. I was angry when I wrote the piece, and I think that anger gave the editorial some of its power, but I wish I had that one sentence back.

Given the serious nature of "Ernest Wayne Dallas Jr.: Two Pictures, One Life," what changes did you have to make in your writing style to strike the proper tone without losing your distinctive voice?

It wasn't a conscious shifting of gears. Our town was mourning that day; that reader I don't have an image of was coping with something awful. I just said what I thought that reader needed to hear in a way that came naturally. The family was on my mind, too, of course, and I imagine that contributed to the tone of the piece.

The Rev. Pat Robertson must look to the opinion writer like a fat fish in a skinny barrel. Your editorial suggests you'll resist taking a shot at him the next time he says something outrageous. Can you?

I hope so; we will just have to see.

What lessons have you learned about the craft over time that might help students and professionals who aspire to write editorials?

I guess it's something I learned as a reporter that applies equally to writing opinion pieces: The more work I do before sitting down to write, the better the piece ends up being. I do not particularly like the fact that this is so, but I believe it is, at least for me. When I do a lot of research on an editorial—reading all the news and opinion pieces I can get my hands on, regardless of viewpoint—I ALWAYS find that the resulting piece is better than the ones I bang out off the top of my head. It's not that I use all the information, particularly; it's that it gives me a feeling of confidence about the subject. It is a good thing to know more than you write; it's dangerous as hell to write more than you know.

Once you've done your research, however, you should proceed confidently (if you are indeed confident; if you aren't, perhaps you should pick another subject). Prepare timidly; write boldly. (Yes, you will screw up sometimes following this formula, but you're going to screw up sometimes anyway. Might as well do it with élan.)

Writers' Workshop

Talking Points

1. Mike Trimble's editorials offer different ways and varying lengths for delivering context to inform the opinions he expresses. How much do you think editorial writers should expect their readers to know about a topic?

2. Notice the way Trimble shaves away ancillary issues to focus the reader's attention in some editorials. In "Ernest Wayne Dallas Jr.: Two Pictures, One Life," he tells readers to put aside "our opinions about this war," and in "The Manchurian Televangelist," he writes that debating the Intelligent Design argument "is not our purpose today." What effect does that narrowing of focus have on the editorials?

3. There's a good chance that, unless they watch TV's "Nick at Night" programs, younger readers aren't likely to catch the meaning of Trimble's imagery in the editorial about the Code Rangers, where "neighborhood Barney Fifes patrol the streets, yearning for a uniform and a whistle . . . " And some readers may miss the meaning behind the phrase "Manchurian preacher" in the Pat Robertson editorial. What do you think about making allusions to pop culture when it's a sure bet some people will get it and others won't?

Assignment Desk

1. Mike Trimble favors editorials that reveal public misbehavior or probe the humorous side of everyday life. Read your local newspaper for a week. Make a list of the stories that lend themselves to the kind of comeuppance Trimble might deliver. Write a lead for one of those editorials.

2. Trimble writes in the first-person, plural voice of "we," arguing that it's a proper voice for the unsigned opinion of the newspaper. If that's not your natural writing voice, try writing a short editorial using "we." When you're done, substitute the word "I" where you've written "we." Compare the two pieces. Write about the difference those words make in editorials.

3. In the "American Pie" editorial, Trimble uses hyperbole and faux outrage to make a point. In the "Ernest Wayne Dallas Jr." editorial, the tone is far more somber, but the effect is just as engaging. Do an X-ray reading of the two pieces. Compare the use of details, analogy, active verbs. What writing devices do the two editorials have in common? Where, beyond the seriousness of the subject, do they diverge?

The Oregonian

Finalist

Rick Attig

Editorial Writing

33. Long Hallways, Hard Steps

MARCH 20, 2005

Summary: Here's an invitation to Gov. Ted Kulongoski to visit the Oregon State Hospital and see for himself its sorry state.

Governor, it's been 30 years since you last toured the Oregon State Hospital.

You need to see it today.

Take this as an invitation, not a criticism. You clearly already understand that a mental health crisis lies behind the haunted-looking facade of the 19th-century J Building, the gray, exhausted face of Oregon's neglected hospital in Salem.

The hospital is only a mile down Center Street from your office at the Capitol. It is a pleasant walk—at least until you take your first step into an abandoned wing. Then the heavy doors clang shut. Sunlight fades. Pigeon droppings crunch beneath your shoes.

From then on, every step you take down the long, echoing hallways of the Oregon State Hospital is a hard one.

In the abandoned hospital wing, you walk past graveyards of old office furniture, a battered upright piano, a corroding X-ray machine and piles of antiquated bed pans. A pigeon carcass lies in the middle of the room on water-stained carpet.

You step warily into a cavernous communal shower plumbed with just one handle to regulate water for all. No modesty shields separate toilets still filthy from the day they were last used. Bathtubs are stuffed with old chair cushions.

Peeling, rot and decay are everywhere. The smell of mold overpowers you. Dried rodent feces crackle underfoot, along with disintegrating asbestos floor tiles and fallen ceiling plaster.

When you look out the barred windows, you see swaths of lawn cordoned off. It's to protect people on the ground from being hit by falling pieces of roofing.

You know the history, governor. A task force urged Oregon to abandon the J Building and most of the other structures at the hospital nearly 20 years ago. Instead, the state has kept pouring money and patients into this place, opening new wards in buildings that should have been torn down long ago.

The fresh layers of plaster, like the yellow smiley faces, the plastic butterflies and the cheerful murals of birds painted on the walls, can't begin to paper over the awful conditions throughout the hospital.

It doesn't get much better when you see the occupied wards.

Governor, take the 200-foot-long walk through the maximum-security ward for the most violent of the state's criminally insane. This bleak stretch of dark cells built more than a century ago is more frightening—more inhumane—than any place still in use in Oregon's prisons.

And this is called a hospital.

Peek in the attic spaces above the remodeled wards. Take a look at the white 5-gallon buckets tipped on their sides. When it rains, staff members trot upstairs to place the buckets under the leaks gushing into the hospital buildings.

Water puddles all along the several miles of spooky underground tunnels that link buildings along the 144 acres of hospital grounds. The tunnels go to an inadequately equipped central kitchen, where orderlies blast-freeze the cooked food, then ship it underground to various hospital buildings, where it is reheated and served.

Disturbing, painful images greet you around every corner. There's a large room crammed with mechanical fans—most of the hospital has no air conditioning and no insulation. The place gets sweltering hot in the summer.

A room with a pool looks so sad and stark it's impossible to imagine anyone happily splashing in the water. A small room where patients are interviewed could hardly be any more austere, containing nothing but a table, two chairs and an empty water pitcher.

A soda machine stands in one corner of the hospital, the happy portrait of people guzzling Coke weirdly juxtaposed against the razor wire atop a security fence.

The newest building on the hospital grounds is the "50 Building," which coincidentally is a half-century old this year. It's worth a visit, governor. The elevator creaks and groans just to slowly make it up two floors.

The wards are terribly overcrowded: rooms designed for two patients contain at least three, sometimes four or even five. This is where Oregon expects its mentally ill to get well.

There's one last stop, governor. Visit the Cremains Building, where there's an abandoned morgue, crematorium and dented copper canisters containing the unclaimed cremains of 3,490 people who died at the hospital.

The battered cans are lined up on dusty shelves in a small square room. Somebody stuck a creepy plastic sticker of a human eye on one wall of the small building—it seems to follow you wherever you step around the room.

Governor, you have shown you understand what's wrong with Oregon's mental health system. You set up a task force on mental health and have endorsed its findings, including moving to more community care and requiring insurers to cover more treatment for mental illnesses. You acted decisively to close the hospital's adolescent ward after this newspaper reported the abuse of teenage patients there.

But you need to see this place. Senate President Peter Courtney, D-Salem, recently toured the decrepit hospital and came away determined to do something about it. Several other legislators also have visited the hospital. The media have swarmed the place.

Yet you have not been inside these dreary walls since you were a young Democratic legislator three decades ago. The years haven't been kind to the hospital or to the thousands of patients who have walked the hospital's long hallways since you were here.

In May, the Legislature will receive a master plan to replace the hospital. Given the state's budget problems, lawmakers will be tempted to leave the costly replacement of the hospital, and the development of more small community mental health facilities, to yet another day.

That would be a tragedy, governor.

Any way you look at it.

Lessons Learned

BY RICK ATTIG

Go look for yourself. That wasn't just the message to the Oregon governor in the editorial, "Long Hallways, Hard Steps," it was also the journalistic lesson from our editorial series on the Oregon State Hospital.

On a gray, drizzly day in November 2005, I joined fellow editorial writer Doug Bates on a day-long tour of the 122-year-old hospital used in the movie "One Flew Over the Cuckoo's Nest," filmed 30 years earlier.

A state senator had invited us to tour the facility with him. We weren't sure what we would get out of the experience, if anything. Near the end of an exhausting day, during which we were confronted by angry patients and stunned by the shabby condition of the hospital, the senator told the hospital superintendent that he wanted to see the "Cremains Room."

We trooped inside a hospital outbuilding and into a small room filled with copper cans, stacked like quarts of paint, containing the cremains of thousands of hospital patients.

That moment was the starting point of what became a 15-part editorial series on the decrepit state hospital, and Oregon's long history of failure to care for its mentally ill. We went back to the hospital again and again to talk to patients, their lawyers and the hospital staff and administration. Through all the editorials, we never forgot those sad, dented copper cans, which said everything about Oregon's treatment of the mentally ill.

Reporters and editorial writers are always talking about getting out of the office. As a member of an editorial board, where there is always another meeting on the schedule, it's particularly hard to get away.

Yet that one-day tour and our editorial series launched many changes: Adolescent patients were promptly removed from the hospital. The Legislature passed mental health parity, a bill that had stalled for more than a decade. Lawmakers funded scores of new community beds. More than 100 families inquired about claiming cremains, and the state began work on a memorial and a more respectful resting place for the deceased patients.

Finally, the governor took our advice, and, unannounced, showed up to tour the hospital. Several patients telephoned us to report that he was there. That day, the governor declared that the hospital must be replaced. Later, the Oregon Legislature agreed.

Sometimes you just have to see it yourself.

Rick Attig, 44, is an associate editor and member of The Oregonian's *editorial board. Attig has won more than 40 state, regional and national newspaper awards. He wrote editorials included in* The Oregonian's *coverage of the U.S. Immigration and Naturalization Service that won the 2001 Pulitzer Prize for public service.*

The Boston Globe

Finalist

Susan Trausch
Editorial Writing

34. From Time to Time

AUG. 12, 2005

When the light is right on Massachusetts Avenue, faint traces of the word "NECCO" can still be seen making their sweet vertical statement down the western corner of the Novartis Institutes for Biomedical Research building in Cambridge.

Charles Sullivan, executive director of the Cambridge Historical Commission, photographed that beautiful ghost of the New England Confectionery Co.—which moved to Revere in 2003—and he treasures the image. Novartis paid to have the old sign scrubbed away, but spokesman Jeff Lockwood says the company has come to accept its haunted corner as "a link to the past."

The past is not always easy to erase from the facades of the present, nor should it be, for it gives texture and depth to a city's commerce and serves as a reminder that time can turn just about every human innovation into an antique.

The past is not always easy to see, either, and requires patience for it to come into focus. Historian Charles Bahne directs the seeker to 31 Church St. in Cambridge—among dozens of places he can name in a minute or so. Lifting the eyes from the entrance to Starbucks, a person might see only orange brick at first, until slowly the words emerge: Ivers & Tucker Carriages.

Those very carriages probably rolled through what is now Central Square and might have pulled up to the Prospect House hotel, currently home to a Curves exercise studio and a Baskin Robbins at 620 Massachusetts Ave. But the specter of 19th-century hospitality still lives on the eastern brick wall of the building, best seen from a few blocks down on the opposite side of the street. High above the blaring traffic and congested sidewalks, pale lettering advertises the Prospect's 1850 amenities: "Boarding and Baiting Stable."

How much the modern pedestrian can miss by focusing on the hurrying feet, or eye-level price tags. The giants of classical music, for instance, are ignored by thousands of people passing 178 Tremont St. in downtown Boston—now the offices of Action for Boston Community Development. Historian and author Susan Wilson urges the busy and oblivious to cross Tremont and go back a century to view the building as Oliver Ditson saw it.

He ran the nation's largest music publishing company there and had the names of Beethoven, Liszt, Schubert, Wagner, Verdi and Gounod carved into the stone on the front of the building. Lower down, the fading name of "Edison" is also visible—fashioned, Wilson surmises, from the usable letters in Ditson's name when the place became home to Boston Edison.

City buildings are like concrete archeological digs, with the layers of history overlapping and ready to tell their tales to people who would but stop to read them. Boston is particularly rich in such visions, and a person looking up from the crooked meanderings of Milk, Broad or Batterymarch Street can feel dizzy taking in the skyline crowded with several centuries.

The juxtaposition of cultures can be dizzying too. A nightclub called "Vertigo" beckons from the ghost ship that is the Cunard Building at 120 State St. And any proper business types haunting the Board of Trade Building at the corner of Broad and State Street would probably be shocked to see the Leeba Salon advertising massages and the full gamut of modern body pampering there.

The sweat and grit of a pre-OSHA America are married to air-conditioned chic at 184 High St.—but diners at the Ottimo Trattoria on a recent afternoon seemed unaware of the hulking Dickensian facade and tower of the Chadwick Lead Works looming over their ziti.

These marriages, no matter how odd, are far better than the divorce a city seems to have with its dying, empty buildings. The faces on the mural of the shuttered South Boston Theatre on West Broadway near F Street seem to be pleading with passersby to go to the movies again. Charlie Chaplin, Humphrey Bogart, and Donald Duck are among the smiling weather-worn crowd refusing to believe that the lights won't be coming up on the small screen.

The crumbling Boston Penny Savings Bank at 1375 Washington St. has the date 1861 carved into its front and looks as though it dropped out of the breakneck competition that has reshaped its industry and changed the institutional names on consumer ATM cards faster than the skyline changed.

The State Street Bank building at 225 Franklin St. still stands proud and tall and occupied, but its title is a misnomer, for State Street is no longer a bank. It is a global financial services company, and its corporate headquarters are over on Lincoln Street. So this landmark might be classified as a living ghost, a 'tweener that reminds people of the old downtown financial district even as it shapes the new one.

But given the swiftness with which businesses gobble each other here and around the world, one can't help wondering whether the State Street name might one day disappear from everything but the top of an office tower.

Will the Borders bookstore on School Street, with its threshold inlay from the Boston Five bank, meld into a third or fourth incarnation in the next 100 years? Will the Jordan Marsh plaque on what is now Macy's become barely legible on a wall in what has long since ceased to be a retail district?

One can imagine the purveyors of electronics, real estate development, entertainment, and everything else that signifies commercial power in 2005 becoming one with Ivers & Tucker. But as long as the world remembers to look at the old names occasionally, and as long as the historians mark the places where the names can be found—and continue to take pictures in just the right light—this brief time that is our own will live on in the city's legacy of stone.

Lessons Learned

BY SUSAN TRAUSCH

Look up! That may sound obvious, but people usually don't do it, particularly if they're journalists on a deadline. They look down at their running feet. They look at the flying seconds on their wristwatches. At best they focus no higher than eye level as they hurry through a crowd, grab a taxi or disappear down a subway hole.

For a day and a half I looked up—way up—to read the old names of Boston and Cambridge businesses, long gone, but still etched on facades above doorways, on stone and steel towers and on exposed brick walls that people hurried by every day but never saw. It was a lesson for the eye, the mind and the heart.

The assignment began with a question in the back seat of a cab as editorial board colleagues and I headed for the State House to interview legislative leaders. "Is the Medieval Manor still with us?" I asked my editor when we passed the old dinner theatre sign on East Berkeley Street. Turns out the theatre is still very much with us, but so much of Boston is not.

"Write about it," said my editor.

I contacted area historians first. I learned the lesson that can be delightfully reassuring in this age of gotcha journalism—people do still like to talk to us and are so generous with their time. They e-mailed me lists of addresses, told me where to stand and at what time of day, described the old hotels and stables, took me back to the 1800s, and wished me well in my 2005 wanderings.

The serendipity of just walking and making my own discoveries after 35 years of living here was as much fun as following the directions of the experts. The Chadwick Lead Works on High Street? Who knew? A paper bag and twine seller right next door? The Penny Savings Bank on Washington Street? What else was I ignoring that was right in front of my face?

Getting out of the office and really looking at a city, feeling its character, noticing the juxtaposition of past and present, understanding that change is the constant of life is the perfect antidote to deadline stress. We tend to become so desk-bound at newspapers, especially in this time of budget crunching and staff cutting. We work the phones more than exercising our senses. We forget that journalism is a license to be curious about small things as well as big ones, about things that are interesting just because they've been there forever.

In the frantic quest to build dwindling readership, newspapers are relying more on what the latest focus group has to say, or on what Wall Street has to say, rather than on the basic curiosity of reporters. If a reporter is wondering about an old sign, or the tower with the stopped clock, or a date on a cornerstone, readers probably are too. And if readers aren't wondering, surprise them! Get them out there, get them walking and talking—and looking up.

Susan Trausch retired from The Boston Globe *in December 2005. She has been an editorial writer and an op-ed columnist. She has also written for* The Globe's *Living pages, business section and Sunday magazine. She has won several awards, including the American Society of Newspaper Editors award for editorial writing 1995.*

PART 6

Watchdog Reporting

Bob Paynter
Watchdog Reporting

If the case of the "Cold-Blooded Liar" seems intimidating in its complexity, consider the story that inspired Bob Paynter to take up journalism in the first place.

During what he describes as "a sometimes-wayward youth," Paynter read "Exodus" by Leon Uris and says he "noted that the story is told by a journalist."

"A decent writer, eager for adventure and with no defensible career ambitions, I naively said to myself, 'You could do that.' Goofy as that sounds now, I was off to journalism school at the University of Missouri within a few weeks."

Compared with an epic like "Exodus," maybe reporting a case as complicated as John Spirko's 20-some-year trek through the legal system looks more manageable.

Paynter credits David Halberstam, John McPhee, Donald Bartlett, James Steele and Bill Marimow with inspiring his interest in investigative work generally—and in justice system failure specifically.

Sandra Livingston, another *Plain Dealer* reporter, did most of the follow-up stories—including reports on court filings and decisions—that followed the original three-part series, Paynter said. He noted that Livingston also played a key role in challenging the state's handling of John Spirko's parole-board hearings, in exploring the likelihood of his winning clemency and in finding and interviewing a long-overlooked potential witness.

In 30 years of work as a journalist, Paynter has earned plenty of national acclaim for taking on topics that don't lend themselves to simplistic treatment. In 1993, he led a team of reporters in a year-long examination of the impact of race on life in the Akron, Ohio, area for the *Beacon Journal.* "A Question of Color" won the 1994 Pulitzer Prize for public service.

In late 1999, Paynter joined *The Plain Dealer* as an investigative reporter, writing about widespread real-estate fraud, inner-city property flipping, bungled property appraisals and the regional economic prospects of Northeast Ohio. He also reported on an unsolved homicide.

Paynter became special projects editor in 2002, supervising and editing investigations of police overtime abuse, problems with court-assigned legal counsel, sexual abuse by priests and questionable government buyouts.

Paynter has won eight first-place awards from the Associated Press Society of Ohio and, as part of a three-reporter team, the Worth-Bingham Prize and the national Sigma Delta Chi Award for investigative reporting for computer-assisted work exposing political fundraising abuses in Columbus.

He has spent his professional life tackling these difficult and complicated stories, and he is just as ambitious in his personal endeavors.

"Lately," Paynter says, "with the nest empty and living just a block or two from Lake Erie, I've decided to take up sailing. As a quest. I almost died the first time out; almost landed on a pile of rocks the second time.

"It's a vast subject about which I'm still quite stupid. But I'm captivated and, with the thaw upon us, eager—if not ready—to go."

—Scott Libin

35. A Cold-Blooded Liar

JAN. 23, 2005

By Bob Paynter

It's no surprise that John George Spirko Jr. landed in a Toledo-area jail cell in early October 1982 . . . just months after being paroled from a Kentucky prison for murder . . . just days after getting the snot beat out of him in a bloody bar fight by a gang of bikers . . . and just hours after waving a sawed-off shotgun in Theresa Fabbro's face in a failed attempt to track down and take revenge on his attackers.

Nor was it especially remarkable that, once again behind bars, Spirko cooked up a pair of exotic schemes—contrived in the volatile psyche of a lifelong liar—to wriggle his way out of this new patch of trouble.

That's the way the 36-year-old ex-con had lived his entire life.

Thirteen years earlier, while in custody in Flint, Mich., after another barroom brawl, a 23-year-old Spirko embarrassed a veteran homicide detective by concocting a detailed, convincing and altogether phony confession to a series of coed murders then filling the local newspapers. Spirko simply wanted to get out of his jail cell for a few hours of coffee and conversation, he later admitted. Further investigation showed that he had nothing to do with what came to be known as "The Michigan Murders."

So, it's little wonder that Spirko's imagination sprang to life again in October 1982, as he faced a felonious-assault charge for the shotgun-waving incident.

But this time, his elaborate flourishes produced far more ominous results—for himself, and possibly for the citizens of Ohio.

In just six weeks, John Spirko talked himself right onto Ohio's death row.

And unless the U.S. Supreme Court or Gov. Bob Taft intervenes, the citizens of Ohio are likely to face the prospect later this year of executing a man for a murder that he very possibly had nothing to do with.

Spirko, now 58, evokes little sympathy. His life of crime and record of spectacular mendacity leave him virtually without credibility. "I'm convictable," he said from death row with a shrug.

Inmate Talks Himself Into Death Sentence

But a months-long *Plain Dealer* examination of the evidence in his case—prompted in part by an extraordinary decision last May by the Van Wert County prosecutor—leads to two conclusions:

- John Spirko's mercurial imagination—and not much else—has brought him to the brink of execution.
- Spirko wasn't the only player in this case to display a casual regard for the truth.

In late 1982 and early 1983, in more than a dozen jailhouse interviews intended to buy himself a short sentence on his new assault charges, Spirko spun for authorities a series of tall tales about the 1982 abduction and murder of Betty Jane Mottinger, the postmaster in Elgin, Ohio, a hamlet of 96 souls not far from the Indiana border.

Spirko's graphic, detailed stories attributed the crime to an ever-changing troupe of vaguely identified dopers, barflies and bikers that he said he knew from Toledo-area taverns. The stories—laced with contradictions, fabrications and factual errors—were almost totally discredited.

Police argued that they contained bits of truth, however. And the stories eventually formed the nucleus of a criminal prosecution that over the next two years got Spirko convicted of kidnapping and aggravated murder in the Mottinger case, making him only the second man sentenced to death in Van Wert County in more than a century.

But the robbery of the Elgin post office, and the abduction and slaying of its postmaster, almost certainly didn't happen the way police and prosecutors said it did, either.

Compelling evidence that they presented to the jury about a mysterious stranger in Elgin on the day of the crime—information that had all but clinched their case against Spirko—almost certainly was wrong. And they knew it.

Some of the least ambiguous evidence they collected during nearly two years of investigation contradicted key elements of their case.

But prosecutors did not reveal that evidence to Spirko's lawyers.

Nor did they share it with the jury.

In fact, it stayed buried in a file drawer—until legal action forced it into the light—for more than a dozen years after Spirko was condemned to die.

* * *

Someone kidnapped Betty Jane Mottinger and robbed her tiny post office at the start of business on Aug. 9, 1982—a crystal clear Monday morning.

All of western Ohio was shocked by such news coming from Elgin, a burg so quiet and remote that old-timers remembered no crimes at all being reported there since World War II.

Elgin is little more than a crossroads in the vast agricultural flatness of John Deere's America. Twenty-two miles due west of Lima, it's on the way to nowhere. Blink twice along Ohio 81 and you're already through it.

The post office is even easier to miss. Housed in a squat, metal-sided hut about 60 yards south of the two-lane highway, the operation was so spare at the time that it had neither a telephone nor running water. It's tucked in the shadow of the grain bins and silos of what in the summer of 1982 was the Elgin Grain Co., the village's sole reason for being.

On the morning of Aug. 9, residents reported seeing a dark-haired stranger standing outside the post office beside a brown, two-tone sedan—possibly a Monte Carlo or a Buick. But nobody witnessed the crime.

Few promising leads had developed by Sept. 19, when shock turned suddenly to horror.

Authorities found Mottinger's skeletal remains wrapped in a paint-splattered curtain and dumped in a soybean field 50 miles from Elgin near the banks of the Blanchard River, just outside Findlay. The body was so badly decomposed from the summer heat that dental records were required to identify the slain postmaster.

Investigators concluded from cut marks to the front of her clothing that Mottinger had been stabbed 13 to 17 times in the chest.

Dozens of postal inspectors—agents of the U.S. Postal Inspection Service, which investigates crimes against post-office employees or property—had descended on the small towns and villages around Elgin right after the kidnapping. They redoubled their efforts now.

But the story of John Spirko's journey onto death row didn't start there. Despite weeks of searching, investigators didn't find a single clue pointing in his direction.

No, Spirko's saga began in the Toledo suburb of Swanton—105 miles north and a world away from Elgin—on Oct. 9, 1982. That's the night Spirko was arrested and jailed after harassing Theresa Fabbro with a shotgun in the parking lot of the Longbranch Saloon, one of his favorite watering holes. It was two days after his bloody whipping at the hands of the gang of bikers.

Out of prison for just two months, Spirko now faced a felonious-assault charge that almost certainly would send him back. His swaggering imagination set to work. And it eventually led to his undoing.

First, Spirko talked his girlfriend, Luann Smith, into hiding $500, a change of clothes and a new 12-gauge pump shotgun inside her 1974 Cutlass and leaving the car around the corner from the jail.

Then he persuaded her to smuggle in two tungsten steel hacksaw blades. And on Oct. 26, after luring a guard to his cell and smacking him in the head with an 8-inch section of iron sawed from his jail bars, Spirko got caught trying to escape. Suddenly, he faced another felonious-assault charge.

Only this time, his girlfriend faced prison time for helping.

Spirko's calculating mind continued to churn. As in Michigan a dozen years earlier, crime stories in the local newspaper apparently helped to spawn another bright idea.

That very week, *The Blade* in Toledo was publishing story after story about developments in what had been a futile effort to solve the Elgin postmaster's murder.

Investigators had been pinning most of their hopes on an obvious suspect. At the time of the crime, Marion "Sonny" Baumgardner was on parole for a similar post-office robbery seven years earlier in Dupont, Ohio, just 30 miles from Elgin. The postmaster in that robbery—also a woman—had been tied up during the crime but had not been seriously injured.

Baumgardner bore an uncanny resemblance to an artist's sketch of the stranger seen in Elgin on the morning Mottinger disappeared, and one witness thought his photo looked like the man.

But Baumgardner had eluded police for weeks.

Then, on Oct. 29, on its front page, *The Blade* reported a crushing blow to investigators. Baumgardner had been arrested, but he had an ironclad alibi for Aug. 9. Witnesses saw him at work that day—in Pasadena, Texas. Baumgardner was cleared of all involvement in the Elgin case.

And after nearly three months, with the trail now cold, investigators were back to "square one."

But to Spirko, then weighing his legal options in the Lucas County Jail, the news served as inspiration.

Investigators weren't looking for him; they had no reason to. He called them. On Oct. 31, just two days after the Baumgardner news.

Spirko got word to federal authorities that he knew something about the Mottinger case. He wanted to cut a deal: Information in return for leniency. For himself and his girlfriend.

His call was like a thunderbolt. Investigators had never heard of Spirko.

But that doesn't mean he didn't inspire suspicion. His credentials were perfect.

* * *

In 1982, Spirko was tall, lean and heavily tattooed—with a dagger on one forearm, the Grim Reaper on the other. He had a rap sheet that stretched back to the second grade, when records in Toledo show that he ran away—the first of many times—and started a fire at a school.

His father, a 300-pound autoworker with an artificial leg, had a violent temper and a tendency to pummel his wife and children during alcoholic rants. Spirko was tagged early on as an incorrigible child with a growing reputation for vile language, impulsive violence and serial lying.

He was convicted of arson, theft, breaking and entering, forgery, interstate transportation of a stolen car and murder—all by the age of 24. And at 36, he had spent all but a few years of his adult life behind bars.

Spirko was paroled from the Kentucky State Penitentiary at Eddyville just 13 days before the Mottinger kidnapping. He had served 12 years of a life sentence for strangling 72-year-old Myra Ashcraft in her Covington, Ky., home while he and his then-girlfriend were stealing her jewelry.

The vote of a single juror reportedly had spared him the death penalty.

On top of all that, Spirko was cocky, fancied himself uncommonly clever, had a big mouth and wasn't very careful about using it.

The new tipster laid out the conditions for his deal right from the start.

First, Spirko demanded probation for his girlfriend, Luann Smith, who had never been in legal trouble until he dragged her into his doomed escape attempt.

Next, he wanted kid-glove treatment for himself.

If he couldn't get his two felonious assault charges dropped—unlikely, he was told, because a jail guard was among the victims—Spirko insisted on doing no more than five years.

And he demanded placement in the federal witness-protection program so he could serve his time in a federal prison.

In return, Spirko would tell authorities everything he knew about the Mottinger case.

The feds agreed.

They promised to recommend probation for Smith and to meet his other demands. And within weeks, as a newly protected witness, Spirko was transferred to the federal penitentiary in Leavenworth, Kan.

For his part, Spirko started to lay out for investigators a shifting, contradictory, ever-evolving but consistently horrifying series of accounts of what might have happened to Betty Jane Mottinger four months earlier— accounts he said he heard about at several Toledo-area parties.

Spirko attributed the crime to a vividly drawn cast of characters—a band of dope-shooting, whiskey-guzzling, obscenity-spewing bikers, barflies and slackers with colorful but hard-to-verify street names like Rooster, Dino and Dirty Dan.

His stories featured detailed scripts—reminiscent of drive-in slasher flicks—studded with coarse dialogue and detailed descriptions of sickening brutality.

Spirko started spinning his tales Nov. 29, 1982, in the first of at least 15 interviews with Postal Inspector Paul Hartman, who was based at the time in Cleveland. The players often changed from interview to interview, and their roles in the drama shifted from one account to another.

But, in essence, Spirko's narrative boiled down to this: A band of vicious losers snatched Mottinger from her tiny post office during what was either a robbery or the botched pickup of a package of mailed drugs, depending on the version. They shoved her into the trunk or the back seat of a car and whisked her off to a "safe house" in the country.

There, they held her prisoner for several hours or several days—bound on a couch in the living room, confined to an upstairs bedroom or tied to a pole in the basement. They taunted her, beat her up, dragged her around by the hair, forced her to perform oral sex and took turns raping her.

Then, as she screamed and flailed and kicked in self-defense, they stabbed her to death so furiously that blood sprayed onto the floor.

Finally, they wrapped her body in a curtain, drove off and dumped it in a soybean field.

* * *

Spirko started off telling Hartman that he first heard about the robbery and murder at a party—and that he'd seen the loot in a bag. But Hartman grew increasingly impatient with his inability to confirm *any* of the accounts. Spirko responded by changing them around and adding still more detail—putting himself closer to the action with each new story.

At first, he had simply heard about the crime from others. Later versions had him witnessing various atrocities and even the murder itself. And, in one account, he even had himself holding Mottinger down (in a cornfield in this version), trying to keep her quiet, when Rooster suddenly stabbed her to death.

The rationale behind the evolving accounts was simple, at least in Spirko's contorted logic. With his girlfriend still not sentenced, he had to keep investigators interested long enough to get what he wanted—probation for her.

"I didn't really care because I didn't do nothin'," Spirko testified during his 1984 trial. "So I didn't figure I'd get indicted."

Spirko said he kept feeding Hartman new versions because "he wouldn't settle for nothin' else. I would tell him one story and . . . the next day, he would come back for another story. And the more I told the more deeper

I got into it, you know. And finally he told me one time, he said 'either you did it,' or, he says, 'or you know who did it.' I don't know if those were his exact words, but it was something to that effect."

Spirko's stories are horrifying, even to an emotionally detached reader more than 22 years later. But they are also shot through with contradictions, fabrications and what appear to be wild guesses—many of them wrong—about the facts of the case.

For one thing, virtually all of the characters in Spirko's dramas were either fictitious or not involved—with either Spirko or the crime. (Spirko said he made up the names, based on people he knew from prison. Investigators maintain they were able to identify several, but eventually cleared them all.)

And there's not a shred of evidence that any of the stories ever happened.

Except for the fact that Mottinger had been stabbed more than a dozen times and that her shroud-wrapped body had been dumped in a Hancock County beanfield—details that were known to anyone in western Ohio who had read a newspaper or watched TV—Spirko's stories easily could have been fiction.

It's possible, for instance, that Mottinger was sexually abused. It's just as possible she wasn't. Her body was so badly decomposed that the prosecution's forensics experts didn't even test her clothing for bodily fluids.

And while it's possible she died in a bloodbath at an isolated farmhouse, investigators could find no evidence of that either.

At one point, they thought they had identified the "safe house" that Spirko had spoken of—a vacant farmhouse near Interstate 75 in Cygnet, Ohio. Postal inspectors descended onto the place in December 1982 and spent three days taking it apart from stem to stern.

They hauled out bedsheets, pillowcases, napkins, trash, magazines, work gloves, matchbooks and drapery cords. They lifted fingerprints from throughout the house, pulled up carpet samples and dug for bloodstains in the weather-stripping around the back door.

They found nothing. Not a drop of blood, not a workable print, not a telltale hair. Not one piece of evidence suggesting that a homicide happened there. All they got for their trouble was a $600 bill for damage from the angry owner.

* * *

Investigators failed to verify much of anything in Spirko's tales. Prosecutors argued during Spirko's 1984 trial that his stories contained several morsels of information that only the killer could have known. Notes of the conversations Spirko had with Hartman leave considerable doubt about that.

But what's striking is how much Spirko *didn't* appear to know about the crime, or somehow failed to mention to Hartman.

Things, for instance, like the loot: Spirko apparently knew nothing about the most obvious items taken during the abduction and robbery.

In addition to $43.86 from the cash drawer and a few money orders, the Elgin post-office robbers took virtually every stamp in the place—more than $700 worth.

And yet during his interviews with Hartman, Spirko specifically said— at least twice—that he never saw any stamps among the stolen items.

Spirko also told Hartman that Mottinger was wearing a gold watch and a gold necklace when she was killed and that he had seen both in the bag of loot.

But in their testimony, Mottinger's family and a co-worker didn't recall her wearing either. When asked about her jewelry, they said that she typically wore three rings—a wedding band, something they described as a "mother's ring" and a tiny pinky ring which, aside from her clothing, was the only personal item found on Mottinger's body.

Spirko said nothing to Hartman about any rings being taken from the victim. Spirko also seemed ignorant about what Mottinger looked like, about how she died and about how her body was prepared for disposal.

Despite hours of interviews over six weeks, no evidence exists that Hartman ever asked Spirko to describe the victim. If he did, it's not reflected in his notes. On two occasions, however, Spirko spontaneously referred to Mottinger as a "fat bitch."

But it's hard to imagine how "fat" would come to mind for someone who had actually seen her. Mottinger was just over 5 feet tall, weighed 104 pounds and was described by friends as "tiny" or "petite."

Spirko also told Hartman that Mottinger's hands were bound behind her back with duct tape when she was killed. But her hands were not bound—with anything—when her body was found.

And he twice told investigators that Mottinger had been stabbed in the back, something her killer would surely know was wrong. She was stabbed in the chest. Investigators found no evidence of wounds to her back.

But that's not all they failed to find.

* * *

Investigators found no Spirko link to Mottinger, no connection to Elgin or to the Findlay area, where her body was found, and no reliable evidence that he had ever been to either place.

Nor did they find a convincing motive. Prosecutors never tried to explain, for instance, why a fresh parolee looking for a place to rob would leave a treasure chest of possibilities like Toledo just after dawn on a Monday morning to scour an unfamiliar rural countryside for a one-room post office that did less than $3,000 in business a year and never kept more than $50 in the safe.

And they never produced a more logical explanation than Spirko's for why he came forward in the first place. Why would a man who was guilty of murder, but had escaped even the hint of detection, voluntarily reach out to police—and risk the death penalty—to bargain down his sentence on an assault charge?

Finally, investigators found no physical evidence linking Spirko to the crime.

No prints.

No murder weapon.

No loot.

And no car for kidnapping and transporting the victim.

In fact, through all his hours of interviews, Spirko gave investigators virtually no evidence in the Mottinger case that they didn't have before they met him.

Except for two things:

The stories, which Hartman recounted for the jury—without regard to fact or fiction—in gruesome detail, and to devastating effect.

And Delaney Gibson Jr.

That may well have been enough.

Gibson and Spirko became best friends while sharing a Kentucky prison cell in the late 1970s.

Although he never set foot in the courtroom, Gibson gave prosecutors an even more delectable suspect than Spirko himself.

And Gibson provided them a critical key to cracking the case—the only strong evidence they ever developed that appeared to link Spirko, albeit indirectly, to Elgin on the day Betty Jane Mottinger disappeared.

Both men were indicted on charges of kidnapping and stabbing the 48-year-old mother of three.

An "eyewitness" testified that she saw Gibson in Elgin on that clear August morning 22 years ago.

No ifs, ands or buts.

Nine men and three women convicted Spirko on Aug. 22, 1984.

But they never heard the whole story.

36. A Mysterious Murder Suspect Emerges, Then Disappears

JAN. 24, 2005

By Bob Paynter

A brown-and-cinnamon sedan eased down Main Street, a misnamed little side lane jutting southward from Ohio 81, and glided to a stop in front of the nondescript, metal-sided blockhouse that served as the Elgin post office.

Betty Jane Mottinger, postmaster for four years, had arrived moments earlier from Ohio City, 10 miles to the northwest, and was already inside.

From her home across the street, Opal Seibert eyed the two-tone vehicle as it crept into town that day. The 30-year resident of Elgin recognized every face for miles around and knew at once when a car or truck didn't belong. This was one of those times.

Sipping coffee in her breezeway, Seibert glanced at the kitchen clock. It was *exactly* 8:30 a.m. on Monday, Aug. 9, 1982.

A lean, clean-shaven stranger stepped slowly from the car and peered around, in all directions, as if to see if anyone was watching. He wore a long-sleeve blue work shirt and glasses. His dark hair was combed straight back.

The man stood there for several minutes, wedged between the car door and the roof, his left arm draped on the door. Seibert's eyes locked onto him from her breezeway.

She never lost sight of the man, except for a few seconds when her view was blocked by a passing truck. And as the truck cleared the post office, the stranger—back behind the wheel—drove off to the south.

Seibert saw no one else in the car as it arrived. She saw no one entering the post office or leaving it and no one else in the car as it pulled away.

Yet five months later, her unwavering memory of that clear, summer morning in Elgin provided a critical key to cracking the most senseless and horrific crime in Elgin's history—the abduction and murder of the 48-year-old postmaster, wife and mother of three.

It was Seibert's sturdy recall that finally gave frustrated investigators their ace in the hole and made her a star witness in the 1984 trial that sent John George Spirko Jr. to death row.

John Spirko, convicted and sentenced to die for kidnapping and murdering Elgin postmaster Betty Jane Mottinger, has been contemplating his fate on Ohio's death row for more than 20 years. "I talked myself into a good one. It's a nightmare." (Photograph courtesy of Chuck Crow/*The Plain Dealer*)

Evidence Tailored to Fit the Crime

More than a dozen years passed before the government was forced to reveal evidence that raised serious doubts about the quality of Seibert's memory—and about the reliability of the postal inspectors investigating the case, the tactics of the prosecutors presenting it to the jury and the caliber of the justice they produced.

By that time, however, Seibert was long dead and Spirko had squandered years on fruitless appeals. Today, the 58-year-old career criminal, who has spent all but a handful of his adult years behind bars, is nearing the end of the line.

Barring last-minute relief by the U.S. Supreme Court or Ohio Gov. Bob Taft, Spirko will likely be executed this year.

But a litany of questions has cropped up about how this bizarre and bewildering case was put together. And some of the most troubling center on just who Opal Seibert saw on that sunny August morning 22 years ago.

In the beginning, her memory promised to be of limited value.

She witnessed no crime. And when combined with what others saw, Seibert's account only contributed to a confused, almost kaleidoscopic portrait of the supposed killer.

Mark Lewis, for instance, who was leaving the Elgin Grain Co. that morning with a Toledo-bound truckload of wheat, said he also noticed the man standing outside the post office. Like Seibert's stranger, the man was wedged between the door and the body of a brownish two-tone sedan, his left arm resting on the door, his right on the rooftop. But there the similarities end.

Lewis' stranger was a husky, slightly pot-bellied man, about 240 pounds, with sandy brown or reddish hair and possibly a light mustache. And instead of long-sleeve and blue, the shirt Lewis remembered him wearing was short-sleeve and green. With orange stripes. About the only feature Lewis and Seibert saw in common was the glasses.

Others in town that morning described other scenarios. But Seibert's memory seemed the firmest. And because of fortuitous developments unfolding 95 miles to the north in a Lucas County jail cell, her stock in one of the biggest investigations in Van Wert County history would suddenly rise in January 1983.

By that point, John Spirko had been filling the ear of Postal Inspector Paul Hartman for more than six weeks with a steady diet of captivating stories about the Mottinger mystery.

Spirko had come forward in late 1982 offering a deal. He was in jail on a pair of unrelated assault charges. In return for lenient treatment for himself and his girlfriend, Spirko volunteered to divulge information about the unsolved postmaster case that he said he picked up at a party.

He had no known connection to Elgin or to Mottinger. Investigators had never heard of him. And much of what he eventually told them turned out to be unprovable or downright wrong.

But with their high-profile investigation going nowhere, they leapt at this new opportunity.

Given Spirko's lengthy and violent criminal record, investigators suspected almost from the day he came forward that he might be involved in Mottinger's death.

Records show they subpoenaed phone records for Spirko and his family and ordered their mail tracked weeks before he started telling Hartman his stories.

And early on in their relationship, the postal inspector struck what eventually looked like pay dirt while searching through Spirko's prison scrapbooks at his sister's home in a Toledo suburb.

Along with dozens of other photos of Spirko's prison buddies, Hartman seized a snapshot of a man who just might pass for Opal Seibert's dark-haired stranger.

The portrait seemed innocent enough. A slight, calm-looking young man in a T-shirt and jeans gazed benignly into the camera as he gently stroked a kitten. But it was the résumé behind the photograph that sparked the imagination.

If John Spirko's rap sheet made him an enticing prospect in the Mottinger case, then Delaney Gibson Jr.'s made him a prosecutor's dream. He was everything Spirko was. And more.

And he had an almost mythical aura about him, a near legendary capacity to engage in criminal mayhem one day, only to vanish the next.

* * *

Gibson and Spirko were cellmates in Kentucky in the late 1970s, when both served time for homicides. Both were paroled—Spirko in July 1982, Gibson five years earlier. And when postal inspectors happened upon Gibson's photograph in late 1982, he had been on the run for more than a year for two other murders.

Gibson was born in 1950 in the mountains of Leslie County, in the coal-field region of southeastern Kentucky. He turned to violence early.

At 16, Gibson and a roving band of friends abducted a 17-year-old girl at gunpoint from a disabled vehicle by the side of a Leslie County highway, hauled her off to the hills and raped her.

He got 15 years.

Gibson stabbed Alfred Metcalf to death in nearby Clay County in September 1972, one month after getting paroled on the rape. He pleaded guilty to voluntary manslaughter, was sentenced to another 15 years and wound up as Spirko's cellmate at the Kentucky State Penitentiary at Eddyville.

Paroled again in late 1977, Gibson returned to Leslie County, where he killed Milton David Couch with a pistol in the summer of 1980. Eight months later, he did the same to R. T. Gray a few miles down the road in Manchester.

Gibson was convicted of the Couch murder on March 26, 1981. But the next day, while awaiting sentencing, he escaped from the Leslie County Jail in Hyden and disappeared.

That was Gibson's status—at large, whereabouts unknown—when investigators in the Mottinger case first ran across his picture in Spirko's photo album.

They assembled more photographs—taken by Kentucky authorities years earlier when Gibson was in custody there—and went to see Opal Seibert in January 1983.

"That's the person I saw," she told them. No doubt about it.

After months of frustration, postal inspectors thought they had finally found their way in the Mottinger killing.

Spirko was shooting off his mouth about the case from his Toledo jail cell. Now they had his murderous former cellmate positively identified as the dark-haired stranger hanging around the Elgin post office on the morning that Mottinger disappeared.

* * *

The Gibson factor changed everything, including Spirko's story line.

His entire relationship with Paul Hartman had been based on lies. No one disputes that. In fact, Spirko later testified, that was the whole point.

The idea was to spin enough intriguing yarns about the Mottinger case to keep investigators in thrall until his girlfriend was safely on probation and his own five-year sentence for a pair of unrelated assault charges was set in stone. Those were his goals for coming forward in the first place.

He had been telling Hartman for weeks about a gang of crazed dopers who kidnapped Mottinger while trying to retrieve a package of drugs from the post office, brutalized her at a country "safe house" and then stabbed her repeatedly and dumped her body in a Hancock County beanfield.

Much of what he related about the circumstances and manner of Mottinger's death had been widely reported in the western Ohio press for months. And Spirko's narratives were jammed with fabrications—including his entire cast of characters—and with grisly details that no one could verify.

But in January 1983, apparently armed with the new Gibson card and ready to play it, Hartman got Spirko to jettison his gang of dopers, disavow everything he had said before and alter his shifting story in a way that would break open the Mottinger investigation.

Hartman denied in a recent interview that he ever coaxed Spirko into anything.

But it's clear from investigative documents that on Jan. 11, 1983, Hartman confronted Spirko with the emerging Gibson theory—at least indirectly—by steering their conversation toward Bear Branch, the tiny mountain community in eastern Kentucky that Gibson called home.

Spirko recalled recently from death row that Hartman was far more blunt than that.

As he started with his usual doper story for the day, Spirko said, Hartman was "lookin' at me and he's smilin' across the table. Then he says, 'You're full of shit. We know who was there. We know who was with you: Delaney Gibson.' "

Spirko said he scoffed at the claim. But Hartman persisted: " 'We've got eyewitnesses.' "

"I don't remember that," Hartman said recently.

But both men agreed at the time that Spirko would sleep on the new development. And sure enough, the next day—Jan. 12, 1983—he concocted an entirely new story, a radical departure from everything he'd said before.

Yes, Spirko told Hartman, it was Delaney Gibson who had killed the Elgin postmaster after all.

During a robbery, Spirko said, Gibson and two cronies had kidnapped Mottinger, raped her and stabbed her to death by the side of a road so she couldn't identify them. Then they told him all about it a few days later.

That was the last story Spirko ever told Hartman.

It was almost certainly a lie as well. Just like the others. But together with Seibert's identification, the new story gave the authorities all they felt they needed: Two months later, Luann Smith—the girlfriend Spirko had been trying to keep out of prison—was given 18 months to five years at Marysville for helping with his failed jail break the previous October. And a few weeks after that, postal authorities declared that the Mottinger murder had been "resolved."

But months passed before indictments were handed down. And nearly a year and a half went by before Spirko was brought to trial.

Delaney Gibson proved a mysterious and elusive quarry, with an uncanny knack for suddenly showing up and disappearing at pivotal moments.

By the time Spirko did go to trial in August 1984, Gibson had become little more than a trick up the prosecution's sleeve.

* * *

The first complication in the investigators' new theory arose three months after Spirko's last chat with Hartman. A bearded Gibson—still on the lam for his two Kentucky murders—was arrested in April 1983 in Canton, N.C., near where he was working incognito as a tomato picker with a troupe of migrant farm workers.

Postal inspectors in the Mottinger case descended on Asheville, N.C., where Gibson was locked up in the Buncombe County Jail.

He promptly told them that his itinerary since escaping from jail in 1981 had included no stops in Ohio, much less Elgin. His wife, Margie, vouched for that.

And both insisted that Gibson had sported the full beard throughout 1982, a fact that might complicate efforts to portray him as Seibert's clean-shaven stranger.

Gibson's supervisor also said Gibson had worn a beard that whole year. If he had ever shaved it, Juan Flores said, he didn't remember when that might have been.

Still, the beard was hardly definitive. Gibson's family and friends could be lying; he could have grown it since the August crime.

And besides, the whole problem became conveniently moot a few months later, after Gibson was shipped back to Kentucky to face his murder charges.

On Aug. 7, 1983, Gibson and several other inmates overpowered a guard and he escaped again, this time from the Clay County Jail.

Just a month later, with Gibson at large and not likely to be available for trial, a Van Wert County grand jury indicted him—along with Spirko—on charges of kidnapping and aggravated murder in the Mottinger case.

But more complications—big ones—soon arose.

Seven days before Christmas in 1983, the FBI arrested Gibson at the John's II Motel outside Montgomery, Ala., and charged him with unlawful flight from the Kentucky murder charges.

Their wild card suddenly back in play, postal inspectors pounced once again—this time on tiny Bear Branch, where Margie Gibson had taken refuge while her husband was on the lam.

For the first time, Hartman asked her about Delaney's whereabouts on the morning of Aug. 9, 1982. Margie Gibson told him a story that would twist the working theory on the Mottinger case into a pretzel.

* * *

Margie told Hartman that she, Delaney and her sister and brother-in-law, Brenda and Michael Bentley, were with their children near the North Carolina migrant camp from Saturday, Aug. 7, until about 6:30 p.m. Sunday, Aug. 8.

If true, that would put Gibson roughly 500 miles away from Elgin on the evening before the crime.

Hartman immediately contacted Bentley, who confirmed the story. Worse, he had receipts documenting activities during the visit.

Worse still, he had photographs. Lots of them. Of Gibson, sporting the full beard that he and his friends had spoken of months earlier.

Over the next few weeks, Hartman shuttled between towns in Kentucky and North Carolina doing interviews and gathering receipts that only compounded the problem.

On Jan. 11, 1984, he obtained 18 photographs from Margie Gibson showing Delaney, herself, their young son and the Bentleys driving go-carts at a North Carolina amusement park that weekend and dining at a McDonald's in Candler, N.C.

Hartman went to Candler. Sure enough, it was the McDonald's in the photos.

He obtained 40 more photographs from the Bentleys, showing basically the same things. Then he called Maloney's Department Store, near the Bentleys' home in Ary, Ky., and confirmed that they had dropped off their film for processing on Aug. 10, 1982.

In photo after photo, there he was: fugitive Delaney Gibson, with a full beard and a thick mop of dark, curly hair, enjoying a family vacation in Maggie Valley, N.C., the night before witness Opal Seibert's clean-shaven stranger slipped quietly into Elgin.

Certainly, it was mathematically possible.

But to complete the scenario, Gibson would have had to straighten his hair, comb it straight back, shave his beard and drive at least nine hours through the night to Elgin—assuming he knew how to navigate the herky-jerky country roads to get there—so he could cruise by Seibert's house at exactly 8:30 on Monday morning.

Then, after kidnapping and murdering Mottinger, he would have to return to his tomato-picking crew and regrow his beard without his boss ever noticing that he'd shaved it off.

Clearly, this was a problem.

It's unclear now who made the decision. But the apparent solution was to stick the fresh photographs in a private file drawer, apparently separate from other investigative documents, where they remained hidden for the next 13 years.

* * *

The new photographs apparently were never shown to Seibert.

It's also unclear whether Van Wert prosecutor Stephen Keister ever saw them.

Prosecutors are required by law to tell defense attorneys about significant evidence that might help their client. Four months before Spirko's trial, Keister did reveal the following: that a Michael Bentley had stated that Gibson was in North Carolina the weekend before the Mottinger killing and "that pictures are purported to have been taken of the weekend in question."

Twice over the next three months, Spirko's attorneys demanded to see "all statements of Michael Bentley." Those statements would have alerted them to receipts documenting the weekend visit and would have proved that the photos were far more than "purported." Dozens had been handed over to Hartman.

And the photos would have shown that Gibson almost certainly was not Seibert's clean-shaven stranger.

But the defense demands went unmet. No photos or Bentley statements were forthcoming. And Gibson—incredibly—was soon unavailable for questioning.

Keister and postal officials decided not to hold him in the Mottinger case. Less than three months before Spirko's trial was to begin, they released Gibson to authorities in Kentucky.

And on July 9, 1984, true to form, Gibson pulled a knife on a deputy at the Bell County Jail and vanished yet again.

Spirko went to trial as scheduled in early August—without his alleged accomplice. Prosecutors called Seibert to the witness stand as planned. And she delivered with rock-solid certainty.

"That there is his face," Seibert testified, as she pulled a years-old picture of a clean-shaven Delaney Gibson from a photo array.

"He had a different hairdo, but that's him," Seibert said. "I don't forget a face."

Keister zeroed in on that certitude in his arguments to the jury.

There had been other witnesses. Prosecutors produced two prisoners who said Spirko had admitted to them that he killed Mottinger. Both later recanted, according to court documents filed by the defense.

And truck driver Mark Lewis testified that Spirko might have been the Elgin stranger—even though Spirko is blond, looks nothing like Gibson, and weighed roughly 60 pounds less than the man Lewis originally described.

Lewis said he was about "70 percent" sure. But he was so shaky on the witness stand that no one asked him to identify the man at the defendant's table. And even Keister acknowledged it would be "silly" to argue that 70 percent is beyond a reasonable doubt.

But Seibert was another matter. She was 100 percent sure, Keister told the jurors. And together with Spirko's stories, Keister argued, Seibert's certainty validated Lewis and made his testimony more than a "70 percent situation."

Spirko and Gibson robbed the post office together and killed Mottinger together, the prosecutor argued. Of those whose photos were shown to Lewis and Seibert, Spirko and Gibson "were the only persons . . . that had any personal connection," Keister said. "These two were the most important persons to each other, the best friends in the whole world."

One of them, Spirko, had said things to Hartman that only the killer could have known, Keister argued. And the other, Gibson, the defendant's closest friend, was positively identified at the scene of the crime. No question.

The prosecutor showed jurors a Kentucky prison photo from the late 1970s showing Gibson's bare-chinned profile. Then he held up an artist's rendering—also in profile—of Seibert's clean-shaven stranger, drawn two days after the crime.

"This is a picture of Delaney Gibson," Keister said, pointing to one. "There is a profile of Delaney Gibson," he said of the other. "I submit to you, it is almost as if the person who made this drawing back on Aug. 11, 1982, had this picture from which to make the drawing.

"You make the comparison. That identification is there. Delaney Gibson was there that morning."

Keister, in a recent interview, declined to discuss any aspect of the Spirko case, citing the passage of time. "It's been 20 years," said the former prosecutor, who left office in 1988. "My memory is fading. And a lot of things have been over the dam."

* * *

It wasn't until the summer of 1997—13 years later—that John Spirko and his attorneys first saw the Gibson vacation photos and other evidence detailing that weekend in North Carolina.

They had been trying to bore into the Mottinger investigative files since shortly after the trial. But postal authorities fought them every step of the way.

A court-brokered agreement finally gave Spirko access to previously undisclosed files in 1996. And for the first time, his attorneys discovered several references to the vacation photos. But no actual pictures. They weren't in the investigative files and postal officials said they couldn't find them.

After a federal judge ordered the missing photos released, postal authorities produced them the next year, just weeks after promising to look for them in Hartman's personal "desk file."

Asked recently if that's where they were found, Hartman said, "I don't believe so." Does he know where they were? "I have no idea." He said he originally put the photos in the investigative case file, "along with everything else."

Meanwhile, in the more than two decades since Gibson was indicted for aggravated murder, Van Wert and federal authorities have never attempted to bring him to trial.

Four months after Spirko was sentenced to death, the FBI arrested Gibson again. This time, agents found him hiding in the false ceiling of his father-in-law's attic, in Bear Branch.

He later pleaded guilty and was sentenced to 40 years in prison for the two Kentucky murders from the early 1980s.

But Ohio authorities didn't place a holder on Gibson to keep him from escaping justice in the Mottinger case if he should ever get out of prison.

And so, when Kentucky released Gibson on parole in December 1998, he walked away a free man—despite the pending indictment.

The next June, Gibson was returned to prison for violating an order to stay out of Clay County, Ky.

But he was paroled again in the summer of 2001, and he has been free ever since, living in Louisville, Ky.

On May 17, 2004, the same day a federal appeals court denied Spirko's next-to-last appeal for relief, Van Wert County authorities dismissed the kidnapping and aggravated murder charges against Gibson.

He declined to return phone messages left with his sister in Bear Branch.

* * *

In 1997, Spirko's attorneys launched a new round of angry appeals based on the Gibson vacation photos. They argued that prosecutors had not only withheld key evidence, but had knowingly presented a false case to the jury.

One federal judge seemed to agree last May, writing that the case against Spirko—built on a "foundation of sand"—left "considerable doubt" about whether he had been lawfully condemned.

Judge Ronald Lee Gilman, of the 6th U.S. Circuit Court of Appeals, noted the "complete absence" of physical evidence against Spirko and other weaknesses in the case. He concluded that if the Gibson photos had not been withheld, the state's star witness and its case would have been seriously undermined and Spirko might have been acquitted.

But Gilman was outvoted 2–1 by his colleagues on the 6th Circuit panel, and the full court declined to take up the matter three months later.

With the exception of Gilman, state and federal appeals-court judges have largely adopted the state's counterargument.

The state's attorneys responded to the new round of Spirko appeals by radically downsizing the stature of one star witness—Opal Seibert—and the role her clean-shaven stranger played in the case.

And in the process, they elevated the stature of another: Postal Inspector Paul Hartman. It was Hartman, during the jailhouse interviews, who produced the really critical evidence that doomed John Spirko, they argued.

But a close look at that evidence suggests that, for whatever reason, not everything that Paul Hartman said in this case was correct.

37. Cop, Criminal Square Off in Jailhouse Duel

JAN. 25, 2005

By Bob Paynter

A pair of movie-star look-alikes waged a war of wits inside the Lucas County Jail as 1982 came to a close.

Day after day, hour after hour, the lifelong con man—with more than a passing resemblance to Nick Nolte—played high-stakes cat and mouse with the veteran postal inspector with a likeness, it was said at the time, to Robert Redford.

Both were highly motivated.

Each was hell-bent on getting the other to play into his hands in what had become a baffling investigation into the murder of 48-year-old Betty Jane Mottinger, the postmaster in a tiny village in western Ohio.

John Spirko was a career criminal only recently paroled from a Kentucky prison, with a long history of trying to manipulate curious cops. He was angling to play investigator Paul Hartman for a sap.

Spirko had found himself back in jail on Toledo-area assault charges in late October 1982, a few months after Mottinger was abducted 100 miles away in Elgin, and five weeks after her body was found. Spirko called officials after reading newspaper stories about the sputtering Mottinger investigation.

He figured he could get lenient treatment on the Toledo cases for his girlfriend and himself by saying he had information about the unsolved murder.

Cop, Criminal in Battle of Wits

Spirko's plan was to tantalize Hartman with lurid, hard-to-prove tales about Mottinger's death—hooking him just long enough to keep his girlfriend out of jail and his own prison time to a minimum.

No hard evidence ever linked Spirko to the crime. Nothing in the months-long investigation pointed to him. And the stories he told Hartman were full of gross fabrications and out-and-out lies.

But the investigator had a role in mind for Spirko as well.

Hartman had never been so deeply involved in a homicide investigation in his 11 years as a postal inspector, although he had interviewed thousands of suspects in lesser cases. He concluded fairly quickly that Spirko was involved "up to his ass" in the Mottinger slaying or knew who was.

Hartman's job was to keep Spirko talking, on the chance that he would either help solve a crime that had confounded postal authorities for months, or implicate himself in the process.

The two men met at least a dozen times in three weeks, often for four, five, six hours or more.

For the most part, there were no witnesses to these conversations. No video cameras. No tape recorders. No stenographers. Just Spirko and Hartman. Criminal and cop. Nolte and Redford.

And based largely on the fruits of those interviews, Spirko was eventually convicted of kidnapping and murdering the rural postmaster and is now on death row. He is awaiting execution—barring an intervention by the U.S. Supreme Court or Gov. Bob Taft—that's likely to come this year.

With his deft handling of Spirko, Hartman was almost single-handedly responsible for closing a case that had frustrated dozens of his colleagues, who collectively spent thousands of hours interviewing more than 3,000 people in 37 states, identifying and eventually discarding nearly 100 suspects along the way.

Whether he actually solved the Mottinger murder, however, is another matter.

* * *

Hartman produced what became the most tangible link between Spirko and the scene of the crime. That came in the form of Delaney Gibson Jr., Spirko's former cellmate and best friend, who was identified by an unwavering eyewitness as the mysterious stranger seen hanging around outside the post office in tiny Elgin, Ohio, moments before Mottinger was abducted.

Not only did Hartman stumble upon Gibson's photo in Spirko's prison scrapbook, he also succeeded—in their final session together—in getting Spirko to tell him that Gibson kidnapped the woman during a robbery, raped her, killed her and then told Spirko about it later.

That was the last in a string of whoppers that Spirko told Hartman.

When evidence later established that Gibson almost certainly was nowhere near Elgin that day—evidence that was never shared with Spirko's jury—the information apparently was buried in a private file drawer and kept from Spirko's attorneys for more than a decade.

And in the late 1990s, when Spirko's attorneys used that newly discovered information to argue that the prosecution had presented a false case to the jury, Hartman took center stage once again.

The state responded to the new round of appeals by asserting that Gibson's alleged role in the crime was meaningless—despite the considerable effort expended to prove it—and that the eyewitness testimony putting him in Elgin was immaterial.

The real foundation of the state's case, the argument continued, was the collection of "statements" that Spirko made, statements that purportedly included a handful of "intimate details" that only the killer could have known—because they supposedly were never made public.

It's an argument, adopted nearly verbatim by a succession of appeals-court judges over the last seven years, that defers to the largely unchallenged trial assertions of Hartman, the man Spirko first encountered in November 1982 in the Lucas County Jail.

But a detailed examination of those assertions, the notes of Hartman's interviews with Spirko and the independent evidence in the case shows that the veteran investigator was wrong on several of his claims and may have overstated others.

And the condition of Hartman's notes raises questions about how some of the more damaging "intimate details" got there in the first place.

Hartman laid out his "intimate details" theory—the essence of which has been repeated in court decisions denying Spirko's appeals—in a sworn statement on Feb. 1, 1983, three weeks after his final session with Spirko.

Among the details Hartman cited was Spirko's revelation that Mottinger's body had been wrapped "in a part of a curtain."

"Public disclosure has not been made that the subject shroud was, in fact, a portion of a curtain," Hartman asserted.

But that's wrong.

It had been publicly disclosed—right under Spirko's nose—and right when he was formulating his plan to trade information about the Mottinger case for leniency.

Just 11 days before Spirko called federal authorities with his proposal for a deal, The Blade in Toledo reported what was described as a significant break in the case on the front page of its local news section.

The shroud around Mottinger's body had been identified as a theater curtain, postal inspectors announced, that "at some time had been cut from a larger piece." The Blade even reported the fragment's precise dimensions.

At least twice in the next week—just days before Spirko reached out to authorities—The Blade described the shroud as "a remnant of a theater curtain."

When prosecutors pressed him during his trial on how he knew about the torn curtain, Spirko replied, "I believe I read that in the paper."

Among other "intimate details" that "have not been released to the news media," Hartman cited the location of stab wounds on Mottinger's body, that Mottinger had been wearing a blouse and slacks when she was abducted and that her purse had been taken along with post-office proceeds during the robbery.

But those details had been in news reports as well.

In fact, almost from the beginning, postal inspectors left little to the public's imagination in this case.

Mottinger's clothing, for instance, had been described in the press in considerable detail (light-colored or white blouse with a design on the front and dark slacks). And Ohio newspapers from Van Wert to Lima and Toledo—not to mention wire services that also fed radio and television reports—had also disclosed the following: what was believed stolen from the post office (less than $50 in cash, stamps and money orders); how Mottinger died (stabbed at least 13 times in the chest); where and how her body was found (wrapped in a tarp—later identified as a curtain—in a soybean field near the Blanchard River in Hancock County, just outside Findlay, roughly 50 miles from Elgin).

Still, Spirko told postal inspectors at least twice that Mottinger had been stabbed in the back—even though she wasn't—and that he knew nothing about stamps having been taken from the post office.

Spirko also twice described Mottinger as a "fat bitch," even though she weighed just over 100 pounds.

Several of Spirko's other descriptions also don't jibe with the facts.

For instance, Hartman said that Spirko's description of the shroud "matches exactly" the material Mottinger's body was wrapped in.

Hartman's notes indicate that Spirko described the shroud as a "gray curtain" made of a heavy "canvas type material."

But everyone who is known to have seen it—investigators who found the body, pathologists conducting Mottinger's autopsy and forensics experts doing tests for both the prosecution and the defense—described the shroud the same way: as a painter's drop cloth.

The cloth was covered with paint smears and spots, literally thousands of them, according to a prosecutor, who said they represented "probably about every color in the rainbow."

And yet, in his description, Spirko never even hinted at paint.

Asked about the omission in an interview recently, Hartman dismissed the paint spots as "minutiae."

"It looked like a gray shroud to me, as I remember it."

Hartman also asserted that Spirko's description of how the slain post-master was wrapped "matches exactly the manner in which the body was prepared for disposal."

In his Dec. 15, 1982, interview, Spirko said he watched as a fictional band of thugs—all either cleared or never identified by authorities—killed Mottinger and wrapped her body in the shroud. According to Hartman's notes, Spirko said they "rolled body onto curtain/flapped curtain end to end over head."

Prosecutors argued during Spirko's 1984 trial that this description was so precise that only the killer could have given it.

As with many of Hartman's assertions, Spirko denied at trial that he ever said it. But even if he did, he somehow left out these facts:

- That after Mottinger was rolled into the shroud, it was attached to her body from the outside with a cord, tied around both her neck and waist.
- That the shroud was further secured from the outside with duct tape, stretched around the body's midsection and legs.
- That inside the shroud, pressed against the body's abdomen and legs, were two concrete blocks.

Spirko mentioned none of those seemingly noteworthy details, according to Hartman's notes. "To me," Hartman said in a recent interview, "the noteworthy detail was that she was put in it [the shroud] in that fashion."

Despite such vagaries and inaccuracies, several other "intimate details" cited by Hartman *do* correspond to facts in the case.

But the way they appear—coupled with the way the interviews were conducted—raise questions about how some of the most significant details found their way into the investigator's notes in the first place.

Among those is the matter of the "pried stone."

* * *

During his interview with Hartman on Dec. 9, 1982, Spirko digressed into a tale about the exploits of his cast of characters during a Florida drug robbery—an episode that had little if anything to do with the Mottinger case.

But at the very end, under a heading labeled "Miscellaneous info," Hartman's notes indicate that Spirko suddenly blurted out that Rooster—one of his fictional characters—had pried a stone loose from a ring on Mottinger's finger after killing her.

This was significant because a tiny, $7.99 "pinky ring" was the only jewelry found on Mottinger's body, a detail that apparently never *was* revealed to the public. And the ring's single rhinestone, not much bigger than the tip of a ballpoint pen, was missing. How it came to be missing was never independently established.

Prosecutors later argued that the mere fact that it was gone could only have been known by the killer and, as a result, was evidence of Spirko's guilt.

But that information was obviously known by investigators as well. And that's exactly where Spirko testified he got it—during hours of give-and-take chatter with Hartman.

"I will never forget the exact words he used," Spirko said of Hartman, during his trial testimony.

"I gave him a couple of fictitious names. And he says, 'The one I want to get a hold of . . . [is] that stinkin' son-of-a-bitch that pried that stone out of her ring.' That's the first time I heard anything about a ring."

Hartman denied at trial that he ever suggested information. And Spirko's reputation for truthfulness is hardly sterling.

But it's impossible to tell where that piece of information—or any other—actually came from, because of the way the interviews were conducted. It's also impossible to know what questions Hartman asked, whether Spirko's answers were recorded accurately or what was said between the two men that wasn't written down.

Not one of their sessions was tape-recorded. Spirko was never asked to write a statement—or to sign any of Hartman's notes—to vouch for the accuracy of any of the accounts. And he was never asked to initial additions or deletions, a standard procedure for validating edited documents.

The technique appears to fall short of accepted police standards, even for the time.

Today, deep into the age of DNA evidence, more police agencies are requiring video or audio recordings of suspect interrogations—especially in homicide cases—because so many documented cases of wrongful convictions have involved faulty confessions.

Researchers say these often occur when investigators, in the process of questioning or prodding their suspects, either deliberately or inadvertently reveal critical information that later shows up in a suspect's statement.

Of the 18 death-row inmates exonerated in Illinois alone, half were originally convicted based on what turned out to be false confessions, or witness statements, said Steven Drizin, staff attorney for the Center on Wrongful Convictions and professor at Northwestern University School of Law.

Notes of even the best police interrogators have been shown to contain significant errors when compared with tape recordings, Drizin said. Notes are also notorious for omitting critical details. "That's why you need taped interrogations," he said.

Hartman testified that he never used a tape recorder while interviewing suspects. He said it hampered his efforts to establish rapport.

He acknowledged on cross-examination that his notes of the Spirko interviews are not verbatim accounts of everything that was said. Rather, Hartman said, they are "my interpretation, as it were, of the words."

And in a recent interview, Hartman said that police officers typically don't ask suspects to initial or sign notes of conversations. In 28 years as a postal inspector, he said, he never did.

But in Spirko's trial, Hartman's notes of more than a dozen conversations were presented as the defendant's "statements." And standards for handling those have been in place for half a century.

* * *

John E. Reid & Associates, Inc., a Chicago firm that trains thousands of law enforcement, government and private investigators every year, is considered one of the nation's leading authorities on investigative techniques.

The traditional procedure for documenting a suspect's version of events is to have him write and sign a statement, said Reid's president, Joseph Buckley, or to have the investigator write a summary of their conversation and have the suspect read and sign it.

"In some cases, you might have a stenographer come in and take it down in shorthand—where it's a question-and-answer process. Then, she would go type it up, the suspect would read it and sign it," Buckley said.

"That hasn't changed," he said. "That has been the case for decades. Forty years. Fifty years."

The purpose, Buckley said, is credibility.

Without a written, signed statement, he said, the validity of the information becomes a matter of whom the jury believes—the police officer or the defendant.

Hartman did none of those things in his interviews with Spirko. Given Spirko's record, credibility with a jury wasn't likely to be an issue.

It would be cop over criminal every time.

A curious fact raises another question about Hartman's interview tactics. In several instances in which Spirko is alleged to have uttered "intimate details" about the case, those very details were added after the original notes were written.

That's definitely the case in one of only two references in the notes to the "pried stone." And it's possible the other was added later as well, according to two documents experts asked to examine portions of Hartman's handwritten notes.

There's no way to tell from the documents whether the critical information was added minutes, hours or even days after the original notes were written. Nor is it possible to tell what prompted the additions.

Hartman disputes that he made any significant additions to his notes.

What is certain, however, is that Spirko never initialed the changes to verify that he was the source of the information.

The most significant examples, in addition to the "pried stone," include Spirko's alleged description of Mottinger's purse and of the clothing the postmaster was wearing when she was killed. Both are among the "intimate details" cited by Hartman.

When he first reached out to federal investigators in October 1982, Spirko said that he knew the identities of three men involved in the crime and that, while at a party in the Toledo area, he had seen a bag that might have contained loot from the robbery.

Spirko described it merely as a sack, made of cloth or canvas, according to notes of that preliminary interview with a different investigator.

By his first interview with Hartman, however, the sack had morphed into a cream-colored bag with "loop handles" and "brown trim around edges," according to Hartman's notes, a description that matched Mottinger's missing purse. That's the description Hartman read to the jury.

But the investigator's handwritten notes show that the words "loop" and "brown trim around edges" were all added sometime after the original notes about the bag were written.

Again, experts say, it's not possible to tell when the additions were made.

The same thing happened with the description of Mottinger's clothing.

In an interview with Hartman on Dec. 10, 1982, Spirko indicated that he had seen Mottinger alive in the basement of a "safe house" after she had been kidnapped.

"The defendant described the victim's clothing, indicating that the postmaster had been wearing dark slacks, a light yellow blouse, which buttoned in the front and bearing a print design," Hartman told the jury.

Spirko insisted at trial that it was Hartman who supplied those details.

And a glance at the investigator's handwritten notes reveals that the entire description—"dark slacks, light yellow blouse, button front, print design"—was added after the original notes were written, and in a different handwriting style.

Again, no way to tell when.

Hartman insisted recently that he had added nothing to his notes, that any changes were nothing more than innocent corrections.

"All these notes were written contemporaneously. They were written during the interviews," he said. "What happened is, obviously, in the course of writing the notes, I went back and added these little notations."

* * *

On Aug. 17, 1984, a week after his original testimony, Hartman was called back to the witness stand on the last day of Spirko's trial. He denied prompting or suggesting any information in his interviews with Spirko.

"For me to have done those things would have violated seriously sound investigative procedure and would have completely destroyed the integrity of the investigation," he testified.

But just a few moments later, while still on the stand, Hartman made the most dramatic addition of all to the notes of his interviews with Spirko.

Asked if Spirko ever actually admitted killing Betty Jane Mottinger, a detail conspicuously absent from his notes and earlier testimony, Hartman said that, as a matter of fact, he had.

Defense attorney Ed Hatcher was stunned.

"Would you like to tell me when he told you that?" Hatcher asked.

"He stated that to me . . . on January 11th of 1983," Hartman replied, the date of his second-to-last session with Spirko.

In an internal memo written sometime after that interview, Hartman asserted that Spirko said to him that day: "Lay it all on me. I killed her."

But defense attorneys had never heard such a claim before.

In fact, in at least two sworn statements made after the Jan. 11 interview—statements in which he summarized his theory of Spirko's involvement—Hartman had mentioned nothing of the sort. Likewise in his testimony—and cross-examination—about the Jan. 11 interview.

And the notes of Hartman's interview for that day—which he had earlier testified were "accurate in all respects"—contained nothing even close to such an admission.

Hatcher pressed him on the notes: "Well, let's take a look and see, OK, on that date. You would have written that down, wouldn't you?"

The investigator calmly replied, "I don't believe that that is in my notes."

Hartman, who retired from the U.S. Postal Inspection Service in early 2000, after nearly three decades in law enforcement, said recently that he didn't need notes to recall the encounter.

Retired postal inspector Paul Hartman has no doubt about Spirko's guilt. (Photograph courtesy of Chuck Crow/*The Plain Dealer*)

"I didn't need to write that down to know that he said it," Hartman said in an interview at his Medina County home. "I remembered it then. I remember it now."

And he remains just as certain that Spirko deserves to die for killing Betty Jane Mottinger.

"It is my belief that he did it," Hartman said. "If and when they execute him, I will have no qualms. No qualms."

* * *

Just days after Hartman's final appearance on the witness stand 20 years ago, Spirko addressed the postal inspector's assertions in a remarkable statement to the jury.

But first, with his conviction freshly on the books, Spirko asked the jury to recommend the death penalty. Even while insisting he was innocent.

"I have never seen Betty Mottinger in my life," he said. "I did not kill Betty Jane Mottinger. I did not kidnap Betty Jane Mottinger. But, I have been convicted for it.

"From what I have heard, a lady that went to work, bothered no one, had a family, a husband that loved her, she was cruelly taken away, brutally murdered. She didn't get no appeal. Nobody gave her that right. Instead, they just stabbed her to death. They probably still out there now laughin' about it; laughin' because I got convicted of it. But she deserved justice, and if that means me, then that's the way it should be. I'm convicted, I should die. It's simple; simple arithmetic."

Spirko blamed no one but himself for his predicament. "I started all this" by reaching out to authorities in the first place, he said. "I put myself in this position."

But then he turned to his battle of wits with the postal inspector.

"I don't actually hold no animosity towards Paul Hartman," Spirko told the jury. "But he did not tell you the truth, not about the statements.

"Why? I can't tell you why. But who am I . . . to call the government liars, the state liars, when I'm a known liar?

"My chances of gettin' up there and telling the truth were nil. But I did tell you the truth. That's the hell of this whole thing. I have told you the truth.

"I feel one thing. I might be bound for hell, but I know Paul Hartman will be right on my tail end. And him and I is going to have a go-around in hell. You can believe that."

38. Painter: Give Me Polygraph in Spirko Case

OCT. 16, 2005

By Bob Paynter and Sandra Livingston

The former house painter who divulged a 15-year-old secret in 1997 about who might have killed an Elgin, Ohio, postmaster is challenging federal authorities to give him a lie-detector test.

John Willier told a Wyandot County investigator eight years ago that the man he painted houses with in Findlay in the summer of 1982 was involved in Betty Jane Mottinger's murder that August and threatened to kill him if he ever told. But federal officials have never contacted him about the allegation.

With death-row inmate John Spirko set to be executed next month for Mottinger's murder, Willier told *The Plain Dealer* on Friday that he is just as willing to talk to officials now as he was in 1997.

Painter Asks for Polygraph

He said he's just as convinced that the shroud Mottinger's body was wrapped in is the very tarp that his boss, Dale Dingus, used on a painting job about the time of the murder.

And he's just as troubled as Jim Bedra—a member of the Ohio Parole Board—that law enforcement officials have never followed up on his assertions about Mottinger's death.

Last week, at Spirko's second clemency hearing before the parole board, Bedra pressed state officials about why they have never reached out to Willier, even though the information he provided about a possible killer has been known for more than eight years.

It's "very strange," Willier agreed on Friday in a telephone interview. "Nobody has got ahold of me."

Mottinger was kidnapped from her tiny, rural post office on Aug. 9, 1982, and was stabbed at least 13 times. Her body, wrapped in a paint-splattered shroud, was found six weeks later in a soybean field a few hundred yards from the rented house trailer where Willier lived.

He was considered a suspect early in the investigation, but investigators lost interest in him in late 1982, as they focused on Spirko.

Dingus, Willier's boss that summer, was running his painting business out of a barn on U.S. 224, also less than a quarter-mile from the spot where Mottinger's body was found.

On Aug. 1, 1997, while being questioned on an unrelated matter by William Latham, an investigator for the Wyandot County prosecutor's office, Willier disclosed that Dingus was involved in Mottinger's kidnapping and murder, both of which followed a botched drug pickup by Dingus and others at the Elgin post office.

In a letter in December from the Avoyelles Correctional Center in Louisiana, where he was serving a 25-year sentence for rape, Dingus told *The Plain Dealer* he had no involvement in Mottinger's death.

On Friday, Willier said authorities investigating the murder showed him a piece of the paint-splattered shroud and he recognized it as part of the dropcloth he and Dingus had been using to paint a Findlay house that summer.

"I am 99-point-nine-tenths sure that that tarp came from that painting job," Willier said. And, he said, besides the owner of the house, Dingus was the only one who had access to the tarp.

"That's the key thing that has me baffled over the years," Willier said. "Look, if this guy—this John Spirko—if he don't know me and I don't know him and he don't know Dingus and Dingus don't know him, how the hell did he get the tarp?"

Willier lives in a small town in Tennessee and works in the cable industry. He declined to discuss the specifics of his 1997 statement to Latham, although he said he stands by it.

But Willier did say he is more than willing to talk to federal authorities—and he's eager to take a lie-detector test about his assertions to Latham, both to finally clear his own name and to help reopen the investigation. He said he offered to take a lie-detector test in 1982 to prove he wasn't involved in the murder, but has never been given one.

"I've been out of trouble since 1988," Willier said, referring to a past scarred by drug involvement and criminal convictions. "I'm very clean now. I'm married. I go to church and everything. I just want this to leave me alone."

But he also expressed some sympathy for Spirko's situation.

"I think about it a lot," Willier said. "It has me bothered. Because what if there is an innocent person there. And what if the guy that actually did it—or guys or whoever—are walking free?"

Parole board member Bedra sounded a similar theme on Wednesday, although not necessarily on Spirko's behalf. Bedra described Willier's story as a legitimate lead, especially in light of 1984 testimony by a forensic scientist called by the defense. The expert testified that paint on the shroud matched paint that Willier and Dingus had been applying to Findlay homes that summer.

Bedra challenged state officials to pursue Willier's story in the interest of justice—for Mottinger and her family.

Everyone agrees that more than one offender was involved, Bedra said. Regardless of whether Spirko is guilty or innocent, he said, "we can all assume that one or more offenders is still out there. I think the state missed a window of opportunity."

Bedra urged officials—especially Van Wert County Prosecutor Charles Kennedy, in whose county the crime occurred—to follow up. "Who knows what you'll find?" Bedra said.

It could not be determined if Kennedy plans to heed Bedra's advice. He could not be reached Friday.

Charles Wille, an assistant Ohio attorney general, expressed skepticism at Wednesday's hearing that any evidence could be found now to corroborate Willier's account.

When asked Friday whether the attorney general's office would try to find Willier, spokeswoman Kim Norris said in an e-mail that a federal judge had already determined that the Willier issues weren't relevant because they didn't prove Spirko was innocent.

Bedra's suggestion followed the videotaped testimony of Wyandot County investigator Latham, who has broken ranks with the law enforcement community to appear on Spirko's behalf at both of his clemency hearings.

Latham has said he found Willier's story far more credible than the prosecution theory that put Spirko on death row.

No physical evidence implicated Spirko, and nothing was found to link the lifelong criminal and admitted con man to Elgin, Mottinger or the area outside Findlay where her body was found.

In fact, investigators had never heard of Spirko until he came forward, saying he had information about the crime he wanted to trade for lenient treatment for himself and his girlfriend in an unrelated case.

Spirko was convicted largely on the basis of his own testimony and a series of jailhouse interviews he gave to former postal inspector Paul Hartman. During both, state attorneys say, he revealed details about the case that only the killer could know—an assertion his attorneys vigorously dispute.

Spirko's lawyers offered an alternative theory at the 1984 trial that Mottinger was murdered in Willier's trailer. Dingus was also living there temporarily about that time.

Latham has said that Willier's story, coupled with recent challenges to Hartman's credibility and the quality of the evidence, raises questions about whether Spirko had anything to do with the Mottinger slaying.

Although he alerted the U.S. Postal Inspection Service about Willier's account several times by phone eight years ago, Latham said no attempt has been made to follow up.

Recently filed court documents show that Latham's calls in 1997 inspired a flurry of memos between postal officials in Washington and Cleveland, where Hartman was based at the time.

The documents had been in Hartman's files, which were made public only recently, after a federal judge's order.

According to the memos, postal officials in Washington seemed ready to come to Ohio to interview Willier.

But Hartman, the investigator most responsible for putting Spirko on death row, was dismissive of the Willier story, telling his boss in one September 1997 memo that "this whole thing sounds like a defense ploy to me."

Describing Willier at the time as a "goofy, 19-year-old kid," Hartman said a fellow investigator described him as so unreliable "that even if you knew it was raining, and Willier told you it was, you'd have to look out the window just to verify the fact for yourself."

In fact, Hartman wrote, "I read this as an ex-convict trying to do a favor for Spirko, a convict; and that Willier has a beef with Dingus."

Still, after speaking with Latham, Hartman recommended that if the Washington investigators wanted to interview Willier they "bring along the polygraph examiner, so that we can work this out and get to the bottom of the entire matter."

But after he spoke to Hartman on Sept. 9, 1997, Latham said he never heard from postal authorities.

Latham met with Willier again, along with Spirko's attorneys, two years later and reported that no one had contacted Willier either.

Willier said on Friday that he has heard nothing from anyone since.

He said he initially talked to Latham in hopes of bringing attention to the issues because things didn't seem right. Now he would like to clarify them for good and move on.

"Just to clear people's minds, hey, let's get it on. Let's do this lie-detector test and then leave me alone from then on for the rest of my life."

39. Taft Must Decide If Doubts Justify Reprieve for Spirko

OCT. 30, 2005

By Bob Paynter and Sandra Livingston

In the six years since executions resumed in Ohio, Gov. Bob Taft has never found a compelling reason to reject a death-penalty recommendation from the Ohio Parole Board.

He's gotten 19 recommendations from the board—all but one advocating execution—and he has followed them every time.

But never before has Taft received a parole board report like the one he got two weeks ago in the case of John Spirko, with so many board members expressing such profound doubt about whether an inmate was guilty.

After two daylong clemency hearings, the board has twice voted 6–3 against clemency for Spirko. But after the second hearing on Oct. 12, the three dissenters didn't just disagree. They gave Taft a litany of what they described as "compelling factors" that raise doubt about whether Spirko should be executed in a little more than two weeks for the 1982 slaying of Elgin, Ohio, postmaster Betty Jane Mottinger.

In only one other death-penalty case during Taft's tenure have three dissenters argued for clemency. But their reasons in that case stemmed from the inmate's youth and his parents' neglect—not from doubts about actual guilt.

In Spirko's case, however, the dissenters raised three basic questions about his 1984 conviction. They questioned the quality of the evidence against him, the fairness of the prosecution and the credibility of the key investigator and primary accuser.

But unless Taft or the courts intervene, John Spirko will die Nov. 15.

Unresolved Issues, Undisclosed Evidence

Three members of the Ohio Parole Board, not convinced that John Spirko committed murder 23 years ago, asked the state's lawyers a series of pointed questions during Spirko's Oct. 12 clemency hearing.

Many of the doubts they raised about the case were fueled by information that was unknown to the jury that convicted Spirko in 1984 and to many of the appellate court judges who have since declined to grant him relief.

Attorneys for the state argued, to the apparent satisfaction of the board majority, that Spirko's own words—to investigators and to the jury—were enough to convict him of robbing the tiny Elgin post office on Aug. 9, 1982, and of kidnapping and fatally stabbing Postmaster Betty Jane Mottinger in the process.

And they produced recent declarations from four of the original jurors that they stand by their verdict.

But that wasn't enough for board members Ellen Venters, Jim Bedra and Sandra Mack. "There is too much residual doubt," they told Gov. Bob Taft in their dissent, "to execute John Spirko."

Question: Why, when dealing with a lifelong liar like John Spirko, does the state's case rely almost exclusively on what Spirko said, not what he did? "Where is the conduct?"—board member Ellen Venters.

Here's What's Known

Spirko was a busy man on Aug. 9, 1982—the day Betty Jane Mottinger disappeared from her Elgin post office—shuttling between various activities in Toledo and Swanton, two hours to the north. And prosecutors never provided a timetable showing how he could have squeezed in a trip to Elgin and back.

Nor did they have any physical evidence linking Spirko to Elgin, Mottinger or the murder scene.

In fact, Spirko never appeared on investigators' radar until nearly three months after the crime, when he contacted them. The career criminal and habitual liar said he had information he wanted to trade in return for lenient treatment for his girlfriend and himself in an unrelated case.

In more than a dozen untaped interviews that followed, Spirko told investigators a series of gruesome, ever-changing tall tales about what he said he knew about the Mottinger murder.

Investigators tried to chase down Spirko's many leads but came up with nothing.

They argued that, embedded among the lies, Spirko's stories contained details that showed he knew things only the killer could know—something they say he acknowledged in a letter to his girlfriend. The letter was as filled with bravado as his interviews.

What's never been clear is where the details came from. Many had been reported in various news outlets before Spirko came forward. And others, Spirko's lawyers argue, might have been supplied—deliberately or inadvertently—by investigators.

One of the details was a description of Mottinger's purse. Spirko first told one postal inspector he had seen a canvas "sack." Two days later, Spirko met with another inspector who had earlier gotten a detailed description of Mottinger's purse from her family. Suddenly, Spirko's vague description radically changed, matching almost verbatim the one given to the inspector weeks earlier, including a precise recitation of the purse's dimensions.

Other descriptions, like the victim's clothing, appear to have been added later to an investigator's notes—in a different handwriting style.

Since none of the key interviews was taped, his attorneys and their experts have questioned whether some of the details were supplied by investigators. The investigators dispute this.

But Spirko never led them to new information to corroborate his stories, a troubling deficiency, according to a national expert on wrongful convictions who appeared before the parole board. And there's plenty that Spirko didn't know.

Twice he told investigators he knew nothing about stamps being stolen from the post office, although more than $700 worth had been taken.

Twice he told investigators that Mottinger had been stabbed in the back, but there was no evidence of back wounds.

Spirko twice described the diminutive, 105-pound woman in his stories as "fat."

It was widely reported that her body was found wrapped in a shroud. Prosecutors claimed that Spirko knew what the shroud looked like (he said it was "gray") and how Mottinger's body was wrapped (shroud "flapped...end to end over head"). But Spirko didn't appear to know the most memorable facts about either.

He said nothing about two concrete blocks wrapped with the body, or about the rope and duct tape used to bind the shroud around her neck, waist and legs. And he didn't appear to know the most obvious detail about the shroud—that it was covered with paint spots, a fact that led every investigator at the scene to describe it as a painter's drop cloth.

(A former house painter disclosed in 1997 that the shroud matched the dropcloth he and his boss used on painting jobs that summer, near where Mottinger's body was found, and that his boss was involved in the crime. Investigators never followed up on the lead.)

Despite what Spirko said and didn't say, evidence of what he did the day of the crime tends to undercut the prosecution's case.

Investigators discovered that Spirko—released two weeks earlier from prison in Kentucky—met for more than an hour with his parole officer in Toledo, although it's not clear at what time.

He went to a doctor's office with his sister that afternoon, also in Toledo. He also called the Kentucky prison from Swanton that afternoon to inquire about his personal belongings. And he signed for a package at the Swanton post office.

Conclusions

The board majority said Spirko knew details of the crime and that he convicted himself with his own words. On matters like the lack of physical evidence, the content of Spirko's statements and the quality of his alibi, the majority deferred to the original jury.

Citing the alibi, the dissenters disagreed. With a "plausible" timetable from Spirko, and none at all from the state, "we are again left with residual doubt," they wrote.

Question: Why did the state put John Spirko on trial and not his friend Delaney Gibson, even though both were indicted and the state claimed it had much stronger evidence placing Gibson at the scene of the crime?—board member Ellen Venters.

Here's What's Known

On the morning of Betty Jane Mottinger's kidnapping, Elgin resident Opal Seibert said she saw a clean-shaven stranger standing outside the post office beside a two-toned car, with one arm resting on top of the open door. She then saw him drive away minutes later, without anyone else leaving or entering the car.

Mark Lewis, a truck driver, saw a man in exactly the same position, also beside a two-toned car, about the same time.

Unless two men in identical cars stopped by the Elgin post office at the same time that morning and stood wedged between car and door in exactly the same manner, it's likely that the two witnesses saw the same man, although they described him quite differently.

A few months later, Spirko was wrapping up his final untaped interview with the primary investigator, Postal Inspector Paul Hartman, when he suddenly—and, until recently, inexplicably—changed his story a final time. His best friend and former cellmate, Delaney Gibson, had killed Mottinger, Spirko now said, and told him all about it.

Not long after, Lewis picked Spirko's photo from a lineup, but said he was only 70 percent sure that was the man he saw that day—hardly beyond a reasonable doubt, even according to the prosecutor.

Seibert picked out an old photo of Gibson. But she said she was 100 percent sure that he was the Elgin stranger—even though Gibson was 20 years younger and half a foot shorter than the man she originally described. She was never asked to identify Gibson in person.

Based on Spirko's stories and Seibert's memory, both men were indicted on capital murder charges in September 1983.

Over the next several months, Hartman gathered extensive evidence—evidence that wasn't disclosed to Spirko or his lawyers for more than a dozen years—indicating that Gibson was nowhere near Elgin the day of the crime and that he didn't look anything like the old photo that Seibert picked out.

Investigators noted at the time, in an internal memo, that the interviews of Gibson had gone nowhere. So, just before Spirko's trial, prosecutors released Gibson to Kentucky to face noncapital charges there.

When Spirko went on trial—alone—in August 1984, prosecutors used Seibert's supposedly unshakeable identification of Gibson to link Spirko to Elgin on the day of the crime.

Gibson, back in Kentucky, was not available to rebut the claim. Spirko and his lawyers contend that prosecutors claimed Gibson was in Elgin on the morning of the crime—despite the undisclosed evidence that he was hundreds of miles away the night before—simply to convict Spirko.

Ohio authorities have never tried to bring Gibson to trial. After serving time for a Kentucky murder, Gibson was paroled in 2001. The Mottinger charges against him were quietly dropped last year.

At Spirko's clemency hearing, Venters wanted to know why prosecutors released the 100 percent suspect before putting their 70 percent defendant on trial. The state's attorneys said they weren't involved in the case at the time and didn't know.

Spirko's lawyers say their client stuck to the Gibson story during the trial—even though it was just as false as the other tales he spun for investigators—because he didn't have the evidence to disprove the state's claim that Gibson was there.

Had they been given the evidence that Gibson was nowhere near Elgin that day, they say, Spirko's final story would have fallen apart, just as all the previous ones had.

Conclusions

The board majority didn't agree that prosecutors intentionally withheld evidence of Gibson's alibi, and said Spirko's lawyers made a "strategic decision" not to pursue it.

The dissenters found the state's persistence in using Gibson's purported presence in Elgin to convict Spirko to be another cause for doubt. Earlier, they had described the tactic as "death by association."

"We cannot ignore the possibility that Gibson was 600 miles away when the offense was committed," they wrote. "This possibility causes residual doubt."

Question: Why would the primary investigator and star witness against John Spirko "reverse his testimony" by declaring recently that he never believed a key piece of evidence used to convict Spirko in the first place? —board member Jim Bedra.

Here's What's Known

On at least three occasions in the past 18 months—twice in tape-recorded interviews—retired postal inspector Paul Hartman disclosed that he never believed that Spirko's best friend, Delaney Gibson, was involved in Betty Jane Mottinger's murder and that he told the prosecutor as much at the time.

The revelation was critical because the prosecution used Gibson's alleged involvement—bolstered by an eyewitness who said she was certain she saw him outside Mottinger's tiny post office at 8:30 a.m. the day of the crime—to help convict Spirko in 1984.

Hartman said he concluded Gibson wasn't involved in part because of evidence that he gathered—including dozens of photographs and several witness statements—that placed Gibson hundreds of miles from Elgin the evening before the crime. That evidence was not provided to Spirko's lawyers until 13 years after their client's conviction.

Hartman later claimed under oath that he made these disclosures to "mislead" a reporter and Spirko's lawyers.

When pressed at Spirko's clemency hearing two weeks ago, state attorneys said they could not explain Hartman's statements about Gibson's role.

But one possible explanation lies in a 22-year-old memo that suggests that it was Hartman who had lured Spirko into implicating Gibson in the first place.

Hartman knew all about Gibson from an extensive background investigation he conducted after learning that the two men had spent time in prison together.

By early 1983, Hartman had already listened to a host of Spirko stories during more than a dozen jailhouse interviews, stories that he had tried in vain to corroborate. Gibson's name had never come up.

But in one of their last interviews, Hartman acknowledged in an internal memo, he steered their conversation to Bear Branch, the tiny Kentucky hamlet that both men knew was Gibson's home. That's just the kind of coaxing that can taint an interrogation, experts say.

Spirko took the bait. The next day, he suddenly changed his story, saying for the first time that Gibson killed Mottinger and told him all about it.

Coupled with the dubious Gibson identification by the state's eyewitness, that story—repeated by Spirko from the witness stand—provided the crux of the state's case. But questions about the source of the Gibson story cast a shadow on other claims Hartman made about Spirko as well.

All of the revelations Spirko was said to have made about the crime—including a purported confession—came during untaped interviews, virtually all with Hartman. With several revelations, most notably a description of the victim's clothing, the critical details appear to have been added later to Hartman's original notes.

Questions have been raised about other details as well.

The state has stressed Spirko's purported knowledge of the "pried stone"—a tiny rhinestone found to be missing from a $7.99 ring found on Mottinger's body.

Given its size and quality, the stone is just as likely to have fallen out during a struggle as to have been pried out. But the fact that the stone was missing was never publicly reported. In his notes and testimony, Hartman said that Spirko told him that one of the characters in his stories pried it loose.

But Spirko testified he knew nothing about a stone until Hartman brought it up, quoting the investigator as telling him that the man he was after is " 'that stinkin' son of a bitch that pried that stone out of her ring.' That's the first time I heard anything about a ring."

Questions about Hartman's notes also figure in the story of Spirko's purported confession.

On the last day of Spirko's trial, Hartman testified that Spirko had confessed to him in early 1983—that during one of their final interviews, Spirko had blurted out: "Lay it all on me. I killed her."

Curiously, Hartman had testified in detail about that interview several days earlier and had never mentioned any such confession. Nor did any mention of it appear in sworn statements Hartman made about the evidence in the case.

His interview notes were silent on the matter as well.

"I don't believe that that is in my notes," Hartman told the jury.

Conclusions

The board majority said it wasn't convinced that any recent Hartman falsehoods proved that he doctored the Spirko interviews or lied during his trial testimony.

The dissenters described Hartman's "apparent deceitful conduct" as "reprehensible," saying it lent credence to claims by Spirko's lawyers that the key witness against their client is not believable.

"We are once again wrought by residual doubt," they wrote.

HOW THIS SERIES WAS PUT TOGETHER

To prepare this series, *The Plain Dealer* examined:

- Hundreds of pages of transcripts and the exhibits from John Spirko's 1984 trial.
- Thousands of pages of investigative documents, disclosed in 1997 after years of litigation and filed in court.
- Briefs and opinions from state and federal appeals courts.
- Dozens of newspaper, magazine and wire-service stories about the murder of Betty Jane Mottinger and the investigation.
- Court documents, news stories and other public records detailing the criminal histories of Spirko, Delaney Gibson Jr. and others.

The newspaper also interviewed Spirko, the lead investigator—retired Postal Inspector Paul Hartman—and:

- Attorneys on both sides in the 1984 trial.
- Investigators in other cases involving Spirko, Gibson and others.
- Spirko and Gibson family members.
- Forensic-document examiners.
- Experts on police interrogation procedures, wrongful convictions and DNA technology.

A conversation with
Bob Paynter

---

*An edited e-mail interview conducted by Poynter Institute faculty member
Scott Libin with Bob Paynter, winner of the ASNE watchdog reporting award.*

**SCOTT LIBIN: Where did the idea come from for your "Cold-Blooded
Liar" series?**

BOB PAYNTER: In June 2004, a friend of John Spirko's e-mailed *The
Plain Dealer* saying that Spirko was about to be executed on flimsy evidence for a 1982 murder he didn't commit, that the prosecution had withheld evidence and that his case would make a great story.

Notes from prison inmates professing innocence or unfair treatment are
not rare. But I'd never received one in a death-penalty case. Plus, I was between projects. And the paper had written virtually nothing about the Spirko
case. So, long shot though it was, I decided to nose around. Just a little.

Where and how did you collect the information?

I figured my efforts would be short-lived. Barring a glaring miscarriage of
justice, far easier to imagine than to find, I didn't see a story at all. I assured
myself I would work the case just long enough to confirm that Spirko was
guilty, then move on. I called his newest team of lawyers and got their take.

One eyebrow rose slightly. I searched out earlier news stories. I studied the appellate briefs and decisions. At first, there seemed plenty to suggest he might be guilty. But a gnawing sensation started to take hold as
well. Spirko's bizarre explanation of how he came to be implicated in the
murder of a rural Ohio postmaster, without having had anything to do
with it, was so much stranger than fiction that it begged for a second look.

And the prosecutors' tactics—both in what was presented at trial and
what was allegedly withheld from the defense—seemed downright offensive. I decided to go to Phase II. I got a full trial transcript, witness lists,
copies of exhibits and appeals-court filings. I got boxes of documents,
assembled by the prosecution and defense teams that were coughed up
during pre- and post-trial discovery. And I waded in. My goal was simple:
Kill that gnawing sensation, or make it grow.

How did you decide what the focus would be?

The focus was easy and obvious: The citizens of Ohio were about to kill a
man for a crime he didn't do. Absent that story line, Spirko's looming exe-

cution didn't stand apart from the others Ohio was carrying out and would have warranted no more than daily news coverage.

The question was: Is it true? Or, do I believe it's true? After all, a jury had convicted Spirko. A judge had sentenced him to die. And at least five layers of post-conviction review had unequivocally allowed those verdicts to stand. Plus, John Spirko couldn't have been less sympathetic.

A career criminal who had spent virtually his entire adult life in prison, Spirko's most recent arrest prior to being implicated in the postal murder had been for threatening a woman with a shotgun after a bar fight and beating a guard with an iron pipe during an attempted jail break. All within weeks of his parole from a 1970 murder conviction. And thanks to his own big mouth, wild imagination and misguided arrogance, Spirko had done far more to implicate himself than the entire investigative team combined.

Still, as I waded deeper into the evidence, that gnawing sensation grew deeper and harder to shake. Despite its perverse logic, Spirko's version of events started to make more sense than the investigators'. It seemed to fit more precisely with verifiable facts. And in the light of once-hidden evidence—evidence concealed from the jury and from defense lawyers for more than a dozen years—the integrity and credibility of the chief investigator grew shakier and shakier.

Increasingly convinced I had a story, the problem became: How in the world can I tell it?

How did you organize your story?

John Spirko had nothing that would make a skeptical reader care about him. Nothing that would elicit sympathy—or even much discomfort—over his fate. Nothing that society would consciously regret losing. Even if he had nothing to do with this murder, he could hardly be described as an "innocent" man. No poor-defendant-abused-by-system approach would ring true in his case, no matter how true it might actually be. About the only thing Spirko could be expected to inspire in a typical *Plain Dealer* reader was revulsion. And maybe curiosity.

Therein lay the organizational key. Central casting could not have invented this man. Abused, beaten and neglected as a child; defiant and unrepentant as a youth; brutal and unfeeling as an adult; wildly grandiose and spectacularly unsuccessful as a manipulator of the system, Spirko fascinated me from the beginning.

Delaney Gibson, his one-time cellmate, and supposed accomplice in the postal murder, was even more intriguing, and added a taste of mystery because his role in the case was crucial and ephemeral at the same time. At some point it occurred to me that if I could hook into readers' fascination with these two characters, I might be able to lead them to what the story was really about: How a failing, high-pressure criminal investigation apparently went bad. How a prosecution was fundamentally marred by hidden evidence and deliberate untruths. How a flawed, self-destructive and unsympathetic man was tried, convicted and sentenced to death more for who he was—and who he chose for friends—than for what he actually did.

In Part One, Spirko's character could help to explain how he got into such a fix. In Part Two, Gibson's exploits could show why investigators were tempted into bending the rules to use him to snare Spirko. And in Part Three, investigator Paul Hartman's interaction with Spirko and Gibson could demonstrate how the good guys can sometimes cross the line. In the beginning, it might have been clear enough to readers who the "Cold-Blooded Liar" was. By the end, not so much.

How many drafts did you do?

Many. I tend to write in pieces. First I organize what I know into key points. Then I summarize each point, along with evidence I can use to make it. I rewrite and reorganize each summary, making each point as concisely and leanly as possible.

Then I start constructing drafts, stringing points together in as efficient and compelling a structure as I can, polishing and condensing as I go. Whenever I add a structural element, I rewrite and recalibrate everything that went before, trying to maintain rhythm and flow. So, by the time I actually have a draft, its innards have been rewritten and reorganized multiple times. Then the drafts get redone. In this case, they probably went through three or four iterations.

What revisions did you make to the story before publishing?

The story was originally built in four parts. My editor, Stuart Warner, wisely counseled three. He also helped with the structural concept of building each story around a central character. As I move my points around and string them together, I don't always leave them in the best spots. Stuart found and set me straight on several structural blind spots, easing narrative flow and eliminating needless repetition.

What role did your editor play?

Stuart is an excellent line editor with a keener eye than mine for needless words and a truer narrative sense. He also has a gentle way of pointing out annoying literary habits. I have an unconscious affinity for introductory clauses, for instance, and for phrases like "for instance." The stories probably still have too many. But Stuart weeded many out.

To what extent did you understand, when you began this project, how big it would become?

I had no idea. As I said earlier, I thought this would be like any number of false conviction tips I've received in the past. Some of those have panned out. But the overwhelming majority don't. And it usually doesn't take long to find out. This one kept getting more intriguing, kept requiring more evidence to examine and more boxes of documents to wade through.

Did you start out with any particular plan or approach in mind, and, if so, how did that hold up or change over the course of the year you spent reporting this story?

Actually, I spent closer to seven months reporting and writing the original series and several more months doing follow-ups later.

The plan all along was to test the possibility that Spirko was wrongfully convicted. Without that, I didn't see a story. What changed over the course of the research was my level of faith in that premise. Even solid criminal prosecutions are acts of theater, with both sides trying to color the evidence to support their positions. Those colorations, in turn, tend to become stronger and less ambiguous the more often they are repeated, summarized and encapsulated in appellate briefs and decisions.

One of the most surprising things about this case was the often substantial difference between these prosecutorial or judicial portrayals and the actual evidence. As I reviewed court filings, I repeatedly came upon references, or descriptions of evidence, that appeared to convincingly confirm Spirko's guilt.

More than once, I was tempted to abandon the project because the evidence, as I was seeing it portrayed, seemed too strong to overcome. But time and again, the reality grew ever more ambiguous and the actual evidence considerably less convincing the deeper I explored.

Summaries of Spirko's statements to investigators are prime examples. When excerpted and quoted by prosecutors and in later appeals, these critical pieces of evidence were portrayed as slam dunks for guilt. But when examined in their entirety and in context, they were anything but, raising far more questions than they answered. Riddled with inconsistencies, factual inaccuracies and suggestions of investigator misconduct, these supposed statements became what I consider to be the most compelling arguments for Spirko's innocence.

What were the biggest surprises you encountered along the way, not just in the actual investigation, but in terms of its effect on you?

I suppose my biggest surprise was the fixation I developed on the victim, Betty Jane Mottinger, and her family. I found myself thinking about them constantly and hoping, praying really, that whatever came of this story, it would do more good than harm.

Clearly, John Spirko was no prize. I met him and interviewed him once. I found him to be humbled by his two decades on death row, but I was determined not to believe a word he said. The thought that a man—any man— might be executed for something he very possibly didn't do, on the basis of such a flawed investigation and prosecution, is the fuel that drove this project.

But no matter how many questions I have about his guilt—and I have plenty—I will never be certain. Absent a smoking gun, I can't be. Mrs. Mottinger's family members have clearly been through a slow-burning hell over the last two decades. They are virtually unanimous in their belief that Spirko killed their loved one and deserves to die for it. As it became clear that I would call that view into question, I knew the story would cause them additional pain. That bothered me more than I expected.

Even though I couldn't share it with them, my solace was this: That the worst possible sin against Betty Jane Mottinger today—and, on some level, the worst thing for her family—would be to execute the wrong man in the name of justice for her. I believe that, but the conviction didn't come quickly or easily. That's probably a good thing.

How would you compare this with other investigative work you've done?

This is not the first time I've questioned a criminal conviction in print. In fact, I'm viscerally drawn to the subject. Our justice system frequently works. But I believe it also errs far more than we care to admit. I'm always on the lookout for a graphic illustration, because I think a bit of humility in the administration of justice makes us all safer. But this is the first time the death penalty was involved. And I believe it's the first story I've ever done where a human life arguably was at stake. For me, that's no small thing. And it's probably more complicated psychologically than anything I've done before.

Can you describe the tone, style or voice you used in your writing?

Not really. I didn't consciously strive for any particular voice or style. As I got deeper into the research, however, I kept recalling "The Thin Blue

Line," Errol Morris' brilliant documentary deconstructing a bogus conviction in the 1976 murder of a Dallas police officer.

Rather than exposing the ugly flaws in the investigation and prosecution of Randall Adams, the film more or less evoked the truth of the matter, in a way I've never forgotten. Essentially, Morris told and retold the story of the police officer's death and its aftermath from an ever expanding set of viewpoints, adding detail and damning perspective with each new telling.

In the viewing, the approach felt understated and straightforward. But without ever being stated directly, its conclusion—that Adams was wrongly convicted because of over-zealous and unethical cops and prosecutors—was both overwhelming and indisputable. While researching the Spirko story, I found a copy on the Internet and watched it again. I can't say exactly how, but I'm sure that film influenced both the tone and the presentation.

Finally, what's the latest?

John Spirko is alive, although still very much in jeopardy. His execution date has been postponed four times since the stories appeared because of lingering questions, most recently in June 2006. At his attorneys' request, Ohio authorities are trying to determine if any of the evidence might contain DNA that could be compared to that of several men whose names have surfaced in the case. That process is ongoing. Barring clemency from Ohio Gov. Bob Taft, Spirko is now scheduled to die on Nov. 29, 2006.

Writers' Workshop

Talking Points

1. The Spirko case unfolded over more than two decades, across thousands of pages of legal documents and along story lines that often crossed in confusing ways. How does the writer's organization of the story make it manageable and understandable?

2. Bob Paynter says he originally planned four pieces for his Spirko series, eventually settling on three at the urging of his editor (other articles would be co-authored). Each of the three pieces focuses on one main character. In what other ways could he have broken up the story?

3. Paynter uses telling detail and shifts in tone to describe people and settings in his story. Identify some examples involving the town of Elgin, Spirko's father and the cast of characters Spirko said killed Betty Jane Mottinger. What effect do these details have on the narrative?

4. There are no clear heroes in the "Cold-Blooded Liar" series. How does Paynter deal with the flawed, unsympathetic natures of Spirko, Hartman and Delaney Gibson? How does Paynter use details to flesh out their personalities?

Assignment Desk

1. Bob Paynter brought readers insight previously unseen about a criminal case that has taken more than 20 years to work its way through the courts. What cases are there in your community or state that could form the basis of such a story? Select one to investigate that hasn't been in the news lately, but that remains on appeal or otherwise unresolved.

2. Paynter's story goes inside the Spirko case to explore possible flaws in the way the criminal justice system functioned. Find another element of government, maybe an agency, program, or department where you live that deserves similar scrutiny. Report on the way it works or doesn't work, showing readers a side of life to which they might not otherwise be exposed.

3. Consider the way Paynter provided context critical to understanding the Spirko case: the defendant's background, the geography and distances involved, professional standards for interrogation of suspects, etc. Review your own reporting and find an example that would benefit from further context. Research and report some additional elements to give greater perspective, helping readers evaluate and interpret the information you have already included.

Los Angeles Times

Finalist

Robin Fields, Evelyn Larrubia and Jack Leonard

Watchdog Reporting

40. When a Family Matter Turns Into a Business

NOV. 13, 2005

Helen Jones sits in a wheelchair, surrounded by strangers who control her life.

She is not allowed to answer the telephone. Her mail is screened. She cannot spend her own money.

A child of the Depression, Jones, 87, worked hard for decades, driving rivets into World War II fighter planes, making neckties, threading bristles into nail-polish brushes. She saved obsessively, putting away $560,000 for her old age.

Her life changed three years ago, when a woman named Melodie Scott told a court in San Bernardino that Jones was unable to manage for herself. Without asking Jones, a judge made Scott—someone she had never met—her legal guardian.

Scott is a professional conservator.

It was her responsibility to protect Jones and conserve her nest egg. So far, Scott has spent at least $200,000 of it. The money has gone to pay Scott's fees, fill Jones' house with new appliances she did not want and hire attendants to supervise her around the clock, among other expenses.

Once Jones grasped what was happening, she found a lawyer and tried, unsuccessfully, to end Scott's hold on her. "I don't want to be a burden to anyone," she told a judge, almost apologetically. "I just wanted to be on my own."

Jones' world has narrowed. She used to call Dial-A-Ride and go to the market, or sit in her driveway chatting with neighbors.

Now she spends her days watching television in her living room in Yucaipa, amid pots of yellow plastic flowers and lamps with no shades. The caretakers rarely take her from her house, except to see the free movie each Friday at the local senior center.

"I'm frustrated, because I don't know my way out," she said, sitting within earshot of one of Scott's aides. "There must be a way out."

Jones' conservator is part of a young, growing and largely unregulated trade in California.

Conservatorship began as a way to help families protect enfeebled relatives from predators and self-neglect. As a final recourse, courts take basic freedoms from grown men and women and give conservators sweeping power over their property, their money and the smallest details of their lives.

But lawmakers and judges did not foresee that professionals would turn what had been a family matter into a business.

In the hands of this new breed of entrepreneur, a system meant to safeguard the elderly and infirm often fails them.

The *Times* examined the work of California's professional conservators, reviewing more than 2,400 cases, including every one they handled in Southern California between 1997 and 2003.

Among the findings:

- Seniors lose their independence with stunning swiftness. More than 500 were entrusted to for-profit conservators without their consent at hearings that lasted minutes. Retired candy company owner Donald Van Ness, 85, did not know what had happened to him until he tried to pay for lunch at a San Diego-area restaurant and was told his credit card had been canceled.

- Some conservators misuse their near-parental power over fragile adults, ignoring their needs and isolating them from loved ones. One withheld the allowance that a disabled man relied on for food, leaving him to survive on handouts from a church. Another abruptly moved a 95-year-old woman to a care home and for a month refused to tell her daughter where she was.

- In the most egregious cases, conservators plunder seniors' estates. One took 88-year-old Thelma Larabee's savings to pay his taxes and invest in a friend's restaurant. Helen Smith's conservator secretly sold Smith's house at a discount—to herself. The conservator's daughter later resold it for triple the price.

- More commonly, conservators run up their fees in ways large and small, eating into seniors' assets. A conservator charged a Los Angeles woman $170 in fees to have an employee bring her $49.93 worth of groceries. Palm Springs widow Mary Edelman kept paying from beyond the grave: Her conservators charged her estate $1,700 for attending her burial.
- Once in conservators' grasp, it is difficult—and expensive—for seniors to get out. Courts typically compel them to pay not only their own legal fees, but those of their unwanted guardians as well. In the 15 months it took Theresa Herrera's grandson to unseat her conservator, almost half of the 92-year-old's $265,000 estate had been exhausted.

"It's really scary," said Mitchell Karasov, a North Hollywood attorney who specializes in elder law. "Would you want that to happen to you? This is what we'll have to look forward to—that we'll be disposable when we no longer have a voice."

There are about 500 professional conservators in California, overseeing $1.5 billion in assets. They hold legal authority over at least 4,600 of California's most vulnerable adults.

Yet they are subject to less state regulation than hairdressers or guide-dog trainers. No agency licenses conservators or investigates complaints against them.

Probate courts are supposed to supervise their work. Yet oversight is erratic and superficial. Even when questionable conduct is brought to their attention, judges rarely take action against conservators.

Three of the past four governors have vetoed legislation that would have provided tougher oversight.

This deeply flawed system is about to be hit by a demographic wave. By 2030, the number of Americans older than 65 is expected to double. Experts predict that as many as 10 percent of them will suffer from Alzheimer's disease.

'She Was Managing'

Helen Jones said she always dreaded the sort of old age she has now, marked by childlike dependence.

Married only briefly and late in life, Jones said she had always done for herself, even as a child in Nebraska, where she scavenged for coal along the railroad tracks to help keep her family warm.

Before Scott entered her life, she kept her financial records in accordion files, paid her bills promptly and knew how much money she had, down to the penny.

She was nearly deaf, and a rare disorder of the nervous system limited her mobility. But she could still make her way to the bank and take her wash to a local laundromat.

"She was managing," said Alice Wilson, a neighbor for more than 30 years. "She's a self-sufficient person."

As Jones' conservator, Scott took over her checking account and put her on an allowance, initially $50 every two weeks.

Scott started making improvements to Jones' pale stucco home, installing central air conditioning, a new refrigerator and a washer and dryer. Scott paid her own sister $1,550 to paint the house.

It pained Jones to see someone else spending her money. So frugal that she still has a red-knit sweater she wore 60 years ago, she even complained when Scott billed her $40 for a Christmas tree. The plastic one in her garage would have done just fine, Jones said.

Decisions about her medical care were another source of contention.

Scott said in court papers that, months after becoming her conservator, she received medical records indicating that Jones had once been diagnosed with schizophrenia.

Scott's staff began taking Jones to a psychiatrist. He prescribed Zyprexa, a drug used to treat schizophrenia and bipolar disorder. Jones refused to take it, saying she did not have either condition.

An aide hired by Scott, Gerlie Kirbac, said one of the conservator's subordinates told her to crush the drug into Jones' food, but she refused.

Kirbac said she also took Jones to the bank so she could check on her money and was fired for it.

"Melodie told me I can't handle Helen," she said. "I said, 'What kind of handle do you want?' "

Scott, 47, whose conservatorship business is the largest in the Inland Empire, said she could not discuss the case because Jones' medical history is private and her complaints are the subject of litigation.

"It would be horribly unethical to breach Mrs. Jones' dignity and right to confidentiality," Scott said in a statement.

In her most recent court filing, a routine list of bills and fees, Scott described Jones as "alert, conversant, obstinate, independent and often paranoid."

She also said Jones suffered from schizophrenia.

Carefully annotating her own copy of the report, Jones circled "schizophrenia" and wrote a comment in the margin: "BS."

Early this year, as Jones struggled to reclaim her independence, she lost her younger brother, Frank Janicek.

He was her last bit of family, her Sunday telephone call. A former Douglas Aircraft worker who served in Africa during World War II, Janicek died of pneumonia in January at 85.

Jones wanted him to have a traditional burial. An earlier experience had left her strongly opposed to cremation.

But upon learning that Jones had a conservator, the funeral home called Scott, who made arrangements for the disposal of Janicek's remains.

In March, a caretaker drove Jones to Riverside National Cemetery, then pushed her wheelchair to a shelter about the size of a bus stop.

A bugler played taps. Two women in dress uniform folded an American flag and presented it to Jones.

She was pleased to see her brother put to rest with military honors.

But she noticed that there was no coffin.

Instead, there was a brass urn containing Janicek's ashes.

Rise of a Profession

The concept of conservatorship dates back at least to medieval England, where guardians were appointed to manage the property of people deemed "lunatic."

In the U.S., California stood for decades as the model for a humane system. The state pioneered legislation in the 1960s and '70s to protect against arbitrary or needless conservatorships. Adults were guaranteed advance notice of court hearings to appoint a conservator, along with legal representation and the right to a jury trial.

Lawmakers assumed the conservator would be a family member or friend.

In 1969, John M. Mills, an economics professor at El Camino College, rented a room in a downtown Los Angeles church and opened what is believed to have been the state's first conservatorship business.

Twenty years later, a court banished Mills from the trade after the state attorney general's office accused him of financial irregularities. By then, he had inspired many others to enter the field.

In most instances, loved ones still act as conservators for incapacitated old people. But professionals now handle about 15 percent of the cases in Southern California.

Although some have only a few clients, others run thriving businesses, managing the lives of more than 100 adults at once. An elite group focuses on wealthy seniors, employing large staffs and commanding rates of up to $135 an hour.

Conservators hold positions of trust on a par with lawyers, accountants and investment firms. In contrast with those professions, however, they don't have to earn degrees or pass licensing exams. Anyone with a clean felony record who pays a $385 state registration fee can go into the business.

Only now is the state moving to impose basic standards. Beginning next year, conservators will need a college degree, experience in the field or certain levels of training. Most current practitioners will not be affected, however.

Conservators find clients by sponsoring breakfasts at senior centers and networking at legal luncheons. Nursing homes call when residents become too addled to pay the rent, wanting a conservator to write checks for them. Hospitals call when patients have outlasted their insurance, hoping that a conservator will move them somewhere else.

Once conservators identify a prospect, they can go to court and initiate a case without the client's approval.

With rare exceptions, they look for people with money. Frumeh Labow, Los Angeles' busiest conservator, sets a minimum of $300,000—enough to guarantee her paycheck for at least a few years, if the client lives that long.

Other conservators have a more modest threshold.

"If the person has six months, the doctor tells me she has terminal cancer and she only has $30,000, I'll take a chance on that," said Jeffrey Siegel, who runs a large Los Angeles practice.

In many cases, professional conservators have done admirable work. Some have saved seniors from con artists or thieving relatives. Others have ensured that lonely adults lived out their last days in dignity.

Many continue to serve clients after their money has run out.

"We're in this business to help people and to protect people," said Ron Patterson, a Bay Area conservator who is president of the Professional Fiduciary Assn. of California. "None of us are here, I believe, to enrich ourselves in any way except the natural way one does in business."

But even some conservators admit they would not want one themselves.

"I can decide who they see. I can put them in a nursing home," said Labow. "It's the biggest imposition on your civil liberties short of being imprisoned."

Quickly in Control

Professional conservators take over with jarring speed. In many courtrooms, they get emergency appointments on the day they ask for them, based on short forms in which they swear that prospective clients cannot care for themselves.

These hasty hearings are meant for cases in which elderly people are in imminent danger. But professional conservators have made them the norm, the *Times* found. More than half of their Southern California cases began this way.

Adults are entitled by law to attend emergency hearings. Yet they were not formally notified in more than half the cases the *Times* examined. Often, judges dispensed with the requirement after conservators told them that prospective wards were too feeble to come to court.

By securing immediate appointments, professionals can gain control over elders before safeguards required in non-emergency cases kick in. For example, in nine of 10 emergency cases, wards were not interviewed by a court investigator before a judge decided they needed a conservator.

The events leading to Jones' conservatorship began in November 2002, when a chance acquaintance, Cindy Gurrola, gave her a ride to the bank. After Gurrola expressed concern for Jones' welfare, a bank employee gave her the business card of a Redlands company that serves the elderly.

Gurrola said she called the number and gave an employee Jones' address. There was no mention of conservatorship or that Jones would be giving up legal control of her affairs, Gurrola said.

About a week later, Jones said, she was napping in her home when a woman walked in and woke her. The woman said she was with "CARE."

Jones said she thought that meant California Alternate Rates and Energy, Southern California Edison's reduced-rate program for seniors.

Jones signed a one-paragraph document, not bothering to read it.

In fact, the woman worked for Conservatorship and Resources for the Elderly Inc., the firm owned by Melodie Scott. The document said that Jones nominated Scott to be her conservator.

"I was sleeping here and someone tapped me on the shoulder and said sign this," Jones said. "And stupid, I signed it, not knowing what I was signing.

"To me, 'conserve' means to save and I thought this was a way of saving me money so I wouldn't have to pay utilities."

The nomination was dated Nov. 22. Eleven days later, Scott filed an emergency request to become Jones' conservator. She said Jones could not keep up with her bills, had a house full of clutter and could no longer manage "the activities of daily living."

Judge Phillip M. Morris granted the petition the next day.

After about a year, Jones decided to fight back. A bank clerk told her that she could not redeem a CD that had matured—only Scott could.

Upset, Jones had her caregiver take her to see paralegal Barbara Seifritz at the Yucaipa Senior Center.

Jones appeared so clear-headed and well-informed that Seifritz was surprised to learn she was under conservatorship. So was Bob Roddick, Seifritz's boss at the nonprofit Inland Counties Legal Services.

At a hearing in March 2004, Roddick told Judge David A. Williams that Jones did not need a conservator.

"She seems perfectly capable of taking care of herself," Roddick said.

"Well, we already have a conservatorship," the judge replied.

"I have it, but I would like to terminate it," Jones told him, confiding her worry that Scott was draining the savings it had taken her 60 years to build.

The judge could have ended her conservatorship on the spot or directed his staff to investigate. He did neither.

He appointed an attorney to review the handling of Jones' finances, but left her in Scott's hands.

By then, Jones had gotten a look at Scott's expense records and saw that her money was going out nearly three times as fast as it was coming in. Scott's firm is spending Jones' money at a rate of $84,000 a year, records show. Her income is about $27,000 a year.

At a hearing in August 2004, court-appointed attorney Donnasue Ortiz challenged the conservator's fees and spending as "excessive."

Scott sought to justify the expenses by saying that Jones was "near death" when she intervened. She told the court that Jones had left a convalescent home "against medical advice," that she was "totally dehydrated and malnourished" and that her garage harbored "thousands of rats," prompting complaints from neighbors.

Jones called Scott's description "one big fabrication." She said that she spent several days in a nursing facility after suffering a fall in October 2002 but that a social worker signed her out, saying she did not need to be there. Two friends who drove her home corroborated her account.

As for rats, three of Jones' neighbors said in interviews that they never saw or complained about any.

In July, with the conservatorship still in place, a frustrated Roddick filed a petition to end it. A judge refused to hear his arguments, saying he had no standing to intervene.

The judge scheduled a hearing for Dec. 2 at which Jones will be represented by Ortiz.

"I don't know how this is going to turn out," Jones said outside the courtroom. "My age is against me and my hearing is against me."

'Chewing Up Estates'

From the moment seniors are entrusted to a professional conservator, the meter is running.

The law allows conservators to spend their wards' money as they see fit and requires them to submit periodic reports. Courts must approve their fees, but state law sets no limit on their compensation beyond that it be "reasonable."

Reports examined by the *Times* show that conservators have billed elderly people for what one described as "drive-by" property inspections and for moving furniture around a room.

Frances Dell, 90, paid her conservator $715 for accompanying her to parties and informing her that her favorite niece had died, among other services. "She needed someone to cry with and mourn her own mortality," the conservator wrote in her bill.

Seniors often pay for layers of helpers hired by their conservators—property managers, home-care supervisors, case managers and more. They pay for flowers, chocolates and other gifts that conservators give them on special occasions.

Among the Christmas presents one woman unwittingly lavished on herself: men's cologne and a stocking with her name embroidered on it, misspelled.

"The word is *conserve*. You're supposed to conserve people's estates," La Mesa probate attorney Richard Schwering said. "Conservatorship is chewing up estates."

The bills pile up even faster when seniors or their families challenge conservators' control.

Wards pay their conservators' legal bills on top of their own because the court does not consider the parties to be adversaries.

Even when conservators oppose their clients' wishes, they are assumed to be looking out for their best interests.

Street-smart and self-made, Charles Thomas built an $18-million empire by investing in Burger King franchises and real estate in some of Los Angeles' toughest neighborhoods. After he was diagnosed with Parkinson's-like symptoms, it became clear he would have to hand over the reins of his businesses.

Thomas had a complex family, with children from several marriages. He picked an outsider—Labow—to be conservator of his estate.

She was appointed in September 1998. Just over a year later, Thomas told his court-appointed counsel that he "wanted Frumeh Labow out of my life."

Labow refused to go, saying Thomas had chosen her before his illness clouded his judgment.

After five years, Labow remained in charge. Thomas had paid $1.1 million in fees to her, the lawyers his relatives had hired to oust her, and the six attorneys Labow had hired to fend them off and manage his holdings.

Suffering from aphasia, Thomas, 70, is no longer able to speak for himself. His family has come to accept that Labow will be a permanent presence in their lives.

"You can't fight them if they're using his money to fight you," said his son, Michael.

'Sarah Could Be Trusted'

Court-sanctioned fees are the only compensation to which conservators are entitled for managing the affairs of their clients.

The *Times* found at least 50 instances in which conservators used their authority over seniors' assets to benefit themselves or their friends, relatives or employers in other ways. Courts approved many of their actions, though often with incomplete information.

A Sacramento conservator hired his live-in girlfriend's firm to auction off his wards' possessions and sell their houses. A San Francisco conservator decorated his apartment with a client's valuable Chinese paintings.

Melodie Scott acknowledges that she let another professional conservator, Sarah Kerley, live rent-free in a client's house in Glendale for months. Kerley was married to Scott's brother at the time.

Scott did not disclose their relationship in her reports to the court. In an interview, she said the three-bedroom, Spanish-style house was in poor condition and that Kerley made repairs in lieu of paying rent and, later on, in exchange for reduced rent.

Scott said she did what she thought was best for the client, Jeanne Ledingham.

"There was no intention ever to take advantage of Ms. Ledingham to the benefit of Sarah Kerley or myself," Scott said. "I thought I was being a hero. . . . This charming little house, this beautiful garden—Sarah could be trusted."

While Kerley was living there, Ledingham paid the utility bills, as well as thousands of dollars to a gardener and a property manager hired by Scott.

Ledingham, who suffered from bipolar disorder, was 51 when Scott took control of her affairs. Scott moved her into a board-and-care and, later, an apartment while Kerley lived in her house.

Ledingham's daughter, a sophomore at a Louisiana college when the conservatorship began, said she was appalled by what happened.

"There were all these people—conservators, attorneys, judges," said Candace Ledingham-Ramos. "No one was looking out for my mother."

Marin Support Services for Elders, a nonprofit group for seniors, was supposed to look out for Florry Fairfield.

Fairfield, a retired real estate agent who had never married, lived with her miniature schnauzer, Daisy, in the quiet Bay Area suburb of Fairfax.

Anne Smith, then director of Marin Support Services, became Fairfield's conservator in March 2001 after telling a court that Alzheimer's-type dementia had left her "clearly unable to handle her affairs or resist undue influence."

Less than a month later, Fairfield, then 82, signed a new will. It was drafted by the lawyer representing Marin Support Services in the conservatorship case.

The will made the organization the main beneficiary of Fairfield's $1.1-million estate and named Smith co-executor.

California law bars professional conservators from inheriting from their wards in such circumstances unless the will was reviewed by an independent attorney or a court. There is no evidence that either step was taken in Fairfield's case.

The law clearly applies to individual conservators. It is unclear whether it applies in this instance because the beneficiary of the will was Marin Support Services, not Smith. Still, experts said, neither conservators nor their employers should become their clients' heirs because it creates a conflict of interest.

"What incentive do they have then to keep the client alive?" said Mitchell Karasov, the elder-law attorney. Every penny spent on the ward's care would reduce the conservator's bequest, he said.

William Kuhns, the lawyer for Marin Support Services, said he drew up the will at Fairfield's request. She decided on her own how to divide her wealth, he said.

"Maybe it gives you the appearance of a conflict of interest, but I've been an attorney for many years, and I'm very comfortable that this was in accordance with her wishes," said Kuhns.

Kuhns collected more than $36,000 for his work on Fairfield's conservatorship and estate.

Four weeks after Fairfield signed the will, a judge deemed her dementia severe enough to disqualify her from voting.

Asked how Fairfield could be too demented to vote, yet able to divide a million-dollar estate, Smith said she could not comment, citing concern for Fairfield's privacy. Speaking generally, she said that people suffering from dementia could still possess the mental soundness to make such decisions.

"Dementia is not a black-and-white disease," Smith said. "People can be very clear about some things and very confused about others."

When Fairfield died, Marin Support Services inherited more than $675,000.

'Lurking in the Shadows'

Even elderly people who have organized their affairs in advance can be pulled into this broken system.

Robert Mushet thought his mother was set.

Dorothy Mushet had signed papers designating her son, then an engineer with Boeing, to make decisions for her if need be. When she began to show signs of dementia, he arranged for her medical care and managed the money she had inherited from his father and earned as a saleswoman for Joseph Magnin Co.

Then, in September 2002, Robert got a call from his mother's nursing home. A Santa Barbara court, he learned, had appointed a professional conservator for Dorothy, then 94.

"I hung up the phone and darn near collapsed," Robert recalled.

His estranged daughter had petitioned for a conservator, saying he had moved Dorothy to the nursing home against her will. The daughter nominated Suzanne McNeely, a leading Santa Barbara conservator.

Robert said he moved his mother because it was dangerous for her to live at home in her weakened state.

With court permission, McNeely moved Dorothy Mushet back into her house and hired her own firm to provide round-the-clock aides for four months, for which she later tried to charge $68,000.

Robert ultimately persuaded a court to make him his mother's conservator, as she had wanted, and to cut McNeely's total bill from $80,600 to about $24,000.

"You brought a matter to court that shouldn't even have come here," Judge J. William McLafferty told McNeely and her attorney.

Though victorious, Robert Mushet said he ran up $50,000 in legal fees. McNeely appealed the judge's reduction in her fee, ultimately settling for a $5,000 increase.

Dorothy died in March 2003. Her son said he felt strangely grateful to her disease for shielding her from the nasty tug of war that poisoned her final months.

"It would've killed my mom if she knew anything about this," he said.

Gerardine Brown, a state parole officer, had little notion what conservatorship was until she retrieved a letter from her mailbox one night in May 2000.

It said a stranger had asked to become her 86-year-old mother's conservator. A judge was set to hear the case 12 hours later in Los Angeles—375 miles from Brown's home outside Sacramento.

Brown got into her car and sped south, driving through the night. "I didn't have time to hire an attorney," she said. "I'm standing there in front of the judge with no idea of what I'm going to face."

Brown's mother, Charlotte Shelton, was a retired biochemist whose work for the Navy broke ground for a woman of her era. Brown—her only child—said she called Shelton regularly, trying to persuade her to move closer to her remaining family as her health failed. Shelton clung stubbornly to her home in Eagle Rock.

Sarah Kerley, the same conservator Scott had let live in a client's house, told the court that Shelton's doctor had asked her to step in. Kerley arranged for a psychiatric evaluation that led to Shelton's involuntary hospitalization in a mental ward. Then Kerley filed papers to become her conservator.

The judge appointed Kerley temporarily while a court-appointed attorney assessed Shelton's condition. The attorney reported three weeks later that he saw no reason why Brown should not assume responsibility for her mother, as long as she did not move her from Southern California. When the judge approved the change, Brown figured the conservator was gone.

Not so. Kerley fought for a continuing role in Shelton's life, challenging Brown on who should pick her mother's doctors and who should be her permanent conservator.

Eventually, Brown said, she agreed that her mother would pay Kerley's fees and those of her attorney if Kerley would stay out of the family's affairs. Just as the settlement was being finalized, Shelton died.

The conservator and her attorney later collected almost $18,000 from Shelton's estate.

Kerley did not respond to requests for comment.

"These people are just lurking in the shadows," Brown said. "It's just chilling to think it can happen to anybody."

Postier v. Marshall

Over 13 days beginning in September 2002, the rarest of scenes played out in a San Jose courtroom.

Lawyers for an elderly woman named Ruth Postier took a professional conservator to trial, accusing him of violating her rights and wasting her money.

Russell Marshall, a well-known Santa Clara County conservator, had secured an emergency appointment to look after Postier, then 77, and her husband, Ed, 80, in August 2000.

Until then, the Postiers had eked by, relying on friends for help. Married since they were teenagers, they had no children or surviving close relatives. They had only Social Security for income, having exhausted their savings from an upholstery business.

Their house was their one real asset, worth more than $500,000 despite its crumbling roof and exposed wiring. It held decades of memories, including a wall of ribbons won by Stardust, their champion Doberman.

In the eight months that Marshall was their conservator, the Postiers chafed at his authority.

After Ed allegedly threatened Ruth during an argument, Marshall moved him into a locked nursing home without the necessary court permission. He later moved the Postiers into separate apartments in an assisted-living complex and put their home up for sale.

Marshall also exhausted their meager resources, incurring more than $50,000 in unpaid bills. He hired a family therapist, paying her $65 an hour not only to counsel the couple, but also to shop for pillowcases, wastebaskets and other household items.

After two months, a court investigator came to check on the Postiers. They complained bitterly about Marshall. Public Defender Malorie Street was assigned to represent the couple and objected when the conservator asked to have his temporary control over their affairs made permanent.

Marshall, in an interview, defended his conduct.

"They wanted me to be their conservator because they wanted to move," he said. He said he had planned the Postiers' expenses carefully and would not have run up debts if Street's opposition had not delayed his efforts to sell their house.

In April 2001, Ed died and the county public guardian took responsibility for Ruth.

After Marshall submitted his final report, Street demanded that the court sanction him for abusing her clients.

When the matter went to trial, a videotape deposition Ruth had given months earlier was shown in court. She could not testify in person, having suffered a stroke that left her speech almost unintelligible. Instead, her worn face appeared on a TV screen, oxygen lines running from her nose.

"Did you want Ms. Street to sue Russell Marshall?" the conservator's attorney asked her.

"Well, he sure didn't do right by me," Postier replied. "He made a mess of my life."

She described how the conservator began removing her belongings from the house as she ate dinner one night.

"Just hauled it out, whether I liked it or not," she said.

Postier said she had never wanted to leave the home she had shared with her husband for so many years. Though they argued often, she once told a friend she wanted their headstone to say, "Ruth and Ed Postier, Together Forever."

She raised trembling, papery hands over her eyes.

"I went through hell," she said.

Superior Court Judge Thomas Hansen found that Marshall had increased the Postiers' indebtedness and moved Ed without proper authority. Nonetheless, he decided Marshall's conduct did not constitute elder abuse.

Hansen awarded Ruth nominal damages of $1, saying it was impossible to measure monetarily what harm, if any, Marshall's actions had caused her.

The judge awarded Marshall and his legal team $75,000. Later, Postier's own lawyers collected more than double that amount, swallowing what was left of her estate.

Street came away stunned.

"That case sent me around the bend," she said. "The statutes designed to protect my clients didn't."

Shortly before Ruth Postier died on May 29, 2003, her caretakers deposited Marshall's check to her.

It was for $1.02.

Damages plus interest.

ABOUT THIS SERIES

Caring for the aged and infirm was once a family affair. Now, it is a business. In documenting this change, reporters Robin Fields, Evelyn Larrubia and Jack Leonard and researcher Maloy Moore examined records of more than 2,400 cases handled by California's professional conservators since 1997. They also conducted hundreds of interviews—with probate lawyers, judges and independent experts as well as people under conservatorship and their loved ones.

To see a photo gallery, share your experience and ask the reporters a question, visit latimes.com/conservators.

Lessons Learned

BY ROBIN FIELDS, EVELYN LARRUBIA AND JACK LEONARD

We knew we would face formidable hurdles in trying to tell the story of how California's adult guardianship system fails the elderly and sick people it is meant to protect.

We were taking readers into an obscure corner of the legal system, one full of jargon and complexity.

This led to our biggest challenge, one that we faced from our first drafts to our last edits: How do you tell the story of being caught in a system without losing the reader in the dull intricacies of that system?

We decided to focus on examples that touched people's lives and pocketbooks in direct, easily explainable ways. It was the smallest, most specific details that made characters come alive. That wasn't as simple as it sounds.

Victims were usually suffering from dementia or other illnesses when their conservatorships started. By the time we learned about a case, frequently the victim was dead. Others were so addled they could not express how they felt.

We met Ruth Postier just weeks before she died. A stroke had left her partially paralyzed and almost entirely unable to speak. She had no relatives who could tell us how she and her husband came to be in the hands of a professional conservator.

Searching for details about her life, we tracked down the couple's friends and neighbors. We learned that the Postiers had married as teenagers and kept show dogs, including a Doberman called Stardust.

A videotaped deposition allowed us to quote Ruth Postier directly. We used the final detail of the story—the damages a judge awarded Ruth in the case—to show how the system values the rights of the elderly and infirm.

The sheer volume of information in our research—culled from more than 2,400 case files—was among our greatest assets but also forced us to make choices. Using extended examples like Postier's was far more evocative than listing all the abuses we unearthed. It was painful to leave out so much of our reporting, but it was more important for readers to empathize with victims than to learn about each episode of wrongdoing.

Helen Jones was a thrifty Midwesterner who wound up in an unwanted conservatorship even though she seemed to have her wits about her.

Her conservator would not talk to us but raised questions about Helen's mental competence in court, saying that Jones was schizophrenic and near death when the conservator intervened. Rather than underplaying these concerns, we tackled them head-on in the piece. In fact, those questions became central issues in telling her story.

Jones was someone who had worked and saved hard so that she would always be independent. She complained about a loss of dignity and control over her life. It's a writing cliché, but we needed to show readers that, rather than just tell them.

It wasn't easy. Jones didn't talk in sound bites. And she was nearly deaf, so interviewing her was lengthy and exhausting. But we went back to her again and again to get the crucial details.

There were the mounting conservator bills. The alleged attempt to secretly give her psychiatric drugs against her will. And the final indignity—her brother's funeral, as arranged by the conservator.

Jones' story provided the backbone of the piece. Still, we struggled to find a way to intermingle more explanatory material about our investigation's findings with the narrative of her case. Ultimately, we wrote the story in 25-inch chunks, each of them focused on a single theme. That gave us a workable structure and sense of pace. It also helped us see what *didn't* need to be in there.

The story triggered a massive response. We got hundreds of calls, e-mails and blog entries. Readers identified with our characters because everyone has elderly relatives or knows someone who faces similar issues.

In the end, the emotion and outrage of our series lived in the characters and individual stories more than in raw statistics.

Robin Fields is a metro reporter for the Los Angeles Times. *Her awards include an honorable mention for outstanding education reporting in the Benjamin Fine awards, and a first place for non-deadline business reporting awarded by the South Florida Society of Professional Journalists in 1998.*

Evelyn Larrubia is a metro reporter for the Los Angeles Times. *She was a finalist for the deadline writing prize awarded by the American Society of Newspaper Editors in 1997, and she received the Livingston Award for Young Journalists in local reporting in 1996.*

Jack Leonard is a metro reporter for the Los Angeles Times. *He was part of the* Times *team that won the Pulitzer Prize for breaking news coverage of the wild-fires that ravaged southern California in 2004.*

The Oregonian

Finalist

Maxine Bernstein and Brent Walth
Watchdog Reporting

41. Flawed Disability Fund Is a Costly Crutch for the City

JULY 3, 2005

A disabled police officer stands guard over Portland Trail Blazers owner Paul Allen at the Rose Garden.

An injured firefighter scrambles up mountains and through woods on his TV show, "Northwest Hunter."

Another disabled firefighter owns an upscale Portland restaurant, aided by city taxpayers who subsidized his training at the prestigious French Culinary Institute in New York.

All have one thing in common: Though clearly able to work, they continue to collect thousands of dollars in benefits each month from the Portland Fire and Police Disability and Retirement Fund.

Disability programs in Oregon and most major U.S. cities serve as a temporary safety net for injured police or firefighters while they are unable to work, moving them off benefits and back to jobs as soon as possible.

Not in Portland.

An investigation by *The Oregonian* found the city's system is an open checkbook, with rules that allow injured police and firefighters to collect checks until they retire, even if they can earn a living in another job.

Although voters tried to fix the system 16 years ago, the newspaper found that the reforms have had little lasting effect in moving people off disability rolls and reducing costs.

Instead, one in nine Portland police and firefighters is on disability, and they go out at four times the rate of their peers statewide. Although injury claims typically close after about a year in other Oregon cities, half the recipients in Portland's $15-million-a-year system have been collecting checks for a decade or more. A claim for lost wages in Portland costs $37,390 a year on average—seven times that of police and firefighters statewide.

The program's costs have doubled in the past decade and are projected to keep rising. And meaningful cost controls don't exist because City Hall has never had to worry about paying the bills: Money for the disability fund comes straight from Portlanders' property taxes—$373 this year for the average house.

"All of the incentives are backwards," said Edward Welch, a workers' compensation expert at Michigan State University. "It's an incredible system. I can hardly believe it."

Nor does it work for the injured. Many police and firefighters say that, once hurt, they find the city no longer wants them, leaving them to collect disability checks even though they could work in some capacity.

"The system is flawed because of its design," said John Hash, a police officer on disability since 1992 who now helps oversee operations of TriMet's light rail. Benefits helped while he couldn't work, he said, but it feels awkward to accept them since he's recovered.

"Ultimately, who's losing in this? The citizens in the city of Portland," he said. "I feel kind of bad for taking it, but at the same time I'd feel stupid for not taking it."

The Oregonian's findings come despite resistance from fund trustees, who voted to block the newspaper's requests for financial and other records and in April sued to prevent them from being released. With the lawsuit still pending, the paper relied on dozens of interviews and previously released fund documents to prepare this report.

Defenders of the system, which voters created in 1948, agree that it needs improvement. But they say police and firefighters who risk their lives in the state's biggest city are deserving. Some suffer grievous injuries from falls, car accidents or gunshots. Many had their careers cut short and hold little hope of returning to any job.

"I truly believe if you're a firefighter or police officer and you're injured on duty protecting Portland citizens, the city has an obligation to maintain your living standards," said Tom Chamberlain, a former trustee on the fund's board and a past president of the Portland Firefighters Association.

City Commissioner Randy Leonard, a former fire union president and past trustee of the fund, says police and firefighters have come to depend upon a system that has proved to be stable, predictable and professional.

"If every bureau in the city ran as well as (the fund), we'd be a very well-run city," Leonard said. "They take caring for taxpayer dollars very seriously."

But the fund has done just the opposite—failing to enforce rules that could rein in costs.

The fund can suspend the benefits of anyone who is capable of working and won't look for a job. It never has.

A fund consultant found last fall that staff did a poor job of tracking medical conditions for the 212 members now out on disability, as required by the city charter. Nor did the fund's staff often know whose responsibility it was to get people on disability back to work.

And police officers have filed and won disability claims that allowed them to sidestep being disciplined or fired, despite reforms intended to halt the practice.

Oversight of the fund comes from a board of trustees dominated by police and fire union members and other bureau officials. Even though the disability fund's staff work as part of the city auditor's office, there has been no city audit of the fund's operations for 11 years.

Fund officials say they don't calculate basic spending benchmarks—such as how long claims stay open or what they cost—because the trustees don't ask them to. The staff did not know that they approved 95 percent of all disability claims until *The Oregonian* filed a public records request to discover the number.

Spending on the disability program is only part of the fund's $86.5 million a year budget, which mainly goes to funding police and fire pensions. But disability costs are growing at a faster rate.

The fund is exempted from property tax limits, which means its tax rate can rise automatically to cover all of its costs. Other government services—still subject to tax limits—get what's left. As a result, the fund consumed $14 million that otherwise would have flowed to schools, libraries and parks over the past eight years.

Fund trustees and officials say they are improving the system. The Fire and Police Bureaus recently have agreed to offer a few light-duty jobs to disabled employees after years of resistance.

But many of these changes come as the fund faces greater scrutiny. In January, the City Council appointed a nine-member citizen task force to study the fund and propose reforms by year's end.

Mayor Tom Potter sat on the fund's board in the early 1990s when he was Portland police chief. As mayor, he serves as its chairman.

Potter said he's determined to fix the system, knows that significant changes will require voters to approve a city charter amendment, and understands that police and firefighters unions could mount campaigns to protect the status quo.

City Auditor Gary Blackmer, who also is a fund trustee, said that as things stand now, the board lacks authority to force police and firefighters off disability if they are able to work.

"If they can be gainfully employed," Blackmer said, "why should we keep paying them?"

Payments Go Back Decades

In November 1967, The Beatles released their "Magical Mystery Tour" album and "The Andy Griffith Show" was the most popular series on television. That same month, Portland police officer Arthur Bell was hurt on the job.

As of the start of this year, records show, he still was collecting a monthly disability check of $3,294.

The exact nature of Bell's 37-year-old injury isn't known. Records aren't available to show when he left work. And Bell won't say. "I respectfully decline to comment," he told *The Oregonian.*

His case illustrates one of the fund's biggest problems—claims that have been open for decades.

As of December, 75 police and firefighters were under what is called the fund's "old plan," covering those hurt before voter-approved changes in 1990. Members of this group receive 60 percent of their base pay, regardless of whether they are able to work and are earning income from another job.

The fund's records show these recipients collected $2.8 million in benefits a year.

Bell, 61, now lives in the south coast town of Lakeside. He co-founded Bell Family Nursery in Aurora in 1979 and sold it in 1999, according to state and county records.

The newspaper used court files, business records and interviews to locate Bell and others like him who have worked in other jobs while continuing to collect benefits. *The Oregonian* found as many as 11 who have worked in construction. Others, who've lived as far away as Hawaii and the Virgin Islands, have been real estate agents, bus drivers or run their own businesses.

- Lawrence Barnum, 61, a police officer injured in 1976, collects $3,294 a month. Today, he's a homebuilder working through his company, Vintage Homes NW of Tigard.

- John V. Pahlke Jr., 59, a police officer injured in 1982, collects $1,163 a month. Pahlke has worked as a registered nurse in Oregon and Arizona since 1986, according to state records. As recently as last year, Pahlke worked at Legacy Emanuel Hospital & Health Center in Portland.
- Leonard Collins, 57, a police officer injured in 1976, collects $3,294 a month. State records show Collins in the past few years has worked as a home inspector and owned a business called Freeway Fix-It Man in Milwaukee.

By comparison, a police officer on the job at least five years makes $5,299 a month today.

Taking Bullet, Benefits

Barnum, Pahlke and Collins all declined interview requests. But one disabled officer said he nearly gave his life protecting the community and deserves ongoing benefits even though he has another job.

Jeffery Brose, 49, a police officer injured in 1980, collects $3,232 a month. Since June 1998, Brose has been licensed as a private investigator in Gresham.

"I took a .357 Magnum right there," Brose said, lowering his shirt collar to reveal a scar on his upper chest. Brose said he had been on the job six months when he was shot on July 31, 1980. He was chasing a prisoner who escaped from the Yamhill County Courthouse, where Brose was off-duty and waiting to testify. Brose went back to work for several years, but he said he never was "100 percent again."

Just because he can work private investigations, Brose said, does not mean he could return to police work.

"What I do is Sunday school compared to what the police on the streets do," he said. "No one shoots at me. I never have to fight. . . . What I do is shuffle a bunch of papers."

Others on disability have far more active jobs, however.

Richard Young said he injured his left knee in training in 1981 as he ran to jump onto a fire truck. Since then, he said he's had five surgeries. He went on disability in 1988 and now receives $4,036 a month in benefits.

Since 1992, Young has starred in his own TV show, "Northwest Hunter," and sold videos called "Northwest Hunter Greatest Hits." The show and videos feature him pursuing mountain goats, white-tail deer and moose in Canada, Alaska and Montana.

Young said his injuries make it impossible to resume firefighting. Hunting is another matter, he said.

"It's a controlled atmosphere," Young, 46, said. "That's the big difference."

Young said the disability board approved what he's doing but added that the fund recently left him with the impression he should "get off TV."

Babette Heeftle, the fund's administrator, declined to discuss Young's case, citing privacy concerns. But she said she doubted the fund's staff would have told him to quit TV.

Young said he wouldn't give up his show anyway.

"I'm not doing anything illegal," he said. "Why should I quit?"

Rules Allow Moonlighting

Among other things, the 1990 reforms were meant to prevent police and firefighters from collecting full benefits while holding outside jobs. The changes set up what is called the fund's "new plan," which allows a higher maximum benefit—75 percent of base salary—but requires members to report any outside income.

Under the plan, benefits are supposed to be reduced based on how much members earn and the status of their disability, although there is a minimum benefit of 25 percent of base pay. As with the state workers' compensation system, benefits are tax-free if the disability is work related.

In other systems, workers who are deemed to have a permanent partial disability but can make a living doing other work usually receive a lump-sum award. Typically, their claims are then closed and disability checks for lost wages stop.

Portland's system allows some disabled workers to hold high-profile jobs, rankling former co-workers.

On Blazers game nights, police Lt. Rex Price works the Rose Garden. Dressed in a dark blazer and tie, he surveys the crowd from an aisle as he keeps an eye on billionaire team owner Paul Allen, seated nearby.

Price, 54, used to patrol the Rose Garden and nearby Lloyd Center when he worked as a Portland police officer. In 1997, while still on the force, he started moonlighting for the Trail Blazers.

Two years later, he went on disability, filing a claim that cited heart disease, but he continues to work for the Blazers. Alice Carrick, who works in the team's personnel department, said Price serves as Allen's "personal escort." His duty is to chaperone Allen "so he knows where he's going... just to be there if he has any requests. Rex knows who to contact if he wants anything done."

Price collects a monthly benefit of $5,320, according to the fund's December report. Police officers say they have complained to the disability fund, wondering how Price can work as a bodyguard but not as a cop.

Portland police Lt. Rex Price (wearing the tie) has been off work since claiming a disability for heart disease in 1999. As of December 2004, he was receiving a monthly benefit of $5,320 despite working as the "personal escort" for Blazers owner Paul Allen (center, next to team president Steve Patterson) at the Rose Garden. (Photograph courtesy of Bob Ellis/*The Oregonian*)

"I'm not security," Price said. "I'm just a facilitator. The pension board has approved what I'm doing."

Retrained But Still Paid

Like other disability systems, Portland's fund helps injured cops and fire-fighters by paying for vocational rehabilitation. The fund has sent one worker to flight instructor school, another to real estate classes and another to improve his private investigator's business.

But unlike other systems, Portland keeps paying after they've landed new careers.

Firefighter Tom Hurley, one of Portland's best-known chefs, benefited from the retraining. At his Northwest Portland restaurant, featured in *Gourmet* magazine last year, Hurley serves up wild Scottish pheasant and other entrees with prices as high as $32.

Contacted by *The Oregonian* on a recent Friday afternoon, Hurley stood in the restaurant's kitchen wearing a blue Fire & Rescue shirt, fixing a broken freezer before an event with a French winemaker.

A fifth-generation firefighter, Hurley, 46, said he fractured his right knee when he fell through a second-story floor that collapsed in a fire. In a subsequent injury, he said, he hurt his back when he was thrown by the force of a fire.

Hurley declined to offer more details, except to say that he worked on and off before going on long-term disability in November 1993. Records from city archives show an independent medical examiner said in May 1995 that he was able to return to work. Instead, the fund's board sent Hurley to another doctor and he remained off work.

State records show that Hurley was a licensed drywall contractor from 1992 to no later than 1995. He said he also worked as an estimator for a construction company.

After that, Hurley took advantage of the fund's vocational rehabilitation program, which helps retrain injured workers in hopes that benefits can be reduced when they go back to work. "I presented a business plan to show them how they could save money by giving me a chance to be retrained," he said.

The fund helped send him to the French Culinary Institute of New York in June 2000 to study classic culinary arts with artisanal baking. Hurley said he wanted to work in the "food capital of the world." He graduated July 26, 2001, according to the institute, which said tuition at the time was about $25,000.

Hurley said the fund subsidized his training. By how much, he would not say. Records from December 2004 said Hurley received $3,948 a month in benefits. Hurley disputed that, putting the amount at about $2,600. Fund officials say Hurley's benefits and how much was spent on his training are confidential.

"Don't Rock the Boat"

When complaints arise about the activities of those on disability, the fund has the power to investigate and suspend benefits if rules are being broken.

It doesn't always happen.

A study by Mercer Human Resource Consulting Inc. concluded last fall that the fund is "reluctant to use this power. This reluctance certainly results in higher costs as some claimants can 'beat the system' and other claimants, when they see this occur, attempt to do the same."

Documents obtained by *The Oregonian* bear this out.

Board minutes show the staff failed to follow up on an anonymous call in 2003 about the activities of a police officer on disability. A board subcommittee decided the staff was under no obligation to check such tips unless they receive at least two anonymous calls or the caller identifies himself.

Heeftle said the fund has no such rule. Instead, each complaint is weighed on its merits. "We will usually err on the side of investigating," Heeftle said.

Earlier, the spouse of a firefighter said she found she couldn't get the fund's staff to look into her concerns when she questioned the extent of her husband's injuries.

In the fall of 2001, Mary Catherine Huben said she met with Heeftle about her husband Brian Runyan, a Portland fire paramedic.

"I know this certainly is going to impact me financially, but I have a problem. He's not hurt," Huben said she told Heeftle. "He did get injured as a firefighter, but he recovered."

Runyan had been off duty since April 1990. He said he hurt himself "lifting heavy patients in awkward positions," and that he has since had two back surgeries. Today he receives $3,229 a month in benefits.

While on disability, Runyan has worked part time as a TriMet bus driver and as a sales associate for a condominium complex in Vancouver. Despite his injury, he is an avid cyclist who finished more than one Cycle Oregon, the weeklong tour that runs hundreds of miles.

Runyan, 58, said he's only able to ride using a recumbent bicycle.

"I have to be able to do the job of a firefighter at 100 percent, so going back, limited duty—that's not an option," Runyan said. "Surgeries can only correct you so much, and will never get you back to where you've been before."

To Huben, Heeftle seemed uninterested. "Honest to God," Huben said, "it was like, 'Don't rock the boat.' "

Citing privacy concerns, Heeftle declined to discuss Runyan's case. "We do listen and take an interest and investigate when needed," Heeftle said. "I'm surprised somebody would characterize it that way."

Runyan later was convicted of assault for repeatedly striking Huben. She got a restraining order and a stalking order against him. They divorced in March 2004.

Huben said her father was a New York City firefighter who was injured when a roof collapsed as he was battling a blaze.

"Nobody should be pulling in (benefits) with no physical disability," she said, "when there are others out there with real physically disabling conditions."

Cost Controls Neglected

Some of the trustees, including Potter and Blackmer, say they worry that the fund doesn't do enough to track whether disabled police and firefighters are reporting their outside income.

The issue surfaced in December, when the fund's board suspended the $2,287 monthly checks firefighter Mark Vrvilo was collecting for a back injury. Vrvilo, 41, had been serving as a medic with the Oregon National Guard in Iraq. He had not disclosed his whereabouts or his income as a reservist. Vrvilo is back from Iraq and has asked for a board hearing to address the matter, said Diana Godwin, one of his lawyers.

Staff at the fund said they discovered Vrvilo's situation only after receiving a tip and searching for him on the Internet.

Bambi Heup, 38, joined Portland police in December 1990. In an interview, she said that in 1992 she was struck with a 2-by-4 while pursuing a thief. The blow broke her nose, and she said that she required brain surgery two years later. She said she worked off and on for years, including doing light duty as recently as 2002 as the bureau's liaison to the disability board.

Heup now co-owns It's Your Logo, a Southeast Portland business that sells embroidered shirts, jerseys and jackets. Records show she bought the business with a partner in August 2003.

The most up-to-date fund records available show Heup receiving a monthly benefit of $3,885.

Heup said her benefits aren't reduced because she has no outside income to report and that the business is not turning a profit. "I'm not employed here," Heup said in an interview at her business. "This is just an investment for me."

The fund's rules contain a potential loophole for people on disability who run businesses. They must report outside income—except for "income from investments such as interest, dividends, rentals and capital gains."

As a result, someone collecting disability could accept a dividend from a business rather than a salary, and avoid a benefit reduction.

Plans to Improve

Heeftle said the fund staff is working to improve case and program management.

Disability costs fell to $13.1 million in 2005, down from $13.3 million a year earlier. Heeftle said the primary reason was outside the fund's control: Police and firefighters filed fewer claims than expected.

One way to reduce costs further is to stop benefits for anyone who is capable of performing outside work but who won't look for a job or retrain. Fund officials say the board has that power but has never used it.

Firefighter Randall Olson is on disability, owns his own business and said he is not reporting any income.

Olson joined the bureau in August 1990. Around 1997 or 1998, he said, he tested positive for hepatitis C, contracted during one of his emergency medical runs. He went on disability in 2000.

Today, Olson, 48, owns and runs Ducks Moorage on the Columbia River along Northeast Marine Drive. "I don't make any money here, but my wife makes a salary," he said. "I'm the president of the corporation."

Because his medical condition is stable, Olson is collecting 50 percent of his firefighter's pay—$2,680 a month, according to city records.

The fund tried to get Olson to take an inspector's job with the Fire Bureau—one that would have further reduced his benefits. He said he refused.

Olson said the fund's staff then suggested he train for a new career. He went to a few vocational rehabilitation meetings and quit. The fund staff then backed off.

"I got very angry about having to go get trained to do something else," Olson said on a recent sunny day as he looked out from his office over the Columbia River. "I'm happy here in my marina."

Lessons Learned

BY BRENT WALTH AND MAXINE BERNSTEIN

Our investigation sprang out of Maxine's watchdog reporting. For years she's covered the obscure and secretive Portland board that rules on police and firefighter disability claims.

As questionable claims piled up, we saw the need for a broader investigation and convinced editors to let us dig deeper. That's one good lesson we learned right away: Look for stories in your own newspaper that continue to raise big questions.

Here are other lessons we took away from this project:

Listen to life stories. As journalists, we're often so hurried that we rush our sources with the list of questions we need answered right this minute. Develop your sources by finding the time to listen to their life stories: where they came from, how they got to where they are and where they hope to go. These personal narratives help you better understand your sources. Plus: When you show this level of interest, your sources are more likely to open up to you on other questions. This approach helped us find stories of police and firefighters in real anguish—men and women whose minor injuries left them with their dreams and identities ruined by a wasteful city bureaucracy.

Read the rules. Laws and regulations govern every public agency. Many reporters don't bother reading them. Our close readings of the rules showed us not only how the disability system worked, but also how it failed. The rules also provided us several entry points to the story and to public records that we would have otherwise missed.

Walk through the front door. In investigative reporting, it's not always possible to approach the target of your story up front, but when you can, you should. We told the city's disability officials what we wanted to look at. Then we told them they could choose to help—or not. As a result, many doors opened up. Some doors slammed shut, too. But they would have closed on us anyway. When officials decided to stonewall us by withholding public records—including how they spent public money—their actions became part of the story itself. (On the records question, we prevailed in court.)

Get organized, and stay that way. We wanted to know what the 160-plus people on long-term disability were doing while receiving benefit checks. For each person, we checked thousands of business records, court files, meeting transcripts and other public documents. We built a database to track our work and our findings. The daily discipline of tracking our progress saved a lot of time and kept us focused.

Build trust. You can try out all the reporting techniques you want, but none of it matters if your reporting team can't work together. We'd never collaborated before. And we brought very different reporting approaches to our work. Early on, we recognized each other's strengths, played to them, and saw how we could learn from one another. We also agreed early on that we would deal with editors as a united front, which means it was up to us to work issues out before airing them in front of others. In the end, this solidarity made all the difference.

Brent Walth, 44, is a senior investigative reporter with The Oregonian. *Walth was a Nieman fellow at Harvard University. He has won several awards including the Gerald Loeb Award for business and financial reporting. He was a 2000 finalist for the Pulitzer Prize for explanatory reporting. He also was part of a team whose investigation into abuses by the Immigration and Naturalization Service won the 2001 Pulitzer Prize for public service.*

Maxine Bernstein, 39, is The Oregonian's *Portland police/major crimes reporter. She has been with* The Oregonian *for eight years. She previously worked at the* Hartford Courant, *covering everything from Hartford police to state lawmakers, business news and the Connecticut congressional delegation.*

PART 7

Hurricane Katrina Coverage

How They Did It

By Butch Ward

This essay, by The Poynter Institute's Butch Ward, draws upon interviews conducted with Stan Tiner, executive editor of the Sun Herald, *and Jim Amoss, editor of* The Times-Picayune.

On Saturday morning, Aug. 27, executive editor Stan Tiner of the *Sun Herald* gathered his staff inside their Biloxi newsroom. A mammoth hurricane called Katrina was bearing down on the Mississippi coast.

"We knew this was going to be a killer storm," Tiner recalled months later. He told the staff to "take care of themselves and their families first, and return as quickly as possible."

Within two days, he would wonder whether he had seen some of them for the last time.

On the morning of Monday, Aug. 29, editor Jim Amoss faced his staff inside *The Times-Picayune* newsroom as Katrina and its 140-mph winds howled outside.

"I told the staff that this was the biggest story of our lives," Amoss remembered later. "We had a tremendous responsibility."

Over the next 12 hours, he learned to what heroic degrees his staff would go to carry out that responsibility.

The wrath of Katrina almost defies exaggeration. Damage estimates of $100 billion. Hundreds dead and hundreds of thousands of people displaced. Entire towns and neighborhoods destroyed and many more thousands of homes damaged. In conspiracy with the city's failed levee system, the storm left 80 percent of New Orleans under water—parts of the city under 20 feet of water. And storm surges of 20 feet and more obliterated entire Mississippi towns.

It was the worst natural disaster in American history. Witness the morning-after headlines on Aug. 30:

"Catastrophe," read *The Times-Picayune*'s Web site.

"Our Tsunami," bannered the *Sun Herald*'s front page.

For the journalists who covered Katrina—and who continue to cover the storm's aftermath—this has been so much more than a professional exercise. Some lost relatives and friends. Many more lost their homes, their possessions. Their worlds—and they—are forever changed.

Appreciating that fact makes the work of these journalists all the more remarkable. Both Amoss and Tiner speak with awe of the dedication and resilience of their staffs. Yes, both staffs had planned how they would publish in the aftermath of a hurricane—they had contingencies for producing a news report online and a newspaper remotely if it became impossible to use their presses.

Covering Katrina, however, required far more than planning. As Tiner said of his journalists' efforts, "Everyone did what they had spent a life preparing to do."

Said Amoss of his staff: "They were so full of energy, heroism and derring-do that sometimes they had to be restrained from risking their lives."

But in addition to being heroic, the work of the Gulf Coast journalists was notable for one other essential characteristic: it absolutely connected with the needs of their audience.

"We gave useful information to people who were on the ground," Tiner said, "trying to survive a disaster. We covered the big story well, too, but no one else had the information necessary for helping people stay alive one more day."

Where to get water. How to apply for a trailer. News about survivors.

"There's no question," Amoss said, "we benefited from the availability of the Internet, which allowed us to gather material and distribute it without [delay] to people who were hungry for it. We were a vital link to their hometown. We were able to be nimble, to adapt to changing circumstances and to reinvent our strategy on the fly."

There's more, of course. Read the columns of *The Times-Picayune*'s Chris Rose, or the first-day dispatches of the *Sun Herald*'s Don Hammack, Joshua Norman and Mike Keller. These are writers working on their home turf, reporting on an upside-down world that is *their* world, talking with people who are neighbors—not strangers. These are local journalists, capable of such excellent work precisely because they are local.

"This was a newspaper story par excellence," Amoss said. "Telling it requires resources that only the newspaper can muster. It flows from the accumulated, layered knowledge of the complex community that only the newspaper staff possesses over time."

For the journalists of the Gulf Coast, the preparation paid off.

The Philadelphia Inquirer

Finalist

Natalie Pompilio

Individual Deadline Writing

42. Thousands Still Have Not Been Heard From

AUG. 31, 2005

NEW ORLEANS—The old shed, Daniel Weber said, the one behind his house. That's where he thinks he will find his wife's body. That's where he thinks the floodwaters sparked by Hurricane Katrina took her Monday after snatching her from his grip.

"Her shirt came off. I couldn't pull her up. The water was rushing so fast," a sobbing Weber, 52, said yesterday. "It's not right. It's not right."

Rosetta Marrero, Weber's wife of 23 years, is one of the many people presumed dead after Katrina battered the Gulf Coast.

The combination of rain, storm surge and multiple breaches in the levee system that had kept New Orleans dry overwhelmed areas of the city yesterday. It was unclear how many remained stranded. Thousands remained unaccounted for last night.

Especially hard hit was the Lower Ninth Ward, one of the city's poorest areas. The rising waters chased many residents to their attics and then the roofs.

Weber and his 44-year-old wife lived in the Lower Ninth Ward. He was trying to pull her to the roof when he lost her. A while back, she had suffered a stroke and her legs were weak, he said.

On Monday, he said, he heard a loud boom, which he believes was the sound of an unsecured barge breaking through the levee near his home. Five minutes later, he said, the water was gushing through their door.

"I said, 'Baby, we have got to get out of here,'" he recalled.

After being rescued from his home by boat, Brian Gayton cries for his grandmother. He lost her in New Orleans' Ninth Ward, a hard-hit area. (Photograph courtesy of Willie J. Allen Jr./*St. Petersburg Times*)

'She's Gone Now'

He punched out a window and climbed outside. Then he reached for his wife. He pulled her onto the roof, and then the water pulled her away.

He floated by himself for 14 hours awaiting rescue, clutching a piece of wood and wondering why he should not let go.

"She's gone now," he said, looking at his cut and bandaged hands. "That's just not fair."

Katrina showed little mercy to the city.

The storm took Weber's wife, his home, and his belongings.

It robbed his neighbors of shelter and their most cherished possessions.

It left 9-year-old Leanna Wallace with cuts on her neck, after she scraped it on a ceiling as water rose in her home.

"We had to put our heads like this," she said, tilting her head to the left. "Somebody had to come rescue us with a boat."

Seeking 'Heartbeats'

Nearby, Iontha Jack, 43, stumbled down the street, glassy-eyed, apparently dazed. She wore only a black T-shirt that reached to her knees. She nervously tugged at it, pulling it lower. "I'm alive, so you all are going to see some leg," she said.

Jack and her brother-in-law did not evacuate because they did not think that the storm "could be that bad."

But it was.

Soaking wet, they sought safety from the dark waters, going to their attic. That's where Jack lost most of her clothes.

"I said, 'Brother-in-law, I am sorry, but the jeans have got to go,'" she said.

The pair floated together, praying until Jack was able to reach a beam in the attic. But her brother-in-law was not as lucky. His foot got caught and he was unable to stay afloat. He drowned.

Jack was one of about 1,500 rescued yesterday by boats of the state Department of Wildlife and Fisheries. Jack got their attention by screaming. Others banged on roofs or signaled with flashlights.

"We are looking for live people at this point, live people and heartbeats," Sgt. Rachel Zechenelly said.

Those rescued were sometimes stunned, sometimes sad, sometimes slightly annoyed. An 80-year-old had to be forcibly pulled from her roof, angry that rescuers would not go into her home to find her purse.

"They're very hungry and very thirsty," Zechenelly said. "That would make an angel impatient."

43. Signs of Desperation Grip a City of Despair

SEPT. 1, 2005

By Natalie Pompilio

NEW ORLEANS—Booker T. Harris, 91, died while sitting in a dirty green-and-white lawn chair, on the back of a truck as it drove him to an evacuation site. His wife, Allie, 93, was sitting in a chair next to him.

About an hour later, Booker Harris was at the city's convention center, a gathering point for people to be evacuated from the city. He was still in his lawn chair, covered by a yellow quilt. His wife was sitting next to him. Hundreds of other evacuees milled around them. Few seemed to notice that Booker Harris was dead or that his wife was crying.

"How did they just leave her like this?" an outraged bystander, Monica Crockett, 47, wondered. "We are all going to start dying one by one, I guess."

On Monday, Hurricane Katrina hammered New Orleans and the Gulf Coast. Yesterday, the horrific effects of the storm's beating became clearer in the city.

Tens of thousands of people are homeless. An unknown number of people are dead, some of the bodies floating in the streets or in flooded homes. The damage to the area's economy—brought on by the storm and continued by hoodlums taking advantage of the chaos—is still unknown.

Yesterday, looters were pillaging sporting-goods stores and pawnshops to arm themselves with guns, witnesses said. Others reported drivers being carjacked by people with machetes.

Also, there were unconfirmed reports by city residents of rapes in the Superdome, which was being used as an emergency shelter.

People were angry—at the storm, at one another and at the government officials and police who they said were doing nothing to help them.

"This is 2005. Nobody should have to live like this," an angry John Murray, 52, said. "This ain't got nothing to do with that hurricane. This has to do with mismanagement."

Hundreds of people rescued from flooded parts of the city were left by their rescuers on the elevated interstate that runs through the city. They walked along aimlessly, some clutching bags of items they had saved from the flooding.

As floodwaters rose in traditionally dry neighborhoods, fleeing residents walked along the streetcar tracks in the middle of stately St. Charles Avenue. Families pushed their elderly in shopping carts; mothers tried to steer their children through an obstacle course of downed oak trees.

Faye Taplin, 65, took a rest on the stone steps of Christ Church Cathedral. Her feet were badly swollen, a marked contrast to her thin ankles.

"If I want to get out of New Orleans, I have to walk. But I didn't think about this," she said, extending one leg to reveal an ailing foot. "It's the only way out. I don't have a ride."

Taplin left her city home, which had never flooded before, when the water was two feet deep in her living room.

A diabetic with high blood pressure, she grabbed her insulin and other medications, as well as a bedspread, soup, cookies and a can opener. She had heard on the radio that people were being evacuated to the central business district miles away, so she began her trek to it.

She soon needed a rest.

"That is as far as you got?" asked a barefoot woman in a housedress who was walking past.

"Yes," Taplin said serenely, with a slight smile.

She was last seen walking back toward her house.

Even if Taplin had made it to a pickup point, there was no guarantee of an immediate evacuation from the city. Catherine Bernard, 49, was shaking with anger as she ranted against the city and its leaders.

"Nobody wants to stop and give us no help," she said. "I never see no storm, no tornado, no hurricane uproot trees like this one."

Bernard and her family had walked about three miles to an underpass in Lee Circle near the central business district.

The group included 14 adults—among them three diabetics, one blind woman and one man in a wheelchair—and four children—including Bernard's 2-year-old grandson, who danced in his diaper and T-shirt, oblivious to the distressed adults.

They and about 100 others had waited three hours for a promised evacuation truck that had not arrived.

"We don't want to be separated," she said, choking back tears. "We were all in the house together and we are going to stick together."

When a caravan of trucks from the Louisiana Department of Wildlife and Fisheries slowly rolled past, the waiting evacuees shouted repeatedly for help.

One woman advised her teenage son to jump into the middle of the street if that's what it would take to stop the trucks. The only response was from a man on the back of one of the trucks, who shouted, "Get to the convention center! "

That's where the Billiot sisters—Kristy, 19, and Jamie, 18—had spent the last five hours. Residents of neighboring St. Bernard's Parish, they escaped their house by boat Monday, then were airlifted from atop a levee to a nearby military base, then finally bused to the convention center.

They had become separated from their parents and a brother, and did not know when they would be evacuated.

Kristy Billiot said they had brought nothing to eat or drink, and nothing had been provided. Their attempt to join the looting of a convenience store ended when police arrived and threatened to start shooting.

"I'm going to go crazy," said Kristy Billiot, whose eyes were swollen from crying. "I hope I wake up and it's a dream."

But it seems to be a nightmare.

A block away from the Billiots, Allie Harris stared into space and munched on crackers, her dead husband in the chair next to her.

44. On the Scene: Ex-Resident "Watched New Orleans Die"

SEPT. 4, 2005

By Natalie Pompilio

My beautiful city is gone.

I call it "my" city because I lived here for almost six years, the longest I've lived anywhere in my adult life.

This is a city that got into my blood, as anyone who has seen my Philadelphia home—decorated with memories from my time here—can testify. Some of my dearest friends live here. Some of my best times were had here.

And last week, I watched New Orleans die.

My friends are alive, but many of them have lost something: their homes or belongings, maybe their jobs.

This is a city of celebration, and now there is only sorrow. The flooding throughout the city, they say, can be blamed on Hurricane Katrina.

But I honestly believe that tears—so many tears shed by so many people in the last few days—have added to the problem.

This is worse than my time in Iraq. There, the language barrier meant I was always a little bit separate. Here, I can understand every word people say to me, and it's killing me. This is the hardest thing I have ever covered.

Maybe it's so hard because I love this city and my friends and I see them all falling apart. Maybe it's the horrible things I've seen in the last few days.

There have been so many "worst moments."

I was interviewing a man when a woman walked up to me, weeping, and said: "Can you write down my name? Because I don't think I'm going to make it."

She had waited at the convention center to be evacuated for about a day without food or water.

"I don't know where my husband and kids are," she said. "They went to a hotel for the storm, but now people tell me the hotel is empty."

I wrote down her name—later lost when the notebook got wet and pages ripped out—and gave her a hug. I tried to comfort her. But what could I do?

There are dogs, dozens, loose on the streets and highways. I have yet to meet a bad one. I pet every dog, diseases be damned, and am always rewarded with wags. The ones that have collars, I try to see where they're from. Some tags have addresses, and the addresses are inevitably underwater. There's no way I can make a call.

Strangers beg for water. They want to know where you're staying and if they can stay with you. They want you to put their names in the paper so their loved ones can find them.

I feel that I've met people who are going to die very soon. They are old and frail and unable or unwilling to evacuate. Some are resigned. Others are angry.

I have seen dead bodies before, many times, in my work as a police reporter. Never have I seen so many at once, and so many treated so callously. In actuality, it's a practicality now as the focus here is not on preserving the dead but saving the still-living.

For the last few days, I haven't been just a reporter and writer. I've been a counselor, a consoler, listener, friend. I start my day with a wad of tissues in my pocket and by the end of the day, there are none.

I have flagged down help for sick people and helped carry them to resting places.

I've tried to coax smiles and laughs from sad-eyed children, succeeding every time I sketch a Snoopy in my reporter's notebook and give it to them.

I wonder, sometimes, if that's crossing some journalistic line. Then I think I really don't care.

I feel bad that I can leave this. I feel bad that I feel bad about losing some of my own belongings in the flood. People have lost their lives or their homes, and I'm upset about a few rings?

I started one story with an anecdote about an elderly man who died while being evacuated, and how his body was propped in a lawn chair in a busy area, covered with a yellow blanket. His wife was sitting next to him.

A National Guardsman said his men could take the wife but would have to send someone back for the man. The soldier asked me whether I could get someone to keep a watch over the body so no one "did something" to it.

Before the Guard drove off, the soldier and I looked at each other. We both had tears in our eyes.

The next day, when I was back in that area with other reporters, I said, "Oh, this is near where Booker T. Harris died, the man I wrote about." And I looked and there he was, still in his chair.

That man had lived for 91 years and this is how it ended.

This piece combines eyewitness reporting with deeply felt first-person commentary. Call it "I"-witness journalism.

On the Scene: Ex-Resident "Watched New Orleans Die"

My beautiful city is gone.

I call it "my" city because I lived here for almost six years, the longest I've lived anywhere in my adult life.

This is a city that got into my blood, as anyone who has seen my Philadelphia home—decorated with memories from my time here—can testify. Some of my dearest friends live here. Some of my best times were had here.

And last week, I watched New Orleans die.

My friends are alive, but many of them have lost something: their homes or belongings, maybe their jobs.

This is a city of celebration, and now there is only sorrow. The flooding throughout the city, they say, can be blamed on Hurricane Katrina.

But I honestly believe that tears—so many tears shed by so many people in the last

Margin annotations:

five-word sentence sets the tone of regret

simple word, now fraught with meaning

telling, followed by showing

echoes the lead sentence

three examples represent the whole

turns possible cliché—"flood of tears"—into something original

good word pairing

war versus natural disaster; compare/contrast

few days—have added to the problem.

This is worse than my time in Iraq. There, the language barrier meant I was always a little bit separate. Here, I can understand every word people say to me, and it's killing me. This is the hardest thing I have ever covered.

Maybe it's so hard because I love this city and my friends and I see them all falling apart. Maybe it's the horrible things I've seen in the last few days.

promises examples of the horror

There have been so many "worst moments."

dialogue puts us there

I was interviewing a man when a woman walked up to me, weeping, and said: "Can you write down my name? Because I don't think I'm going to make it."

delivers with first example

She had waited at the convention center to be evacuated for about a day without food or water.

she lets her source tell part of the story

"I don't know where my husband and kids are," she said. "They went to a hotel for the storm, but now people tell me the hotel is empty."

sometimes a tiny detail can convey more emotion than a devastated landscape

I wrote down her name— later lost when the notebook got wet and pages ripped out— and gave her a hug. I tried to comfort her. But what could I do?

she has become a participant/ observer

There are dogs, dozens, loose on the streets and highways. I have yet to meet a bad one. I pet every dog, diseases be damned, and am always rewarded with

phrase reveals her character

wags. The ones that have collars, I try to see where they're from. Some tags have addresses, and the addresses are inevitably underwater. There's no way I can make a call.

Strangers beg for water. They want to know where you're staying and if they can stay with you. They want you to put their names in the paper so their loved ones can find them.

I feel that I've met people who are going to die very soon. They are old and frail and unable or unwilling to evacuate. Some are resigned. Others are angry.

I have seen dead bodies before, many times, in my work as a police reporter. Never have I seen so many at once, and so many treated so callously. In actuality, it's a practicality now as the focus here is not on preserving the dead but saving the still-living.

For the last few days, I haven't been just a reporter and writer. I've been a counselor, a consoler, listener, friend. I start my day with a wad of tissues in my pocket and by the end of the day, there are none.

I have flagged down help for sick people and helped carry them to resting places.

I've tried to coax smiles and laughs from sad-eyed children, succeeding every time I sketch a Snoopy in my reporter's notebook and give it to them.

Margin annotations:

every good intention hits a dead end

an example of how people turn to the news media in a crisis

her street credibility does her no good

short inventory of key roles

so much better than "I cried a lot"

reminds me of word "gone" in lead

general to specific

she makes the ethical concerns transparent

I wonder, sometimes, if that's crossing some journalistic line. Then I think I really don't care.

I feel bad that I can leave this. I feel bad that I feel bad about losing some of my own belongings in the flood. People have lost their lives or their homes, and I'm upset about a few rings?

she lets the reader listen in as she thinks out loud

she retells a powerful anecdote from an earlier story

I started one story with an anecdote about an elderly man who died while being evacuated, and how his body was propped in a lawn chair in a busy area, covered with a yellow blanket. His wife was sitting next to him.

details help us see

A National Guardsman said his men could take the wife but would have to send someone back for the man. The soldier asked me whether I could get someone to keep a watch over the body so no one "did something" to it.

in this context she can reveal her emotional reaction

Before the Guard drove off, the soldier and I looked at each other. We both had tears in our eyes.

one full name has special power

The next day, when I was back in that area with other reporters. I said, "Oh, this is near where Booker T. Harris died, the man I wrote about." And I looked and there he was, still in his chair.

That man had lived for 91 years and this is how it ended.

lead gives us the name of a city—"gone"; end gives us one man whose life is—"ended"

Roy Peter Clark is senior scholar and vice president of The Poynter Institute.

Lessons Learned

BY NATALIE POMPILIO

I didn't have the luxury of working the phones or reading the wires or searching the Internet after Hurricane Katrina smashed into New Orleans.

The city didn't have electricity and most phone lines were down. I had left my computer and rental car behind during a hurried evacuation of *The Times-Picayune,* where I had been staying. What remained was back-to-the-basics reporting at its most basic: hitching rides with others or traveling by bike and on foot, carrying only a notebook and pen, scrawling handwritten stories across unlined sheets of paper and then searching, every night, for a way to get the words to the outside world.

It was like a reporting boot camp, and even though I've been doing this for 10 years, I learned a lot.

The first lesson, perhaps, was that I could do it. I could live without constant news updates. I didn't need my phone as a crutch. When I sat down to write my first story in longhand, I thought, "This will never work. I'm nothing without my keyboard." But I did it—actually, I wrote two that way that night—and later dictated each word and punctuation mark over the phone to my editors.

I learned that it's impossible to separate myself from the job I do. During Katrina, I broke some so-called "journalism rules:" I shared what food or water I had with strangers. When I had a car, I gave people rides. I took down phone numbers so I could call scattered family members later to report their loved ones were alive. I hugged and rubbed the backs of more sobbing people than I could count. I don't regret that. I only wish I had been able to do more. The details that made me cry, made me scream, even made me smile, they went into my stories. I have to believe that writing and recording them made a difference.

And Katrina reminded me of how lucky I am to do this job. A lot of us print reporters, we're curmudgeons. We blow out the candles and curse the darkness. We bemoan the state of the industry and the future of journalism and the fact that we'll never get wealthy writing for newspapers.

But we forget how privileged we are. My job has taken me to places many people will never see and offered me a chance to experience things few people will. I have been welcomed into the homes of mourning families. I've been told stories that began, "I never told anyone else this before . . . "

Midway through the first day in New Orleans, with most of the city under water, I was walking away from the Lower Ninth Ward with a reporter friend. We had just spoken to a man whose wife had been swept away from him by the flood waters and a woman who had listened to her brother-in-law drown near her in their attic. We had talked to men who had taken a rowboat so they could rescue strangers from rooftops. Their stories were chilling and awe-inspiring and it was up to us to make sure people heard them.

I said to my friend, "I know it may sound inappropriate, but I love my job on days like this."

He understood. I think real journalists do.

Natalie Pompilio writes for The Philadelphia Inquirer *and also serves as a fellow with the Dart Center for Journalism and Trauma. She has co-authored a book, "More Philadelphia Murals and the Stories They Tell," which will be released by Temple University Press in fall 2006.*

SunHerald

■ Finalist

Margaret Baker, Don Hammack, Mike Keller, Anita Lee and Joshua Norman
Team Deadline Writing

45. 'Our Tsunami'

AUG. 30, 2005

By Anita Lee, Don Hammack, Joshua Norman and Margaret Baker

BILOXI—Hurricane Katrina devastated South Mississippi on Monday with a force not seen since Camille 36 years ago, sweeping aside multi-million-dollar casinos, burying the beach highway and killing at least 50 people in Harrison County.

"This," said Biloxi Mayor A. J. Holloway, "is our tsunami."

At least 50 people are confirmed dead in Gulfport and Biloxi.

Katrina raged ashore in Mississippi at dawn and terrorized the Coast until winds subsided after 3 p.m., leaving massive damage in her wake. Monday night, communications were down and transportation systems demolished. Katrina also crippled medical services.

Beleaguered emergency personnel awaited reinforcements from the federal government and other states to shore up assistance.

"We are still in the search-and-rescue mode," Holloway said. It will be days before the costs of Katrina, in lives and property, are known.

Katrina's tidal surge swept away bridges that had linked the three Coast counties.

Along the waterfront, the storm surge obliterated businesses, homes, community landmarks and condominiums. It swept away the concrete Eight Flags display marking the Gulfport-Biloxi boundary on the beach.

Countless treasures washed from homes joining streams of debris that settled 5 feet high on residential streets off the beach.

New sets of stairs to nowhere joined those Camille left when she washed away waterfront mansions on Aug. 17, 1969. Katrina will forever be compared to Camille in many ways. Camille cost the Coast 144 lives and more than $6.5 billion in property damage in current dollars.

A revitalized and growing Mississippi Coast had even more to lose. In Biloxi, Holloway said at least five casinos are out of commission.

Grand Casino Biloxi washed across U.S. 90. Treasure Bay's pirate ship was beached. At least three other casinos were out of commission, Holloway said.

Beau Rivage still stood, while Hard Rock Casino, scheduled to open in early September, was heavily damaged. The signature guitar, said to be the world's largest, stood.

"Highway 90 is destroyed," Holloway said. "It's something like I've never seen before. I saw a disaster. Water did not get this high for Camille."

Most of the residents who lost their lives were on Point Cadet, at the southeastern tip of Biloxi's peninsula.

In Gulfport, the storm surge crossed the CSX railroad tracks, a line old-timers say Camille did not cross.

Hancock and Jackson counties did not fare any better. Communications were all but severed during Katrina.

Before telephone contact was lost Monday morning, Hancock County officials reported that a foot of water swamped their Emergency Operations Center, which sits 30 feet above sea level. The back of the Hancock County courthouse, where the center is located, gave way.

"Thirty-five people swam out of their Emergency Operations Center with life jackets on," said Christopher Cirillo, Harrison County's Emergency Medical Services director.

"We haven't heard from them. The only person we can raise on the radio is the sheriff in his car."

Jackson County's Emergency Operations Center also began to disintegrate shortly after Katrina raged ashore. The roof was peeling off by 7:30 a.m., forcing officials to evacuate to the courthouse across the street.

As soon as the wind subsided, looters struck. They stole cars, radios, liquor, furniture, generators and anything else they could find.

A furious Harrison County Sheriff, George Payne, was heard on the police scanner telling his deputies to make room in the jail.

In neighborhoods, shell-shocked residents burst into tears and embraced, consoling one another.

The atmosphere, at times, was surreal.

Brothers Jesus and David Diaz walked up Biloxi's St. Charles Avenue in a daze.

"What are you looking for?" they were asked.

One of them said, "Our house."

46. It Could Have All Gone Wrong

AUG. 30, 2005

By Don Hammack

GULFPORT—It must have been a completely plausible plan at the time to Mike Petro and his family.

They lived at 1514 18th Avenue, just east of downtown, just off the beach, just south of the railroad tracks, right off Second Street. He and his wife Andrea, his 30-year-old son, twin 13-year-old daughters, a 6-year-old daughter, a dachshund and a cat thought they'd be able to beat Hurricane Katrina and leave town early Monday morning.

Having disregarded mandatory evacuation orders, it nearly proved a fatal mistake.

When Katrina slammed into the Central Gulf Coast in the early morning hours, ruining what we like to call our little slice of heaven, the Petros' power went out, interrupting their last-minute packing scheme. Then they heard the water, a strange rumbling train sound.

Their house, more than 100 years old and not built on the cheap like modern ones, began to be ripped apart at the seams.

The family began to move for shelter, angling across the intersection one house north of their lot.

Petro got knocked down by a piece of his house. It plunked him down on a slab of something, he said, while his wife and kids were being herded up the street by the storm surge.

The rest of the family wound up pushed to another house on the east side of 18th. Mike Petro's slab helped him make it up and across 18th Street, and he needed the help. He'd had hip replacement surgery recently and he moved with a noticeable limp.

"I was afraid for the kids," said Petro, his voice cracking for the first time. "You can beat the hell outta me . . . "

As he stood on the listing porch that was two houses north of the intersection of 18thAvenue and Second Street, he nearly apologized for setting up shop in a neighbor's severely damaged house, using a piece of debris as a cane. He said he was going to leave them a note of thanks.

"I was scared to death by the end," he said. "But they weren't," meaning the dachshund, which they'd managed to keep with them, and a cat that they hoped would be back after expending one-ninth of its allotment of good fortune.

His wife joined him after he was interviewed, having crossed the street. Mike Petro sat on the threshold to the borrowed house, she squatted in front of him. They grasped each other's faces with two hands, sharing a moment they nearly robbed themselves of by poor decision-making the night before.

Around him, even as the back end of Katrina's feeder bands continued to hack at the coastline, recovery had begun. Two young Seabees who lived in the brick house just south of the railroad tracks were climbing over the piles of debris on 18th.

There was a lot of debris. A mess of maroon upholstered pews and the organ from St. Peter's By the Sea was instead by the railroad tracks. The Episcopal church moved east several years ago when the Grand Casino purchased the old church, with enough slot-machine coin to build a beautiful new building, one that's apparently been demolished.

Also among the debris was the house just north of the Petro's and in it, apparently an 85-year-old woman and a younger man. They were in the house Sunday night, neighbors said, and Monday morning there was evidence of what had been, but only if you knew what there was when it started out.

There was a perfectly clean, silver oxygen bottle, the green paint on it not so much as smudged as it lay among the pickup-sticks wreckage underneath it, but with no hose to lead back to a possible victim.

The Seabees crawled all over the place hollering for survivors. They'd survived Katrina, with water up to their waists in the first floor of their brick rental.

Petty Officer Third Class Jesse Good said he'd been the target of an insurgent mortar attack while stationed in the Middle East with NMCB 7.

"I haven't seen nothing like that in Iraq," said Good, 22.

It didn't appear there was much for them to hope for in their search.

There was an ironic sign of hope among the wreckage. Lying on the sidewalk north of where the debris field began trailing off, lay a brightly colored, hand-painted, thin wooden plaque.

It certainly had been attached to some kitchen wall someplace just 24 hours earlier.

"If you're lucky enough to live by the beach you're lucky enough."

It just didn't seem too lucky Monday morning for the vast majority of South Mississippians.

Mike Petro and his clan found a sliver, but there wasn't much else.

47. Short Trip Outside an Eye-Opener

AUG. 30, 2005

By Joshua Norman and Mike Keller

BILOXI—When the winds that tore buildings in half and crushed tin roofs like aluminum foil finally subsided, we could not help but try to see the damage of Katrina on a broader scale.

We decided to venture out, not knowing how far we would get or what we would see along the way.

Ostensibly, the goal of the walk was to find our cars before the looting we heard about on the police scanner turned into grand theft auto. We had parked them on the second floor of Edgewater Mall's concrete parking garage and did not know if they would still be there.

We knew that the well-being of the cars was a minuscule thing in an event that took so many people's lives and homes. But they were ours and they were all we had.

At around 4:45 p.m., we started our brief journey. It was the first breath of open air in nearly 24 hours. The wind that greeted us out the door was sporadic, but surprisingly intense when it kicked up.

Of the buildings we passed along the way, a very small minority looked as they had just 12 hours earlier.

Power lines drooped ominously. The TV station across the road was trashed. Parts of its roof and the insulation that used to sit beneath it were scattered everywhere. Satellite dishes had folded like tacos.

We briefly walked along the CSX railroad tracks past broken pine trees, avoiding downed power lines that possibly coursed with electricity.

We passed an apartment complex to our south where a young woman frantically asked us if we knew whether Keesler Air Force Base was still open. She needed to get there. We didn't ask why. We told her that all the news coming over the scanner told her drive would be impossible.

Beyond the woman, the movie theater's 30-foot sign was sprawled on the ground. At first we did not know what it used to be, but the foot-long letters made us understand.

After the sign, we came across a small group of looters who greeted us with a bag full of liquor. "Go and get yours," one said. "There's plenty of it."

An officer with Biloxi Police Department stopped us. "Go home," he called over the bullhorn from inside his car. We showed him our press badges. "I don't care who you are," he said. "We are under orders to arrest anyone on the street. We have a curfew in effect."

We pleaded to let us get to our cars as other groups of wandering people were pushed back over the railroad tracks by another squad car.

"All right, go straight to your car and get going," he said. "If we let you guys wander around then other people are gonna do it, too."

We waded through the pond that used to be the mall's northern parking lot, past more twisted tin and cushions from unseen furniture and found our cars. Our walk was cut short by the hard hand of martial law. We inched back along the debris-strewn road and decided to postpone any more walks in Biloxi for the near future.

Lessons Learned

BY MARGARET BAKER, DON HAMMACK,
MIKE KELLER, ANITA LEE AND JOSHUA NORMAN

Once you've evacuated for a hurricane, it's hard to return.

That became clear to us at the *Sun Herald* on Aug. 29. Five reporters at the *Sun Herald* wrote the main story and sidebars on that day when Hurricane Katrina hit. Four of us bunked in the office the night before. The fifth reporter stayed at the county's emergency operations center.

But the other journalists, who also braved the storm and desperately wanted to help, were stuck in the suburbs. They had no routes through the mountains of debris, downed power lines and trees.

Those of us near shore took what lessons we had learned as journalists and hit the streets as soon as the debris stopped flying.

Basic technology proved our biggest obstacle—and our salvation. Management had planned well. It sent a team to publish the newspaper over to our sister Knight Ridder newspaper, *The Ledger-Enquirer* in Columbus, Ga. They printed the newspapers there and flew them back to Biloxi. As a result, we never missed a day of print publication.

Still, we lost power, telephone service and, at times, our Internet connection. A technology team at the *Sun Herald* helped us get our stories out against all odds.

Any success we had with our coverage can be attributed to relying on fundamentals. Here's a list of basic things to keep in mind when you find yourself facing an impending disaster:

Keep a timeline. Before a hurricane, or other foreseeable disaster possibility, it's valuable to start a timeline that shows what public agencies are doing to prepare, especially the time and date evacuation orders are issued. You won't have to piece this together later when time is short and questions arise.

Think online. Through crisis blogs and message boards, newspapers can relay information to frantic relatives in other states and counties. When vast numbers of your readers have evacuated, many are following developments on the Internet.

Reporters brought in lists of people who wanted friends and relatives to know they were alive. Our area had bizarre phone limitations. It would let us call Alaska. But we couldn't call across the street. So triangular means emerged to get damage reports out and back in from message boards.

Be compassionate. Objectivity is important, but it shouldn't overshadow empathy in a disaster.

Quite often, shell-shocked survivors turned to us for comfort. One of us consoled survivors in search of lost relatives as first responders pulled bodies from the rubble.

Knight Ridder managed to rush in supplies—gas, food, water and ice—before the Red Cross, Salvation Army, FEMA and other relief organizations had arrived. So we gave out lots of water.

It was also heartening to see how eager people were for newspapers. With our established carrier routes in disarray, many of us loaded up copies and handed them out as we worked. Distribution points also were set up at buildings where people gathered in the days after the storm.

Be flexible. You can never have too many ways to get out a story. Internet connectivity came and went, as did cell phones. Satellite phones are expensive, but necessary. When you finally find your source in the field, remember to ask their schedule so you can hunt them down if the telephone fails.

Take time to take care of yourself. Disaster turns reporters into war correspondents—without the training or time to adjust. Take breaks from work. Talk about problems you are having with colleagues, friends or professional counselors.

If you get mentally or physically sick, you are not doing anyone any good. Your urge will be to keep working constantly. Fight that.

Take a day off here and there. Get your mind off the disaster. If you can, take that day to get out of the disaster zone. Seeing normal life helps put things in perspective more than you would expect.

Margaret Baker, a senior staff writer, joined the Sun Herald *in 1994 as a crime reporter in Jackson County. Over the years, she has won local, state and regional awards for her news reporting. A resident of Biloxi, Baker and a colleague lost their home to Hurricane Katrina on Aug. 29, 2005.*

Don Hammack covers South Mississippi transportation issues for the Sun Herald. *Prior to Hurricane Katrina, he was a sports writer for the newspaper. He has won numerous Mississippi Press Association awards for sports writing. He was the* Sun Herald's *Employee of the Year in 2004 for the paper's nationally recognized crisis blog during Hurricane Ivan.*

Mike Keller joined the Sun Herald *on Aug. 1, 2005, 28 days before Katrina came ashore. He moved to South Mississippi from New York City. He covers the environment, energy and business. Keller previously spent six years as a cartographer and geographic analyst. He was a United Nations peacekeeper in East Africa and a staff demographic analyst for one of the 2004 presidential candidates.*

Anita Lee, a staff writer for the Sun Herald, *has been a reporter or editor since 1987. She has received state and regional awards for in-depth reporting, feature writing and as a project editor. She was previously a finalist for the Scripps Howard Foundation's public service award.*

Joshua Norman began working at the Sun Herald *less than two months before Hurricane Katrina hit South Mississippi. He stayed at the* Sun Herald's *building, where he reported throughout the storm and was one of the first reporters on the ground once it passed. Since then, Norman has been busy writing about a wide variety of subjects, from housing issues to minority communities to dolphins, in addition to covering the community of Pass Christian.*

A conversation with
Stan Tiner

An edited interview with Stan Tiner by Poynter faculty member Butch Ward. Stan Tiner has been the executive editor of the Sun Herald *in Biloxi, Miss., since 2000. Ward asked him to recall the scene in his newsroom on the day Katrina hit land.*

STAN TINER: Every time another person showed up in the newsroom, there was incredible delight and relief that someone else was living. We knew this was going to be a killer storm, and we had told everyone during a staff meeting on Saturday to take care of themselves and their families first, and return as quickly as possible. But because everyone was living by the Camille standard—they knew how far in Camille had come and where those water lines were—and they said, "if it stood then, then I'm immune from death." They had a sense of invulnerability. So people stayed in the danger zone. We had no way of knowing how many of our staff we might have seen for the last time at our meeting on Saturday.

So the initial impact of seeing someone walk into the building, elevated our sense of being a newsroom to that of a true family.

Of course, the initial excitement at seeing someone arrive was tempered quickly as people eventually got to see their homes, or what was left of them. There were just waves of emotion: the thrill of seeing someone alive and the pain of knowing they were suffering.

We quickly got out of the newsroom to report on the storm's impact. Remember, there was no information coming to us; we were limited to what we could go out and see ourselves.

I had driven the 10 miles from my house to the office, weaving around all kinds of debris in the road, seeing the looters. I ran into a Gulfport policeman who told me, "The city's gone." He said he hadn't seen it himself, but that's what someone had told him on the radio. He told me that two restaurants on the same street as the newspaper had been destroyed. When I asked him about the newspaper building, he said he didn't know. So it wasn't until I came around the corner and saw the building standing that I knew whether it had been destroyed or not.

I drove down to the beach—or as close as I could because of the devastation. People were wandering around, looking like they had been in a nuclear blast. Their eyes had that blank stare like soldiers after a battle. They were asking for food and water because their houses had been destroyed.

When I got to Highway 90, it literally had been turned upside down—the water had gotten under the roadway and played around with it for a while and then literally flipped it over.

In the newsroom, we never lost the professional air. Everyone did what they had spent a life preparing to do. Everybody knew it was the biggest story of our lives. Nobody ever came out and said that, but we all knew it that it was.

This brought home very well the value of a local newspaper. We really had the home-field advantage. We knew where things were, who to talk to, where shelters would be located. We were serving this community at a level that nobody else could. One of the best stories came when the mayor came to our newsroom. He looked really impacted, eyes big. His city had just been wiped off the face of the earth. It was very emotional. He told us he had stayed at City Hall and watched as the water rushed through like a river.

"This is our tsunami," he said. And that became our headline the next day and one used by newspapers around the world.

He told us 50 people were dead. That was the first official death count. But the point is he came to us—he knew he could tell us his story and that we would tell the world.

We gave useful information to people who were on the ground, trying to survive a disaster. We covered the big story well, too. But no one else had the information necessary for helping people stay alive one more day. We delivered the paper free to people for six months. I'll never forget the reporters and photographers out delivering papers. They were connecting with real people, making the kind of difference people say they get into the business for—to help others. But most of us don't get to really do that.

We never missed an edition and the Web site never went down. On Saturday we had sent a group of people to the paper in Columbus, Ga., and told them if you don't hear from us again, put out a newspaper. That Saturday, we put out the regular Sunday paper, and on Sunday, we published the Monday paper. We printed the Tuesday paper on Tuesday morning and distributed it that afternoon.

After the storm, there was no electricity. We had generators going, and initially a few cell phones and a little Internet access. When people from Knight Ridder showed up, they had some satellite phones and they set up WiFi so that by Tuesday, we could communicate more easily.

The newsroom was incredibly hot. It's always hot in September in South Mississippi, but we had had record heat the whole month. There were holes in the roof, dripping water. It was like a rainforest. People were arriving from all over the country and camping out in the building anywhere they could find a space—under desks, in the hallways. We just made do.

BUTCH WARD: Did anything about your staff surprise you?

I learned during all this how good my staff was. We're a small paper in a place that people don't pay much attention to. But I watched how the staff rose to the challenge, willing to work around the clock. And their journalism was impressive.

I had the easiest job in the place—I just stood back and cheered them on. In a situation like that, you're either going to do well or you're not. When the day came, they were able to do it very well. It reminded me how the editor's most important job is to hire good people. Hire them and turn them loose. And they'll come through for you.

Did anything surprise you about yourself?

I think a kinder, gentler Stan came out, because I was more understanding of the human needs of the staff than I had been before. I can be pretty demanding. But I found out it was necessary to be extremely mindful of the people's needs. Even if they played a critical role at the paper, there were times when they needed some down time.

I learned to pace myself. You can't do everything right now. I came to believe in journalism triage. We'd examine all the stories around us on a given day—and there were hundreds every day—and say, if the staff can do 25 or 30 stories today, which ones are critical to keeping our community alive and going for one more day? What are we capable of pulling out and how important was that coverage to the community?

And those were the stories we did.

The Times-Picayune

Finalist

Chris Rose
Commentary/Column Writing

48. Are You Nuts?

NOV. 6, 2005

It has been said to me almost a dozen times, in exactly the same words: "Everyone here is mentally ill now."

Some who say this are healthcare professionals voicing the accumulated wisdom of their careers and some are laymen venturing a psychological assessment that just happens to be correct.

With all due respect, we're living in Crazy Town.

The only lines at retail outlets longer than those for lumber and refrigerators are at the pharmacy windows, where fidgety, glassy-eyed neighbors greet each other with the casual inquiries one might expect at a restaurant:

"What are you gonna have? The Valium here is good. But I'm going with the Paxil. Last week I had the Xanax and it didn't agree with me."

We talk about prescription medications now like they're the soft-shell crabs at Clancy's. Suddenly, we've all developed a low-grade expertise in pharmacology.

Everybody's got it, this thing, this affliction, this affinity for forgetfulness, absent-mindedness, confusion, laughing at inappropriate circumstances, crying when the wrong song comes on the radio, behaving in odd and contrary ways.

A friend recounts a recent conversation into which Murphy's Law was injected—the adage that if anything can go wrong, it will.

In perhaps the most succinct characterization of contemporary life in New Orleans I've heard yet, one said to the other: "Murphy's running this town now."

Ain't that the truth?

Here's one for you: Some friends of mine were clearing out their belongings from their home in the Fontainebleau area and were going through the muddle of despair that attends the realization that you were insured out the wazoo for a hurricane but all you got was flood damage and now you're going to get a check for $250,000 to rebuild your $500,000 house.

As they pondered this dismal circumstance in the street, their roof collapsed. Just like that. It must have suffered some sort of structural or rain-related stress from the storm and now, two weeks later, it manifested itself in total collapse.

Now I ask you: What would you do if you watched your home crumble to pieces before your eyes?

What they did was, realizing their home now qualified for a home-owner's claim, they jumped up and down and high-fived each other and yelled: "The roof collapsed! The roof collapsed!"

Our home is destroyed. Oh, happy day. I submit there's something not right there.

I also submit that if you don't have this affliction, if this whole thing hasn't sent you into a vicious spin of acute cognitive dissonance, then you must be crazy and—like I said: We're all whacked.

How could you not be? Consider the sights, sounds and smells you encounter on a daily basis as you drive around a town that has a permanent bathtub ring around it. I mean, could somebody please erase that brown line?

Every day I drive past a building on Magazine Street where there's plywood over the windows with a huge spray-painted message that says: I AM HERE. I HAVE A GUN.

OK, the storm was more than two months ago. You can take the sign down now. You can come out now.

Or maybe the guy's still inside there, in the dark with his canned food, water and a gun, thinking that the whole thing is still going on, like those Japanese soldiers you used to hear about in the '70s and '80s who just randomly wandered out of hiding in the forests on desolate islands in the South Pacific, thinking that World War II was still going on.

The visuals around here prey on you. Driving in from the east the other day, I saw a huge, gray wild boar that had wandered onto the interstate and been shredded by traffic. Several people I know also saw this massive porcine carnage, all torn up and chunky on the side of the road.

It looked like five dead dogs. Directly across the interstate from it was an upside down alligator.

I mean: What the hell? Since when did we have wild boars around here? And when did they decide to lumber out of the wilderness up to the interstate like it's some sort of sacred dying ground for wildebeests?

Just farther up the road a bit are all those car dealerships with rows and rows and rows of new cars that will never be sold, all browned-out like they were soaking in coffee for a week, which I guess they were.

All those lots need are some balloons on a Saturday afternoon and some guy in a bad suit saying: "Let's make a deal!"

Welcome to the Outer Limits. Your hometown. Need a new car?

Speaking of car dealers, no one epitomizes the temporary insanity around here more than Saints owner Tom Benson, who said he feared for his life in a confrontation with a drunk fan and WWL sportscaster Lee Zurik at Tiger Stadium last Sunday.

Admittedly, the shape of Lee Zurik's eyebrows have an oddly discomfiting menace about them, but fearing for your life?

Just get a good set of tweezers and defend yourself, Tom. Get a hold of yourself, man.

Maybe I shouldn't make light of this phenomenon. Maybe I'm exhibiting a form of madness in thinking this is all slightly amusing. Maybe I'm not well, either.

But former city health director Brobson Lutz tells me it's all part of healing.

"It's a part of the human coping mechanism," he said. "Part of the recovery process. I have said from the beginning that the mental health concerns here are far greater than those we can expect from infectious diseases or household injuries."

The U.S. Army brought Lutz onto the USS Iwo Jima a few weeks ago to talk to the troops about how to deal with people suffering from post-traumatic stress. They were concerned, primarily, with the dazed-out-looking folks who wander around the French Quarter all day.

"I told them to leave those guys alone," Lutz said. "They may be crazy, but they survived this thing. They coped. If they were taken out of that environment, then they could *really* develop problems. Remember that, in the immediate aftermath of all this, the primary psychiatric care in this city was being provided by the bartenders at Johnny White's and Molly's."

Interesting point. I mean, who needs a psychology degree? All anyone around here wants is someone to listen to their stories.

I thanked Lutz for his time and mentioned that our call sounded strange. It was around noon this past Thursday.

"Are you in the bathtub?" I asked him.

"Yes," he said. "And I'm having trouble coming up with sound bites."

Like I said, we're all a little touched by Katrina Fever.

My friend Glenn Collins is living in exile in Alabama and one Sunday afternoon he went to a shopping mall in Birmingham. He went to the Gap and was greeted by a salesclerk with a name tag that said "Katrina."

He left immediately. He went next door to the Coach boutique, where he was greeted by a salesclerk with a name tag that said "Katrina."

He kinda freaked out. He asked the woman something along the lines of: What's with all the Katrinas? And she blurted out: "Oh, you know Katrina at the Gap? She's my friend!"

"I wish I was making this up," he told me. "I mean, what are the odds of this?"

He needed a drink, he said. So he went to a nearby Outback Steakhouse and ordered a beer but the bartender told him they don't sell alcohol on Sundays.

"But I'm from New Orleans!" he pleaded. "Don't you have a special exemption for people from New Orleans? Please?"

They did not. So he drove across three counties to get a drink. He said to me: "The Twilight Zone, it just keeps going on and on and on."

49. 1 Dead in Attic

NOV. 15, 2005

By Chris Rose

I live on the island, where much has the appearance of Life Goes On. Gas stations, bars, pizza joints, joggers, strollers, dogs, churches, shoppers, neighbors, even garage sales.

Sometimes trash and mail service, sometimes not.

It sets to mind a modicum of complacency that maybe everything is all right.

But I have this terrible habit of getting into my car every two or three days and driving into the Valley Down Below, that vast wasteland below sea level that was my city, and it's mind-blowing A) how vast it is and B) how wasted it is.

My wife questions the wisdom of my frequent forays into the massive expanse of blown-apart lives and property that local street maps used to call Gentilly, Lakeview, the East and the Lower 9th. She fears that it contributes to my unhappiness and general instability and I suspect she is right.

Perhaps I should just stay on the stretch of safe, dry land Uptown where we live and try to move on, focus on pleasant things, quit making myself miserable, quit reliving all those terrible things we saw on TV that first week.

That's advice I wish I could follow, but I can't. I am compelled for reasons that are not entirely clear to me. And so I drive.

I drive around and try to figure out those Byzantine markings and symbols that the cops and the National Guard spray-painted on all the houses around here, cryptic communications that tell the story of who or what was or wasn't inside the house when the floodwater rose to the ceiling.

In some cases, there's no interpretation needed. There's one I pass on St. Roch Avenue in the 8th Ward at least once a week. It says: "1 dead in attic."

That certainly sums up the situation. No mystery there.

It's spray-painted there on the front of the house and it probably will remain spray-painted there for weeks, months, maybe years, a perpetual reminder of the untimely passing of a citizen, a resident, a New Orleanian.

One of us.

You'd think some numerical coding could have conveyed this information on this house, so that I—we all—wouldn't have to drive by places like this every day and be reminded: "1 dead in attic."

I have seen plenty of houses in worse shape than the one where 1 Dead in Attic used to live, houses in Gentilly and the Lower 9th that yield the most chilling visual displays in town: low-rider shotgun rooftops with holes that were hacked away from the inside with an ax, leaving small, splintered openings through which people sought escape.

Imagine if your life came to that point, and remained there, on display, all over town for us to see, day after day.

Amazingly, those rooftops are the stories with happy endings. I mean, they got out, right?

But where are they now? Do you think they have trouble sleeping at night?

The occasional rooftops still have painted messages: "HELP US." I guess they had paint cans in their attic. And an ax, like Margaret Orr and Aaron Broussard always told us we should have if we weren't going to evacuate.

Some people thought Orr and Broussard were crazy. Alarmists. Extremists. Well, maybe they are crazy. But they were right.

Perhaps 1 Dead in Attic should have heeded this advice. But judging from the ages on the state's official victims list, he or she was probably up in years. And stubborn. And unafraid. And now a statistic.

I wonder who eventually came and took 1 Dead in Attic away. Who knows? Hell, with the way things run around here—I wonder if anyone has come to take 1 Dead in Attic away.

And who claimed him or her? Who grieved over 1 Dead in Attic and who buried 1 Dead in Attic?

Was there anyone with him or her at the end and what was the last thing they said to each other? How did 1 Dead in Attic spend the last weekend in August of the year 2005?

What were their plans? Maybe dinner at Mandich on St. Claude? Maybe a Labor Day family reunion in City Park—one of those raucous picnics where everybody wears matching T-shirts to mark the occasion and they rent a DJ and a SpaceWalk and a couple of guys actually get there the night before to secure a good, shady spot?

I wonder if I ever met 1 Dead in Attic. Maybe in the course of my job or maybe at a Saints game or maybe we once stood next to each other at a Mardi Gras parade or maybe we once flipped each other off in a traffic jam.

1 Dead in Attic could have been my mail carrier, a waitress at my favorite restaurant or the guy who burglarized my house a couple years ago. Who knows?

My wife, she's right. I've got to quit just randomly driving around. This can't be helping anything.

But I can't stop. I return to the Valley Down Below over and over, looking for signs of progress in all that muck, some sign that things are getting better, that things are improving, that we don't all have to live in a state of abeyance forever but—you know what?

I just don't see them there.

I mean, in the 8th Ward, tucked down there behind St. Roch Cemetery, life looks pretty much like it did when the floodwater first receded 10 weeks ago, with lots of cars pointing this way and that, kids' yard toys caked in mire, portraits of despair, desolation and loss. And hatchet holes in rooftops.

But there's something I've discovered about the 8th Ward in this strange exercise of mine: Apparently, a lot of Mardi Gras Indians are from there. Or were from there; I'm not sure what the proper terminology is.

On several desolate streets that I drive down, I see where some folks have returned to a few of the homes and they haven't bothered to put their furniture and appliances out on the curb—what's the point, really?—but they have retrieved their tattered and muddy Indian suits and sequins and feathers and they have nailed them to the fronts of their houses.

The colors of these displays is startling because everything else in the 8th is gray. The streets, the walls, the cars, even the trees. Just gray.

So the oranges and blues and greens of the Indian costumes are something beautiful to behold, like the first flowers to bloom after the fallout. I don't know what the significance of these displays is, but they hold a mystical fascination for me.

They haunt me, almost as much as the spray paint on the front of a house that says 1 Dead in Attic. They look like ghosts hanging there. They are reminders of something. Something very New Orleans.

Do these memorials mean these guys—the Indians—are coming back? I mean, they have to, don't they? Where else could they do what they do?

And—maybe this is a strange time to ask—but who are these guys, anyway? Why do they do what they do with all those feathers and beads that take so much time and money to make? What's with all the Big Chief and Spy Boy role-playing?

As many times as I have reveled in their rhythmic, poetic and sometimes borderline absurd revelry in the streets of our city, I now realize that if you asked me to explain the origins and meaning of the Mardi Gras Indians—I couldn't do it.

I have no clue. And that makes me wish I'd been paying more attention for the past 20 years. I could have learned something.

I could have learned something about a people whose history is now but a sepia mist over back-of-town streets and neighborhoods that nobody's ever heard of and where nobody lives and nothing ever happens anymore; a freeze frame still life in the air, a story of what we once were.

50. Can We Live Upstairs, Too?

DEC. 4, 2005

By Chris Rose

Each time I go to Maryland to visit my children-in-exile, my daughter Katherine asks me the same thing: "Daddy, is everything in New Orleans broken?"

My first impulse is to tell her: "Only our hearts, darling. In a million little pieces. But our spirits shall endure."

But Katherine, being 6, isn't much for purple melodrama or lofty sentiment. She just wants to know if her swing set is OK.

So I tell her that a lot of things are, in fact, broken, but that most of her stuff—that's what counts to a child, right?—is fine. Except for the swing set, oddly enough. It's history. But that's a small price, I tell her.

I try to teach my kids that they are the lucky ones, the fortunate few, and they saw all that stuff on TV so I think they get it.

I think.

They see the piles of donated clothes at their schools in Maryland, and the table where students were raising money to buy backpacks for Katrina kids and so they know: There are folks out there a lot worse off than us.

On TV, they saw the images of people sitting in baskets dangling from ropes out of helicopters and they thought that looked pretty scary but pretty fun all the same and they wish they had done that.

"No you don't," I tell them and leave it at that.

Katherine and my son Jack recently asked me for status reports about their favorite places. The zoo: good. The Aquarium: not so good. Creole Creamery: good. This is important. After all, who would want to live in a town without ice cream?

I try to paint a somewhat accurate picture of what life looks like here, filtered through their lenses; I want them to understand, in some small way, what they will come home to one day soon.

They need to know what will be different in their upside-down world. The fewer surprises, my thinking goes, the smoother it will all go down.

They seem to grasp the situation best by an accounting of their friends. Where *are* their friends, they want to know? Who will be here when they come back to New Orleans?

I tell them that Walker and Olivia and Margot are like us: They're all here and safe and settled in their own homes.

I tell them that Casey, Helen and the twins—Sisson and Tappan—all lost the first floors of their homes in the flood but that they are going to live upstairs in their houses and they will be in school with us in January.

They think this sounds cool, this living upstairs thing.

"Can we live upstairs?" Jack asks me.

Hmm. "We can pretend," I tell him. "How about we make believe we live upstairs?"

He thinks this sounds like a good game.

Then I tell them that Lexi and Mila have moved away and they won't be coming back. Same for Miles and Cecilia. Ditto Charlie. They're gone.

They don't like this news, but they process it and they have been aware for a while that lots of families are spread around the country like them, living in new places and going to new schools. Hurricane Kids, just like them.

They don't like the idea that they never said goodbye to Lexi and Mila and Miles and Cecilia and Charlie. I tell them we'll find these kids and we will tell them goodbye. I promise them that we will find these kids. So they can say…goodbye.

Continuing on the list of friends, I tell them that Sean is up the air but that he will probably be coming back.

"Why is Sean up in the air?" Jack asks me. He's 4. I try to picture what he is picturing. Sean. Up in the air.

That sounds even cooler than living upstairs. I guess it sounds like he's dangling under a helicopter. I don't know. Sometimes I wonder how we're able to communicate with our children at all.

Katherine asks me about the specific fates of two other friends, Juliet and Nadia. I tell her that, truth is, I have no idea what happened to Juliet and Nadia. Not a clue. Vanished. They're just gone and we don't know where to or for how long and maybe we'll see them again and maybe we won't.

I don't know.

Kids don't work so well with uncertainties.

"Will you find Nadia for me?" Katherine asks.

I tell her yes, I will find Nadia. But I don't know where Nadia is. I can't even find my barber; how am I going to find some kid who used to live in Gentilly and is now cast to the fates?

Where the hell did everybody go?

Man, it's a hell of a thing that went down here.

Juliet, Nadia—are you out there? Somewhere? Anywhere?

If you are, Katherine says hello.

And goodbye.

While the writer wanders through the landscape like a lost pilgrim, he uses an anchor in the single phrase that also serves as the title.

1 Dead in Attic

heavy with meaning—an island is surrounded by water

I live on The Island, where much has the appearance of Life Goes On. Gas stations, bars, pizza joints, joggers, strollers, dogs, churches, shoppers, neighbors, even garage sales.

pay attention to how he uses capital letters to turn a phrase into a noun

specific signs of normal life

Sometimes trash and mail service, sometimes not.

It sets to mind a modicum of complacency that maybe everything is all right.

upscale phrase in contrast with simple language above— "Life Goes On"

he does it again

But I have this terrible habit of getting into my car every two or three days and driving into the Valley Down Below, that vast wasteland below sea level that was my city, and it's mind-blowing A) how vast it is and B) how wasted it is.

turns a cliché into an interesting word cluster

adds humanity and universality

My wife questions the wisdom of my frequent forays into the massive expanse of blown-apart lives and property that local street maps used to call Gentilly, Lakeview, the East and the Lower 9th. She fears that it contributes to my unhappiness and general instability and I suspect she is right.

key place names

Perhaps I should just stay on the stretch of safe, dry land

Uptown where we live and try to move on, focus on pleasant things, quit making myself miserable, quit reliving all those terrible things we saw on TV that first week.

That's advice I wish I could follow, but I can't. I am compelled for reasons that are not entirely clear to me. And so I drive.

I drive around and try to figure out those Byzantine markings and symbols that the cops and the National Guard spray-painted on all the houses around here, cryptic communications that tell the story of who or what was or wasn't inside the house when the floodwater rose to the ceiling.

In some cases, there's no interpretation needed. There's one I pass on St. Roch Avenue in the 8th Ward at least once a week. It says: "1 dead in attic."

That certainly sums up the situation. No mystery there.

It's spray-painted there on the front of the house and it probably will remain spray-painted there for weeks, months, maybe years, a perpetual reminder of the untimely passing of a citizen, a resident, a New Orleanian.

One of us.

You'd think some numerical coding could have conveyed this information on this house,

there it is again—
a sign that carries
the theme

so that I—we all—wouldn't have to drive by places like this every day and be reminded: "1 dead in attic."

I have seen plenty of houses in worse shape than the one where 1 Dead in Attic used to live, houses in Gentilly and the Lower 9th that yield the most chilling visual displays in town: low-rider shotgun rooftops with holes that were hacked away from the inside with an ax, leaving small, splintered openings through which people sought escape.

turns the phrase
into a noun

an establishing
shot feels
cinematic

leads us to this
realization

Imagine if your life came to that point, and remained there, on display, all over town for us to see, day after day.

Amazingly, those rooftops are the stories with happy endings. I mean, they got out, right?

But where are they now? Do you think they have trouble sleeping at night?

turns to questions
in an effort to
make sense
of it all

The occasional rooftops still have painted messages: "HELP US." I guess they had paint cans in their attic. And an ax, like Margaret Orr and Aaron Broussard always told us we should have if we weren't going to evacuate.

a different sign

Some people thought Orr and Broussard were crazy. Alarmists. Extremists. Well, maybe they are crazy. But they were right.

short, short, short,
punch, punch,
punch

Perhaps 1 Dead in Attic should have heeded this advice.

more fragments

more
questions

But judging from the ages on the state's official victims list, he or she was probably up in years. And stubborn. And unafraid. And now a statistic.

I wonder who eventually came and took 1 Dead in Attic away. Who knows? Hell, with the way things run around here—I wonder if anyone has come to take 1 Dead in Attic away.

And who claimed him or her? Who grieved over 1 Dead in Attic and who buried 1 Dead in Attic?

Was there anyone with him or her at the end and what was the last thing they said to each other? How did 1 Dead in Attic spend the last weekend in August of the year 2005?

What were their plans? Maybe dinner at Mandich on St. Claude? Maybe a Labor Day family reunion in City Park—one of those raucous picnics where everybody wears matching T-shirts to mark the occasion and they rent a DJ and a SpaceWalk and a couple of guys actually get there the night before to secure a good, shady spot?

I wonder if I ever met 1 Dead in Attic. Maybe in the course of my job or maybe at a Saints game or maybe we once stood next to each other at a Mardi Gras parade or maybe we once flipped each other off in a traffic jam.

the questions and fragments reflect the uncertainty and devastation

poignant dreams of normality

count how many times he repeats this phrase

this phrase hooks us back toward the beginning

another repeated phrase

three again

1 Dead in Attic could have been my mail carrier, a waitress at my favorite restaurant or the guy who burglarized my house a couple years ago. Who knows?

My wife, she's right. I've got to quit just randomly driving around. This can't be helping anything.

But I can't stop. I return to the Valley Down Below over and over, looking for signs of progress in all that muck, some sign that things are getting better, that things are improving, that we don't all have to live in a state of abeyance forever but— you know what?

I just don't see them there.

I mean, in the 8th Ward, tucked down there behind St. Roch Cemetery, life looks pretty much like it did when the floodwater first receded 10 weeks ago, with lots of cars pointing this way and that, kids' yard toys caked in mire, portraits of despair, desolation and loss. And hatchet holes in rooftops.

But there's something I've discovered about the 8th Ward in this strange exercise of mine: Apparently, a lot of Mardi Gras Indians are from there. Or were from there; I'm not sure what the proper terminology is.

On several desolate streets that I drive down, I see where some folks have returned to a

writers tend to use three examples to represent the whole

the isolation of this sentence carries weight

saves the most important detail until last

introduces the festival that represents the most carefree expression of life in New Orleans few of the homes and they haven't bothered to put their furniture and appliances out on the curb—what's the point, really?—but they have retrieved their tattered and muddy Indian suits and sequins and feathers and they have nailed them to the fronts of their houses.

a sign of the value of the past and hope for the future?

The colors of these displays is startling because everything else in the 8th is gray. The streets, the walls, the cars, even the trees. Just gray.

contrast

So the oranges and blues and greens of the Indian costumes are something beautiful to behold, like the first flowers to bloom after the fallout. I don't know what the significance of these displays is, but they hold a mystical fascination for me.

effective imagery and alliteration

They haunt me, almost as much as the spray paint on the front of a house that says 1 Dead in Attic. They look like ghosts hanging there. They are reminders of something. Something very New Orleans.

it's back!

Do these memorials mean these guys—the Indians—are coming back? I mean, they have to, don't they? Where else could they do what they do?

more questions still

And—maybe this is a strange time to ask—but who are these guys, anyway? Why do they do what they do with all those feathers and beads that take so much time and money to make?

took cultural history of his city for granted

What's with all the Big Chief and Spy Boy role-playing?

As many times as I have reveled in their rhythmic, poetic and sometimes borderline absurd revelry in the streets of our city, I now realize that if you asked me to explain the origins and meaning of the Mardi Gras Indians—I couldn't do it.

I have no clue. And that makes me wish I'd been paying more attention for the past 20 years. I could have learned something.

I could have learned something about a people whose history is now but a sepia mist over back-of-town streets and neighborhoods that nobody's ever heard of and where nobody lives and nothing ever happens anymore; a freeze frame still life in the air, a story of what we once were.

another powerful image

Roy Peter Clark is senior scholar and vice president of The Poynter Institute.

Lessons Learned

BY CHRIS ROSE

If you titled an essay "Lessons Learned from Covering Katrina," you'd need a whole book, not a page or two, to tell the story.

The ways in which the natural and man-made disasters of the summer of 2005 turned the city of New Orleans and its newspaper upside down are too many to count.

The story is too big. And it continues today, changing every day, getting bigger every day as we wrestle with the consequences and the future.

I can best address only what happened to me. And here is the formula for success that I learned: Cut your veins open and bleed onto the page. Turns out, people really like that. (And so, it appears, do the folks who give out awards.)

A disaster story like this generally has two means of entry:

A) The numerical, in which we measure the size of the storm, the number of casualties, the number of homes destroyed, the amount of money needed to fix it, how strong the levees need to be, etc., stories doled out in mass, weight and volume.

B) The pathos, the stories of loss and sorrow told by the victims: Meet John Doe, he lost everything, this is his story (with the obligatory photo of him holding a precious and mud-caked memento in his hands).

When I first got back into New Orleans, a week after the storm, the blunt force of the event hit me so hard that I immediately turned into one of the zombies walking around this city, staggering about in disbelief at the endless vistas of carnage and destruction.

Finding my way into the story was an exercise in fumbling and stumbling. Where to begin to document this one? What do you say that even remotely captures this?

Though I never contrived to do so, I fell into a pattern of writing personal stories rather than seeking the stories of those around me. The swell of emotion inside of me was too large to allow me to get outside of myself and go check in with the citizenry at large.

I basically fell into the pattern that every resident who came back to this city fell into: Just try to survive, wing it, improvise, make it day to day, sift through the physical and emotional rubble and come out of it alive and stronger. Put the pieces back together.

In the process, I became the city's poster boy for post-traumatic stress disorder. I documented my breakdowns, my setbacks, my fears and the minute, and often excruciating, details of living in a city in ruin.

Yes, reporters spend much of their time cataloguing human suffering and physical destruction, but nothing prepares you to do it in your hometown.

By trying to find the words to describe this—and failing often—it turns out that many readers felt like they were looking in the mirror when they read my stories.

I was not afraid to cry. And not afraid to write about it. I was not afraid to cower in fear, nor to document it. I was not afraid to vent barrels of anger and frustration. I howled at the moon with all the ferocity I could muster. And it turned out the readers were with me—all the way.

One of the biggest stories in the Katrina aftermath is the psychological toll on the survivors. The anxiety, depression and confusion. Since I suffered all of that—suffer it still—I give voice in the newspaper to the mental state of an entire community.

To be blunt: Everyone here is whacked by this thing. And they are comforted to know they are not alone.

The story consumed me, consumes me still. There is not a single action one can initiate in New Orleans that is not colored by Katrina and its aftermath. Everything is different. The simplest functions of shopping, having dinner with friends (they moved away), filling a prescription (wow, the line is long!), getting a haircut (where is my barber?), eating out (are they open yet?) or even finding a parking space (anywhere you damn well please; what does it matter?) lead you to reminders, lessons, memories and sorrow.

From the beginning, I just tried to document the truth of what has happened here in the barest human terms. Our history, our culture, our future, our dreams have all been dissected and laid bare by this.

Our hobbies, our pets, our kitchen appliances—everything is a story. Where is my mail? Is it safe for kids to be here? Are we going to have Mardi Gras? Is crime getting better or worse?

It's all just about living day to day, and wondering what adventure each new morning brings.

I don't believe I have ever been more honest in my life. I don't even know what objective journalism is anymore. I have approached this "assignment"—boy, there's a relative term—more as a resident of the city than as an employee of the newspaper.

I have done my best to try to understand it but I find I ask more questions in my stories than I can answer. But then, that is what the readers are doing.

By putting their fears and anger and occasional comic absurdities in print for them to read, they have felt less isolated in all of this. And they have responded. They tell me—in 20,000 e-mails, no less—that they feel like somebody understands, because they see it laid out in print in an institution they know and trust (now more than ever)—their hometown newspaper—and they realize that, in the end, we're all in this one together.

The healing power of journalism at work! Who knew there was such a thing?

Chris Rose is columnist for The Times-Picayune *in New Orleans. For his coverage of Katrina and its aftermath, Rose won the National Headliner Award from the New Jersey Press Association. He was a member of the team that won the Pulitzer Prize for public service. Rose was a finalist for the Pulitzer Prize for distinguished commentary, the Scripps Howard award for commentary and the Michael Kelly Award, presented by Atlantic Monthly Media. His post-Katrina columns have been collected into a book, "1 Dead in Attic."*

The Times-Picayune

Finalist

Terri Troncale
Editorial Writing

51. It's Time for a Nation to Return the Favor

NOV. 20, 2005

The federal government wrapped levees around greater New Orleans so that the rest of the country could share in our bounty.

Americans wanted the oil and gas that flow freely off our shores. They longed for the oysters and shrimp and flaky Gulf fish that live in abundance in our waters. They wanted to ship corn and soybeans and beets down the Mississippi and through our ports. They wanted coffee and steel to flow north through the mouth of the river and into the heartland.

They wanted more than that, though. They wanted to share in our spirit. They wanted to sample the joyous beauty of our jazz and our food. And we were happy to oblige them.

So the federal government built levees and convinced us that we were safe.

We weren't.

The levees, we were told, could stand up to a Category 3 hurricane.

They couldn't.

By the time Katrina surged into New Orleans, it had weakened to Category 3. Yet our levee system wasn't as strong as the Army Corps of Engineers said it was. Barely anchored in mushy soil, the floodwalls gave way.

Our homes and businesses were swamped. Hundreds of our neighbors died.

Now, this metro area is drying off and digging out. Life is going forward. Our heart is beating.

But we need the federal government—we need our Congress—to fulfill the promises made to us in the past. We need to be safe. We need to be able to go about our business feeding and fueling the rest of the nation. We need better protection next hurricane season than we had this year. Going forward, we need protection from the fiercest storms, the Category 5 storms that are out there waiting to strike.

Some voices in Washington are arguing against us. We were foolish, they say. We settled in a place that is lower than the sea. We should have expected to drown.

As if choosing to live in one of the nation's great cities amounted to a death wish. As if living in San Francisco or Miami or Boston is any more logical.

Great cities are made by their place and their people, their beauty and their risk. Water flows around and through most of them. And one of the greatest bodies of water in the land flows through this one: the Mississippi.

The federal government decided long ago to try to tame the river and the swampy land spreading out from it. The country needed this water-logged land of ours to prosper, so that the nation could prosper even more.

Some people in Washington don't seem to remember that. They act as if we are a burden. They act as if we wore our skirts too short and invited trouble.

We can't put up with that. We have to stand up for ourselves. Whether you are back at home or still in exile waiting to return, let Congress know that this metro area must be made safe from future storms. Call and write the leaders who are deciding our fate. Get your family and friends in other states to do the same. Start with members of the Environment and Public Works and Appropriations committees in the Senate, and Transportation and Appropriations in the House. Flood them with mail the way we were flooded by Katrina.

Remind them that this is a singular American city and that this nation still needs what we can give it.

52. Guarding the Borders

DEC. 6, 2005

By Terri Troncale

Pre-Katrina Orleans Parish levee inspections were so cursory that the only chance the city had of staying dry was if nature left it alone.

As long as hurricanes veered far enough to the east or west of New Orleans, people were safe. That is a poor method of flood protection, though, as Hurricane Katrina so devastatingly demonstrated.

The more New Orleanians find out about the way the levees were built and inspected, the clearer it is that no agency charged with protecting the city was doing a good job of it. Inspection teams from the Army Corps of Engineers, Orleans Levee Board and state Department of Transportation and Development clearly were more focused on lunch than on levee oversight.

They'd do a quick check of the levees along Lake Pontchartrain and the Mississippi River, see what they could of the outfall canals from their cars, then head to lunch. They covered more than 100 miles of levees in five hours or so. Apparently they couldn't bother spending the time to scrutinize floodwalls when crab cakes with champagne dill sauce and white chocolate mousse were waiting.

A former corps engineer who worked in other states said that he did more painstaking inspections of levees that safeguarded cattle. There is no way to properly inspect a levee system of New Orleans' size and complexity in five hours, he said. When he was on inspection teams in Missouri and California, they typically covered no more than 10 miles per day.

Given what the federal government's regulations say inspectors are supposed to do, it's no wonder his team only managed to cover short distances in a day. Among other things, inspectors are supposed to look for signs of seepage or sand boils; subsidence; animal burrows; encroachments such as fences, patios and pools and trees and shrubs whose root systems could undermine the levees' stability. There is a grading system to rank the seriousness of problems spotted during the inspections.

That would require thorough inspections, though. Eyeballing the 17th Street Canal from the Old Hammond Highway does not qualify as thorough.

Sadly, the damage done to the canal by Katrina's storm waters is easy to see from the highway now.

It is a shame that New Orleanians were led to believe that they were safer than they were. A flood protection system billed as being able to stand up to a Category 3 storm buckled under a Category 3 storm.

Not only were annual inspections a joke, canal floodwalls were barely anchored in mushy soil. Luck seems to have been about the only thing standing between the city and massive flooding, and luck almost always runs out. That happened here Aug. 29.

What the city needs is a flood protection system that is built to stand up to killer storms—at least Category 3 storms by next hurricane season and eventually Category 5 storms. Then, New Orleanians need to be assured that the corps and other agencies charged with making sure levees are in good condition actually do the job properly.

53. Out with the Old, in with the New

DEC. 31, 2005

By Terri Troncale

Rarely have so many people in one place been so eager for a new year to begin.

When 2005 turns to 2006 at midnight tonight, Hurricane Katrina will be last year's sorrow. We will say farewell and good riddance to the most painful months many of us will ever experience.

Of course, it is not that simple. People here will be in mourning for some time to come over what this storm did to our families, our homes and our neighborhoods. We will still feel wounded and vulnerable when the new year begins—and for who knows how long into the future. We have lost too much to get over it in mere months.

But reaching the end of 2005 gives us a dividing point, a line of demarcation between the tragedy of Katrina and the future. Perhaps it is merely illusion today, but as we move through 2006, our focus will shift more and more from destruction to recovery.

At least it should. The fate of greater New Orleans depends on so much more than individuals' desire to return and rebuild.

* * *

Above all, our fate depends on whether President Bush and Congress follow through on the promise delivered by reconstruction czar Donald Powell to build the "best levee system known in the world." Congress approved $2.9 billion of $3.1 billion requested by the White House to repair breaches in canal floodwalls, shore up some levees with stone and concrete and complete long-delayed levee work in West Jefferson, Plaquemines and St. Charles parishes.

Regrettably, lawmakers rejected the administration's request for $300 million to build pumping stations along Lake Pontchartrain to keep storm surge from pouring into New Orleans through drainage canals. Katrina demonstrated in catastrophic detail the risks posed by the drainage canals. The new pumps are crucial, and Louisiana's congressional delegation needs to make them a top priority when Congress reconvenes after its holiday break.

The $3.1 billion in levee work will make much of New Orleans safer than it was when Katrina struck. But eastern New Orleans, the Lower 9th Ward and St. Bernard Parish still would be vulnerable to a storm of that magnitude, and the entire region would be at risk from more powerful hurricanes. For the long-term, the metro area needs a protection system that can stand up to the worst storms, keep storm surge out of the lake and out of our homes.

One of the biggest disappointments in Congress after Katrina was the blockage of Rep. Richard Baker's legislation authorizing the government-backed purchase of flooded homes. The Baton Rouge congressman's plan would give much-needed financial relief to homeowners, prevent massive foreclosures and spark the wholesale redevelopment of damaged neighborhoods. It is the most comprehensive rebuilding plan on the table, and it is essential to the future health of Lakeview, Gentilly, Broadmoor and other hard-hit neighborhoods.

Rep. Baker worked doggedly to try to get the measure passed before Congress adjourned for the holidays, but resistance from the White House and from key lawmakers kept the bill bottled up. Alabama Sen. Richard Shelby, who chairs the Senate Banking Committee, has promised to make the bill a priority early in 2006. Louisianians and their elected representatives need to keep the pressure up to make sure that happens.

* * *

While strong leadership in Washington is crucial to South Louisiana's future, we are in desperate need of leadership and vision here at home—and that is proving much harder to find.

Gov. Kathleen Blanco seems to empathize with storm victims, but she has shown little willingness to break with old-time politics and make the bold reforms needed post-Katrina. During a special session last fall, her legislative allies helped kill a bill to create a unified, professional levee board for the Mississippi River and Lake Pontchartrain basins. In addition, the governor backed the diversion of money from South Louisiana to an equestrian park and other questionable capital projects in areas untouched by Katrina or Rita.

Despite the vital issues facing South Louisiana in the post-Katrina world, Gov. Blanco also had to be pressured into calling a special session early in the new year. She was silent as her legislative leaders dismissed the need for the session, saying they saw nothing urgent that needed to be dealt with. Perhaps if House Speaker Joe Salter and Senate President

Donald Hines spent any time in the New Orleans area, they would understand the urgency.

First, lawmakers need to revisit Sen. Walter Boasso's legislation to scrap the patronage-riddled local levee boards sprinkled across the metro area for a single, professionally run board.

Beyond that, lawmakers need to chop away at the wasteful duplication in Orleans Parish government. The city is burdened with superfluous law enforcement agencies and an excess of elected minor political offices—including seven elected tax assessors. This tangle of institutions, which was an impediment to the city's growth before Katrina, is almost a criminal misuse of precious resources now.

On the city level, Mayor Ray Nagin and the City Council simply must start working together. New Orleans desperately needs its elected leaders to put aside personal agendas and agree on a vision for the city. The mayor and his staff must communicate better with the council and with the public, and the council must be willing to compromise. They must all have the gumption to make tough decisions about how to rebuild this flood-ravaged city.

* * *

None of us could have imagined Aug. 28 where we would be today. Who could have fathomed entire parishes emptied for weeks on end by flooding? Who could have fathomed having all of our friends and family scattered across the continent? Who could have known that there were so many heroes living among us?

These are the most trying times any community could face. And yet we are still a community—far-flung and battered, but a community of people who have shown great strength and resilience. We need the same selflessness and dedication from our leaders, and we need it now.

Lessons Learned

BY TERRI TRONCALE

The first thing I saw the morning after Hurricane Katrina hit New Orleans was a *Times-Picayune* photographer paddling a kayak in front of our building.

The newspaper's building was an island. Chest-deep floodwaters surrounded it. The red kayak was our only boat. If we were going to cover the aftermath of Katrina, and of course we were going to cover this story, we would have to abandon the building and find dry land.

That is what we did. Not long after breakfast on Aug. 30, 250 staffers and family members were loaded into open-backed delivery trucks and driven across the Mississippi River.

Half a dozen trucks kept going toward Houma and, eventually, Baton Rouge. Three others, including the one I was in, stopped at our satellite office on the river's West Bank. There, 10 of us asked for a truck to take back into the city.

We knew that my house and others hugging the river were dry, and we knew that someone had to tell the story from inside New Orleans.

That decision, made in a moment's time in a parking lot, has influenced every word I have written about Katrina. Being on the ground in New Orleans, when the city was submerged, when flooded-out residents were roaming Interstate 10 without water, food or shelter, gave me a personal view of the devastation and of the government's anemic response.

That is the greatest lesson I took from this experience. I have never ascribed to the ivory tower approach to the editorial page. But it is rare as an editorial writer to have such an intimate view of a subject.

Our first experience when we crossed back over the Mississippi into New Orleans that Tuesday morning was the looting of a Wal-Mart store. I sat at my dining room table an hour later and wrote an editorial rebuking the police officers who allowed—and even participated in—the looting. I dictated the piece from my neighbor's house, where there was a working phone. We used that phone the rest of the day to dictate stories and transmit photographs.

With water continuing to pour into the city, we evacuated my house late that night. We headed across the Mississippi again to a spot we could count on to stay dry while we slept. We spent the next few days moving from house to house in the city, reporting on the deteriorating conditions at the Superdome and Convention Center. We scavenged water and food from the homes of friends and coworkers who had given us their keys. We wept at the sight of hundreds of desperate people, some of them dying, who were exposed to the stifling late summer heat with little or no water.

The editorials written from inside the city in those first days by me and deputy editorial page editor Dante Ramos were a plea for help for suffering New Orleanians. After the immediate crisis passed, our editorials shifted to the long-term recovery of the region—the federal assistance that would be needed, the state and local political reform that would be essential.

As is evident in the three editorials printed here—"It's Time for a Nation to Return the Favor," "Guarding the Borders" and "Out with the Old, in with the New"—we have taken on inertia, mismanagement and corruption at all levels of government.

It is now seven months after the storm, and I have written about nothing other than Katrina and its aftermath. I can't foresee a time yet when that will change.

The emotion of the early weeks after the storm has faded over time. But the memory of helpless people abandoned to their own devices hasn't.

The Thursday after the storm, Sept. 1, people who had walked out of their flooded neighborhoods were still stranded on Interstate 10. One family pushed a wheelchair holding an elderly woman dressed in pink pajamas. She had died, and they had covered her head with a bag to shield her.

It was a heartbreaking sight, and I will carry it with me every day that I cover this story.

Terri Troncale is the editorial page editor at The Times-Picayune. *She has worked as an editorial writer in Alabama, where she was a finalist, along with three co-workers, for the 1994 Pulitzer Prize in editorial writing for a series on the needs of Alabama public schools. She also has received numerous awards during her career from the Alabama Associated Press, Alabama Press Association, Louisiana Press Association and Louisiana-Mississippi Associated Press.*

A conversation with
Jim Amoss

An edited interview with Jim Amoss by Poynter faculty member Butch Ward. Jim Amoss has been editor of The Times-Picayune *in New Orleans since 1990. They started by discussing how the newsroom decided how to cover the aftermath of Katrina.*

JIM AMOSS: You have to remember that the discovery of what had happened came in several waves. First there was the hurricane windstorm—and it was ferocious. It blew in six or seven windows in our building, which is quite a fortress—a big, hulking, fascist-looking, thick-walled building that exudes strong shelter. During past storms, lots of people had flocked to it to seek safety.

This was the strongest storm I had ever sat through—windows blowing in had never happened before.

We had placed computers powered by generators near the core of the building, and we planned to produce newspapers with those generators after we lost power, which we knew would happen. We also planned to use those computers to put our work on the Internet or to transmit our work to remote presses if need be.

This plan still all made sense when the storm arrived late Sunday night into Monday morning. And so in late morning, or early afternoon, we gradually emerged from the building. Winds were still strong, but you could walk outside without facing too much danger. Some of our bravest journalists ventured out, some in boats and some in trucks, and what they immediately observed was that it had been a ferocious windstorm that had caused great damage. But this is what we had planned for—to stay in the building and dispatch our staff from there.

So we began to dispatch staff members to parts of the city that we knew others wouldn't go to because they wouldn't know where to go—we knew the national media would focus on downtown and the French Quarter, and that's what they did. And they were reporting that New Orleans had dodged another bullet.

In other parts of the city, our people—especially our photographers—were finding another story. Along the eastern edge of the city—in the Lower Ninth Ward, in St. Bernard's Parish—the Industrial Canal levee had collapsed. They found horrific sites: violent water, buildings destroyed and many people trapped on rooftops. People in private boats already were trying to rescue stranded residents. The photographers alternated from shooting photos to joining in the rescue.

So in mid-afternoon, the photographers came back to the office and reported that the eastern edge of the city was disastrously flooded, and that there would likely be a great loss of life.

At this point, we still had no reports from the northwest side of the city along Lake Pontchartrain.

When we gathered for a news meeting between 7 and 7:30 that Monday evening, for a news meeting in near-darkness—the only light was powered by generators—we had decided to produce a fully paginated PDF online version of the paper. There simply were no residents to deliver a paper to, and we had this diaspora outside New Orleans that argued for distributing this information across America.

When we started the meeting, we were deciding how to best report the apparent duality of the situation: that the city had been saved, but that the Lower Ninth Ward and St. Bernard's Parish had been devastated. But that soon changed.

That afternoon at about 2 p.m., James O'Byrne, the features editor, and Doug MacCash, the arts critic, had taken bicycles and rode them along the railroad tracks to Canal Boulevard, which runs from Lake Pontchartrain to downtown New Orleans. What they found was a rushing torrent—waves cascading toward downtown—and they realized that something disastrous had happened.

Watching this, it dawned on James that his home had been destroyed too. He put down his notebook and let that thought sink in. Then, after a few moments, he picked it up and started scribbling again.

He then pulled out a camera and immediately saw the flashing light that meant his battery was low. So he turned to the people with them on the bridge and asked, "Does anyone have a AA battery?" Suddenly a man jumped off the bridge into the water, swam 50 feet to his house (which is under, surrounded by seven feet of water), goes inside (closing the door behind him) and comes out holding a Ziploc bag filled with batteries in his teeth.

For six hours, James and Doug rode along the railroad tracks, taking notes and shooting photographs, reporting on the breach of the 17th Street Canal. What they saw was a truly disastrous urban inundation—it was a real triumph of first-hand reporting.

So we were in the midst of our news meeting that evening when James and Doug burst in and told us what they had—the whole city was being inundated by the breach. We radically rethought what we would say in the next day's paper, and went with the headline, "Catastrophic."

All of us had family and friends scattered away from New Orleans—and it wasn't until they went on nola.com that they learned the true dimensions of what had happened.

This facet of the story—the inundation that followed the hurricane and the flooding—no one had any experience covering something like that, or the implications of what it would mean to our city.

BUTCH WARD: So what does the editor do at this point?

The main task at this point is the orchestration of coverage. We tried to deploy our forces in such a way that we avoided redundancy and maximized our effort to cover the thousands of stories that must be told—and to deploy the staff in a way that's safe. They were so full of energy, heroism and derring-do that sometimes they had to be restrained from risking their lives.

We had to make sure our communications worked—that we actually could harness all of this information into a newspaper and an online report.

We told our reporters and photographers to keep us constantly informed—we needed to get information to our readers as soon as we saw it. And so we were able to publish hundreds of dispatches that told people what was going on as it was happening.

On Monday morning, I told the staff that this was the biggest story of our lives, and that it was absolutely vital that we tell it as only we can tell it. We had a tremendous responsibility—this was a newspaper story par excellence. Telling it requires resources that only the newspaper can muster. It flows from the accumulated, layered knowledge of the complex community that only the newspaper staff possesses over time.

There's no question we benefited from the availability of the Internet, which allowed us to gather material and distribute it without having to wait, to people who were hungry for it. We were a vital link to their hometown. We were able to be nimble, to adapt to changing circumstances and to reinvent our strategy on the fly.

What surprised you about your staff?

Their emotional resilience and stamina at a time when they had lost everything. Scenes like the one with James O'Byrne on the bridge, realizing he had lost his home, were replicated over and over. People who had no idea what had befallen their possessions or, in some cases, their families, were there putting out the newspaper. In a way, I think that helped to sustain them over time.

What surprised you about yourself?

My ability to crowd out the darkest thoughts of what would happen to the newspaper, to my family, to my city. Plunging into newspapering was a form of therapy. It was quite a blessing. I could see the difference in family members who didn't have that to help them through it all.

I also was surprised at how grief would come to me unexpectedly; how riding in the car and hearing a radio report could bring me to tears.

PART 8

Community Service Photojournalism

Todd Heisler

Community Service Photojournalism

Todd Heisler fell in love with photography at the age of 15. His high school photography class exposed him to the immediate gratification and creative communication that came with making photos.

He realized he could do something with his photography when he attended Illinois State University and worked on *The Daily Vidette.* An internship with *The Pantagraph,* in Bloomington, Ill., offered him more experience in photojournalism.

After school, Heisler got a job working for Copley's Chicago newspapers, a chain of small weekly community papers. At Copley, "I learned to do the small things well," Heisler said. He photographed the prom, people who lost their house in a tornado, and just daily life.

That experience taught him about balancing his personal vision with how he dealt with the subjects he photographed. The personal vision involved knowing what he wanted to say with his photos. Dealing with people made it personal from a human standpoint.

"In community newspapers, I learned that I would take a photo of someone and I would see them again," Heisler said. "I saw the impact it would have on them and the community. The best advice someone gave to me is that every assignment is important to somebody."

Rocky Mountain News

Heisler also learned to find the beautiful in everything and to make beautiful photographs. The Copley newspapers had been built around great photojournalism. The foundation of the chain was a weekly photo section.

Mike Davis at Copley became a mentor for Heisler. He worked at *National Geographic,* the White House and now works at *The Oregonian.* "Davis would say to us: approach your community as if you were doing a book of the community," Heisler recalled. "It meant finding the beauty in everything. No idea was too mundane."

In 2001, Heisler moved to the *Rocky Mountain News.* That's where he learned that the emphasis on photojournalism was on the *journalism.* "What I really learned at the *Rocky* was that it can't just be about beautiful pictures," he said. "It has to say something about the story, the place. It has to take people to another place. My challenge when I came to the *Rocky* was to find the beauty (in what I photographed)—and have my pictures say something."

"Final Salute" shows how well Heisler, 34, addressed that challenge. The photos he made during that project capture beauty in all the major— and the minor—scenes that occurred when a Marine came home for the last time. He wanted the people who see those photographs to reevaluate the way they see their world. His powerful images earned him not only the ASNE community service photojournalism award, but the Pulitzer Prize as well. His partner, Jim Sheeler, also won the ASNE non-deadline writing award for "Final Salute," which is featured in Part 2 of this book. Sheeler, too, won a Pulitzer Prize for the story.

"Final Salute" bears witness to Heisler's growth professionally and personally. "It changed the way I thought about my subjects," he said. "It made me learn to put down the camera more. And try to find out where they were coming from, who they were as people—especially with this project. It made me think more of my role as a human being."

—Aly Colón

Marine Maj. Steve Beck prepares for the final inspection of 2nd Lt. James J. Cathey's body, only days after notifying Cathey's wife of the Marine's death in Iraq. The knock at the door begins a ritual steeped in tradition more than two centuries old, a tradition based on the same tenet: "Never leave a Marine behind." When the wars began in Afghanistan and Iraq, Maj. Beck expected to find himself overseas, in the heat of battle. He never thought he would be the one arranging funerals for his fallen comrades.

54. About "Final Salute"

The "Final Salute" photos made by Todd Heisler capture the story that begins with an ending, the dreaded knock at the door. Through moving photographs, Heisler shows the cost of war, the impact of the loss of a single life and the caring spirit of the Marine Corps. His pictures represent the iconic images of our time.

They track Maj. Steve Beck and his men as they help their fallen Marines and the families left behind through their final time together. They invite a viewer in to see a world unseen before this story:

Stunned faces peer out the oval windows of a passenger jet as Marines in dress blues board the cargo hold to unload the casket of one of their fallen brothers. A widow lies on a bed before her husband's casket on the night before his funeral, listening to what would have been the music for her formal wedding celebration, her face lit by the glow of her laptop screen.

John Temple, publisher and editor of the *Rocky Mountain News*, noted that his paper has published many powerful photo essays. But "never before have I been to story meetings where tears fell from every person in the room as they looked at the rough edit."

He described Heisler's work as a "sensitive, dignified and unflinchingly truthful record of this important era in our nation's history."

—Adapted from the *Rocky Mountain News* ASNE contest entry

A conversation with

Todd Heisler

An edited e-mail interview conducted by Poynter Institute faculty member Kenny Irby with Todd Heisler, winner of the ASNE community service photojournalism award.

KENNY IRBY: Where did the idea for "Final Salute" come from?

TODD HEISLER: At the start of the Iraq War, I was an embedded journalist. *Rocky Mountain News* writer Jim Sheeler was focusing on the home front. The idea for "Final Salute" was created from our passion in covering different facets of the war, and from an interest in putting names with casualty numbers.

For Sheeler, it started in March 2003 at Fort Logan National Cemetery in Denver, when he covered Colorado's first casualty of the Iraq War, Marine Thomas Slocum. Sheeler discovered that the man who buried Slocum was a Marine. As he covered more funerals, he noticed the Marine stare. He wanted to get behind that stare and learn more about how the Marines prepared for, and conducted, funerals.

After approaching local Marine commanders, he met Maj. Steve Beck, who was responsible for death notifications. Beck was very quizzical at first about Sheeler's intentions. But after reading his stories about the Marines that Beck himself had brought home, he eventually opened up. I met Beck shortly thereafter, and the three of us formed a collaboration that started the journey that resulted in "Final Salute."

How did you decide what the focus would be?

Our original plan for the story was to follow a Marine from the moment his casket arrived at the airport to his burial. Unfortunately, the first family we encountered did not want to talk with us. We were able to observe everything from the outside, but there was no way to do the story the way we intended.

Because we couldn't do an in-depth story, we took the time to learn more about the process from Maj. Beck. We also learned more about him, how his experiences had a profound effect on him, and how close he and the Marines had become with the families.

It was then that we realized there was so much more to this story. It was Maj. Beck who encouraged us to wait and see where the story would take

Jo Burns cries as she and her husband, Bob, opened the boxes containing their son's uniforms from Iraq—boxes delivered by Maj. Steve Beck. "For me, having all this back is a good thing," she said a few minutes later. "I want to remember. I don't ever want to forget, or to stop feeling." Bob Burns then took her hand. "I don't want to forget either," he said. "I just don't want to hurt."

us. It was obvious at that point that he would be a great focus to the story, but he was very apprehensive about being in the spotlight. In the end, the focus became how he guided the families through their grief.

How did you organize your story coverage?

We kept in touch with Maj. Beck on a regular basis. He would call us if there was an event, or if he was planning to visit a family. If there was a casualty, he would introduce us to the family shortly after the notifications had been made. In that case, Sheeler and I would do a daily story for the paper, and continue our coverage for the project.

How long did it take to build a relationship with the family members?

Each family was different. Some families, like the Burns family, had a level of trust with us because Sheeler had written a story about them previously. Throughout the entire process, we had to build trust with Maj. Beck. As we built trust with him, he would help us earn trust with the families.

In Katherine Cathey's case, Sheeler and I initially spent about four hours at her home talking with her about her husband. When we were leaving her house around midnight, she said, "I know this might sound weird, but you guys made my night." We ended up spending the next five days or so with her, building the relationship. Our philosophy was to spend as much time as possible with the families—just *listening*. The families just wanted to talk about their loved ones, and have their stories told, and you can't put a time frame on it.

Tell me about the revisions you made. What was the editing process?

In early August 2005 we had a meeting with all the top editors to show them what Sheeler and I had documented to that point. I created a loose edit of photographs while Sheeler read quotes from his notebook. *Rocky Mountain News* editor and publisher John Temple later said it was the only news meeting he had ever attended in which everyone was crying.

Even though the story was strong and had an impact, photo director Janet Reeves and I did not think we were completely finished. It was a good story, but it didn't quite live up to our expectations. It wasn't there yet.

Janet and I had some conversations about scenes Sheeler was writing about that we didn't see in the photos. Our plan was to have Sheeler write, and Janet and I would create a manageable edit with the photos. We had no idea how the story would end.

About a week later, we learned that 2nd Lt. Cathey had been killed. His story became a major part of "Final Salute."

I think having the time to reflect on the work and receiving feedback from my editors, especially Reeves, changed my approach. At the end of our first presentation to the editors, I remember Temple saying, "This (story) is like a prayer." His comment stayed with me the whole time I was shooting—and later when Reeves and I were going through hundreds of outtakes.

What role did your picture editor play?

Janet Reeves is an amazing advocate. As my coverage started taking shape, she went out of her way to make sure we stayed committed to the story. After our first big meeting to discuss the project, she kept track of the things we were hearing but weren't seeing. When it came down to the final weeks of editing, she and I basically locked ourselves in the studio with a dozen storyboards and piles of prints to create the final edit.

What role did your writing colleague, Jim Sheeler, play in the process? How did the collaboration between you work?

The whole process was a collaboration of mutual respect. He has always been a photographer's favorite reporter to work with because he works

After arriving at the funeral home, Katherine Cathey, moaning softly, pressed her pregnant belly to her husband's casket. Two days after she was notified of Jim's death in Iraq, she found out they would have a boy. Born on Dec. 22, 2005, he was named James Jeffrey Cathey Jr.

like a photojournalist—he looks for scenes and moments. While many writers are content just getting a little color and rely on phoning the rest in, Sheeler is there for the long haul. At times, he even pushed me to stay longer than I thought necessary.

I knew when he needed the space to sit and talk with someone, and he knew the right moments when he needed to step back and just observe. If he saw something, or felt something would happen, he would tell me. We learned together, and spent long drives and downtime in hotel rooms sharing thoughts and ideas on the project. When things got emotional, it was good to have someone to talk to who was witnessing the same things I was.

Early on in the process, we decided together that the story would not be complete unless we both felt we were finished. When we started finalizing the piece, he gathered amazing quotes that he knew wouldn't make the final draft and wrote poignant captions. During the weeks it took him to write the story, he surrounded himself with my photographs. The project was so successful because it's hard to tell where the photographer ends and the writer begins.

Given the U.S. government ban on documenting the "fallen soldiers," how did you negotiate the access that allowed you to be on the runway for the body transport photograph?

There is a great deal of confusion and misconception about the ban on documenting this scene. While there is a ban on photographing "fallen soldiers" at military bases, there is no such rule at commercial airports. It is ultimately the family's decision whether a photographer will be welcomed on the tarmac with them.

It also depends on the casualty assistance officer, and whether he or she is willing to have journalists there while he, or she, takes care of the family. Usually, airport officials, casualty assistance officers and family members alike were not willing to grant access to multiple news organizations at the same time. Since we were working with Maj. Beck, and we talked with the Catheys days before the arrival, we rode in with the family.

How much time did you put into the coverage?

We worked on the project on and off for about nine months, while doing daily assignments.

What were some of the ethical challenges that you faced? How did you overcome them?

The night before the burial of her husband's body, Katherine Cathey refused to leave the casket, and asked to sleep next to his body for the last time. The Marines made a bed for her, tucking in the sheets below the flag. Before she fell asleep, she opened her laptop computer and played songs that reminded her of "Cat," and one of the Marines asked if she wanted them to continue standing watch as she slept. "I think it would be kind of nice if you kept doing it," she said. "I think that's what he would have wanted."

While Maj. Beck was open to me photographing some very private moments, including fallen Marines at the airport, he was very protective of the grieving families. He told me many times a sensational view of their grief could be devastating to his career. He had a legitimate concern and I was considerate of it. At the same time, I couldn't candy-coat a very serious situation.

Through the entire process, we all became very close, and at times it was difficult to balance my need to make intimate photographs with my feelings for the subjects. In the end, this challenge made the final piece that much better. It made me reflect on how I was presenting the people in the story, how I was representing their grief and whether I was being sensational or stripping them of their dignity.

How did you organize your final photographic narrative?

After printing out about 100 prints, photo director Janet Reeves and I read through the first draft of the story and selected key themes we wanted to represent. There were concrete scenes we knew would be in the final edit. But we looked for other things, like sense of place and different types of

Marines lift the flag off the casket of Lance Cpl. Evenor Herrera, preparing to fold it for the last time and present it to Herrera's parents, Blanca and David Stibbs, center. After watching so many scenes of grief, the Marines involved say the cries of the family never leave their mind. "It's almost enough to wish that you could take his place, so these people wouldn't hurt so much," said Sgt. Kevin Thomas.

emotion. We did not want every photograph to be of someone crying, because that was not a true representation of the whole experience.

Later, we arranged about 12 storyboards, and started tacking on photos that we knew were our obvious leads—that was the easiest part. It was the quieter, transitional photos that took the longest to agree upon. Once we had the edit down to about 50 photographs, we met with the designer and a handful of editors to discuss the progress we made.

Editor and publisher John Temple asked everyone to pick the photos they absolutely couldn't live without and there was a great deal of discussion about which shots should stay. Along with the designer, we organized the package by facing pages, and started to see what would fit. We decided the photographs would follow the same structure as the written story, with some minor exceptions.

What are the more memorable lessons you learned during this assignment?

One of the most important lessons is that the families want these stories told—they want their loved ones to be remembered. I also learned how important it is to be judicious with the number of frames I make.

Were there any major surprises for you while reporting this story?

We knew the story would draw some attention, but we had no idea we would receive thousands of e-mails, letters and phone calls from people in the military and civilians from all around the world.

Why do you do what you do as a photojournalist?

Working on "Final Salute" re-instilled my faith that one photograph can make people stop, if for just a few seconds, and reflect on the world and the time they live in. I want my photographs to give people a better understanding of our community, to shed new light on subjects people might have overlooked and give a voice to those who might not otherwise be heard. Even in the bigger stories I have done, I have always tried to find beauty in the everyday, even mundane things, to make people reevaluate the way they see the world.

What outcome had you hoped for when covering this story?

We thought "Final Salute" would strike a nerve, but we had no idea what nerve that would be. We did not want it to be seen as a political statement, but instead as a contemplation of the loss felt in our community—and in communities across the country. We published the Web version of the project, including the written piece in its entirety, the day before "Final Salute" hit the newsstands on Veteran's Day.

Sheeler and I started receiving e-mails immediately. To this day, we have received more than a thousand e-mails, letters and phone calls. The vast majority has been positive, from people both for and against the war. I consider the story a success because so many people have reached out to us—about the war, the women and men fighting in Iraq and the families left behind.

How different was this story from the kinds of stories that you have covered during your career?

I never had a story take me on a journey the way "Final Salute" has. I have done many long-term, in-depth projects and essays. But they were about broader topics, and none required the level of commitment of "Final Salute." I covered new ground during this project; building on the skills I developed over the years doing community journalism. I never took a single subject this far.

What advice can you offer younger photographers when it comes to being a visual reporter?

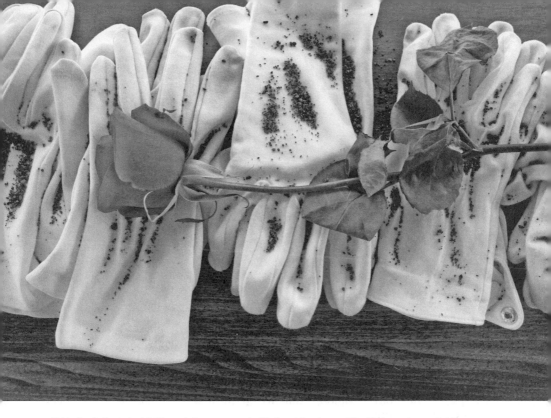

At Lt. Jim Cathey's burial, his casket was covered with the white gloves of the Marines who carried him, sand they brought from the beaches of Iwo Jima and a single red rose.

When I was in college, I heard a great piece of advice that has always stuck with me: "Be a person first, a journalist second and a photographer last." It's important to truly care about your subjects and take time to put the camera down and listen. The photos you do not make can be as important as the ones you do make. Think about how important that assignment is to *them*. Learning to do the small things very well helped me when it came time for big assignments like covering the war in Iraq. Learn to work with writers well and be open to their ideas. I have always tried to make the relationship with reporters less adversarial and more collaborative.

Learn more about the work of the 2006 ASNE winners and finalists in an e-learning course at News University (www.newsu.org). See and hear from the photojournalists and the judges as they discuss the honored work, and explore ways to strengthen your picture editing and critical thinking—improving your own photojournalism. The course, "Community Service Photojournalism: Lessons from a Contest (2006)," is at www.newsu.org/asne2006. *NewsU is a journalism-training project of The Poynter Institute funded by the John S. and James L. Knight Foundation.*

The Oregonian

■ Finalist

Bruce Ely
Community Service Photojournalism

55. About "Sidelines"

Bruce Ely wanted to capture something different. Having photographed professional basketball, the best college football teams and many Olympians, Ely remained attached to his community as a photojournalist. That connection prompted him to create a photo column he dubbed "Sidelines: A Different View of Prep Sports."

The column captures those moments that define everyday life for most people. Weekly, in black-and-white photos, Ely offers revealing, intimate moments. Not about stars or starters. But about those who love the game and those who watch the game. It is about teens who learn valuable lessons about giving, sharing and helping one another, and exceeding their own expectations or abilities.

"Sidelines" provides photographs that represent the fabric of communities, slices of life people experience individually but few see collectively.

Ely's photos show the beauty and the pain, the humanity and the vitality of the people he photographs. Viewers get drawn into the mud with runners negotiating an onerous, cross-country course. They go into a locker room before the big game. They weigh in before a wrestling match. See a snowboarder close up, laughing in spite of a broken wrist.

These are the photos of everyday Americana—the weird, the wonderful and the uninhibited moments that exemplify high school sports.

—Adapted from *The Oregonian* ASNE contest entry

Bruce Ely is a photojournalist at The Oregonian. *He joined the paper in early 2000. His awards in 2005 include: first place Sports Feature— Best of Photojournalism (photograph of synchronized swimming team from "Sidelines" column); second place Sports Portfolio—Pictures of*

An underwater speaker guides members of the Tualatin Hills Synchronized Swim Team as they move grace-fully through the water and appear to effortlessly defy gravity. "It requires a high level of synergy to be suc-cessful," says coach Linia Vaz De Negri. "Being upside down, not seeing, not hearing—they really need to have a good feel for each other out there."

the Year International, first place editing Newspaper Recurring Feature—Best of Photojournalism (editing of "Sidelines" column). His 2004 awards: second place portfolio—National Headliners Awards (portfolio of work from 2004).

Lessons Learned

BY BRUCE ELY

It's hard to believe, but I used to be a high jumper back in high school. I jumped 5 feet, 10 inches—which is completely average.

I was never good enough to get my picture in my hometown paper, *The Spokesman Review.* I wasn't good enough. My team wasn't good enough. Just like most newspapers, space in the sports section goes to the biggest and best athletes in the community.

I am sure every sports photographer out there has gone to an event and come back with a great picture—only to have it not published because it wasn't of the winner. Some of the best moments in high school sports often do not involve the biggest schools or best athletes. How do we get these telling pictures in our paper? This is the idea I started with when I went to the sports department to pitch a photo column called "Sidelines."

High school sports are not just about the action. Although, I guess some would disagree. With this column I am trying to show the culture surrounding these sports—away from the action. Each week we try to take a look at a sport or team that does not get coverage in our newspaper. Students are participating in sports other than basketball, football and tennis.

Once a week, I am given a day to work on the column—shooting and researching. Fortunately, I am not asked to cover an event for the daily paper while shooting for a "Sidelines" picture.

After starting the column last fall, we have published 48 "Sidelines" columns. We decided to put the column on hold during the summer while school is on break.

Having a dedicated space in the newspaper each week comes with an added level of pressure. There are many critics of the column—inside and outside the newsroom. We always hope to get e-mails and phone calls that tell us how wonderful our work is. It doesn't always work out that way, though.

Here is a portion of an e-mail I received from a cheerleader regarding a "Sidelines" picture. The picture was of a dejected quarterback after a playoff game:

> It is hard to understand the reasoning behind posting a picture of my quarterback and fellow cheerleaders like that, three days after the fact. No other reasoning can be drawn except that the picture was meant to cause pain and humiliate. You should be ashamed for

your self for what you have done. If you are a holy man, God does not except this kind of behavior and you have rightfully earned your spot in hell. But if you are not a holy man, which would not surprise many, you have earned your place with the other scum of the earth.

You must be a sad troubled man to have such a small, unimportant column in the newspaper. And by your appearance, it obvious that you could not be new to the journalism business, you are way too old for that. So it looks as if your career has developed into shattering the hearts and souls of young aspiring athletes; in a small column run only once a week. It must be a nice feeling. Getting back at all the jocks who more likely than not, never knew or cared about your worthless existence.

Sincerely,
Your Cheerleader Friend

Here is another response about the same picture:

Bruce—I just wanted to thank you for the "Sidelines" picture you ran on December 6. My son, Stephen Scott, is the lineman in the middle on the bench. Your picture said it all. My son was very moved by the picture. He has it in his room to remind him of an awesome season, the friends he met, the highs and the lows . . . and the dreams for the next year. Thank you for being there and capturing the moment.

Laurie Scott

I wanted to create the photo column called "Sidelines" because I wanted the community to witness the moments that define everyday life for most people. The weekly, black-and-white photo column is intimate and revealing. It isn't about the stars or starters.

It's about those who love the game and those who watch the game. It is about teens who learn valuable lessons about giving, sharing and helping one another, and exceeding their own expectations or abilities.

Bruce Ely is a photojournalist at The Oregonian.

The Seattle Times

Mike Siegel

Community Service Photojournalism

56. About "What's Best for Baby M?"

What happens when the government takes a child away from his or her parents? Usually it takes place behind closed court doors. The public rarely sees what happens.

When Washington State opened the system, photographer Mike Siegel and reporter Jonathan Martin found a homeless couple whose child had been seized by the state at birth. Siegel and Martin remained persistent over a two-year period in documenting the couple's attempt to regain custody of their daughter, known by the state as "Baby M."

Siegel gained the trust of the couple. He obtained access into an extraordinarily intimate view of their lives. Siegel also developed his own contacts inside the government. This enabled him to get behind courtroom doors, often over the objections of skittish bureaucrats.

He persisted in making pictures that needed to be made: in court, during parental visits, at counseling sessions, during drug testing. Siegel spent countless hours with the couple—where they ate, slept and lived—even as their lives began to unravel.

His pictures allow viewers to witness the searing pain of separation. The photos about what happened in the case of "Baby M" help us understand a crucial problem in the community and the dedication of those helping to address it.

—Adapted from *The Seattle Times* ASNE contest entry

Mike Siegel has been a staff photographer at The Seattle Times *for 19 years. He has won several awards in 2006, including second place for the Casey Medal and first place from the Society of Professional Journalists for News, and 2 second places for Photostory and Spot News.*

Liz Campo says goodbye to her daughter after a supervised visit. Caseworkers noted that her boyfriend, Mike Testa, seen through the back window, seemed aloof during some family sessions.

Lessons Learned

BY MIKE SIEGEL

The headline read: "What's Best for Baby M?"

> *"One of the most profound powers exercised by the state of Washington is the decision to take a child from its parents because of abuse or neglect. In an unprecedented look inside the dependency-court system, this is the story of one couple, Liz and Mike, and their daughter, Baby M."*

> —*The Seattle Times*, Dec. 4, 2005

I began covering this homeless couple in August 2003. The assignment that summer day was ordinary: Photograph a homeless woman in the juvenile court parking lot with all her personal belongings stuffed in the back of a Toyota pickup. The story as I understood it at the time was about this homeless woman who, with her boyfriend, was trying to get their baby back. At the end of this initial assignment, it was apparent that this was more than a single image or a simple story. Reporter Jonathan Martin and I followed the couple for the next 28 months.

When working on a long-term story like this, I learned that not all the images I produced would run in the newspaper. After shooting for several months, I remember photo editor Fred Nelson telling me I had some very good images. But he also said the photographs would get even better, and some of the moments I had already captured may not be published. As I continued to shoot, the images became more powerful and revealing.

One valuable lesson I learned was the importance of developing a close working relationship with Jonathan Martin, the reporter. During the next two-plus years, Jonathan and I both made regular contact with the couple. We kept each other apprised as to what new information was emerging. The first time Mike assaulted Liz, I got a call from Mike telling me he was about to be arrested by the local police. I dropped what I was doing that day and made the picture of Liz crying on the couch. I also took notes and some of those notes I collected were included in the story.

During the 28 months I covered Mike, Liz and Baby M, I attended court hearings, court-appointed parenting classes, visitations with Baby M, drug tests and the couple's everyday life in their attempt to win back custody of Baby M. I attended these hearings, evaluations and supervised visits with the couple's consent.

The pictures I captured during the 28 months didn't happen overnight. The more hours I spent with the couple, the more comfortable the couple became with the cameras and me. Sometimes I attended yet another hearing knowing that the photos wouldn't always be great and would probably never be used. But I knew it was important to be around the couple as much as possible. The lesson I learned here was how important it was to make the couple as comfortable with me as possible, given these sensitive situations.

Capturing true emotion, without the camera intimidating the subjects, became another lesson well-learned. When it came time to make the tough emotional pictures, I was able to. A few times during the process Liz's lawyers objected to me being there. Each time, Liz told her lawyers that I would be staying. One of those lawyers would later praise the photographs and story.

I hit several roadblocks along the way. One time, while attempting to visit Liz during a visit with her daughter, the social worker called building security to have the reporter and me removed. The mother had invited us. We never wanted to upset the visitation or the staff at Child Protective Services. Lesson learned: Get the social worker's permission before the visit, not during the visit.

During our coverage of Baby M, I made the necessary time to work on this story, whether it was late at night or on weekends. This was important. Sometimes the best pictures don't happen between 9 and 5.

This story about Baby M stood out with readers. My photographs of Baby M won praise from the juvenile court judges, social workers, lawyers, child advocates and the state itself. Many readers said they had simply not read anything like it.

The story is now part of the training materials for the King County Court Appointed Special Advocate programs. One reader wrote: "I read every word, studied every picture and cried when I was finished."

Mike Siegel is a staff photographer at The Seattle Times, *where he has worked for 19 years. He has also worked at four other newspapers and at United Press International.*

Los Angeles Times

Finalist

Brian Vander Brug
Community Service Photojournalism

57. About "Southeast Homicide"

A chilly December morning in South Los Angeles. An unidentified body, a bullet hole in the head. A detective examines the body.

This familiar scene reflects the stuff of countless crime scenes. But from it, *Los Angeles Times* photographer Brian Vander Brug fashioned an original visual story. He offers a penetrating look at a single murder and the team of homicide detectives who were determined to solve it.

Vander Brug, along with *Times* staff writer Jill Leovy, earned an extraordinary degree of trust among detectives. This trust allowed Vander Brug to gain the access that sets his photos apart. He's there when the body is found. He's there when suspects are interrogated. He's there when one of them confesses.

His presence enables him to make powerful photos. These photos capture frustration, despair and hopelessness generated by the murder of Jerry Lee Wesley Jr., who was cherished by his family, liked by his co-workers and who happened to be sitting in his Chevrolet Suburban on the wrong street at the wrong time.

Vander Brug's photo images offer a window into the high homicide rate that has roiled the community and serve as a major impetus for change.

—Adapted from the *Los Angeles Times* ASNE contest entry

Brian Vander Brug is a staff photographer at the Los Angeles Times. *His work on "Mortal Wounds," a series on homicide in South Los Angeles, earned several first place awards, including: community service photojournalism, the American Society of Newspaper Editors (2004); domestic news picture story, National Press Association Best of Photojournalism (2003); photojournalism and Scripps Howard National Journalism Award (2003). A photograph in that series, "A*

Dorothy Wesley wipes away a tear as she and her husband, Jerry Wesley Sr., look at a mug shot with detective John Zambos, right. Muriel Bryant-Manolesakis, Wesley Sr.'s sister, stands in the back.

Hole in Her Life," won first place, portrait, Pictures of the Year International (2003). In 2003, Vander Brug was named Los Angeles Press Club Journalist of the Year (photojournalism) for "Mortal Wounds."

Lessons Learned

BY BRIAN VANDER BRUG

The proposal from my reporter friend was simple: Show up for work every day inside a Los Angeles Police Department station and document the work of the homicide detectives who worked there. The project would be known as: "Inside Access: Southeast Homicide."

We would work without the knowledge of the department's media relations office and their red tape. But it would be with the blessing of the division chief. The station brass promised unfettered access. There were only a few ground rules, like not messing up evidence or interfering with witnesses.

We were off the daily schedule at the *Los Angeles Times*. It allowed us to roll on all the 187 calls. We would be invited inside the crime-scene tape when detectives called, day or night, to investigate a case. It was going to be great. I thought it would be pretty easy, as we expected to catch seven or eight murders during the rest of the year.

Southeast homicide was one of the busiest detective squads in one of the most violent areas of the city. Seventy murders were on the books when I joined the project just before Thanksgiving. Not a week had gone by when the first call to a murder scene at 101st and Figueroa Streets came in.

On the morning of Dec. 1, I was on the roof cleaning out my rain gutters when the phone rang with the news of the first homicide. I thought for a second about not rolling. After all, I'd have plenty of chances to shoot murder scenes for the project, and a series of powerful storms was forecast for the coming days. The gutters had to be ready. But I was anxious to get into the story. I jumped down the ladder and was on the road. Luckily I made it to the city before the crime scene was taken down. It would be our only murder for the rest of the year.

One of the most important things you can do when working on a story like this is to be ready to go all the time. You have to have a family that knows what you do. They need to understand when you disappear during dinner, or take off in the middle of the night.

Equally important is to have the support of your editors at the paper. They need to be willing to have you off the schedule and deal with having one less body to shoot dailies.

The ability to be there anytime is key.

I couldn't be on another assignment and still be available to work on the project. If I had missed the opportunity to photograph the crime scene and the first hours of the investigation, the project would have been dead photographically.

Our original idea was to focus on the detectives themselves. We wanted to weave a story about them as people, how they deal with the staggering loss of life at the hands of others. With seven or eight cases to work on, we could pick and choose. But the story changed as we had only one homicide to cover. It is important to keep an open mind and photograph everything, as you never know what twists and turns await you.

Patience is also something needed in large quantities. Police detective work can be very glamorous, much like you see on television . . . for about an hour. After that it involves interviews, phone work, paper work and hours, days and weeks spent in the office at a desk in front of a computer. All very boring stuff that doesn't yield great pictures.

I needed to overcome a lot of tedious desk-sitting while waiting for the photographic opportunities to present themselves. You have to be there all day—every day. Some days absolutely nothing would happen. That is hard to deal with as a photojournalist. But by being there every day with your subjects, you get to know them. And they get to know you.

The detectives really got the sense we cared about what they do. Personal relationships developed. A level of trust was established early. When we were with them as they investigated the first and only murder case, they weren't worried about us violating the law, or the few ground rules set for the access they'd granted us.

They did their job solving the crime and we got our story, which was also their story. We were there when the coroner zipped Jerry Lee Wesley into a body bag. We were there when detective John Skaggs notified a father that his only son had been killed. We were there when detectives apprehended a suspect and interviewed him about his involvement. We were there when a family laid their loved one to rest.

So were our readers.

Brian Vander Brug is a staff photographer at the Los Angeles Times.

Suggested Readings

RECENT RESOURCES

Adam, G. Stuart and Roy Peter Clark. "Journalism: The Democratic Craft." New York: Oxford University Press, 2005. The authors narrow the gap between the classroom and the profession with this collection of classic readings, writing instruction, study guides and exercises.

Baranick, Alana, Jim Sheeler and Stephen Miller. "Life on the Death Beat." Oak Park, IL: Marion Street Press, 2005. A handbook for obituary writers.

Boynton, Robert S. "The New New Journalism." New York: Vintage Books, 2005. Conversations with some of America's best nonfiction writers on their craft.

Brady, John Joseph. "The Interviewer's Handbook." Waukesha, WI: Writer Books, 2004. Brady describes interviewing techniques used by professional journalists and writers.

Clark, Roy Peter. "Writing Tools: 50 Essential Strategies for Every Writer." New York: Little, Brown and Company, 2006. Writing advice from the sub-atomic to metaphysical levels.

Clark, Roy Peter and Don Fry. "Coaching Writers." 2nd edition. New York: Bedford/St. Martin's, 2003. Guidelines on how to improve communication between editors and reporters.

Conrad, Mark. "The Business of Sports: A Primer for Journalists." Mahwah, NJ: Lawrence Erlbaum Associates, 2005. An exploration of sports business topics most relevant to journalists.

Goldstein, Norm, ed. "The Associated Press Stylebook and Briefing on Media Law." New York: Basic Books, 2004. AP's rules on grammar, spelling, punctuation, capitalization, word usage and more.

Gutkind, Lee and Annie Dillard. "In Fact." New York: W. W. Norton & Company, 2005. A collection of creative nonfiction.

Harrigan, Jane and Karen F. Dunlap. "The Editorial Eye." 2nd edition. New York: Bedford/St. Martin's, 2003. This updated edition deals with both the technical and management elements of professional editing.

Hennessy, Brendan. "Writing Feature Articles." Burlington, MA: Focal Press, 2006. An introduction to feature writing.

Houston, Brant, Len Bruzzese and Steve Weinberg. "The Investigative Reporter's Handbook." Boston: Bedford/St. Martin's, 2002. Valuable advice and tools for investigative reporters.

LaRocque, Paula. "The Book on Writing: The Ultimate Guide to Writing Well." Oak Park, IL: Marion Street Press, 2003. Useful tips about many aspects of writing.

Ludwig, Mark D. "Modern News Editing." Ames, IA: Blackwell, 2005. A handbook for media writers and editors.

Mencher, Melvin. "Melvin Mencher's News Reporting and Writing." 10th edition. Boston: McGraw-Hill, 2006. A guide to writing well and reporting accurately.

Plotnik, Arthur. "Spunk & Bite." New York: Random House Reference, 2005. A writer's guide to punchier, more engaging language and style.

Pumario, Jim. "Bad News and Good Judgment." Oak Park, IL: Marion Street Press, 2005. Useful tools for reporting sensitive issues in a small-town newspaper.

Reed, Robert and Glenn Lewin. "Covering Business." Oak Park, IL: Marion Street Press, 2005. A guide to reporting on commerce and developing a business beat.

Roush, Chris. "Show Me the Money: Writing Business and Economic Stories for Mass Communication." Mahwah, NJ: Lawrence Erlbaum Associates, 2004. Advice and examples on being a business journalist.

Scanlan, Christopher. "Reporting and Writing: Basics for the 21st Century." New York: Oxford University Press, 2000. Chip Scanlan's practical guide to professional journalism skills.

Smith, Sarah Harrison. "The Fact Checker's Bible." New York: Anchor Books, 2004. A manual on how to get the facts right.

Summer, David E. and Holly G. Miller. "Feature and Magazine Writing: Action, Angle and Anecdotes." Ames, IA: Blackwell, 2005. Practical advice and the basic elements of magazine writing.

Titchener, Campbell B. "Reviewing the Arts." Mahwah, NJ: Lawrence Erlbaum Associates, 2005. Helpful suggestions on how to produce all types of art reviews.

Weingarten, Marc. "The Gang that Wouldn't Write Straight: Wolfe, Thompson, Didion, and the New Journalism Revolution." New York: Crown Publishers, 2005. A look at the origins and rise of New Journalism.

WRITING AND REPORTING ANTHOLOGIES

Belkin, Lisa, ed. "Tales from the Times: Real-Life Stories to Make You Think, Wonder, and Smile, from the Pages of *The New York Times.*" New York: St. Martin's Griffin, 2004. A collection of human-interest stories from *The New York Times.*

Flippin, Royce, ed. "Best American Political Writing 2005." New York: Thunder's Mouth Press, 2005. The fourth volume in this series focuses on magazine writing.

Garlock, David, ed. "Pulitzer Prize Feature Stories." Ames: Iowa State Press, 2003. Twenty-five Pulitzer Prize-winning feature stories published from 1979 to 2003.

Harrington, Walt. "The Beholder's Eye." New York: Grove Press, 2005. A collection of some of America's finest personal journalism.

Kincaid, Jamaica, ed. "The Best American Travel Writing 2005." Boston: Houghton Mifflin, 2005. This anthology includes well-written stories about travel.

Lupica, Mike, ed. "The Best American Sports Writing 2005." Boston: Houghton Mifflin, 2005. Examples of excellent sports writing.

Mills, Eleanor, et al., eds. "Journalistas: 100 Years of the Best Writing and Reporting by Women Journalists." New York: Carroll & Graf, 2005. A collection of stories written by women during the 20th century.

Orlean, Susan, ed. "The Best American Essays 2005." Boston: Houghton Mifflin, 2005. This series has become a showcase for the country's finest writing.

Penzler, Otto. "The Best American Crime Writing 2005." New York: Harper, 2005. An annual anthology of nonfiction crime stories originally published in magazines.

Remnick, David, ed. "Life Stories: Profiles from *The New Yorker.*" New York: Random House, 2001. A compilation of some of the best profiles to appear in *The New Yorker.*

Silverman, Matthew and Greg Spira. "Best Baseball Writing 2005." New York: Carroll & Graf Publishers, 2005. These twenty-five baseball stories mark the beginning of a new anthology series on baseball writing.

Sloan, Wm. David and Laird B. Anderson. "Pulitzer Prize Editorials: America's Best Writing, 1917–2003." 3rd ed. Ames: Iowa State Press, 2003. Historical and recent Pulitzer Prize winning editorials.

Weiner, Jonathan, ed. "The Best American Science and Nature Writing 2005." Boston: Houghton Mifflin, 2005. Some of the year's finest writing on a wide range of scientific topics.

CLASSICS

Blundell, William E. "The Art and Craft of Feature Writing." New York: Plume, 1988. A step-by-step guide to reporting and editing.

Brande, Dorothea. "Becoming a Writer." Los Angeles: J. P. Tarcher; Boston: distributed by Putnam Publishing, reprint of 1934 edition, 1981. Timeless writing advice from 1934.

Franklin, Jon. "Writing for Story." New York: Plume, 1994. Lessons about how to write dramatic nonfiction.

Harrington, Walt. "Intimate Journalism: The Art and Craft of Reporting Everyday Life." Thousand Oaks, CA: Sage, 1997. Award-winning articles are used to describe the process of combining traditional feature writing with in-depth reporting.

Murray, Donald M. "Writing to Deadline: The Journalist at Work." Portsmouth, NH: Heinemann, 2000. Murray helps journalists understand the writing process.

Snyder, Louis L. and Richard B. Morris, eds. "A Treasury of Great Reporting." New York: Simon & Schuster, 1962. Historical examples of great reporting and writing.

Stewart, James B. "Follow the Story: How to Write Successful Nonfiction." New York: Simon & Schuster, 1988. Stewart illustrates the techniques of compelling narrative writing.

Strunk, William, Jr. and E. B. White. "The Elements of Style." Illustrated edition. New York: Penguin Press, 2005. A classic reference book on the rules of usage and the principles of composition.

Zinsser, William. "On Writing Well." New York: Harper Resource, 2001. The 25th anniversary edition of a respected writing guide.

David Shedden, director of the Eugene Patterson Library at The Poynter Institute for Media Studies, compiled this listing.